In 1930, a Los Angeles string band gained a broad regional following under the name "The Beverly Hillbillies." Three decades later, the name would reappear as the title of a wildly popular television show, featuring essentially the same family of clownish mountaineers depicted in the long-running comic strip *Li'l Abner*. In 1972, the leering rapists in the film *Deliverance* would lend the hillbilly a darker and more threatening aura ("it did for North Georgians," said one journalist, "what *Jaws* did for sharks"). To this day, the portrayal of southern mountain people as at once comically and threateningly premodern and ignorant is one of the most pervasive images in American popular culture. Typically associated with the Ozarks or Appalachia, the hillbilly is filthy, lazy, uncivilized, drunk, and impoverished not only economically and culturally but also genetically.

In this pioneering work of cultural history, historian Anthony Harkins argues that the hillbilly—in his various guises of "briar hopper," "brush ape," "ridge runner," and "white trash"—has been viewed by mainstream Americans simultaneously as a violent degenerate who threatens the modern order and as a keeper of traditional values of family, home, and physical production, and thus symbolic of a nostalgic past free of the problems of contemporary life. "Hillbilly" signifies both rugged individualism and stubborn backwardness, strong family and kin networks but also inbreeding and bloody feuds.

Spanning film, literature, and the entire expanse of American popular culture, from D. W. Griffith to hillbilly music to the Internet, Harkins illustrates how the image of the hillbilly has consistently served as both a marker of social derision and regional pride (witness the expression "I ain't no flatlander"). He traces the corresponding changes in representations of the hillbilly from late-nineteenth-century America, through the Great Depression, the mass migrations of southern Appalachians in the 1940s and 1950s, and the War on Poverty in the mid-1960s, to the present day. Harkins also argues that images of hillbillies

Hillbilly

A Cultural History of an American Icon

Hillbilly

Anthony Harkins

OXFORD
UNIVERSITY PRESS

2004

OXFORD
UNIVERSITY PRESS

Oxford   New York

Auckland   Bangkok   Buenos Aires   Cape Town   Chennai
Dar es Salaam   Delhi   Hong Kong   Istanbul   Karachi   Kolkata
Kuala Lumpur   Madrid   Melbourne   Mexico City   Mumbai   Nairobi
São Paulo   Shanghai   Taipei   Tokyo   Toronto

Published by Oxford University Press, Inc.
198 Madison Avenue, New York, New York 10016

www.oup.com

Oxford is a registered trademark of Oxford University Press

Library of Congress Cataloging-in-Publication Data
Harkins, Anthony.
Hillbilly : a cultural history of an American icon / Anthony Harkins.
   p. cm.
Includes bibliographical references (p.) and index.
ISBN 0-19-514631-X
1. Mountain people in popular culture—United States.   2. Whites in popular culture—
United States.   3. Popular culture—United States.   4. United States—Civilization.
5. United States—Race relations.   6. Group identity—United States.   7. Whites—
Race identity—United States.   8. Mountain people—United States—Public opinion.
9. Whites—United States—Public opinion.   10. Public opinion—
United States.   I. Title.
E184.M83H37   2003
975'.00943—dc21   2003041974

Portions of chapter 3 have been reprinted with permission in revised form from
"The Significance of 'Hillbilly' in Early Country Music, 1924–1945," *Journal of Appalachian Studies* 2
(Fall 1996): 311–22.

Chapter 6 has been reprinted with permission in revised form from
"The Hillbilly in the Living Room: Television Representations of Southern Mountaineers in
Situational Comedies, 1952–1971," *Appalachian Journal* 29 (Fall 2001–Winter 2002): 98–126.

9   8   7   6   5   4   3   2   1

Printed in the United States of America
on acid-free paper

To Charles R. Harkins

In Memoriam

acknowledgments

Over the many years that I have worked on this project, I have incurred many debts, both personal and professional, that I am grateful to have the chance to formally acknowledge. This book began as a dissertation and many of my greatest influences have been my professors at the University of Wisconsin-Madison. As both mentor and friend, Paul Boyer has greatly influenced this manuscript. Not only did he urge me to pursue this topic despite my initial reservations, but the energy and scholarly rigor that he brings to his writing and teaching also inspired me to become a cultural historian. His many thought-provoking comments and questions, penetrating readings of my chapters, and above all, his unflagging support and good humor, immeasurably improved my work. Steve Kantrowitz encouraged me to expand my analysis to more fully address the major issues and tensions in American history and offered his steady friendship. As seminar instructor, teaching mentor, and reader, Jim Baughman was a model of effective research and teaching, always urging me to ground my claims with concrete evidence.

In addition to these readers of the entire manuscript, a number of friends and colleagues also read and commented on portions of this project at an early stage in its development. I am grateful to Tracey Deutsch, Laura McEnaney, Charlie Montgomery, and Bethel Saler for their helpful comments and suggestions. I also want to thank the many scholars who have spoken with me and helped me clarify my thinking, especially Bill Cronon, Archie Green, Jim Leary, Bill Malone, David Roediger, Anne Mitchell Whisnant, and David Whisnant.

This work is appearing in print largely because of the support and expertise of the editorial staff at Oxford. I thank Niko Pfund for his unflagging commitment to this project, Susan Ferber for her unparalleled editorial suggestions as well as calm guidance, and Stacey Hamilton for her assistance with the book's production. I also thank the outside readers of the original manuscript, both those who remained anonymous and those who did not (Dwight Billings, Erika Doss, David Hsuing, and Scott Sandage), for their incisive commentary and suggestions. My efforts to address their concerns and to reach for what they saw as the project's full potential has made this a far better book.

I am also deeply appreciative of the many individuals who have shared difficult to find or unpublished materials with me, often allowing me to see their notes for their own forthcoming publications. First, I owe an enormous debt of gratitude to Jerry Williamson. Going far beyond the bounds of mere scholarly collegiality, Jerry opened up to me his vast collection of hillbilly-related materials, allowing me to roam at will through his extensive files and view his copies of rare films. He also freely offered his valuable insights into the hillbilly identity, helped me find accommodations during my stay in Boone, North Carolina, and has continued to offer his invaluable support and insights in the ensuing years. I am extremely grateful to him for his many kindnesses and suggestions. I also thank the following people who all provided me with their own scholarly work or other research materials: Terry Bailes, Tom Bené, Simon Bronner, Jim Clark, Stephen Cox, Jon Harris, Tom Inge, Angie Maxwell, Michael McKernan, John McCoy, Ronnie Pugh, David Whisnant, Adam Wilson, and David Zercher. Finally, I am most appreciative of Paul Henning's willingness, despite health problems, to participate in an extended telephone interview. His candor and infectious warmth in recalling his years working on *The Beverly Hillbillies* and other programming made for a thoroughly enjoyable and informative conversation.

This research project has entailed significant expense in acquiring illustrations and republication permissions and traveling to far-flung archives and libraries, and I gratefully acknowledge the institutional support and research assistance I have received. My sincere appreciation to the University of Wisconsin-Madison's Department of History for research travel and conference presentation funds and the Princeton University Committee on Research in the Humanities and Social Sciences for their generous grant that allowed me to acquire the array of artwork that enriches the text. I am grateful to John Blazejewski for the expert job he did photographing the majority of these images. I also wish to express my gratitude to the many librarians and archivists who have assisted me along the way. In particular, I thank Stephen Goddard of the Spencer Museum of Art, University of Kansas; Steve Green of the Southern Folklife Collection at the University of North Carolina-Chapel Hill; Ronnie Pugh, formerly of the Country Music Foundation; Ned Irwin of the Archives of Appalachia at Eastern Tennessee State University; Dean Williams of the Appalachian Collection at Appalachian State University; Kate Black and Bill Marshall of the Appalachian Collection and Special Collections at the University of Kentucky; Harry Rice and Gerald Roberts of the Hutchins Library at Berea College; Ann Wright of the Asheville Public Library; Randy Roberts of the Western Historical Manuscript Collection of the University of Missouri-Columbia, and the library staff at Firestone Library of Princeton University. For assistance during my research in the Los Angeles area, I thank Ned Comstock at the Cinema-Television Library at the University of Southern California; the staff at the Margaret Herrick Library at the Academy of Motion Picture Arts and Sciences (particularly Kristine Kreuger); Brigitte Kueppers, chief archivist of Special Collections at the Theater Arts Library at the University of California, Los Angeles, and the extremely helpful proprietors of Eddie Brandt's Saturday Matinee in North Hollywood, California, for their great assistance in finding the many obscure hillbilly films held in their vast collection.

My travels were made infinitely more enjoyable and affordable through the kindness of friends and family who generously allowed me to stay with them during my research trips. I sincerely thank Anne and Chris Kenyon, my mother, Shanna MacLean, Harry and Katherine Petrequin, and David Zercher. Above all, I am indebted to Andrew Cypiot for not only allowing me to stay in his small apartment for over a month but also for conducting valuable research for me. I could not have completed the California portion of my research without his help and friendship.

Throughout the many years it took to bring this project to fruition, I have relied heavily upon friends and colleagues for guidance and support. I am very grateful that Susan Ballard, Steve Burg, Joe Cullon, Judy Cochran, Rob Good, Dan Graff, Charlotte Haller, Katherine Ledford, Charlie Montgomery and Linda Curchin, Paul Murphy, Doug Reichert-Powell, Sue Rosenthal, Bethel Saler, James Siekmeier, Kevin Smith, Lisa Tetrault, David Zercher, and, last but certainly not least, the "Lake Pawtuckaway Gang" (Sam Broeksmit, Andrew Cypiot, Pat Connors, John Gregg, Jeff Speck, Mark Van Norman, and Adam Wilson) have all been a part of my life. I especially thank Janet Davis and Jeff Osborne, Steve Hoelscher and Kristin Nilsson, and Mark and Paula Van Ells and their children for their many kindnesses, including last-minute babysitting, home-cooked dinners, and general assurances that we would all survive this process of completing dissertations and publishing our first books (which, remarkably, we all have).

My family has been my greatest inspiration and source of support. I thank my mom for her help and good cheer during my research trip to Asheville and in subsequent conversations, Sean for his many hours of computer advice and assistance, Sue and Tom for their assistance in acquiring Mountain Dew materials, and Michael and Barbara for their unfailing support and help with keeping our house in running order. Thank you to my sisters Sue and Tammy for their love and support over the years. To my dad, Charles Harkins, to whom I dedicate this book, I offer my heartfelt gratitude for his many years of financial and mostly emotional support and encouragement, even during the times when he wondered exactly what I was investigating and if I would ever complete the task. It is my greatest regret that he could not see the fruition of these many years of labor, but I am comforted by the fact that he at least knew it would be published one day. My children, Chloe and Owen, deserve my gratitude for their calm acceptance of the countless times their daily activities were interrupted by my writing schedule and for keeping me firmly grounded when the work threatened to overwhelm me.

Finally, to Tracy, I owe more than I can ever repay. This book has truly been a joint effort and in dozens of ways, and she has contributed nearly as much to its final form as have I. Not only did she read the entire text and make valuable editorial and conceptual suggestions, but she also devoted hours to proofreading, put together the bibliography, and helped solve dozens of computer glitches and crises. She sacrificed countless weekends and evenings to take care of the kids and the house so that I could have precious writing and research time, and she visited with me hillbilly-related locations in North Carolina and Tennessee. Along the way, she undoubtedly learned far, far more about the hillbilly than she ever thought possible or desirable. But despite the strain of sitting through dozens of hillbilly films and television shows, her intellectual and emotional support and her love have never wavered. It is due to her Herculean efforts that I have finally been able to complete this project, and I present this book to her with all my love.

contents

Contents
xii

Hillbilly

introduction

Race, Class, Popular Culture, and "the Hillbilly"

In 1930, a Los Angeles string band gained a broad regional following under the name "The Beverly Hillbillies." Thirty-two years later, the name would reappear as the title of a wildly popular television show. Essentially the same family of savage mountaineers were featured as the Hatburns in the 1921 film *Tol'able David*, the Scraggs of Al Capp's long-running comic strip *Li'l Abner* (beginning in 1934), and the unnamed mountain rapists of the 1972 movie *Deliverance*. And sixty-eight years after his inception in the early years of the Depression, the lazy, isolated, and cantankerous comic strip mountaineer Snuffy Smith was still appearing in hundreds of newspapers nationwide. As these examples attest, the portrayal of southern mountain people as premodern and ignorant "hillbillies" is one of the most lasting and pervasive images in American popular iconography, appearing continuously throughout the twentieth century in nearly every major facet of American popular culture from novels and magazines to movies and television programs to country music and the Internet.[1]

Although the hillbilly image has remained relatively unchanged, the meaning of these representations and the word itself have continuously evolved over the past century in response to broader social, economic, and cultural transformations in American society. The key to the "hillbilly"'s surprising ubiquity and endurance from 1900 to the dawn of the third millennium has been the fundamental ambiguity of the meaning of this term and image. In its many manifestations, "hillbilly" has been used in national me-

3

dia representations and by thousands of Americans within and outside the southern mountains to both uphold and challenge the dominant trends of twentieth-century American life—urbanization, the growing centrality of technology, and the resulting routinization of American life. Consistently used by middle-class economic interests to denigrate working-class southern whites (whether from the mountains or not) and to define the benefits of advanced civilization through negative counterexample, the term and idea have also been used to challenge the generally unquestioned acceptance and legitimacy of "modernity" and "progress." The media hillbilly thrived during the 1930s in an era of economic and social collapse, but it also reemerged in the 1960s at a time of widespread questioning of the price of "progress" and the social equity of the "affluent society." Uniquely positioned as a white "other," a construction both within and beyond the confines of American "whiteness," the hillbilly has also been at the heart of struggles over American racial identity and hierarchy. Finally, in the same oppositionally dualistic way, southern mountain folk both denounced it as a vicious slur and embraced it in defense of their value system and in celebration of their cultural heritage. Thus, while often dismissed as a debased and trivial "mass" culture stereotype, the hillbilly has instead served at times of national soul-searching and throughout the twentieth century as a continually negotiated mythic space through which modern Americans have attempted to define themselves and their national identity and to reconcile the past and the present.

This book examines the cultural and ideological construct "the hillbilly" (and its antecedent and fellow traveler "the mountaineer") rather than the actual people of the southern mountains or even the purportedly "true-to-life" representations of these people in popular literature, photography, and academic studies. Nonetheless, it is, of course, impossible to completely separate these three socially constructed categories—the southern mountain people, the efforts to represent the "real" southern mountaineer, and the image of the "hillbilly"—that have intertwined dialectically throughout the century. As mass media increasingly permeated American culture, the distinction between image and reality became increasingly blurred. Inundated by stereotypical portrayals of shiftless, drunken, promiscuous, and bare-footed people, living in blissful squalor beyond the reach of civilization, many Americans outside the southern mountains came to see little or no difference between the "real" southern mountaineers and their cultural image.

In response to such widespread acceptance of these pejorative portrayals, writers, photographers, and artists who were ostensibly sympathetic to the mountain people created a distinct but parallel construction, the stalwart, forthright, and picturesque mountaineer. But this construct was premised on the same notion of a mythic white population wholly isolated from modern civilization. As a result, images of noble mountaineers intended to delegitimize hillbilly caricatures actually reinforced these portraits and perpetuated the idea that the southern mountain people were a separate "race" in, but not of, white America. At the same time, many southern mountain folk, often trapped in regional low-paying industrial work or forced to migrate outside the mountains to survive, embraced elements of both the rugged and pure mountaineer myth and the hillbilly label and its implied hostility to middle-class norms and propriety, in the process intensifying the national perception of their status as an American "other."

Because the hillbilly image/identity has always been a site of contending attitudes toward modernity, it has occupied a mythical far more than a concrete geographic locale. True, producers and audiences alike most often associated this image with the regions of southern Appalachia and the Ozarks. Yet although there has always been great topographical, social, and cultural diversity within and between these two areas, the creators of such images freely combined the two regions into a single fantastical place. Because the physical locale of hillbilly portrayals is often unclear or unstated, in the minds of many, the image is not confined exclusively to these two regions, and the label has historically been applied to literary and cultural figures from upstate New York to western Washington State. Indeed, most cultural consumers, to the extent they considered the matter at all, conceived of "hillbillyland" as, at best, an amorphous area of the upper South and, more often, as anywhere on the rough edges of the landscape and economy.[2]

What defines the hillbilly more than geography are cultural traits and values. In this regard, "hillbilly" is no different than dozens of similar labels and ideological and graphic constructs of poor and working-class southern whites coined by middle- and upper-class commentators, northern and southern. These derisive terms were intended to indicate a diet rooted in scarcity ("clay eater," "corn-cracker," "rabbit twister"), physical appearance and clothing that denoted hard and specifically working-class laboring conditions ("redneck," "wool hat," "lint head"), an animal-like existence on the economic and physical fringes of society ("brush ape," "ridge runner," "briar hopper"), ignorance and racism, and in all cases, economic, genetic, and cultural impoverishment (best summed up by the label "poor white," or more pointedly, "poor white trash"). Many of these derogatory labels were used interchangeably as putdowns of working-class southern whites, especially those who had migrated to southern and midwestern urban centers. But they were also reappropriated by some as badges of class and racial identity and pride. "Hillbilly," "redneck," "cracker," and recently even "poor white trash" have all been embraced to mark an "oppositional culture" against a hegemonic middle-class culture and the relative gain in status of African Americans and other minority social groups. Nor are the humorous elements of the word and image "hillbilly" unique; all these labels (even one as crude as "poor white trash") historically had ostensibly comical overtones, not only for middle- and upper-class whites in positions of authority but also, in a different context and with a different intent, for working-class whites.[3]

"Hillbilly" is the most long-lived of these rural working-class slurs and the one most widespread in popular culture. It was the only one of these terms adopted as a label for what would later be called country music; the only one used to denote a genre of cartoons and comic strips; the only one to appear in the title of a television series (one that also became one of the medium's most popular and influential shows); and arguably the most prevalent of these terms in motion pictures. Its prominence partly stemmed from the fact that most Americans saw it as *primarily* a benignly humorous (if somewhat condescending) term and characterization. Even "redneck," though increasingly used as a comical term beginning in the mid-1970s and moving more fully into that camp with the success of Jeff Foxworthy's "You might be a redneck . . ." joke books and comedy routines, nonetheless continued to carry a connotation of virulent white racism to a far greater extent than did "hillbilly." Yet, "hillbilly" could also evoke degradation, violence, animalism, and carnality, as well as more positive conceptions of romantic rurality, cultural and ethnic purity, pioneer heritage, and personal and communal independence and self-sufficiency. Indeed, I argue that through most of the twentieth century "hillbilly" remained the most semantically malleable of these labels and therefore the term that resonated most broadly with audiences both nationally and in the southern hill country.

The continuous popularity and ubiquity of the hillbilly portrait stems from the dualistic nature of this cultural conception: it includes both positive and negative features of the American past and present, and incorporates both "otherness" and self-identification. These dualisms allowed these images to gain popularity not only with a "mainstream" nationwide audience but also with many in southern mountain society who embraced the positive features of this identity while rejecting its negative aspects. On the one hand, "the hillbilly" personified characteristics associated with the nation's founders and settlers, which many Americans saw as endangered by a modern, industrialized, and increasingly atomized society. Such elements included the pioneer spirit; strong family and kin networks ruled by benevolent patriarchs; a clear sense of gender roles; a closeness to nature and the land; authenticity and purity; rugged individualism and a powerful sense of self; and the "horse sense" of average people as opposed to scientific and bureaucratic ways of thinking.

On the other hand, each of these features could be defined by its negative flip side in order to evince the anachronistic incompatibility of such values to twentieth-century America. The pioneer spirit could also reflect social and economic backwardness; strong kin connections might mean inbreeding, domestic violence, and bloody feuds; rugged individualism could also be interpreted as stubbornness and an inability to adapt to changing conditions; closeness to nature could stand for primitiveness, savagery, and sexual promiscuity; and purity and common sense might actually indicate ignorance and a reliance on unscientific and dangerous childrearing, medical, dietary, and religious practices. Thus, "the hillbilly" served the dual and seemingly contradictory purposes of allowing the "mainstream," or generally nonrural, middle-class white, American audience to imagine a romanticized past, while simultaneously enabling that same audience to recommit itself to modernity by caricaturing the negative aspects of premodern, uncivilized society.

The hillbilly image's duality grew out of and was inextricably linked to its white racial status. Much recent scholarship has correctly complicated notions of white racial identity and illuminated the historical construction and significance of "whiteness" in its American context. Historians and other scholars have explored the way various European ethnic groups used claims to whiteness to gain social and economic privilege and to define and disempower nonwhite racial "others." They have also highlighted white fascination with African-American culture and the interconnectivity of "black" and "white" racial and cultural categories. Yet these authors have focused less on the contested nature of white identity itself. The evolution of "the hillbilly" offers a fascinating and revealing insight into the internal conceptual divisions within the broad category of "white America." Despite their poverty, ignorance, primitiveness, and isolation, "hillbillies" were "one hundred percent" Protestant Americans of supposedly pure Anglo-Saxon or at least Scotch-Irish lineage, which countless commentators of the late-nineteenth- and early-twentieth centuries, greatly concerned by waves of Southern and Eastern European immigrants, took pains to prove. Thus, middle-class white Americans could see these people as a fascinating and exotic "other" akin to Native Americans or Blacks, while at the same time sympathize with them as poorer and less modern versions of themselves.[4]

This status of the "white other" generated concern and interest from religious, social, and political reformers throughout the twentieth century. To the mountain folk's would-be redeemers of the Progressive Era, their "hard shell" Protestantism and pioneer ancestry were both a ready explanation for their supposed primitiveness and a potential salvation for a nation threatened by non-Protestant invasions as well as the enervating forces of mass industrialization and bureaucracy. Similarly, midcentury critics and defenders of the southern mountain people saw them respectively (and at times simultaneously) as the vestiges of a dangerously atavistic culture or as the guardians of a rugged individualism and traditional ways of life. Their advocates of different decades consistently argued that these latter qualities were desperately needed as an antidote to the ills of modern America, whether the conformist tendencies of the 1920s, the economic crisis of the 1930s, or the mindless consumerism of the post–World War II "affluent society." During the War on Poverty of the 1960s, images of impoverished and exploited white Appalachians also provided "cover" for liberal politicians promoting government aid programs primarily designed to benefit urban nonwhites.

The hillbilly's whiteness, however nondefinitive, was also central to its longevity in popular media, for it allowed the image to serve as a seemingly apolitical site for often highly charged political struggles over the definition of race, class, gender norms and roles, as well as the nature of mass culture. Because producers could portray images of poverty, ignorance, and backwardness without raising cries of bigotry and racism from civil rights advocates and the black and minority communities, the crude and often negative hillbilly stereotype continued long after cultural producers had abandoned previously accepted yet equally offensive and racist stereotypes. Similarly, images of hillbilly families and kin networks could be used both to challenge supposed norms of male breadwinners and submissive female domesticity and to uphold these "traditional" gender roles by negative example. For critics of mass culture who saw it as a corrosive force that pandered to the lowest common denominator and undermined "legitimate" art, the hillbilly was the perfect symbol of worthless "kitsch." While at times condemning the crudely stereotyped nature of hillbilly portraits in country music, comic strips, film, and television, these critics also denounced the consumers of such images as mindless rubes and interpreted the huge audiences some of these characterizations garnered as conclusive proof of the mass media's inherent baseness and national cultural decline. Regardless, millions of viewers and listeners embraced the image and conception of the hillbilly because it allowed them to come to terms with the ambiguities in their own lives in a time of rapid and often disorienting change. Thus, for over a century, the hillbilly's ambiguous signification allowed it to resonate in strikingly distinct ways with reformers, cultural creators, disseminators, critics, and popular audiences both within the southern mountain region and the nation as a whole.[5]

Each chapter of this book centers on the construction of "the hillbilly" in a particular (usually nonprint) medium and in separate but overlapping time periods and shows how each cultural format—shaped by institutional constraints, the personal attitudes of producers and creators, and popular expectations—transformed its identity and meaning.[6] Illuminating the multifaceted and contested nature of the shape-shifting, historicized "hillbilly" and its inextricable linkages to large-scale historical processes and events, I strive to do justice to sociologist Richard Dyer's recognition of the "complexity of representation" with its "unequal but not monolithic relations of production and reception . . . [and] its tense and unfinished, unfinishable relation to the reality to which it refers and which it affects."[7]

Chapter 1 traces the pre-twentieth-century literary and visual antecedents of the hillbilly representation in America through the separate but overlapping traditions of the New England rustic yokel, the poor white of the southern backcountry, and the mythic frontiersman of Appalachia and Arkansas. Although authors and social commentators used the conception of the mythic mountaineer in varying ways, in all cases, they ignored the reality of late-nineteenth-century economic and social upheaval in the region and instead defined the hill folk as a people forever trapped in an unceasing past. Chapter 2 follows the evolution of the word and the image of "hillbilly" from its first appearance in print in 1900 to the end of World War I, concentrating in particular on jokebooks and the new mass medium of motion pictures. Though the meaning of the hillbilly began to take on more explicitly comical overtones by the mid-1910s, "hillbilly" remained a relatively uncommon and thoroughly ambiguous label throughout this era.

The next three chapters center on the construction of the image in different media during the Depression years of the 1930s—the hillbilly's cultural epicenter—and its aftermath. Chapter 3 examines the central role of "hillbilly" in commercially recorded rural white music from its origins in the early 1920s through World War II. Both a fabrication of music industry producers and promoters and an outgrowth of a tradition of farcical performances by folk musicians, the "hillbilly" label was ambivalently accepted by musicians and fans alike as long as the image evoked a nostalgic sense of a mythic mountaineer. By the late 1930s, however, the growing power of a derisive hillbilly stereotype led musicians and the burgeoning country music industry to gradually abandon the image and label for the more unambiguously positive cowboy identity and "country" label. Nonetheless, as "hillbilly" and string-band music became interwoven in the popular imagination, its meaning shifted from one denoting only threat and violence to one that primarily signified low humor and carefree frivolity. Chapter 4 analyzes the appearance in 1934 of three cartoon characterizations that would shape the graphic image of the hillbilly for decades to come: Paul Webb's *The Mountain Boys* cartoon in *Esquire* magazine, Billy DeBeck's character "Snuffy Smith" in his *Barney Google* comic strip, and Al Capp's *Li'l Abner*. Emerging in the depths of the Great Depression, this burst of hillbilly imagery reflected not only public fears of economic collapse and social disintegration but also the sudden popular fascination with all aspects of mountain ways of life and the increasing importance of the entertainment industry. By crystallizing long-developing conceptions of mountaineer backwardness and social degeneracy and presenting a more sanguine vision of the durability of the American people and spirit, these images mirrored the complicated mix of emotions and attitudes of Depression-era audiences. Chapter 5 focuses on the depiction of the hillbilly in motion pictures, the dominant media of the midcentury, from 1920s silent films through the postwar *Ma and Pa Kettle* series. Strongly influenced by other media portrayals, including Broadway plays, Webb's cartoons, and country music and vaudeville performers, film presentations of mountain folk followed the same trajectory as other media, moving from a near-exclusive focus on violence and social threat to a growing emphasis on farcical comedy. With the advent of an era of postwar prosperity, the hillbilly image lived on only in the domesticated version the Kettles embodied and on the fringes of the film industry. Yet, later films would show that early-twentieth-century conceptions of mountain folk as depraved savages remained just under the surface of this supposedly light-hearted fare.

My last chapters examine the postwar hillbilly and its uses and meanings, paying particular attention to the early 1960s, when the mountaineer, largely absent from public consciousness for nearly two decades, reemerged on the national stage. Chapter 6 considers television programs of the 1950s and 1960s (particularly *The Real McCoys, The Andy Griffith Show,* and the phenomenally successful *The Beverly Hillbillies*) that featured hillbilly characters and settings. Generally dismissed as crude entertainment aimed at rural and small town audiences, these shows reflected social concerns about the massive postwar migration of Appalachian mountain folk to Midwestern and Mid-Atlantic industrial cities, as well as the renewed attention paid to impoverished and isolated white mountain folk living in the midst of "the affluent society." By presenting hill people as colorful inheritors of folk traditions or as safely domesticated comic buffoons, who remained morally upright despite the venality that surrounded them, these programs helped alleviate public concerns about economic and social inequality by both minimizing the plight of the people of the southern mountains and portraying their poverty as simply another aspect of their folk culture. The epilogue examines the continuing importance of the hillbilly conception in the American imagination, ranging from the enormous influence of the book and film *Deliverance* (1972) and its aftermath to the diverse permutations of the hillbilly in cyberspace. By the late twentieth century, the image's former prominence had indisputably waned, a result of the steady decline of a rural populace that had historically represented both threatening and foolish backwardness to the urban public, the growing cultural and political influence of southern mountaineers both within and outside the mountain region, and the increasing unacceptability of broadly defined racial and ethnic stereotypes. Nonetheless, such diverse examples as the Hillbilly Days festival in Pikeville, Kentucky, contemporary country musicians who proudly call themselves and their music "hillbilly," caricatures of President Bill Clinton, and various permutations of "the hillbilly" on the Internet all suggest that the term and image still resonated as an ambiguous marker of both social derision and regional and personal pride.

Finally, I close with a postscript on the remarkable plan to resurrect *The Beverly Hillbillies* as a "reality" show and the reaction to these plans by people in and beyond the southern mountains. Whether it materializes or not, such programming proves yet again that over a century after its first appearance in print, "hillbilly" continues to serve as a mythic cultural space through which Americans struggle to define themselves and their heritage.

chapter one

From Yankee Doodle to "Devil Anse"
Literary, Graphic, and Ideological Progenitors, 1700–1899

The twentieth-century hillbilly image had its origins in three related but separate literary and illustrative traditions that reach back at least as far as the colonial era: portrayals of the rural rube; conceptions of poor whites of the southern backcountry; and images of the inhabitants of the southern mountain regions. Initially distinct, these three strands slowly coalesced through the nineteenth century into a new icon of complex and ambiguous geographic, racial, and cultural significance. Primarily situated by the end of the century in the newly labeled region "Appalachia," this new national "type" combined cultural elements from New England, Arkansas, and the southeastern mountains, all mediated through the self-interested preconceptions of northeastern journalists and illustrators. The image's racial identity was equally unstable. Partly based on denigrating antebellum portrayals by abolitionists, slaveholders, and African Americans alike, all of whom positioned so-called poor whites beyond the bounds of true "whiteness," the new identity also drew from post–Civil War missionaries' and writers' accounts that celebrated the mountain people (although they remained uncertain what to call them) as proud inheritors of a pioneer past who were essential for preserving American civilization. These spatial and racial inconsistencies and the image itself grew out of the dramatic changes in the United States as a whole, and the southern mountains in particular, as a still primarily agricultural society rapidly transformed into an urban-dominated industrial power. As Appalachia was "discovered" by both industrialists and a general reading public, the meaning of the people this image supposedly represented shifted dramatically from slightly isolated but generally unremarkably rural folk, to picturesque survivors of an earlier era, to dangerous moonshining and feuding savages who needed to be reformed or eradicated.

Rustic Yokels and Poor Whites in Literature and Nonfiction Writings, 1776–1867

The oldest and most diffuse predecessor of the twentieth-century hillbilly icon is the rural rube. A nearly universal cultural character, its American examples date back to the earliest years of New England colonization and were drawn from the British stock theatrical character "Hodge," an archetypal Yorkshire countryman characterized by a mix of provincialism, cunning calculation, and quick but crude rejoinders. From these beginnings emerged the Yankee "type" who appeared throughout the eighteenth and first half of the nineteenth centuries and under a variety of names, including Yankee Doodle, Brother Jonathan, Jack Downing, Deuteronomy Dutiful, Solon Shingle, and Rip Van Winkle, in plays, almanacs, newspapers and journals, short stories, as well as cartoons and genre paintings. These images were most prominent in the decades between 1820 and 1850, a time of intense economic and social change comprising the beginnings of the industrial revolution, the rapid growth of cities, and the increasing tensions over the potential abolition or spread of slavery. They reflected both interregional animosities and attempts by those with social and cultural power (particularly New York city urbanites) to solidify the new social order by denigrating rural people and an agricultural way of life many of them had only recently left behind. The standard representations of writers, artists, and actors of figures with gangling bodies, ill-fitting or old-fashioned clothes, peculiar dialect, and simple grins closely matched later hillbilly counterparts. So did the deliberate ambiguity of these characters, who were simultaneously objects of ridicule (to Europeans or American townsfolk) and deriders of the pretensions and values of their supposed social superiors. In this regard, the Yankee bumpkin always wore a "mask of foolishness," a natural simplicity that belied an innate shrewdness and tenacity.[1]

Although this character prefigured aspects of the hillbilly, as it spread from New England over the course of the first half of the nineteenth century it increasingly became associated more with political and financial deception and a "get ahead at any price" mentality than its simple rube origins. Transformed into the character of Brother Jonathan, the personification of the United States that preceded Uncle Sam as the national symbol, it came to celebrate the strength, courage, and individualism of the American common man and therefore became too generic to serve as an explicit model for the later hillbilly image. More directly connected were two other images that overlapped with the rustic Yankee but were more explicitly linked on both a geographic and social map with the later characters: the "poor white" and the "mountaineer."[2]

One of the earliest depictions of the social category writers and scholars would later label "southern poor whites" is from the account by William Byrd II of Westover of his 1728 expedition to survey and map the disputed Virginia–North Carolina boundary line. Written by an elite Virginia planter who was educated in the finest schools in England, Byrd's narrative is replete with scientific discussions of the flora, fauna, and geography of the region and descriptions of the Native Americans he and his party encountered. It also includes a detailed and unflattering account of the white settlers of the North Carolina backcountry.[3] Byrd's portrait of the men and women he encounters in the Dismal Swamp border region (near present day Norfolk, Virginia) introduces many of the standard tropes that would come to define southern rural whites for the next several hundred years:

> Surely there is no place in the World where the Inhabitants live with less Labour than in N Carolina. It approaches nearer to the Description of Lubberland than any other. . . . The Men, for their Parts, just like the Indians, impose all the Work upon the poor Women. They make their Wives rise out of their Beds early in the Morning, at the same time that they lye and Snore, till the Sun has run one third of his course, and disperst all the unwholesome Damps. Then, after Stretching and Yawning for half an Hour, they light their Pipes, and, under the Protection of a cloud of Smoak, venture out into the Open Air; tho', if it happens to be never so little cold, they quickly return Shivering into the Chimney corner. . . . Thus they loiter away their Lives, like Solomon's Sluggard.[4]

Byrd's strangely ambivalent perception of the backwoods people he encounters reflects the ambiguity that would thereafter always characterize hillbilly imagery. Clearly appalled by the conditions of the rural inhabitants, whom he views as unhealthy, slovenly, and utterly averse to work, Byrd's outrage primarily stems not from their impoverishment but rather from their rejection of his self-perceived "natural" order: the need for hard work and purposefulness, the economic and physical dependence of women upon men, and the proper distinction between white men and Indians. Although on the surface he seems genuinely horrified by their behavior, his imagery of prolonged stretching and yawning and protective smoke clouds has an exaggerated, cartoonish quality and suggests an attitude more of satirical derision than moral condemnation. Here, then, are the root elements of an intentionally *comical* stereotype that would be exploited repeatedly by later chroniclers of southern poor whites, in general, and the hillbilly caricature, in particular.

Over the next two centuries, in both explicitly fictional and ostensibly nonfictional narratives, northern and southern commentators solidified Byrd's literary construction of a benighted class of southern rural poor whites. Charles Woodmason, a mid-eighteenth-century itinerant Anglican preacher, shared many of Byrd's conceptions of the slothfulness of the southern rural whites, but without his comic overtones. Writing in 1766, Woodmason condemned the poverty and "extreme Indolence" of the white farmers and herders of the South Carolina backwoods whom, he fumed, "delight in their present low, lazy, sluttish, heathenish, hellish Life, and seem not desirous of changing it."[5] An account nearly a century later of the men and women of the South Carolina backcountry illustrates the persistence of this critique. The 1847 article "The Carolina Sand-Hillers" describes these rural folk as "peculiar in dress and looks," wearing always the "plainest homespun . . . often without shoes . . . with slouched hats of cheapest texture . . . as distinct a race as the Indian." Like Byrd and Woodmason, the author stressed that "[t]he ruling idea uppermost in their minds seemed to be hatred of labor." Unlike the local Indians who at least have "personal daring," the author lamented that the "sand-hillers" have no personal ambition or "energy of character" and thus will forever be condemned to a life of mere subsistence.[6]

Aimed at a northern audience and designed to exhibit the catastrophic social effects of slavery on whites and blacks alike, "The Carolina Sand-Hillers" reflects the staying power of this imagery into the mid-nineteenth century and the ease with which it could be deployed to new political ends. Indeed, the ideological construction of a base class of southern poor whites served the interests of both opponents and proponents of slavery. For abolitionists, who advocated the immediate emancipation of all slaves, and free-soilers, who simply opposed the spread of slavery into the western territories, the existence of such a group proved the destructive effect of slavery on social morals and human industry and the inordinate economic power of the planter elite. It also served as an implicit warning of the disastrous consequences of the spread of slavery into nonslaveholding regions and its debilitating effect on the work ethic of otherwise stalwart white farmers. For slaveholders, particularly those at the apex of southern society, the idleness of rural working-class whites justified the "peculiar institution" and made clear the need for a planter-led economic and social hierarchy. Planter D. R. Hundley wrote, for example, that "poor whites" were "the laziest two-legged animals that walk erect on the face of the earth . . . [and exhibited] a natural stupidity or dullness of intellect that almost surpasses belief." To abolitionists and proslavery ideologues alike, therefore, southern poor whites utterly lacked industry, intelligence, social propriety, and honor, the essential ingredients for political and social equality and thus should not be trusted with political decision-making.[7]

Northern and southern middle- to upper-class commentators perceived this class of people as so utterly degraded that they challenged their assertion of "whiteness," the one claim southern working-class whites had to political equality, "normative" status, and social superiority to free and enslaved blacks. Like Byrd and the author of "The Carolina Sand-Hillers," journalists and travel writers repeatedly compared "poor whites" unfavorably to other supposedly inferior people of color, be they enslaved blacks, Indians, or even Mexican peasants. Through a variety of arguments, including genetic inferiority, excessive interbreeding with "nonwhites," and environmental factors, such as the destructive influences of the southern climate, rampant disease, and a woefully inadequate diet, these writers asserted that "poor whites" were neither truly "white" nor clearly "nonwhite" but instead, a separate "'Cracker' race" in all ways so debased that they had no capacity for social advancement. This attitude is clear in an 1866 article from the Boston *Daily Advertiser* that proclaimed that this social class had reached depths of "[s]uch filthy poverty, such foul ignorance, such idiotic imbecility" that they could never be truly civilized. "[T]ime and effort will lead the negro up to intelligent manhood," the author concluded, "but I almost doubt if it will be possible to ever lift this 'white trash' into respectability."[8]

Contempt for working-class whites was almost as strong among African Americans as among middle-class and elite whites. Enslaved African Americans invented derogatory terms containing explicit versions of "whiteness" such as "(poor) white trash" and "poor buckra" (a derivative form of the West African word for "white man"). Although relations between slaves and nonelite southern whites were complex, many slaves deeply resented the role of poor whites as overseers and patrol riders and adopted their owners' view that elite southern planters were socially and morally superior. Many also believed that blacks, enslaved and free, formed a middle layer of social respectability between the planter aristocracy at the top of the social system and the "poor whites" at the bottom. The construction of a "poor white" and "white trash" social and cultural category thus allowed black slaves to carve out a space of social superiority, as well as permitted the white planter elite to justify enormous economic and social inequality among whites in a supposedly democratic society.[9]

Images of Mountain People – Appalachia, 1780–1865

In addition to ostensibly accurate depictions of actual rural white people, a second influential stream of literature about impoverished southern whites was the stories by writers collectively labeled (by later scholars) "southwestern humorists," which freely blended historical reality with literary invention. They featured characters who, in both look and deed, were important prototypes for the coming hillbilly persona. Ransy Sniffle of Augustus B. Longstreet's 1835 collection *Georgia Scenes, Characters, Incidents &c., in the First Half Century of the Republic* was one of the earliest and most enduring of these literary figures. An emaciated little man, Sniffle's standard condition of utter listlessness is only aroused by the vicarious thrill of watching a bloody fight that he helps provoke. Longstreet thus established the literary genre of debased poor whites as con men who intentionally profit from others' misfortune, a tradition carried on in the following decades by a host of writers, including William Gilmore Simms, Richard Hildreth, Harriet Beecher Stowe, and, most fully, by Johnson J. Hooper in his depiction of Captain Simon Suggs. Early illustrations of Suggs with his disheveled clothes, bearded face, long angular nose and facial features, sallow expression, and wide-brimmed hat, prefigure the standard hillbilly iconography used by later illustrators and movie makers (fig. 1.1).[10]

Figure 1.1
Hillbilly Progenitor #1: Simon Suggs. Frontispiece illustration by F. H. Darley, Johnson J. Hooper, *Adventures of Captain Simon Suggs, Late of the Tallapoosa Volunteers* (Philadelphia: T. B. Peterson, 1845). Courtesy of Princeton University Library.

SIMON SUGGS.

Despite these writers' significant influence on the as yet unborn hillbilly persona, none described people explicitly from or in mountain environs. The sole exception was the first poor white character from the Appalachian mountains, Sut Lovingood, created by Tennessee journalist George Washington Harris and published in the mid-1850s in various Tennessee newspapers and William T. Porter's national humor magazine *The Spirit of the Times*. Immoral, racist, depraved, and mean-spirited, yet utterly vital and free of nearly all constraints of social propriety and status, Sut positively revels in his own animalism and crudeness. Harris describes him as a "queer looking, long legged, short bodied, small headed, white haired, hog eyed, funny sort of a genius" who is part of a ridiculously large and absurdly named family composed of sixteen children (with appellations such as Phineass, Zodiack, and Jane Barnum Lind), a filthy but fecund mother, and a bestial father, Hoss. Human nakedness (both physical and psychological) is at the core of nearly all of Harris's tales, which often feature Sut or another character being stripped bare or engaging in (implied) fornication. Most of the stories also involve brutal pranks Sut gleefully pulls on people in positions of authority and power or, in a few cases, on black congregants. Just as often, though, Sut is the victim of his own avarice or gullibility and is forced to "act the fool," a role he recognizes for himself as a self-described "nat'ral born durn'd fool." He is a rawer and more cutting counterpart of Yankee Doodle and other northern antecedents, and his capacity to recognize and embrace his own foolishness (and that of all humans) imbues this otherwise merely grotesque and obscene figure with his lasting cultural significance and makes him a far richer character than the examples of poor whites discussed earlier.[11]

Harris's depiction of Sut and his family and neighbors in the Frog Mountains of eastern Tennessee solidified the characterizations of Longstreet, Hooper, and others into the standard tropes of the twentieth-century American hillbilly—lazy, slovenly, degenerate people who endure wrenching but always comic poverty, embody an uncivilized state of raw physicality and sexuality, and possess an almost superhuman fecundity. But for several reasons, Harris's work remained only a precursor to rather than the first example of the hillbilly image. First, Harris used the mountain settings of his stories more as a colorful background than as an intrinsic element of the character's persona and larger literary meaning. Second, although Harris's Lovingood stories were initially quite popular with newspaper and magazine readers, his strident politics (a potent mixture of rabid secessionism and radical libertarianism), use of thick dialect and tortured grammar, and his unapologetically rough and unseemly content clashed with the dominant "genteel tradition" of literature and literary criticism of the late-nineteenth century. Mark Twain greatly admired Harris's humor but accurately predicted, in his 1867 review of *Sut Lovingood*:

Yarns Spun by a "Nat'ral Born Durn'd Fool," the first publication of Harris's tales in book form, "Eastern people will call it coarse and possibly taboo it." Until William Faulkner and Erskine Caldwell in the 1930s, Harris had few literary followers and his work fell out of print. Although devotees of Sut have become more prominent since the book's republication in 1966, he remains on the fringe of cultural respectability and critics have remained uncertain where to place Harris and his alter ego on the cultural spectrum.[12]

Graphic artists' attempts to depict Sut in the 1850s make clear that no standard image of a southern mountaineer yet existed and that, in fact, most urban Americans had absolutely no idea what such a person should look like. Most illustrations in mid-nineteenth-century magazines presented Sut in working- and even middle-class urban attire of the era (such as a swallow-tailed coat and a high shirt collar) or the riding costume of the rural gentry. The work of Justin O. Howard, a New York political cartoonist commissioned to draw the accompanying illustrations for the original 1867 edition of *Sut Lovingood*, came closest to an accurate depiction of a hardscrabble southern mountaineer *and* to the standardized depiction of the hillbilly in the twentieth century. He presented Sut as a long and lean figure with an elongated nose and hands, bare feet, and attire consisting of ill-fitting overalls and a slouch hat who looks on bemusedly as his naked father flees from a swarm of angry bees (fig. 1.2). Yet Howard's late nineteenth century counterparts did

Figure 1.2
Hillbilly Progenitor #2: Sut Lovingood.
Illustration by Justin O. Howard,
George Washington Harris, *Sut Lovingood: Yarns Spun by a 'Natu'ral Durn'd Fool'*
(New York: Dick and Fitzgerald, 1867), 25.
Courtesy of Princeton University Library.

not adopt his characterization, instead presenting Lovingood as a nondescript rural rube or a Huckleberry Finn look-alike. This diversity of depictions shows that by the turn of the century a nationally recognized iconographic stereotype of southern mountain folk had not yet been established.[13]

A second major strand from which the hillbilly image would develop was literary portrayals of people (nearly all male) of the southern mountains, initially and predominantly defined as the southern Appalachian region but later also encompassing the hill country of Arkansas and Missouri. Although some antebellum depictions of southern mountain folk emphasized their primitive brutality, antebellum writers and artists more often praised their hunting and fighting prowess, celebrating them as stalwart frontier folk capable of thriving in a hostile wilderness. These representations of the mountain folk added two important new elements to the developing hillbilly persona: a conflation of the land and the people into an indivisible cultural construct; and a conception of innate violence, represented by the omnipresence of guns and rifles.

One of the earliest descriptions of the southern mountaineers comes from a 1780 announcement to the people of Virginia from British Major Patrick Ferguson about the dangers of the "Back Water men" who had marched from eastern Tennessee to the South Carolina border and would defeat his troops a week later at the Battle of King's Mountain in South Carolina. Ferguson warned urban Virginians that they should join the Tory forces "[u]nless you wish to be eat up by an inundation of barbarians . . . who by their shocking cruelties and irregularities, give the best proof of their cowardice and want of discipline." Ferguson's belief that town-dwelling Virginians would be swayed by descriptions of their fellow countrymen of the western frontier as "barbarians" provides a striking example of the conception of the "otherness" of southern mountaineers as early as the late eighteenth century.[14]

A closely related but more heroic cultural construction of the mountain folk was the glorified backwoods frontiersman, largely based on the real or imagined exploits and personalities of Daniel Boone and David Crockett. Boone, in particular, became a leading symbol of American masculine prowess after leading settlers through the Cumberland Gap into Kentucky, fighting and killing Indians, and taming a savage wilderness. First immortalized in John Filson's widely read "The Adventures of Col. Daniel Boon" of 1784, Boone was celebrated by numerous subsequent authors and was the major inspiration for the quintessential literary hero of the American wilderness, Natty Bumppo of James Fenimore Cooper's series of novels *The Leatherstocking Tales*. Through the literary reincarnations of Filson, Cooper, and others, Boone became the embodiment of a national myth, "the man who made the wilderness safe for democracy" and who best symbolized the regenerative potential of the frontier. As a cultural icon, therefore, he generally lacked the intrinsic ambiguity of the later hillbilly identity.[15]

Crockett was a more direct progenitor of the hillbilly persona. Although, like Boone, he represented the heroic frontiersman, Indian fighter, and big game hunter, in his own day he also symbolized backwoods ignorance and rough humor. Elected repeatedly to the Tennessee state legislature and the U.S. House of Representatives, he was nonetheless ridiculed by more cosmopolitan legislators for his backcountry origins. Ironically, his eventual mythic status was largely the product of the Whig Party which used Crockett (with his full consent) as a "real live" backwoodsmen to denounce the Democratic Party of Andrew Jackson, supposedly a fellow frontiersman. After the real David Crockett died in Texas defending the Alamo, the mythic "Davy" Crockett, a mixture of superhuman frontiersman and comical hick, lived on in the popular *Crockett Almanacs* series of the 1840s and 1850s, plays such as James Kirke Paulding's *The Lion of the West* (1831) and Frank Murdock and Frank Mayo's *Davy Crockett; Or, Be Sure You're Right, Then Go Ahead* (performed continuously from 1872 through 1896), and numerous twentieth-century film and television incarnations.[16]

Figurative depictions and the cultural meanings of Boone and especially Crockett would become important components of the emerging mountaineer, if not strictly hillbilly, image. Later artists and stage and screen costume designers would incorporate buckskin, fur or coonskin caps, and long-barreled rifles into their representations of these characters (fig. 1.3). In addition, the idea of figures who carve civilization out of a hostile wilderness would live on throughout the twentieth century in more positive accounts of mountaineers as spirited but noble people who preserve pioneer skills and ways of life in an industrial-era frontier. Finally, in moving late in life to a new western frontier—Boone left Kentucky to spend his final years in east-central Missouri and Crockett traveled through much of Arkansas on his way to Texas—Boone and Crockett's actual lives represent the symbolic conflation of the separate regions of the hillbilly's origin ("Appalachia" and "the Ozarks") into a single mythic space.[17]

Travel accounts of antebellum visitors to the southern Appalachian mountains were less mythologized sources of the developing image of the southern mountaineer. These writings suggest that, whereas most urban commentators found the mountain landscape awesome in its beauty and primitiveness, they saw the people of the southern uplands as quaint but not markedly different from the rest of rural Americans. The few examples of mid-nineteenth-century writings on the southern mountains intended for a popular audience such as "A Winter in the South" paint a similar picture. This fictionalized travelogue by "Porte Crayon" (the pen name of writer and

Vol.I. "*Go Ahead!*" No.3.

Davy Crockett's ALMANACK, OF WILD SPORTS IN THE WEST, Life in the Backwoods, & Sketches of Texas.

O KENTUCKY! THE HUNTERS OF KENTUCKY!!!
Nashville, Tennessee. Published by the heirs of Col. Crockett.

Figure 1.3
Davy Crockett: The original media-fabricated
hillbilly. Cover illustration by unknown illustrator,
Davy Crockett's Almanack, v. 1, no. 3 (Nashville,
1837) (copied from Ambrose Andrews portrait
of James Hackett playing character Nimrod
Wildfire in James Kirke Paulding's *The Lion
of the West*). Center for American History,
University of Texas at Austin. CN 10458.

illustrator David Hunter Strother) relates the journey of Squire Broadacre
and his family through the mountains of Virginia, Tennessee, and North Carolina. While Strother's physical descriptions of local people suggest the beginnings of a developing visual stereotype, unlike later accounts, the mountain folk are not presented as degraded or immoral. Though the illustration
accompanying the description of Squire Broadacre's guide, Mr. Jones, and
captioned "the Mountaineer" portrays a somewhat sinister figure, his position on horseback and costume of heavy cloth coat and pointed shoes more
closely resembles images of mountain men of the American West or European vagabonds than the barefoot, suspender-clad hillbilly to come (fig. 1.4).
The author presents neither Jones nor any other local inhabitant as listless,
impoverished, drunken, hot tempered, or suspicious of strangers—all standard tropes of the hillbilly image—but instead stresses their hospitality and
the region's abundance of food. The bearded face and tattered clothing of another mountaineer the Broadacres encounter, Kan Foster, point to a developing stereotype (fig. 1.5). In the text, however, rather than warily aiming a
rifle at the "intruders," he welcomes his visitors to his tidy and attractive
home. Strother's descriptions of Mr. Jones and Kan Foster thus suggest that
prior to the Civil War, the literary image of southern mountaineers was one

From Yankee Doodle to "Devil Anse"

THE MOUNTAINEER.

Figure 1.4
Typical portrayal of a southern mountaineer prior to hillbilly stereotype. "The Mountaineer." Illustration and text by David Hunter Strother, "A Winter in the South," *Harper's New Monthly Magazine* 15 (November 1857): 725.

KAN FOSTER.

Figure 1.5
"Kan Foster": Mountaineer as ragged but upright and inviting host. Illustration and text by David Hunter Strother, "A Winter in the South," *Harper's New Monthly Magazine* 16 (December 1857): 173.

of poor but upstanding rural folk, not the ignorant and hostile men and women of postbellum literature.[18]

Frederick Law Olmsted's *A Journey through the Backcountry*, published in 1860 and perhaps the most influential antebellum depiction of the people of the southern mountains, also offers no indication that they were notably different than nonelite whites in the rest of the South. As in his other

Hillbilly

writings, Olmsted intended this book to be a condemnation of the slave system and the limits it imposed on economic development. He saw such negative effects even in the mountain regions of Tennessee, North Carolina, and Virginia, areas without large-scale plantations and with relatively few slaveholders. Although Olmsted routinely described the working-class mountain folk he encountered as "coarse," "ignorant," and "dirty," and complained of their laziness and subsequent poverty, he attributed these traits to the slave economy rather than, as later writers would, cultural and genetic characteristics of a unique race of mountain people.[19] In short, even by the eve of the Civil War, interpreters of the southern Appalachian mountain people still did not believe that these people constituted a subset of nonelite southern whites, let alone a separate "race," culturally distinct and socially isolated from American civilization.[20]

Images of Mountain People—Arkansas and the Ozarks, 1820–1900

During the same years writers and social commentators were beginning to write about the land and people of southern Appalachia, adventurers, outdoorsmen, and humorists were also discovering the other primary locus from which the hillbilly image would grow: the hill country of Missouri and Arkansas. Because of its limited population and relative isolation from the rest of the nation even well after the Civil War, Arkansas rapidly acquired a reputation as the home of violent and primitive squatters living in near-wilderness conditions. Henry Rowe Schoolcraft, a geologist and student of Indian culture who traveled through the mountains of Missouri and Arkansas in 1818–1819, was one of the first visitors to report on the state at length. Schoolcraft described how "[t]he inhabitants . . . pursue a similar course of life with the savages, having embraced their love of ease, and their contempt for agricultural pursuits . . . [and] their mode of dressing in skins." He also lamented that, when hunting season came, the men abandoned their household and farming duties to the women. Mirroring the critique of William Byrd and others, he thus defined frontier Arkansans as an uncivilized people, who inverted "proper" race and gender hierarchies.[21]

Later visitors reinforced the idea of Arkansas as a violent and primitive land. English geologist George Featherstonhaugh called parts of the state a "sinkhole of crime and infamy," while German sportsman Frederick Gerstaecker presented a land populated by hard-drinking and lazy backwoodsmen, who were prone to violence and thrilled by the rugged sport of bear hunting. Humorous writings such as Charles Fenton Noland's columns on "Col. Pete Whetstone" and Thomas Bangs Thorpe's famous "The Big Bear of Arkansas," both widely circulated in *Spirit of the Times* in the 1840s, solidified the backwoods conception of the state. Not all of these travelogues, adventure stories, or tall tales were based on the mountainous region of the state, nor were they absolutely unique to Arkansas or even the old Southwest. Collectively, however, they laid the groundwork for the notion that lazy, potentially dangerous, and impoverished people populated Arkansas and the South more generally.[22]

Perhaps the most direct link between southwestern popular culture and the coming hillbilly image is "The Arkansas Traveller," a written tale, humorous oration, instrumental and lyrical song, and pictorial image that has appeared continuously since the mid-nineteenth century.[23] Most likely the creation of Colonel Sandford Faulkner, an elite Arkansas politician during its first years of statehood, the well-known tale is an ostensibly humorous retelling of an encounter between a party of Arkansas politicians, who have lost their way in the mountains during an 1840 campaign tour, and a poor squatter continuously sawing away at the same tune on his fiddle in front of a primitive log cabin.[24] The squatter responds to each of the visitors' requests for assistance with verbal puns, negative replies, and indifference. A sampling:

> Traveller: "As I'm so bold, then, what might your name be?"
> Squatter: "It might be Dick, and it might be Tom; but it lacks right
>   smart uv it."
> Traveller: "Sir! will you tell me where this road goes to?"
> Squatter: "It's never gone any whar since I've lived here; It's always
>   thar when I git up in the mornin'."

Finally, the traveler (representing Colonel Faulkner himself) achieves his ends by seizing the fiddle and playing the end of the tune that the squatter has forgotten. The grateful homesteader, joyful that he finally recalls the closing melody, invites the travelers in for food and drink.[25]

Published as music in 1847, and with accompanying dialogue in 1862 or 1863, "The Arkansas Traveller" appeared in various forms throughout the next century and a half. It was also depicted in pictorial form, first as a painting by Edward Washbourne (c. 1855) and then as engravings based on the painting, most famously in two Currier and Ives prints of 1870. These drawings depict many of the elements that make up the twentieth-century image of the hillbilly lifestyle: a ragged man with a long beard wearing a coonskin cap; animal pelts on the walls of a dilapidated log cabin; an impoverished family consisting of a woman smoking a corncob pipe and six slovenly children; dogs lazing in the dirt; a sign for "whisky" over the doorway with an inverted "ᴢ" denoting backwoods ignorance; and the mountains looming in the background (fig.

Figure 1.6

The Arkansas Traveler.

Leopold Grozelier engraving of Edward Washbourne painting, 1859.

1.6). The ambiguity of the cabin man's actions and attitudes would also later be replicated in the hillbilly persona. At first wary of outsiders and surly, the squatter later shows excessive hospitality. He is depicted as impoverished and ignorant but at the same time as living in total comfort in the wilderness. Likewise, the squatter symbolizes frontier laziness and idleness, as he sits and plays the fiddle while neglecting his crops and household duties. This indolence is juxtaposed against the purposefulness and urgency of the traveler. Yet it is the squatter who holds all the cards, and both participants know it. Like hillbilly characters to come, the squatter simultaneously "plays the fool" and takes advantage of the traveler, his social and economic "better."

As the audience for the "Arkansas Traveller" in its various forms grew from an Arkansas political elite to a statewide audience to a national readership of humor magazines and sheet music, the characters' significance changed. In the earliest extant printed version of the text from 1876, the opening scene introduces "A lost and bewildered Arkansas Traveler [who] approaches the cabin of a Squatter, about forty years ago, in search of lodgings."[26]

From Yankee Doodle to "Devil Anse"

Radically transforming its original meaning, the version published in the *Arkansas Traveler's Song Book*, in New York in 1864, represented "an Eastern man's experience among the inhabitants of Arkansas." The introduction further noted that the traveler's encounter with this backwoodsman was so upsetting he "has never had the courage to visit Arkansas since!"[27] Like Sut Lovingood's early illustrators, the New York artist had no idea what an Arkansan squatter should look like and drew a gypsy-like figure, barefoot, in loose fitting clothes, and with a bandanna tied around his head akin to depictions of impoverished transients (fig. 1.7). When writer H. C. Mercer described the tale in 1896, its meaning had changed yet again. In this version, both the squatter and the traveler were portrayed as products of the wilderness, one a rugged pioneer, the other a degraded squatter, and the message of the juxtaposition of class between the two was largely eliminated. Because both figures were now attired and described as frontiersmen, the story implied that all Arkansans fit into this category.[28]

The transformations in meaning of this song-story reveal the nationalization of a regional stereotype—"Arkansas" was becoming instantly recognizable shorthand for the half-comic, half-savage backwoodsman, a popular

Figure 1.7
A New Yorker's conception of the Arkansas Traveler frontiersman as European gypsy. Cover drawing by unknown illustrator, *Arkansas Traveler's Song Book* (New York: Dick and Fitzgerald, 1864).

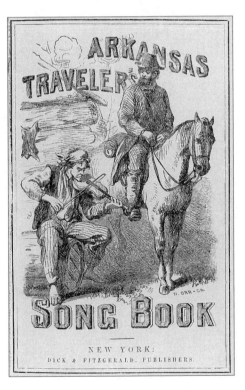

cultural icon growing as familiar to Americans as the noble Indian Chief in full headdress or the lazy plantation slave. Superimposing the shiftlessness and degeneracy of the symbolic poor white upon the frontiersman and hunter of earlier accounts of Arkansas woodsmen, this musical tale reflects the slow conflation of these two images from which the hillbilly would emerge in the following decades.

"Local Color" and the Construction of a Mountain "Other":

The Discovery of "Appalachia," 1865–1890

By the time the Arkansas Traveler was becoming iconicized in the decades immediately following the Civil War, descriptions and images of rustic rubes, impoverished southern whites, and frontier inhabitants had developed for well over 100 years and were well established in American culture. These separate depictions not only would continue to appear in various cultural formats throughout the twentieth century, but they also began to coalesce into a new self-contained image linked to a specific geographic locale—the dualistic icon of the hillbilly-mountaineer. The new creation was largely the result of the emergence of the "local color" writing in the 1870s and 1880s, a literary genre that grew out of the new, popular nineteenth-century magazines (such as *Lippincott's, The Century, Scribner's, The Living Age*, and above all, *Harper's New Monthly Magazine*) that catered to a newly expansive urban middle-class readership. Unlike early-nineteenth-century naturalists and scholars who wrote their travel accounts for a specialized scientific community and who viewed their work as objective analyses of natural, geological, and climactic conditions, local color writers, like the new magazines in general, intended their work primarily as entertainment. Characterized by a conversational style and tone and described by their authors as "daguerreotypes," "sketches," or even "hurrygraphs," local color's principal function was to increase sales by emphasizing "the peculiarities of life in a little-known corner of the nation."[29]

Although the array of local color writers and writings was too diverse to constitute a formal literary "movement," they shared a vision of the exoticism and "otherness" of their subjects. In an age of faith in American, and more generally Western, intellectual, cultural, and social superiority over the other "races" of the world, these writings were designed to show not cultural difference so much as cultural hierarchy—to celebrate modernity and "mainstream" progress and values by emphasizing the inferiority and alien nature of alternative cultures and societies, be they exotic, picturesque foreign locales and peoples or ethnically and geographically distinct societies in the United States, such as Louisiana Cajuns, Georgia blacks, or rural New Englanders of coastal Maine. These sketches tended to focus on antebellum and preindustrial America, both in order to romanticize the past and to point out the benefits of modern industrial society.[30]

It was in this context that a coherent place—"Appalachia"—and a unique people—the Appalachian "mountaineers"—reached national consciousness. Between 1870 and 1890, local colorists published over ninety travel sketches and 125 short stories about the region. The attitude of these authors is best summed up by the title of one of the first pieces describing the region, "A Strange Land and a Peculiar People." Despite his provocative title, Will Wallace Harney devoted far more time to his travel difficulties than to descriptions of the contemporary inhabitants of southeastern Kentucky. Nonetheless, his article introduced the idea of Appalachian "otherness" and established the region as a rich source of picturesque local color. Although Harney soon abandoned Appalachia as a literary source, he was succeeded in the following two decades by a host of other writers, including Charles Dudley Warner, Rebecca Harding Davis, Frances Hodgson Burnett, and James Lane Allen.[31]

Of greatest importance in terms of the nationalization of the Appalachian mountaineer image was the extremely popular short stories and novels of Mary Noailles Murfree (pen name Charles Egbert Craddock), the writer who almost single-handedly established the genre of "Southern Mountain fiction." Although scholars have questioned the accuracy of her human portrayals in such works as *In the Tennessee Mountains* (1884) and *The Prophet of the Great Smoky Mountains* (1885), the general reading public regarded them as factual. Murfree's writings solidified earlier notions about the eastern Tennessee mountains, and the Appalachian Mountain region more generally, as a land of illiterate but moral and proud people living in total isolation from modern America, but she infused her characters with a general tone of melancholy. Her plaintive approach helped redefine the mountains as a region existing in a perpetual past, the opposite of the energized, fast-paced world of urban industrializing America. The fact that most readers and reviewers believed that her antebellum-era stories documented contemporary conditions in the mountains underscores just how successful she was in establishing this conception of the mountains and their people.[32]

Although Murfree presented a somewhat more accurate and sympathetic portrait of mountain people and society than did many local color writers, all of these writers recapitulated and expanded upon the themes of earlier literary portrayals of poor whites and backwoodsmen. For example, James Lane Allen commented that although many Kentucky mountaineers had in the past left the mountains for rumored wealth in the West, they had "nearly all come back," unable to "cope with the rush and vigor and enterprise of frontier life. Theirs, they say, is a good lazy man's home." The writers' descriptions of human figures also reflected this general notion of Appalachian "otherness" and backwardness and resemble earlier portraits of Augustus B. Longstreet and George Washington Harris. Harney claimed that the "natives" have "marked peculiarities" of human anatomy and that all featured "elongation of the bones, the contour of the facial angle . . . and harsh features." Taking her cue from these local colorists, anthropologist Ellen Church Semple in an influential 1901 article described the mountaineers as having "thin bony faces, sallow skins, and dull hair," and lamented that they "retained little of the ruddy, vigorous appearance" of their "vigorous" forebears.[33]

The illustrations that accompanied these serialized travel accounts and short stories mirrored the text and reflected the slow emergence of a new stand-alone mountaineer persona. At first, these depictions differed little from antebellum illustrations. For example, mountain guide Jerry Browning in Rebecca Harding Davis's fictionalized 1880 account of a summer holiday in the mountains of western Virginia and West Virginia is the model of a trustworthy and proud backwoodsman, expertly cradling his rifle across his chest as he looks stoically ahead (fig. 1.8). In Allen's 1886 story "Through Cumberland Gap on Horseback," however, the pictorial representation of mountaineers—drawn by leading regional sketch artist E. W. (Edward Win-

JERRY BROWNING, OUR GUIDE.

Figure 1.8
"Jerry Browning": The epitome of the mountaineer as stalwart backwoodsman. Illustrator unknown, Rebecca Harding Davis, "By-Paths in the Mountains," *Harper's New Monthly Magazine* 61 (July 1880): 176.

Figure 1.9
Mountaineers as simpletons.
Illustration by E. W. Kemble captioned
"Native Types"; James Lane Allen,
"Through Cumberland Gap on
Horseback," *Harper's New Monthly
Magazine* 73 (June 1886): 53.

sor) Kemble—moves dramatically toward a hillbilly image. Kemble depicts two hill folk as plainly dressed, humorous simpletons whose dim-witted faces contrast sharply with the evocative descriptions of the natural beauty of the mountains (fig. 1.9). Allen's extended portrayal of these two mountaineers (whom he labels "native types") attempting to sell a "bag of small, hard peaches" (a stark contrast to the bounty of food Strother reported in 1857) could well have been written by Byrd about his "lubberlanders" 150 years earlier: "Slim, slab-sided, stomachless, and serene, mild and melancholy, they might have been lotus-eaters. . . . If they could sell peaches, they would be happy; if not, they would be happy." One should be careful not to read too much into a single line or an illustration by an artist with a penchant for portraying mountaineers as comic stereotypes, but, regardless of their typicality, they do reveal the emergence of a new conception of the people of the southern mountains, one that would become increasingly recognizable in the following decades.[34]

Like their male counterparts, images and depictions of mountain women underwent a similar, if less prominent, metamorphosis. Portrayed in antebellum accounts, such as "A Winter in the South," as unremarkably Victorian or as typical matrons of small farm homesteads, by the 1870s and 1880s, local color writers increasingly cast female characters and nonfiction subjects as one of several types: the beautiful but ignorant mountain lass; the overworked and crudely attired drudge who struggles to care for her oversized family; or (as illustrated by Kemble) the bonneted, toothless crone who lives

A MOUNTAINEER DAME.

Figure 1.10

Mountain woman as pipe-smoking crone.
Illustration by E. W. Kemble captioned
"A Mountaineer Dame"; James Lane Allen,
"Through Cumberland Gap on Horseback,"
Harper's New Monthly Magazine 73
(June 1886): 62.

out her remaining years smoking a corncob pipe awash in a haze of melancholia (fig. 1.10). In his 1889 "Comments on Kentucky," Charles Dudley Warner encapsulates this life cycle: "The girls marry young, bear many children, work like galley-slaves and at the time when women should be at their best they fade, lose their teeth, become ugly, and look old." Somewhat less of an explicit caricature than her male counterpart and far less often featured in turn-of-the-century magazine illustrations or frontispieces of novels, the "mountain woman" nonetheless reflected the same trend of merging conceptions of "poor whites" and backwoods pioneers into a new "poor mountaineer" persona.[35]

Moonshining, Feuding, and the Emergence of the Savage Mountaineer, 1880–1900

Even though local color writers firmly established the "fact" of Appalachian otherness, for the most part, their vision was of a picturesque landscape and colorful, even quirky men and women oddly out of step with modern society. More of a curiosity than a concern, this fictionalized Appalachia served primarily to point out the benefits of advanced civilization and to offer northern urbanites a welcome sojourn in a mysterious (but ultimately safe) wilderness from which they could return refreshed to their place in the cosmopolitan social order.

Beginning in the 1880s and accelerating rapidly in the 1890s, however, a strikingly different conception of the region developed—a notion that the people of the southern Appalachian mountains (and eventually of the southern mountains more generally) were not just out of step with but actually were a threat to civilization. The new ideological construction of the mountains as a land of lawlessness, cursed by the twin "evils" of "moonshining" and "feuding," was not entirely without foundation. Organized resistance to federal excise tax collection and violent, interfamilial conflicts did indeed develop in the southeastern mountain region in the last two decades of the century. Small farmers in this region had long converted a portion of their corn crop to alcohol for personal consumption and to trade or sell to rural neighbors and townspeople. The federal government had sporadically tried to collect excise taxes on this product since the late eighteenth century (the "Whiskey Rebellion" of 1794 in western Pennsylvania is the most famous example of upland opposition to these attempts), but not until the Civil War did they make a concerted effort to require licenses for and collect revenues from all distillers, no matter how small. Southern mountain farmers, who depended on the sale of corn whiskey to supplement their meager incomes and saw its production as a long-enjoyed right, deeply resented what they viewed as the unwarranted and dangerous intrusion of centralized power into properly local affairs. Many of these small-time distillers, increasingly labeled "moonshiners" and "blockaders" in the popular press, as well as much of their clientele, held deep grievances against the often heavy-handed methods and sometimes corrupt and illegal practices used by agents to enforce the law.

These tensions and animosities climaxed during the 1890s when the combination of economic depression, the expansion of nationalizing market forces and urbanization into previously exclusively rural locales, and the spread of local prohibition legislation threatened the livelihood of many mountain distillers in northeast Georgia and elsewhere in the region. The result was the rise of semiformal organized efforts to maintain local control over liquor production through collective violence. In a region where many white men also felt threatened by increasing black political and social autonomy and the growing number of women moving into the industrialized paid workforce, such collective opposition was often closely tied to concerns about perceived challenges to white supremacy and traditional morality. These efforts by "white caps" and "night riders" to enforce the economic, social, and racial status quo largely ended by the late 1890s, as federal authorities arrested and broke up resistance organizations and as modernizing forces continued to erode rural life. But by this time, the image of mountaineers as lawless "moonshiners" forever battling "revenooers" had become firmly entrenched in the popular imagination and would remain a central component of the hillbilly mythos from that time forward.[36]

At the same time that moonshine-related violence was drawing widespread government and press attention, local, and often, interfamilial conflict in the southeastern uplands (particularly eastern Kentucky) was also garnering national headlines. From the 1870s through the first decade of the next century, regional and national newspapers reported on dozens of family-oriented conflicts, forty-one between 1874 and 1893 alone. Although most of these disputes lasted only briefly and involved few casualties, some, such as the Martin-Tolliver conflict called the "Rowan County War," continued for over three years and resulted in twenty deaths. Journalists initially tended to view such conflicts as first a southern, and later a Kentucky phenomenon, the inevitable result of ongoing political power struggles and a uniquely violent past. By the mid-1880s, however, a series of murders in Appalachia shifted the focus from the entire state to the mountains, in particular. Increasingly, newspapers of both political parties, most influentially the Democratic *Louisville (Ky.) Courier-Journal* and the Republican *New York Times*, condemned the people of the mountains as degenerate barbarians whose conflicts stemmed not from political or economic disputes but from cultural, or even genetic, traits inherited from their wild Scottish highland ancestors. Reporters' shift in terminology from *vendetta* (with its Corsican context) to *feud* in labeling these battles, and their references to the disputing parties as family *clans*, underscored this new emphasis on Scottish heritage.[37]

Newspapers such as the *Courier-Journal* and the *Times* argued that the mountain people threatened national economic prosperity and social stability, not just that of eastern Kentucky. The only solution to this crisis, they asserted, was regional "progress" in the form of industrialization, railroad construction, and the growth of towns and cities. Eager to attract northern capital and to portray their region as a secure investment opportunity, regional news reporters and elites defined any local people who opposed industrial "progress" as backward and deviant—in other words, as white savages on par with African and Native Americans and opponents of European imperialism worldwide. A *Baltimore Sun* editorial of 1912, responding to a deadly shootout in the mountain town of Hillsville, Virginia, most explicitly expressed this argument. The paper thundered:

> There are but two remedies for such a situation as this, and they are education and extermination. With many of the individuals, the latter is the only remedy. Men and races alike, when they defy civilization, must die. The mountaineers of Virginia and Kentucky and North Car-

olina, like the red Indians and the South African Boers, must learn this lesson.[38]

Somewhat more severe in its prescription than most discussions of southern mountaineers, this editorial is nonetheless representative of hundreds of similar press accounts in its conflation of the actions of a single family with the entire regional population and in its comparison of southern mountaineers to other "primitive" peoples beyond the pale of civilization.

Although these accounts insisted that industrial development was the only solution to inherent mountain violence, historian Altina Waller and others have argued convincingly that, in reality, these violent outbreaks in the 1890s most likely resulted from the climax of the region's post–Civil War economic and social transformation. The advent of extractive industries (such as lumbering and iron and coal mining) and construction of railroad lines needed to bring these products to national markets, increases in land speculation and rising rates of absentee land ownership, and decreasing agricultural opportunities all led to a violent struggle between forces advocating modernization and those fighting to maintain local autonomy and a traditional agrarian system. Most Americans, unaware of the tremendous changes taking place in the southern mountains, however, had no reason to question the position of myriad press accounts that the widespread "lawlessness" of eastern Kentucky reflected a cultural and genetic inheritance of the southern mountain people. Thus, by the turn of the century, the idea that the southern mountaineers were a race of violent savages who threatened the progress of the rest of America had become firmly entrenched in the American psyche.[39]

Of all the conflicts in the southern mountains, none fired the public imagination more than the Hatfield-McCoy "feud" of the 1880s. Neither the first, longest, nor bloodiest interfamilial conflict in the southern Appalachians, the two families nonetheless rapidly became household names, a dubious distinction that has lasted for over 100 years. Countless articles and several books, most notably New York *World* journalist T. C. Crawford's *An American Vendetta: A Story of Barbarism in the United States* (1889), presented a portrait of "Devil Anse" (William Anderson) Hatfield and "Old Ranel" (Randolph) McCoy and their relatives as savage and isolated mountain people living in "Murderland" to whom family loyalty mattered above all else and who were ready, even eager, to use deadly violence against rivals and law enforcement officials. The actual conflict had much more to do with economic disputes and interstate rivalry than a "culture of violence," but most accounts eschewed any such political and economic analysis and instead presented it as a prime example of the irrational violence and dangerous ignorance of all rural people of the region.[40]

Iconography that solidified a new, more degraded and violent image of the mountaineer powerfully reinforced this vision. The frontispiece of Crawford's *An American Vendetta* featured a rendering by a *New York World* illustrator of "Devil Ance" [*sic*] as a tough-as-nails, rifle-toting mountain patriarch with a flowing dark beard and a wide-brimmed hat (fig. 1.11). Predicting the importance of these visual representations in creating the iconic savage mountaineer, in his preface Crawford asserted that the illustrations "caught in a most striking manner the spirit and character of the people and country" and "alone give a value to the book, whatever may be said about the rest." Hatfield may not have fully consented to this representation of himself, but he became quite a media celebrity and actively participated in contrived photographs taken long after the feud violence had ended. He posed repeatedly for cameramen with his rifle always at the ready ("Armed for Action" in the words of one caption) or with bandoleers of shotgun and rifle cartridges strapped across his waist and chest. In 1897, "Devil Anse" accepted the request of an itinerant photographer to pose with his family with their guns prominently displayed (fig. 1.12). Widely reprinted in the ensuing decades, these photographs of the Hatfields as grim-visaged desperadoes came to represent the image of all mountain folk to "modern" Americans. Hatfield even

Figure 1.11

The construction of the ominous mountaineer: "Devil Anse" Hatfield. Frontispiece illustration by Mr. Graves; T. C. Crawford, *An American Vendetta: A Story of Barbarism in the United States* (New York: Bedford, Clarke and Company, 1889).

From Yankee Doodle to "Devil Anse"

Figure 1.12
The crystalization of mountaineers as violent
feudists: "Devil Anse" Hatfield (bottom row, second
from left) and his family, 1897. Photographer unknown.
Courtesy of West Virginia State Archives.

played a role in later film depictions of mountaineers. Prior to the shooting
of the 1915 mountaineer spoof *The Cub* in the Virginia mountains, director
Maurice Tourneur traveled to Mingo County, West Virginia, to meet "Devil
Anse," apparently to lend authenticity to his portrayal of his mountaineer
characters. Film scholar Jerry Williamson speculates that Hatfield was such
a prominent symbol of the mountains to the national public, he may have
served as the origin of the archetypal hillbilly of later films, cartoons, and
other popular culture forms.[41]

The new conception of a savage mountaineer feudist quickly spread beyond the specific context of the Hatfield-McCoy conflict to fictional accounts

of Appalachian life by John Fox, Jr. and a host of lesser talents. Through his dozens of short stories and novels, most famously *A Cumberland Vendetta* (1895), *The Little Shepherd of Kingdom Come* (1903), and *The Trail of the Lonesome Pine* (1907), Fox presented his vision of the chasm that separated civilized society and the degraded culture of violent and backward mountain moonshiners and feudists. The accompanying illustrations in these works reinforced this concept of the ignorant, degenerate mountaineer. For example, a drawing accompanying Fox's 1892 short story "A Mountain Europa" portrays the heroine's father as an unkempt moonshiner leaning on his gun (fig. 1.13). Drawn, perhaps not surprisingly, by E. W. Kemble, the picture is the earliest I have discovered that brings together nearly all the visual tropes of the later iconic hillbilly: a surly disposition, barefeet, long scruffy beard, suspender-clad overalls, shapeless oversized felt hat, moonshine jug or flask, and long-barreled rifle. Although this iconic hillbilly would not be universally recognized until the 1930s, the textual and iconographic portrayals in sensational newspaper accounts and the novels of John Fox, Jr., and others collectively established the public perception of savage and degenerate mountaineers.[42]

Figure 1.13

The emergence of the iconic hillbilly. Illustration by E. W. Kemble captioned "Dad"; John Fox, Jr., "A Mountain Europa," *Century Illustrated Monthly Magazine* 42 (October 1892): 846.

Appalachia as Problem, Appalachia as Solution: Responses to the Feudist Image, 1890–1900

Turn-of-the-century writers, scholars, and benevolence workers offered various responses to this new conception of the dangerous mountaineer. Some writers, for the most part unfamiliar with the mountains and their people, accepted this stereotype without question. University of Chicago sociologist George Vincent, perhaps the most egregious case, reiterates in "A Retarded Frontier" (1898) the standard claim that in the "quiet pools in the mountains of Virginia, North Carolina, Kentucky and Tennessee . . . the frontier has survived in practical isolation until this very day," — a "fact" based on his four-day excursion through the eastern Kentucky mountains and the "vivid" stories of "Miss Murfree, Mr. John Fox, Jr., and other writers." The disconnection between myth and reality was so great, however, that even Vincent acknowledges "we had heard so many stories of the ignorance of the mountaineers that we were somewhat disappointed by their familiarity with a good many things we had expected them not to know" and suspects that the townspeople's stories about backward backwoodsmen are "jests" which "have about them a suggestion of newspaper origin." Likewise, author Charles Dudley Warner found it hard to reconcile the standard reports that all mountain people are "ignorant . . . idle, vicious, and cowardly" with his own experience in the region of "nothing but kind treatment . . . [with] little evidence of demoralization." But in the end, to these writers, and perhaps to large numbers of their readers, the ideological power of the myth of white mountain savages was too strong to offset their doubts about its veracity.[43]

Not all writers accepted so readily the moonshiner-feudist stereotype. In his 1896 piece "The Moonshiner of Fact," Francis Lynde critiqued novelists' eagerness to typecast the people of the southern mountains (and the rest of the South). After five full days searching for "local color" from Virginia to Louisiana, his main character "Pencraft" finally spots what he considers to be a family of "Southern types" whom the narrator informs him are probably Georgia mountaineers. "Mountaineers? Not moonshiners?" Pencraft asks excitedly. "Why certainly," comes the wry reply. "All mountaineers are moonshiners. Didn't you know that?" Oblivious to the narrator's deliberate exaggeration, Pencraft proceeds to write a story of bloodthirsty men and women "whose regard for human life was a minus quality . . . [and] to whom all strangers were 'revenuers' and as such to be killed without compunction." Lynde's cautionary tale concludes with a heavily armed Pencraft visiting the mountains of eastern Tennessee, only to discover how inaccurate his portrait had been. "These people are poor and ignorant and simple and primitive — anything you like along that line," Pencraft atones, "but they're as hospitable as the Arabs, as honest as they are simple, and as harmless as unspoiled country-folk anywhere."[44]

Not surprisingly, people from mountain communities raised some of the strongest criticisms of the degenerate mountaineer stereotype. Ministers J. T. Wilds and J. H. Polhemus, both of whom had served in the southern mountains, angrily challenged an 1895 address reported in the *Missionary Review of the World* that accused the mountain folk of carrying on murderous feuds, "moral looseness," and an utter ignorance of the outside world and Christianity. Wilds even suggested the mountain people used outsiders' expectations of native ignorance for their own ends for they are "[s]ome of the keenest minds and sharpest wits . . . [and] are forever hoodwinking strangers and commenting among themselves upon the ignoramuses who come from the cities ready to believe everything they hear." The reaction of the Berea College student choir, composed largely of mountain youth, to a campus lecture by author John Fox, Jr., in 1896, also reflected an intense native antagonism toward a damning mountaineer portrait. The students found Fox's patronizing recitation of readings, songs, and stories about Appalachian mountain folk so offensive that they denounced him as "anything but a gentleman" and threatened to tar and feather him. Despite their vehement complaints, however, Fox went on to a highly successful career as a novelist and a national circuit lecturer and became *the* definitive source on southern mountain society in the public imagination.[45]

Polhemus, Wilds, and the Berea students all sought to defend the reputation of the mountain people by presenting them (and in the latter case, themselves) as no different than other American citizens. But the dominant response of a wide array of nonfiction writers, who "discovered" Appalachia in the late nineteenth century and set out to "redeem" the mountaineer, was *not* to deny the "otherness" of mountain culture but rather to argue that its distinctiveness offered positive traits turn-of-the-century America desperately needed.[46] Like many Progressive reformers, they decried the regimentation and bureaucratization of the American people in the face of large-scale industrialization and unionization and worried that the growing power of an elite plutocracy in business and government threatened cherished American values of individualism, freedom, and democracy. Many of these men and women also feared that the Anglo-Saxon Protestant people (or "race" in their contemporary terminology) and their culture, which they believed were the very heart of America, would be engulfed by alien hordes of newly arriving non-Protestant immigrants from eastern and southern Europe and blacks swelling northern and southern cities. In addition, to counteract the "effeminacy" and "neurasthenia" they felt plagued the American middle class, many Progressives promoted the curative powers of the "strenuous life" that could reconnect urban people to the land and the rigors of their pioneer ancestors. To many reformers, therefore, the people of Appalachia represented a pure and untapped source for offsetting these social ills. As historian Allen Batteau summarizes, "Darkest Appalachia was seen as a place where young men could bring out their pioneering blood, as an area 'in need' of the civilizing influences from New England, and as a population that could save America from its latest impending crisis."[47]

Central to the idea of Appalachia as national salvation was the racial and religious pedigree of the people — in short, their "whiteness." According to this argument, the people of the southern mountains were the purest exemplars of the "race" whose ancestors had emigrated from the British Isles in the colonial era. At a time when political and intellectual leaders in America loudly advocated the theory of Social Darwinism, the superiority of the Anglo-Saxon people, and the strict hierarchy of the world's races, it is not surprising that these authors stressed the genetic, linguistic, physical, and cultural "Anglo-Saxonism" of the Appalachian people. Anthropologist Ellen Churchill Semple described them in 1901 as "the purest Anglo-Saxon stock in all the United States," and Reverend Samuel Wilson, president of Maryville College just outside of Knoxville, Tennessee, celebrated their "tide of rich red Teutonic and Celtic blood." Their "vigor and tenacity" clearly denoted the high fecundity of the mountain people that he and others argued could help offset the decreasing birth rate among middle-class white Americans and prevent "race suicide."[48]

In promoting their vision of southern mountaineers as "one hundred percent Americans," social "redeemers" challenged the prevailing idea that Appalachians were descendants of European rabble. Perhaps the most explicit example of this argument is an 1882 unsigned article bluntly entitled "Poor White Trash." A chronicle of the author's sojourn in the eastern Kentucky mountains, it presented shockingly backward people, "who plough with a stick and fight with a club, think the earth to be flat and their ancestors gods. . . . who, in many cases, neither read or write . . . and who often can barely count to ten." "These," the writer lamented, "are the 'no account' people, the 'poor white trash.'" Historian John Fiske's *Old Virginia and Her Neighbors* (1897) gave this theory a scholarly imprimatur. Asserting that the southern backcountry was settled by paupers and petty criminals forced to the margins of civilization by the power of the tidewater slaveholding aristocracy and their own degenerate heredity, Fiske concluded "[t]here can be little doubt that the white freedmen of degraded type were the progenitors of a considerable portion of what is often called the 'white trash' of the South."[49]

In response to such moral and genetic critiques of the mountain people's ancestry, promoters of the "noble" mountaineer worked to recast this heritage, arguing that the mountaineers were in their current uncivilized state not because they were the descendants of the human flotsam of Europe or were inherently violent but because the physical isolation imposed by the Appalachian mountains had preserved them in an earlier state of social evolution. Put most poetically by Josiah Stoddard Johnston in 1899, the Appalachians were "a vast Sargasso, a dead sea surrounded by an ocean of life," where the mountain people had been "wrapped in a Rip Van Winkle sleep and covered with a Lethean gloom." Johnston, like countless others of this era, stressed the pioneer heritage and lifeways of the people and their Elizabethan dialect and culture, arguing that the mountain natives were in some sense actually living in the past. In the often-quoted words of Berea College president William Frost, they were "our contemporary ancestors." Not only did geographic and temporal isolation explain such aberrant behavior as feuds and moonshine, these authors argued, but it was also a great asset for it had preserved social, cultural, and physical qualities and a racial purity that had built the America they cherished and feared was fast disappearing.[50]

Efforts by the mountain folk's self-perceived defenders to repudiate the "poor white trash" or "mean white" label also led them to introduce, beginning in the early 1880s, a new and theoretically more positive designation for Appalachian denizens—"mountain whites." The timing of this term's emergence and the expansion of benevolence efforts in the mountains is significant, because it coincided with a dramatic increase in racial violence throughout the nation and white benevolence workers' growing weariness with the limited advances of Reconstruction-era efforts to aid African Americans. The construction of a class of "mountain whites" and the significant growth of settlement schools and missionary programs in the Appalachian region gave many reformers the chance "to turn with a clear conscience away from blacks to aid Appalachia" and its citizens, who, unlike African Americans and southern "poor whites," had the cultural and racial qualities to rise out of their impoverished and benighted state.[51]

The supposed racial and religious purity of the "mountain whites" was a major selling point for such benevolence efforts, and Berea president Frost celebrated the fact that the region was "[u]ncontaminated with slavery" and populated not by "Catholics, nor aliens, nor infidels" but rather "Americans of the Americas."[52] Yet despite such efforts to resuscitate "mountain whites" as a legitimate social and cultural category clearly separate from "poor whites" and "white trash," it increasingly became synonymous in the public's mind with these stigmatized labels and cultural constructions. In the *Missionary Review of the World* address that so angered Polhemus and Wilds, for example, Mrs. S. M. Davis argued that there were "three classes" of illiterate southern whites—"'bankers' [people from the coastal sand banks], 'crackers,' and 'mountain whites,' often called 'Scotch-Irish heathen,' four million of whom live in North Carolina, Tennessee, Virginia, Kentucky, etc." These men and women, she wrote, were "[u]tterly illiterate, and their condition, intellectually and morally, it is difficult adequately to describe." Even in his pamphlet "Classification of Mountain Whites" of 1901, Reverend Robert Campbell recognized that "there is something about the name, or its associations, that savors of condescension." As members of the benevolence community began to sense the growing negative connotations of the term, they moved away from its usage.[53]

By 1914 (if not earlier), Presbyterian missionary Reverend Samuel Wilson rejected "mountain white" for the more acceptable label "mountaineer," arguing vehemently that the former term "implies peculiarity and, inferentially, inferiority . . . [and] sounds too much like 'poor white trash,' the most opprobrious term known in the South." Proclaiming that there were "no mountain blacks, or browns, or yellows" he wondered how it would sound "to hear the inhabitants of the Buckeye State spoken of as 'Ohio whites!'" Wilson's statement not only ignored the substantial numbers of Native Americans, African Americans, and, by this late date, even Southern and Eastern Europeans living in the Appalachian region, but it also defined "whiteness" as so normative and central to the conception of the contemporary civilized American, that to use the label "white" was actually to deny the legitimate "whiteness" of the mountaineers and emphasize their similarity to other culturally marginalized peoples. Yet at the same time, Wilson used such "colorized" language to stress the urgent need to solve the "white problem" of "[h]ow . . . to bring these belated and submerged blood brothers of ours, our own kith and kin, out into the completer enjoyment of twentieth century civilization and Christianity?" His simultaneous rejection and use of a colorized label perfectly illustrates the ambivalent conception of these people as a "white other," a group both within and outside of "normative" American society.[54]

Although the fundamental contradictions in the cultural construction of the southern Appalachian people persisted throughout the twentieth century, the label "mountain whites" steadily lost favor through the 1910s and was rapidly replaced by potentially more heroic and romantic terms, particularly "highlanders" and "mountaineers." Though the Scottish origins of the term "highlanders" would seem to contradict the widespread notion of their "Anglo-Saxon" cultural and biological inheritance, this made little difference to the emerging image of mountaineers as "a romantic people" situated "securely in the heroic past." In the end, the mountain folk's defenders struggled to repudiate the portrayal of all mountaineers as primitive savages and to promote instead a positive vision of noble and culturally and genetically "pure" people capable of social uplift. But their cultural and geographic rather than economic and political explanations of present-day conditions merely revamped mythic conceptions of a homogeneous and backward society. Perhaps those who sought to redeem the mountain people viewed the replacement of "mountain whites" with "mountaineers" and "highlanders" as a great victory. And indeed, although "highlander" died out as a label after World War I, mountaineer remained the predominant term used to describe the people of the southern hill country through much of the twentieth century. But at the same time that "mountaineer" was replacing "mountain whites," a new term was emerging that was destined to become universally recognized, conflate disparate regions of the South into a single cultural space, and reinforce with a vengeance negative connotations only hinted at in the term "mountain white."[55]

chaptertwo

The Emergence of "Hillbilly," 1900–1920

By the start of the twentieth century, the conflation over the previous two hundred years of rustic yokel, "poor white," and mountaineer images and ideas had set the stage for the emergence of a new amalgamated cultural icon, the "hillbilly." Although the home of the iconic late-nineteenth-century mountaineer of local color literature and sensational press accounts was ostensibly "Appalachia" (itself less a clearly identifiable locale than a newly constructed cultural space developed by urban northeastern novelists, book publishers, magazine editors and writers, and their middle-class readership), the first uses of the term "hillbilly" in print referred to the people in the bordering areas of Georgia and Alabama and the southwestern hill country of Arkansas and Missouri. From its origins as a regional label, the word and image would slowly spread nationally through the works of joke book writers, professional linguists, popular authors, and motion picture producers and directors. First appearing in print at the dawn of the new century, the term's rise accompanied but did not immediately impact the simultaneous phenomenon of the rapid spread of mountain moonshiners and feudists and their wives and daughters in pre–World War I silent films. Yet by the mid-1910s, as interest in this genre waned, the characters' once exclusive meaning of violent and lawless people who posed a serious threat to the "proper" late-Victorian social order shifted to include a parallel vision of still backward but now comic backwoods folk who served as ridiculous foils for modern Americans, all with almost no change in their outward appearance.

As in the past, what accounted for the image's initial appeal and what made such a dramatic transformation possible was the word's and image's on-going ambiguity and thus malleability. Partly, these characters were popular with early twentieth-century audiences because they satisfied their basic desire, in the words of a 1907 *Baltimore Sun* article on film's appeal, for "anything in which there is a hearty, healthy laugh or where the heart thrills and the breath catches." But as strangely mixed white Anglo-Saxon Americans, who lived and acted as stereotypically violent, sexual, and primitive people of color and who simultaneously occupied a heroic past and a degraded present, the mountaineer/hillbilly could also be used to both uphold the superiority of modern civilization and provide exhilarating scenes of murder and mayhem that did not threaten the "proper" social and racial order. They thus served as a conduit for many Americans struggling to come to terms with rapid industrial growth and a wave of new technologies, burgeoning and increasingly racially and ethnically diverse cities, ever more blatant class divisions and tensions, and challenges to "traditional" social mores and gender roles that accompanied the rise of a new consumption ethos.[1]

Alabama Sand-Hillers and Slow Trains in Arkansaw—

the Birth of the "Hillbilly" Label at the Turn of the Century

For a word that would become almost universally used and would permeate all aspects of American culture, the etymological and cultural origins of the term "hillbilly" are remarkably murky. The most credible theory is that Scottish highlanders either in their native country or in the New World linked two older Scottish expressions, "hill-folk" and "billie" (a synonym for "fellow" or "companion"). Although it is unclear when this elision took place, the term was likely part of rural southern vernacular by the late nineteenth century. William Nathaniel Harben's use of the expression "passle o' hill-billies" without quotation marks and as a passing reference in his novel *Abner Daniel* (1902) suggests, as folklorist Archie Green has argued, that he probably heard the term while growing up in Whitfield county in northern Georgia.[2] African Methodist Episcopal minister R. S. Lovinggood's inclusion in a 1907 published sermon of "hill billy" in a list of words (including "sheeny," "dago," and "nigger") that must be avoided because they "stirred up race hatred" indicates the term's derogatory and racial connotation was well known, at least among African Americans, by this date.[3] A more definitive pre-1900 use of "hillbilly" in the vernacular suggests other interpretations of the word. In a photograph of a large group of men and women in a woodsy setting in West Virginia hand labeled "'Camp Hillbilly,' August, 1899," the use of quotation marks around the words Camp Hillbilly, the participants' obviously middle-class attire of suits, high-collar dresses, straw hats, and bonnets, and the relaxed group pose of the gathering suggest that "hillbilly" here is meant to be humorous and to point out the incongruity of this group of middle-class city folk in their backwoods holiday setting. The photograph thus emphasizes by inversion the lower class, impoverished, and nonurban meaning of the term. But it also might have been meant by the author to show that beneath their city clothes, these campers had much in common with "hillbillies."[4]

Although these examples seem to suggest a general familiarity with the term across the southern mountains and even parts of the Midwest, the author of the 1900 *New York Journal* article that marked the term's first known appearance in print stressed both the novelty and the allure of this persona to Americans outside the region. Political correspondent Julian Hawthorne emphasized that when his local "interlocutor" "refer[red] familiarly to the Hill-Billies, I was obliged to ask him to explain," and then went on to use the term eight times in the brief article. Hawthorne's ensuing definition perfectly captures the term's intrinsic ambiguity: "a Hill-Billie is a free and untrammeled white citizen of Alabama, who lives in the hills, has no means to speak of, dresses as he can, talks as he pleases, drinks whiskey when he gets it, and fires off his revolver as the fancy takes him." Clearly derogatory and accentuating the poverty and improper social behavior of its subject, it also suggests more admirable attributes of freedom, self-identity, and independence—as did the article's focus on the political importance and autonomy of mountain folk who happily accept free liquor and campaign payouts from one candidate only to vote for his rival.[5]

Such standoffishness is further highlighted in the accompanying illustration by famed political cartoonist Homer Davenport, perhaps the first published pictorial representation of figures labeled "hill-billies" (fig. 2.1). Defined by their long-limbed bodies, scraggly beards or mustaches, oversized felt hats, and full-length trench coats, these backwoods folk look up expectantly but noncommittally (with arms akimbo or folded in front or behind rather than outstretched) at the huge figure of railroad magnate Collis Huntington as he prepares to try and buy their votes. Regardless of Hawthorne's or Davenport's exact intent in so prominently constructing a textual and visual definition of "hill-billie," the multiple possible interpretations show just how ambiguous, and therefore potentially malleable, the term and its image were. This article also shows that the term was beginning to be presented to readers and viewers far outside the mountain South, an audience who likely had far less sense of the full range of meanings of the label than did the West Virginians of "Camp Hillbilly."

Figure 2.1

"A free and untrammeled white citizen of Alabama": The birth of the labeled-as-such "Hill-Billie." Homer Davenport, "Uncle Collis and the 'Hill-Billies': Illustrating the Troubles of a Good Man in the Far South," *New York Journal*, April 23, 1900, 2.

The word's next appearance in print extended its scope to the mountainous region of Arkansas and Missouri, an association that intensified the word's satirical and derogatory connotations. Humorist Charles S. Hibler's 1902 pamphlet *Down in Arkansas* offered an extensive discussion of the hillbilly, through the adventures of a Boston capitalist, a Philadelphia lawyer, and a Kansas City real estate agent who visit the Ouachita Mountains of western Arkansas in hopes of making a killing by buying cheap land and selling it to lumber and mineral interests. Most of the story revolves around the already-hackneyed theme of the slowness of "Arkansaw" trains, but here the image is explicitly connected to the mental and physical slowness of the mountain inhabitants. When the three ask the conductor why the train is four hours late arriving in Kansas City, he replies: "In a sense, fellers, this train's really yesterday's train. . . . Er long stretch of our road runs through Arkansaw an' them Hill Billies down thar ar more or less behin' time; we run slow like so's to give 'em time to get up, an' get ther business." Later in their travels, the threesome become lost in the woods and captured by some of these "hill billies" who suspect they are revenuers. Their native guide explains the origins and the characteristics of these strange backwoodsmen:

> Though as yet unheralded, the Hill Billy has a traditional history, reaching onto the dim and distant past. . . . The Hill Billy is a character in many respects unlike any other on the globe, and to do him justice would require the facile pen of a Dickens. . . . The Hill Billy, ever true to his principle of exclusiveness, never looks beyond his own beloved hills for his bride. As a result, the species has remained pure and undefiled. . . . The Hill Billy is proud in his poverty, contented with his environment, happy in his seclusion.

These themes of complacent poverty and geographic and social stasis would be perpetuated in almost all subsequent depictions of this persona.[6]

Down in Arkansas appears not to have been widely read or distributed but the same cannot be said of Thomas Jackson's *On a Slow Train through Arkansaw*, printed the following year. A widely traveled railroad brakeman, Jackson published his book just in time to take full advantage of the huge influx of train travelers visiting the 1904 Louisiana Purchase Centennial Exposition (World's Fair) in St. Louis, and used his railroad connections to aggressively market the book through railroad station newsstands and hawkers. As a result, Jackson's publication sold a staggering seven million copies by 1950. Surprisingly, *On a Slow Train* has very little to do with Arkansas or southern mountaineers and is largely a haphazard retelling of standard jokes, puns, and minstrel stage quips. However, both the title and the fact that Jackson set the first pages in the state reemphasized the connection between backwardness and Arkansas. Equally influential was the widely replicated cover illustration depicting a tall, lank, and bearded figure with rifle, hound dogs, and oversized hat perched on a stump on his barely cleared land in front of his log cabin home. The cover reference to "Sayings of the Southern Darkies" and "Best Minstrel Jokes" illustrates how Jackson saw this new iconic mountaineer as closely related to similarly stereotypical images of slow-witted African-American rustics ruled by animal appetites (fig. 2.2). Jackson's work spawned a slew of imitators, including Andrew Guy Chilton's *Through Arkansas on the Hog* (1908) and George Beason's *I Blew in from Arkansaw* (1908). It also generated strong opposition within Arkansas, best exemplified by Mrs. Bernice Babcock's diatribe *The Man Who Lied on Arkansas and What It Got Him* (1909). But the damage had been done, and the widespread notion that the state was peopled by slow (and slow-witted) bumpkins thrived well into the post–World War II era.[7]

Of the many works that built upon the base established by Jackson and

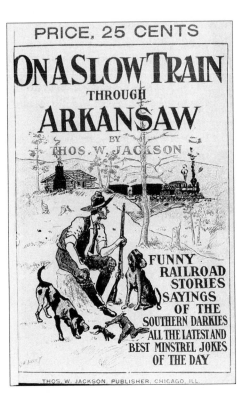

Figure 2.2
The original mass-produced Ozarks
hillbilly. Cover illustration, artist unknown,
Thomas Jackson, *On a Slow Train through
Arkansaw* (Chicago: Thos. W. Jackson
Publisher, 1903).

his predecessors, Marion Hughes's *Three Years in Arkansaw* (1904) most significantly furthered the hillbilly image. A jack-of-all-trades, who had worked in five states as a farmer, hotelkeeper, and lawyer, Hughes spent three years in the mountain towns of Horatio and Hatton Gap, Arkansas, in the late 1890s. His book is a strange combination of tall tales, ethnic and racial jokes, and a careful assessment of local social and economic conditions. It also added important visual and literary elements to the emerging hillbilly image and further combined mountain and poor white constructions. Hughes's detailed discussion of hogs, including raising and slaughtering them, also added to the linkage between swine and poor whites, a central visual trope of the hillbilly image. His focus on the importance of pigs as a food source also emphasizes the inhabitant's primitive living conditions, and his story of the original settlers of the state hints at much darker relations with animals. Describing the founders as an Irishman and a white woman whose children were raised on the milk of their black slave and their goat, he writes, "That is why the natives of Arkansaw possess so many peculiarities that the human race or the descendants of Adam does not possess." Along with separating

Arkansans from the rest of humanity, Hughes hints at both miscegenation and bestiality.[8]

Further stressing their closeness to the dirt and their animality, Hughes consistently associates the hill people with extraordinarily high fecundity, early marriage, and a near complete lack of social etiquette. For example, he describes a typical bride responding to the minister's question whether she will marry the groom: "she stopped picking wool, studied for a minute; took the snuff stick out of her mouth; turned around, spit a stream of tobacco juice into the fire, and said, 'I reckon.'" The description of the bride represents yet another standard trope in hillbilly imagery—mannish, homely, uncouth, and meagerly attired women. Hughes describes one old woman who "had her sleeves rolled up until you could see the hair under her arms. Her dress came just a little below her kneecaps, and was a Mother Hubbard . . . made of Flour sacks of different brands" so that she advertised "Early Riser" and "Pillsbury's Best" on the front and back of her dress. The crude accompanying cartoon of this supposedly typical Arkansan doing her wash while farm animals scrounge around underfoot (fig. 2.3) and his constant references to women's (and men's) use of liquor and tobacco (whether smoked, chewed as "chaw," or on a snuff stick) unabashedly illustrated their vulgarity, filth, and social crudity.[9]

Figure 2.3

"Typical" slovenly and impoverished Arkansan woman. Marion Hughes, *Three Years in Arkansaw* (Chicago: M.A. Donohue & Company, 1905), 24.

INTERIOR OF A TYPICAL ARKANSAW HOME

Figure 2.4
"Interior of a Typical Arkansaw Home."
Marion Hughes, *Three Years in Arkansaw* (Chicago:
M. A. Donohue & Company, 1905), 35.

All the aforementioned visual tropes are brought together in Hughes's cartoon of an indoor scene of the "typical Arkansaw home" with far too many children, animals of all sorts, an old-before-her-time mother, and a shiftless father playing his fiddle (fig. 2.4). The accompanying text describing how the man ignores his family's needs while his wife struggles to light a fire to warm "the barefooted, half-naked children . . . shivering with cold" centers on the familiar themes of rural poverty and social isolation of these people. Yet because of the legacy of comical presentations of Arkansans or perhaps because, unlike Appalachia, the region lacked a consistent effort by missionaries and reformers to emphasize the "plight" of the local inhabitants, here these conditions are presented as deserving only humorous derision, not sympathy or moral outrage.

This sense of mocking laughter at poverty, antisocial behavior, and animal living, as well as his ambiguous relation to the local people and the hillbilly myth he helped create, is well captured in the bit of doggerel with which Hughes closes the book:

I have lived in 16 States
But of all I ever saw
There is no place like living
Down in old Arkansaw

Hillbilly

They all wear homemade clothing
Both the men and females
While the children with dirty faces
All go in their shirttails

The men drink moonshine whiskey
The women chew and dip
And the big gals go barefooted
With tobacco on their lip. . . .

All are free-hearted
And respect the moral law
Is the reason I love to live
Down in old Arkansaw.[10]

Because he spent many years living in rural Arkansas and because of his working-class and transient life experiences, Hughes thought of himself as part of these people and had a grudging admiration for their raw way of life, their hardiness, and their straightforwardness. At the same time, he presented them primarily as humorous and satirical caricatures precisely because of their "otherness"—the degree to which their clothing, appearance, life ways, and values differed from a middle-class urban norm. Although Arkansans harshly condemned Hughes's book as yet another vicious attack on the people and character of their much maligned state (one writer, strongly refuting his "slurs," suggested that Hughes be placed in a zoo as the missing link between man and ape), *Three Years in Arkansaw* was widely read in and outside the state. It played an important role both in reinforcing outsider conceptions of Arkansan backwardness and in establishing a figurative image of the hillbilly as an extension of crude animalism.[11]

Among those who read Hughes's work and both spread and legitimated the term were linguists and folklorists. University of Arkansas professor Joseph W. Carr acknowledged his indebtedness to Hughes's book in a 1904 article in the journal of the American Dialect Society that cited words peculiar to the Ozarks region of Arkansas. Carr's wordlist included the first scholarly reference to "hill-billy," defined as an "[u]ncouth countryman, particularly from the hills," as in the quotation "You one-gallused *hill billies*, behave yourselves." Two years later, Carr offered a second definition of the term that now distinguished poor whites geographically and culturally: "The swampers & the hill-billies don't hit it off very well." Over the next three years, references to the word "hillbilly" were recorded in southwest Missouri, east Alabama, and west Georgia, and, by 1917, Kentucky, Kansas, and Louisiana.[12]

What accounts for the emergence of the term "hillbilly" in the years immediately after 1900? Although there is no single definitive answer, one can surmise that the consequences of many of the economic and cultural developments that led to the establishment of the mountaineer icon helped spawn the slightly later hillbilly incarnation. As the denuding of Appalachian hillsides and the shrinkage of mountain farms and household economies drove tens of thousands of previously self-sufficient mountaineers into tenancy or work in the burgeoning coal mines, and especially, cotton mills, reports on the subsequent impoverishment of the region once again brought the mountaineers into the national spotlight. Critics of the new company towns and textile factories that sprang up all over the Piedmont region in the early twentieth century railed against the low pay, poor living and working conditions, and particularly the widespread practice of employing children, some as young as nine years old. In response, industrialists launched a public relations campaign designed to illustrate the backward and unhealthy life ways of hill people and the supposed advantages of town life and to present themselves as agents of benevolence. Building upon the by-then well-established vision of hopelessly isolated and irrationally violent mountain people, propagated in local-color novels by Mary Murfree, John Fox, Jr., and others and by the spate of news accounts on "feuds," these defenders of the textile industry added new layers to the conception of mountaineers, presenting them as a diseased, illiterate, undernourished, sexually promiscuous, and degenerate people. The "mountaineer" thus became both a useful foil for industrial exploitation and a potent symbol of unsanitary and immoral white poverty. Although neither anti–child labor advocates nor cotton industry apologists appear to have used the term "hillbilly" itself in their writings or speeches, their debate formed the ideological backdrop against which the word and image emerged.[13]

Broader political and social movements may also help explain the timing of the appearance of "hillbilly." The Democratic mobilization against the Populist Party in the late nineteenth century and the imposition of systematic racial segregation had reestablished an atmosphere of racialized class tension that the Populists had struggled to overcome. The followers of 1911 Democratic Mississippi senatorial candidate James Vardaman, for instance, adopted the semantically and chronologically similar (first in print in 1893) label "rednecks" for themselves precisely to emphasize their commitment to white supremacy. Perhaps the slightly later appearance of "hillbilly" and its related visual caricature was also connected to the rise of Populism and the perceived need by economic and social elites to discredit southern working whites who potentially threatened the corporate political and economic order. Or the term's slow emergence in print may have owed more to the ideological atmosphere of the Progressive Era. To self-conscious urban reformers eager to apply scientific reasoning to the social problems associated with urbanization and industrialization, the hillbilly stood for everything they were working to eradicate—unhygienic living conditions, societal backwardness, and animalism. Likewise, to newly arriving urbanites—either transplanted native-born farmers or immigrants from southern and eastern European villages—the hillbilly represented a way of life and cultural values from which they sought to escape. None of these factors can single-handedly explain the sudden appearance of "hillbilly" in print in the early 1900s, but these forces and movements collectively contributed to a social and cultural atmosphere that encouraged the growth of the stereotype.[14]

Nonetheless, one must be careful not to overstate the prevalence of "hillbilly" in American culture prior to World War I. In the early 1900s, the term was still far from universal, and the idea of the hillbilly, although becoming more concrete, was still very much in flux. Even in the southwestern mountains, the word was not at all common in the years surrounding 1900. It is important to note that the word "hillbilly" never appears in Hughes's book and is mentioned only once in *On a Slow Train through Arkansaw*. The preeminent Ozark folklorist Vance Randolph also found that "hillbilly" was not widely used before 1915. Even the absence of a standardized written spelling of the word reflected its still-evolving nature. Until the 1930s, "hill-billy(s)," "hill billy(s)," and "hillbillie(s)," all appeared in print, sometimes with different versions of the word in the same sentence or paragraph. If pre–World War I writings on mountain folk are to be taken as representative of national attitudes, most Americans still saw the mountaineer far more as a potential threat than a comical throwback.[15]

Southern Mountaineers in Early Motion Pictures, 1904–1920

The slow growth of the term's use and the evolving meaning of the mountaineer image can best be traced through the relatively new medium of silent motion pictures. Reaching a far larger and more diverse audience (some 40 million a week by 1922) than either joke books or local color novels and heavily reliant on simple stories of struggle between good and evil, and civilization and savagery, films would profoundly influence the depiction and meaning of the hillbilly persona throughout the twentieth century. Prior to World War I, only one motion picture used the word in its title, promotional copy, or interior title cards, the aptly named *Billie—the Hill Billy* of 1915. Despite the near total absence of the term "hillbilly" in early motion pictures, however, many movies were set in the mountains or about mountaineers. Jerry Williamson, the leading scholar on southern mountain films, has tallied more than 400 movies made between 1904 and 1920 set in the mountains and featuring the "colorful" lives of mountain men and women, and another seventy-six such films produced between 1920 and 1929. A significant number were created by the primary movie companies of the day, including Biograph, Edison, and Vitagraph, directed by important directors including D. W. Griffith, and starred such leading film personalities as Mary Pickford. Indeed, the first film produced explicitly about mountain people, Biograph's 1904 short *The Moonshiner*, proved to be such a success that the company was still advertising it four years later as its biggest money maker—"the most widely known and most popular film ever made." The success of *The Moonshiner* led to such a steady increase in the number of mountaineer-themed films that film studios released seventy such films in 1914, averaging more than one new movie a week.[16]

All one- or two-reelers until just prior to World War I and shown in nickelodeons to largely working-class and ethnic audiences, these films featured highly melodramatic storylines and nearly nonstop action, including horse chases, characters falling or leaping from cliffs, and fighting of all forms. Standard plots, involving feuding families, battles between moonshiners and revenuers, and love triangles that pitted urbanites against mountaineers, ensured that nearly every film featured one or more killings. The death toll in some was even higher. In *The Last of Their Race* (1914), the killing is so wanton that by the film's end only two adversaries of once large rival clans remain standing. Even in our own age, when film images of real and fictional violence have become routine, the amount of violence in the nearly 500 mountain films released through 1929 is staggering—over 200 murders, 500 assaults with guns, axes, or hand-to-hand combat, and 100 attacks on women.[17]

These films' spectacular violence and action almost invariably revolved around storylines of sexual desire and conquest. Mirroring and often based on the stories of local color novelists such as Charles Neville Buck, Murfree, and Fox, Jr., these plots often took the form of a love triangle between a primitive but alluring mountain girl, a man from outside of mountain society working with industrial interests to "modernize" the region (usually a valley farmer or a professional such as a revenue agent, an engineer, or a surveyor), and a potentially violent mountain man who also covets her. As unambiguous melodramas, these stories nearly always conclude with the outsider besting his mountain rival and bringing his female prize back to the city or lowlands, proving the superiority of modern, urban, capitalist America to primitive backwoods society. These plots also strongly suggested that properly virile modern men, despite their years of formal education and positions in the bureaucratic social structure, could still triumph on the frontier. In a surprising number of cases, however, once in the city, the mountain woman discovers that her urban partner is weak, cowardly, or untrustworthy and realizes that true happiness lies with her native suitor in her beloved mountains. Yet despite the alternative endings of these films, the underlying theme remained the same: the propriety of male dominance, with strong, virile men winning out over weak or self-centered ones.[18]

Shockingly, given late-Victorian-era conceptions of feminine gentility and propriety, the violence in these films was perpetrated not only by mountain moonshiners and feudists but also by their wives and daughters. Many mountaineer silents featured women shooting and killing men, including law officers and elders of rival families. In one extreme case, Griffith's *The Mountaineer's Honor* (1909), a mountain mother actually shoots her own son dead rather than see him dishonorably hanged. In addition to shooting guns and holding captives at gunpoint, many women in these films successfully disguise themselves as men to participate in all-male activities such as running moonshine and lumbering or to avenge the shooting of a family member. Similarly, a number of films portrayed "wild mountain women" who refuse to be controlled by those at the top of the social hierarchy (be they fathers, priests, landowners, or other elites). Such transgressive behavior by women, however, was rarely allowed to last long, and the mountain vixen inevitably ends up married to the male lead.[19]

Clearly, film directors and producers intended such portrayals of manly gun-toting women and wild mountain girls as warnings of the dangers of crossing social and gender boundaries at a time when the more socially liberated "new woman," suffragettes, and the ever-growing number of women working outside the home, were challenging traditional gender mores and male control of public spaces. From this perspective, the films' closing scenes, featuring socially dominant men once again firmly in charge, symbolized the restoration of the "proper" social order. The same case can be made for the typical victory of the urban modern man over the backward mountaineer. But as many audience studies have shown, the filmmaker's intended meaning is not the only message derived by audiences. Nickelodeon audiences may have come away with an opposite set of messages: the thrilling possibility of transgressing gender and class boundaries and norms; the excitement and allure of life in the wilderness in contrast to the crowded and regimented nature of industrial America; and the secret satisfaction of challenging and even besting (no matter how briefly) the forces of social order and control. It is this very ambiguity in the possible meaning of the mountaineer that made these silent films so popular and that sustained mountaineer/hillbilly characters throughout the century and across the cultural spectrum.[20]

Central to the acceptability of such violent and titillating images was the unique status of the characters as people both beyond and within the confines of a seemingly endangered contemporary whiteness. On the one hand, the setting of these films in the far away (both geographically and chrono-logically) southern mountains cushioned their potential social threat. Self-appointed middle-class urban reformers of the Progressive Era, deeply con-cerned about burgeoning urban populations of "undesirable" Southern and Eastern European immigrants and concomitant increases in crime and poverty, were alarmed by the rapid spread of penny arcades and nickelodeons in working-class and immigrant city neighborhoods and the presumed threat they posed to the Victorian social order by encouraging loosened sexual stan-dards and wanton violence. In the words of a 1910 *Good Housekeeping* arti-cle, the nickelodeons and the films they presented served as "a primary school for criminals. . . . teaching obscenity, crime, murder, and debauch-ery for a nickel." In response to these criticisms, the film industry in 1908 es-tablished a censorship council, the National Board of Review, which deemed scenes of murder, gun battles, and raw sexuality unacceptable if set in mod-ern urban settings. But they attracted less attention if based in mysterious for-eign lands, the "Wild West" of half a century earlier, or the isolated country of Appalachia and the Ozarks. On the other hand, similarly violent acts by African Americans, Latinos, Chinese, and Native Americans, or even newly arrived Southern and Eastern Europeans, would have been too threatening to the racial order to have passed the censors' ban. What made mountaineer films acceptable was the race of the perpetrators; despite their status as near-savages ruled by animal lusts, the mountaineers were clearly "white" (and moreover, Anglo-Saxon Protestants). Thus, as in late-nineteenth-century lit-erary and news accounts, contemporary white Americans living and behav-ing as pioneer forebearers and as people of color was central to the image's appeal.[21]

The promotional copy for Pathe's 1920 film *Forbidden Valley* made this contradictory status explicit: "The last stand of primitive white men in Amer-ica; the last frontier of the land where men make and enforce their own laws; such is The Forbidden Valley in the heart of the Kentucky mountains." The combination of the words "primitive" and "white" is instructive, for it points to the "white other" nature of mountaineer characters in these films. The ex-plicit use of "white" in the film's promotional copy was unusual; most adver-tisements and reviews of these films lacked specific racial references to the mountaineers, assuming a character's whiteness unless explicitly stated oth-erwise. However, descriptions of their centuries-old social customs, ancestral feuds, and pioneer life ways, all indirectly signified the mountain folk's his-torically privileged racial status, since they alluded to their American colo-nial (hence, "white" Northern European) heritage. Mountain characters also differed from their nonwhite counterparts because they were allowed to act like modern whites in these films: fathers and elders exercise authority over their children and wives; the few black and Indian characters are shown in unmistakably subservient roles; and most important, mountain women can romance and marry white outsiders.[22]

At the same time, however, mountaineer characters' viciousness, ignorance, and primitiveness mirrored the portrayal of nonwhite characters in numerous other silent films. Race and notions of proper racial hierarchy were central to both the narratives and ideological underpinnings of many silent film producers and directors, most notably, Kentucky native D. W. Griffith. In the same way Griffith consistently used characters of African, Chinese, Latino, and Indian descent to show the latent violence in all people of color, the dangers of interracial sexual desire, and the superiority of whites through narratives of nonwhite servitude, he incorporated mountaineers, coded as "nonwhite," to highlight the superiority of "normative" white society. All of the six films he made for Biograph with explicit mountain settings center on the violence of his mountaineer characters in feuds, assaults, murder, or as participants in the Civil War. The themes of intercultural relationships and the desire of white male leads for nonwhite or mountaineer women are another striking similarity. While Griffith-directed films sometimes portray a theoretically permanent union between mountain women and the non-mountain men who take them back to the city or lowlands, they just as often show mountain women unable or unwilling to assimilate into "white" society and implicitly or explicitly argue that they are best off "with their own kind." Finally, the sheer number of films by Griffith (and his contemporaries) that feature white male sexual interest in mountain women suggests the same sorts of fascination with miscegenation that dominate other Griffith silents.[23]

The characters' costuming and labeling in promotional copy also suggest their liminal whiteness. The appearance of most mountain characters differs little from their "white" counterparts in other films of the era. No figures appear with excessively long beards, oversized and tattered hats, granny dresses, bare feet, or any of the other markers of the cartoonish hillbilly that would subsequently be established. Instead, most characters are dressed in ordinary turn-of-the-century clothing with a slightly rural look. Male leads, even ones portraying moonshiners or feudists, often are dressed in suit coats, boots, and even ties, and female characters generally wear long, bustled dresses. Instead of using clothing to emphasize the chronological and cultural separateness of these people, the film companies used descriptors such as "pioneer," "frontier," and "feudal days" in their promotional copy and the ubiquity of long-barreled Winchester rifles and bowie knives.

However, scruffy, shabbily dressed protohillbillies did begin to appear in silent films of the 1910s, usually in supporting roles. The male leads in

Griffith's 1911 *The Revenue Man and His Girl*, for example, dress as early-twentieth-century contemporaries, but the supporting cast of mountaineers involved in a shootout with the revenue agent is presented as bearded men who brandish rifles and walk with the slumped-over posture of later cartoon hillbillies. As was true in literary illustrations, the comical hillbilly caricature in film did not suddenly appear overnight but evolved and filmmakers played an important role in its evolution.

Solidifying Ambiguity: Film Parodies and the Emergence of "Hillbilly" in the World War I Era

The mountain films by Griffith and others primarily portrayed deadly serious mountain characters and the full-blown comic hillbilly persona did not emerge until well after World War I. Yet as the appearance of these supporting characters suggests, more humorous readings of this image began to appear in the 1910s. As early as 1911, film companies began releasing a small number of films that parodied the melodramatic storylines and acting of the mountaineer genre. Films such as *Ferdie's Family Feud* (1912) and *The Contents of the Suitcase* (1913) featured naive city folk or travelers who comically stumble into the midst of family feuds and moonshine rings, a storyline used repeatedly in the years to come. Other movies were explicit burlesques, featuring characters with ridiculous names, such as the feuding families the Higginses and the Judsons or revenue agent Snitz, and starring leading silent comedy stars such as Fatty Arbuckle, Buster Keaton, and Harold Lloyd. By the end of the decade, a number of comedies began to play on audiences' established preconceptions (largely derived from the earlier movies) about mountaineer backwardness. In *Miss Deception* (1917), a refined city woman deliberately plays on her snobbish family's fears that an extended stay with her uncle in the Kentucky mountains will transform her into a primitive savage by returning from her visit in the guise of an egregiously uncouth yokel. Likewise, the humor in *Her Primitive Man* (1917) centers on a woman artist visiting the mountains to make some "primitive sketches" of the natives who instead sketches a college graduate whom she takes to be the title character.[24]

Though greatly outnumbered by the sea of feuding and moonshining "shoot-'em-ups," these comedies reveal that the exclusive conception of mountaineers and their culture as a legitimate threat to modern civilization was beginning to dissipate. In its place was emerging a parallel but distinct interpretation of the mountaineer as a humorous hillbilly persona, an idea that drew on earlier comical writings about the southern mountains, particularly the Ozarks region. Amazingly, however, the iconography hardly changed.

The same storylines and images that once denoted palpable brutality were now used to suggest comical and absurd characters and situations. Where once the mountaineers as "white others" formed a colorful scenic backdrop for the proving of middle-class white male virility and, ultimately, superiority, they now also served as comic foils for bumbling urban naïfs in standard "fish-out-of-water" plotlines.

The rise of comedic portrayals of mountaineer feudists and moonshiners was both a natural development in the evolution of all ethnic and racial images and reflected specific changes in film audiences and the film industry in the 1910s. The gap between a laughable fool and a blood-thirsty savage in myriad American ethnic and racial stereotypes has often been bridged with astounding ease, since the former is simply a more benign form of the latter's racist essence. Thus, just as the dim-witted and carefree minstrel character Jim Crow transformed into the knife-wielding urban "coon" and the simian Irish brutes of Thomas Nast's cartoons transmogrified into feisty but harmless leprechauns, so did the cartoonish hillbilly readily emerge from the savage mountain outlaw.[25] The turn to parody also reflected the decreasing popularity of the hackneyed plots and stereotypical characters of mountaineer melodramas. Director Maurice Tourner warned in 1918: "If the photoplay is to advance, we must throw the whole impossible crew [of stock characters] overboard . . . [including] the moonshiners with their regulation feud and all the rest." The "Exploitation Angles" section of the film industry trade journal *Motion Picture World* (MPW) counseled theater operators to downplay feud and moonshine plots of mountaineer films and instead emphasize stars and locale. More tellingly, numerous letters to the *MPW* from exhibitors show that moviegoers were now rejecting standard feud films. Complained one angry Illinois exhibitor about *The Kentuckians* (Paramount/Famous Players Lasky, 1921): "my patrons said it was awful, so I guess they were right; quite a few walked out on it." Recognizing audiences' declining interest in the subject, studios steadily reduced the number of "mountain films" they produced annually, from a highpoint of 70 in 1914 to 49 the following year to only 18 by 1920 (a trend that continued throughout the following decade).[26]

Audiences' declining interest in mountaineer films after 1914 also reflected broader film industry transformations. By the late 1910s, the one- or two-reelers of pioneering companies like Biograph were rapidly being outpaced by the new feature-length "photoplays" of independent producers, designed for the self-perceived sophisticated tastes of the middle-class clientele of the "refined" picture palaces, not immigrant and working-class audiences of old-fashioned nickelodeons. This trend accompanied the film industry moving its center of operations from the East Coast to Hollywood beginning around 1914. As the locale of wilderness scenes shifted from the southern mountains to the western range and California foothills, and as the cowboy movie became a steadily more prominent film genre, the cattle rustler and the sheriff and his posse increasingly replaced the moonshiner and revenue agent. By 1919, even a movie with as reliably a "mountaineer" title as *A Moonshine Feud* would feature a heroine named Texas and a shootout on horseback across a western prairie.[27]

With the shift in motion pictures and American culture from the conception of mountain people as exclusively dangerous savages to the new vision of mountaineers as simultaneously menacing threats *and* backward clowns came the gradual increase in the use of the term hillbilly. The mid-1910s, which saw the first use of the term in serious nonfiction literature, were an important watershed in the term's solidification. In *The Southern Mountaineers* (1914), Presbyterian minister Samuel Tynedale Wilson used the term "hill billy" ironically in order to counter the assertion that all southern mountaineers were moonshiners. "In the Tennessee legislature," he wrote, "the 'hill billy' legislators were the ones who really passed and enforced the prohibition law." A pamphlet published in Asheville, North Carolina, used the word in its opening sentence but also revealed its ambiguous meaning: " 'The Hill Billy' or 'American Mountaineer' is the name given to the people living in the mountains of the Southern States. Whether the name is used as a term of reproach, intended as a compliment or employed only to describe, I do not know." The author's conception of the mountain people is equally ambivalent. On the one hand, he praises their Anglo-Saxon purity and generally strong work ethic and acknowledges the extreme hardships of their mountain existence, as well as the excesses of the prevalent stereotype. On the other hand, he regularly refers to them as unhealthily inbred and insular, quick to take offense, and "peculiar." He concludes that, in order to help this class of people, he has "on purpose, omitted many things of a ludicrous nature." These two examples, however, were the exception to the rule. None of the major nonfiction works in the early twentieth century describing the society and culture of the southern mountains include the word "hillbilly," even as an example of a grossly inaccurate slur. It remains unclear whether the term's absence from these texts reflects the authors' views that it was a derogatory label unworthy of comment or that it was not yet common enough to need to be repudiated. Regardless, the omission of "hillbilly" once again reveals that the term was not the universally known label it would become in the following decades.[28]

The mid-1910s also marked the first use of the term in the titles of popular entertainment. As discussed above, *Billie—the Hill Billy*, the only film to use "hillbilly" in its title prior to U.S. involvement in World War I, was released in 1915. Far from the burlesque connotations the word would later hold, however, here "hillbilly" referred to a grim and oppressive Ozarks mountaineer who tries to crush his children's spirit and keep them isolated from civilization. Following a common storyline, the mountaineer's daughter is rescued by marriage to a visiting urbanite who takes her home to live with his mother. Despite the prominence of the novel word "hillbilly," the film's negative characterization of the mountain people and the idea of urban outsider as savior differed little from countless other mountaineer films.[29] Also in 1915 came the first use of the term "hillbilly" in the title of a nationally circulated printed work, William Aspenwall Bradley's *Harper's* article "Hobnobbing with Hillbillies." In contrast to its farcical title, Bradley's article is striking for its lack of humorous anecdotes and scenes and the degree to which it perpetuates rather than diverges from a typical local color account. Nor does Bradley use the word "hillbilly" anywhere in the body of the article, instead relying on terms such as "pioneers," "mountain people," "mountaineers," and, in an obvious homage to William Frost's phrase, "contemporary ancestors." In this overview of his journey through the southern mountain region, Bradley emphasizes the familiar themes of the backwardness of the people, the way they live as their colonial and frontier-era ancestors did, and, above all, their propensity for lawbreaking and almost casual violence. Bradley refers repeatedly to "famous" feuds of the past half-century and reports how his "own moral sensibility" became "dulled after a while," as he "shakes hands with a minister of the Gospel who has killed his man and served a term in prison" or has dinner with "an affable host . . . known to have committed at least three murders." These encounters become so commonplace, he reports, that his discomfort soon "wears away and one comes to take quite as a matter of course any lurid sort of personal past or family pedigree."[30]

Dozens of other accounts of the region and its people over the previous decades featured all of these same themes, but this work reflected halting but discernible shifts in the underlying tropes of the mountaineer identity. Unlike earlier accounts, Bradley often notes the incursion of the coal mining and lumbering industries in much of the region, the way coal towns and railroads are breaking down the insularity and primitiveness of the people and the land, and the subsequent despoilment of the natural beauty. Most strikingly, Bradley acknowledges the way the national press has distorted the image of mountain people and perpetuated negative stereotypes. When he reaches the small town of Hillsville, Virginia, where a courthouse shootout focused national media attention three years earlier and prompted the *Baltimore Sun* to call for education or extermination, Bradley plans to avoid referring to the event, certain that local townspeople will rather not discuss it. However, he is surprised by both the local people's willingness, even eagerness, to discuss the specifics of the case and the modernity and peacefulness of the town itself. He reports that the townspeople remain indignant about the "flights of fancy in which they [northern newsreporters] indulged in order to create the requisite local color so sadly lacking in reality." Bradley thus acknowledges the national media's deliberate distortions of mountain society and the industrial transformation of the region, while perpetuating standard tropes about mountain violence, lawbreaking, and backwardness. The townspeople's surprising willingness to discuss the case, akin to the willingness of the Hatfield clan to brandish weapons for newspaper photographers, might also reveal their secret pride in playing a central role in a national media event. Nonetheless, during his journey through the region, Bradley is only dimly aware of the way local residents use the mountaineer stereotype for their own ends and embraces the long-entrenched view of isolated and backward mountain people.[31]

Although Bradley's use of "hillbilly" does not indicate a new humorous interpretation of the local inhabitants, he does discuss the idea of the laziness and idleness of the people in a way that moves beyond the realm of staid anthropological commentary and into farce. For instance, he describes an encounter with a Tennessean, "unshaven and unshorn" whose "black eyes laughed out at us with impudence and easy good-humor from a wilderness of curly black beard angled elf-locks beneath a tattered hat" and who gleefully announces "'You-uns have come to lazy man's land.'" Bradley begins to doubt this pronouncement when he awakens at four-thirty the next morning to find all the hotel's guests already up and breakfasted. But when he finishes his morning meal and exits the hotel, the sight confirms his suspicions:

> . . . there was practically the entire male population sprawled about the court-house steps across the way or seated on chairs along the sidewalk, while over every fence bobbed a feminine bonnet. Not in the whole town did we see a single person who seemed to have anything to do, and yet there was not one who had not risen at four in the morning to do it.[32]

Bradley's article marks a clear transitional stage in the conception of the mountain people and the emergence of a hillbilly stereotype. Still reliant on earlier local color and news accounts that stressed the pioneer and frontier nature of mountain life, the violence and lawlessness of the inhabitants, and their ignorance and isolation from the modern world, his account nevertheless acknowledges the way extractive industries and transportation networks were transforming the people, and the deliberative distortions by the press in order to reinforce widespread preconceptions of mountain "otherness" (although he fails to recognize his own role in the creation of this mountain mystique). Finally, by incorporating comical representations and anecdotes into an ostensibly realistic account, Bradley points the way to a dominant image of the people as slovenly and antiprogressive buffoons—though this latter meaning of "hillbilly" would not emerge completely until the 1930s. For the first two decades of the century, hillbilly was not widely used, and when it was, it was intended as a synonym for mountaineer, although one that emphasized the negative aspects of this figure.

The most fascinating example of the term's mid-1910s usage, and the one that best illustrates the still unformalized nature of the term "hillbilly," is the monthly literary magazine written and published beginning in 1914 by students at Asheville High School in North Carolina, simply entitled *The Hillbilly*. One might expect a cartoonish mountaineer with a slouch hat and rifle as the cover illustration. Instead, the title page of the first several years' editions featured a highly stylized female visage in the manner of Aubrey Beardsley with flowing tresses and exotic neckwear (fig. 2.5). The use of gothic print for article and poem titles, the high quality of the paper, and the lack of any discussion of the meaning or significance of the magazine title all indicate

Figure 2.5

A strangely incongruous blending of "hillbilly" and late-Victorian design. *The Hillbilly* (Asheville, North Carolina), June 1917, 1. Courtesy North Carolina Collection, Pack Memorial Public Library, Asheville, North Carolina, and Asheville High School.

that "hillbilly" had not yet developed the stereotyped meaning that it later would but instead was used as a nearly apolitical regional marker. The unselfconscious use of the title results in sentences and sentiments that seem incongruous to modern readers, such as the following commentary on the potential legacy of the magazine: "The Hillbilly is like a young man who has yet to win himself a name, and who sees before him a great work in behalf of humanity."[33]

More than ten years would pass before this publication began to adopt more standardized mountain imagery. In 1927, having become more a class yearbook than a literary journal, *The Hillbilly* featured regional images of log cabins, waterfalls, and young people backpacking in the mountains. Not until 1933 did it depict highly stylized representations of mountain men and women engaged in crafts such as quilting and basketweaving (fig. 2.6) and not until 1939 did the cover feature a classic hillbilly stereotype of a backwoods ectomorph with overlong beard, barefeet, slouch hat, rifle, and whiskey jug (see fig. 4.1). These changes might have been the result of new student artists or the whims of different journalism instructors, but it is striking to note how, at the journal's inception, there was a near complete divorce between the derogatory meaning of the term and its use in a refined literary journal by self-

Figure 2.6

The Hillbilly metamorphosing: A stylized folk image of the 1930s. *The Hillbilly,* Asheville High School Yearbook, 1933, 95. Courtesy North Carolina Collection, Pack Memorial Public Library, Asheville, North Carolina, and Asheville High School.

perceived urbane students of this modern city at the base of the Blue Ridge Mountains.[34]

By the start of the 1920s, the term "hillbilly" and its attendant imagery as a descriptor of the people of the southern mountains was starting to appear in a variety of American cultural forms from jokebooks, to motion pictures, to high school literary journals. But with few exceptions, it was still largely limited to regional usage. Furthermore, its meaning was still very much in flux, with various writers and artists using the term to denote hardworking pioneering Americans, degenerate and vicious lawbreakers, slow-witted and comical backwoods rubes, or often some combination of all three. Initially, self-perceived defenders of the mountain people, particularly of the southern Appalachian region, studiously avoided the use of hillbilly, believing that it reinforced negative conceptions of senseless violence and degradation. Instead, they embraced the labels "highlander" and "mountaineer," which they argued better represented the heroic and pure nature of these people with their noble colonial heritage and unique folk culture. This quasi-mythic mountaineer construction remained strong into the 1920s and would persist in a somewhat muted form in American culture throughout the twentieth century.

Yet as films and other mass media continued to promote conceptions of thick-headed yokels or savage feudists and the public need grew for characters that could both prove by negative counterexample the benefits of life in modern industrial capitalism and challenge the social limitations it imposed, the hillbilly slowly but steadily grew in the national consciousness.

chapterthree

Country Music and the Rise of "Ezra K. Hillbilly" in Interwar America

By the early 1920s, although magazines, novels, and films were rife with commentary on "mountaineers" and "mountain whites," public use of the term and iconography of "hillbilly" was still quite rare and its meaning was still very much in flux. The enormous success of commercially recorded rural white music, today commonly labeled "country music," played a central role in putting the word hillbilly and its image squarely on the national cultural map. Country music's identity was so completely entwined with the "hillbilly" concept that between its commercial origins in the early 1920s and its emergence as a major cultural force in the 1950s it was nearly universally known as "hillbilly music." Beyond nationalizing the term, country music also replaced the term's dominant pre–World War I association with violence and threat with a new principal denotation of unpretentious humor, carefree frivolity, and grassroots authenticity.

Both in practice and as a cultural category, "hillbilly music" was suffused with ambiguity. Officially promoted as "white" folk music and performed by and for predominantly rural and small town southerners who looked back nostalgically to a simpler agrarian life, it was, in fact, an amalgam of African-American and Euro-American traditions and the product of modern industrial capitalism and cutting-edge technology. Its social meaning was also hotly contested by those inside the country music "subculture" who performed and listened to the music and the promoters, producers, and journalists who represented outside commercial interests. Many in the latter group used the term to disparage both what they deemed a base and formulaic genre and the culture from which it developed. Musicians and their audiences, on the other hand, held a more complex view. While recognizing the term's derisive connotations, they also warily adopted the label as a marker of personal and cultural pride that reflected their sense of divided identity between a rural past and the industrial present. In the Depression Era, with its general celebration of "the folk" and journalistic accounts of the "hillbilly craze" sweeping Broadway, such a stance resonated, although at times uneasily, with the national zeitgeist. By the beginning of World War II, however, the growing power of an instantly recognizable derogatory hillbilly stereotype led musicians and the increasingly lucrative country music industry to repudiate the label and adopt the more marketable term "country music" and its singing cowboy image. Nonetheless, the term became irrevocably entwined with string-band music in the popular imagination, and many performers and listeners continued to embrace the cultural ambiguity inherent in the "hillbilly" label and persona.

Hillbilly Semiotics and the Birth of Commercial Country Music

The origins of the rural music played by white performers that would come to be almost universally labeled "hillbilly music" lay deep in the American past. Often seen as rooted nearly exclusively in Anglo-Celtic musical traditions, rural music was, in fact, in the words of leading country music historian Bill Malone, "a remarkable blending of ethnic, racial, religious, and commercial components with both Old World and American origins." Although folksongs, dance tunes, and ballads brought by seventeenth- and eighteenth-century colonists from the British Isles formed the core of this musical heritage, French, German, and Spanish musical styles and instrumentation, and religious music traditions from British psalm-singing to congregational music to the emotionalism of Pentecostal revivalism of the turn of the century, all made vital contributions to this evolving cultural amalgam. In the southern United States, in particular, this rich cultural mix became deeply imbued with a great array of African-American influences, including the introduction of the five-string banjo and the guitar, spiritual and gospel singing traditions, and ragtime, blues, and jazz styles.[1]

Often associated with rural simplicity and traditionalism and seen as a pristine survival of preindustrial America, country music instead was the product of a continuous interaction between "folk" and commercial cultural influences and the steady expansion of industry and technology into even the most remote reaches of the South. Tunes composed by professional Tin Pan Alley songwriters beginning in the late nineteenth century and recorded or performed by touring vaudeville and minstrel troupes or smaller "tent repertory" shows, and entertainment provided by circuses, chautauquas, and the "physick" wagon of traveling medicine shows all became part of rural America's evolving musical heritage. Steady rural migration to small towns and cities since the mid-nineteenth century introduced thousands of rural Americans to urban cultural forms and styles that they then incorporated into their own musical repertoires. The enormous impact of industrial change on working-class southerners, especially the deep penetration of railroads, is reflected in the titles and lyrics of many country songs, including "Wabash Cannon Ball," "Waiting for a Train," and "The Wreck of the Old 97," as well as in the musical imitation of train sounds. Several post–World War I songs also commented on the impact of industry from the liberating potential of the automobile ("On the Dixie Bee Line") to the hardships of cotton mill work ("Weave Room Blues," "Spinning Room Blues").[2] Although this diverse musical tradition developed in the South and elsewhere in rural America over two centuries, it did not gain national prominence until the wide diffusion of phonographs and the rise of the recording industry beginning in the late nineteenth century and particularly, the explosive growth of radio broadcasting in the early 1920s. By the end of 1922, 510 radio stations were broadcasting in the United States (89 in the South), and radio sales rose so dramatically in this decade (nearly fifteenfold) that, by some estimates, nearly a third of the homes in America had a radio by 1929 (and two-thirds of homes by 1933). The frictions resulting from this blending of ultramodern technology with supposedly old-fashioned folk culture mirrored the profound social conflicts of this decade over prohibition, immigration policy, public morality, and regional versus national identity that were all part of the country's wrenching transformation from an older culture rooted in local social and economic institutions to a newer society defined by urbanity, mass production, and mass consumption. These tensions were at the heart of debates over the production, reception, and categorization of "hillbilly music" in the broader popular culture.[3]

A central figure in both the commercial "discovery" of rural southern folk music and the establishment of the "hillbilly" label was Ralph Sylvester Peer. A talent scout and, later, producer for Okeh records, Peer is widely credited with naming and launching the boom in "race" records—blues songs and spirituals by black performers that sold in the thousands. The great success of these recordings in the sluggish recording industry of the 1920s, and the growing awareness by New York–based recording companies of the potential size of black audiences and the number of southern black musicians who could sustain the sales of "race" music, led Peer to initiate the first field recordings of folk musicians in Atlanta in 1923.[4] Primarily intent on recording black musicians, Peer also recorded Fiddlin' John Carson—a renowned Atlanta-based fiddler who had been performing on local radio station WSB—but only because he had an unexpected vacancy in his recording schedule and could not find any black musicians to fill the gap. Describing Carson's singing as "plu perfect awful," Peer released only his unaccompanied fiddle tunes on an uncatalogued and unlabeled record without advertising and only for the Atlanta market. When to his surprise the album sold out within a few months, however, he brought Carson to New York to record.[5] Despite his obvious distaste for what he considered base music and musicians (asked later in life to recollect the early "hillbillies" he recorded, he replied "I tried so hard to forget them, and you keep bringing them up"), he immediately recognized its commercial potential. He conducted numerous recording field trips for Okeh, and later Victor Records, throughout the southern states, most famously a 1927 session in Bristol, Tennessee, where he recorded two of the most influential acts in country music history, the Carter Family and Jimmie Rodgers. Two years earlier in New York, he also recorded a string band from Galax, Virginia, that he dubbed "the Hill Billies," the first commercially recorded band to bear that name.[6]

Although Peer and his colleagues recognized the marketability of the music of Carson, the Hill Billies, and similar performers, it was initially so new to them that they were unsure how to categorize it. From the mid-1920s through the mid-1930s, nearly all of the major recording companies that produced what is now considered "country music" (including Victor, Vocalion, Okeh, and Columbia) used a wide variety of labels, including "Songs from Dixie," "Old Southern Tunes," "Old Time Singin'," "Old Familiar Tunes," and even "Native American Melodies." Even by 1930, after the term "hillbilly" was widely being used on the radio, by the press, and by many performers, only Okeh records labeled their selections with this heading; Decca and Bluebird (a lower-end subsidiary of RCA Victor), the major distributors of country music in this decade, did not adopt the label "hillbilly" until 1936.[7]

Regardless of the chosen label, however, all were intended to signify racial "whiteness" by differentiating this music from works by black performers sold under the rubric "race music." Record company catalogs reinforced the whiteness of the music and performers in numerous ways, including using terms such as "Dixie" and "Native American" as substitutes for "white" in section titles and featuring explicitly racialized songs such as "Run Nigger Run" and traditional minstrel show selections such as "The Old Log Cabin in the Lane." Ralph Peer was explicitly aware of the racialized nature of the labels he coined, later describing Okeh records as the place where "I invented the hillbilly and the nigger stuff." The widely shared conception of country music as white music played nearly exclusively by white performers for white audiences would persist throughout the century, reinforced by exhibitions of whiteness through the expropriation of blackness.[8] Mirroring the broader culture at a time when *Amos and Andy* was the most popular program in America, the

Grand Ole Opry country music show often ended broadcasts in the 1920s and 1930s with a black-dialect comedy routine and the WLS *National Barn Dance* aired a minstrel theme show in 1937. These and other country music radio programs and traveling shows regularly featured blackface comedians with names such as "Lasses and Honey," "Greasy" Medlin, and "Slo 'n' Ezy," a tradition that hung on in a few cases into the early 1960s.[9]

Yet producers and musicians' racial construction of the music was also strangely contradictory, both denying and acknowledging the interracial reality of southern folk music. As the 1923 Atlanta recordings by Peer attest, many of the field recording sessions were integrated, with black gospel quartets and blues singers exchanging musical ideas and taking turns at the microphone with white fiddlers and string bands. Such integration reflected the enormous influence of African-American musicians and musical styles on many early (and even post–World War II) country musicians. Uncle Dave Macon, Dr. Humphrey Bate, Jimmie Rodgers, and Hank Williams are only the best known of the myriad country performers who learned many of their songs and stylings from black musicians. Even the long history of country music stars, including Macon, Rodgers, and Roy Acuff who began their careers by "blacking up" in medicine shows and traveling troupes reflects the great impact of black culture on country performers. The sizable number of early country performers who made their reputations playing blues songs long popular among black musicians further reflects this fruitful cultural exchange. Nonetheless, these white artists recognized the importance to the music industry (and thus to their careers) of maintaining racial distinctions, a fact made clear by the Allen Brothers' 1927 lawsuit against Columbia Records for $250,000 for damaging their reputations by issuing their recording of "Chattanooga Blues" as part of its "race" series.[10]

Even though the commercial music industry and white musicians all sought to distinguish their music clearly from that of black performers, because recording executives and journalists viewed country music as a strange outgrowth of the same exotic rural southern culture that produced the blues and jazz, they often associated white country music and musicians with their black counterparts in both record company publications and press accounts. Early record catalogs often listed white and black rural musical selections in separate categories but on facing pages. Beginning in the mid-1930s, Bluebird Records began listing their selections as "Hill Billy and Race Records," simultaneously separating and unifying these musical forms, a custom that several other labels and music industry periodicals soon adopted. Perhaps the clearest example of this synchronous racial merging and dividing is what folk music scholar Archie Green has called "the semi-official baptismal narrative" of country music, Kyle Crichton's 1938 article "Thar's Gold in them Hillbillies." Ostensibly about the rise of hillbilly music and musicians, the cover page incongruously features photographs of three female black blues singers alongside one of white country performer Jimmie Davis, and the text repeatedly, but without explicit acknowledgment, links white and black performers, emphasizing the strange and almost other-worldly status of each. Although "hillbilly," both as a label for a musical genre and for its performers, clearly denoted "whiteness," therefore, it constituted a strangely mixed cultural and racial category, simultaneously distinct from and akin to African-American and other nonwhite images.[11]

By the early 1920s "hillbilly" also had a comical connotation, deriving partially from the emerging national stereotype but just as strongly from a farcical tradition in much early country music. Groups that performed at the Georgia Old Time Fiddlers' Conventions in Atlanta in the 1910s and 1920s, for example, used names such as the "Moo Cow Band," the "Simp Phony Orchestry," and the "Lick Skillet Orchestra." The festivities were emceed by "Professor Aleck Smart" who dressed in the standard vaudevillian costume of the rube comedian—undersized striped pants, top hat, and frock coat. In addition to ensuring audiences of a foot-stomping good time, these names were also designed to mock the "high art" pretensions of newly wealthy Atlantans, who attended both the fiddler conventions and the operatic festivals. Many musicians in these contests who later commercially recorded their music borrowed directly from this comedic tradition in naming their acts and incorporating certain tropes, particularly "moonshining," that would come to be linked to the hillbilly image. Gid Tanner and the Skillet Lickers recorded musical skits entitled "A Corn Licker Still in Georgia" and "Kickapoo Joy Juice" (a label later embraced by Al Capp in his Li'l Abner comic strip); Fiddlin' John Carson sang "John Makes Good Licker" and even gave his performing daughter Rosa Lee Carson the stage name "Moonshine Kate."[12]

The hillbilly label and identity thus fit easily into a tradition of humorous and self-satirizing songs, band names, and even stage personalities. By February of 1925, the Atlanta-based string band George Daniell's Hillbillies broadcast on local radio station WSB and later that year Uncle Dave Macon of the touring vaudeville act "Uncle Dave Macon and his Hillbillies" performed and recorded "Hill Billie Blues" (an updated version of W. C. Handy's "Hesitation Blues") that opened "I am a billie and I live in the hills." By the mid-1920s, even the print media had begun to associate country music and the "hillbilly" label. Stephen Vincent Benét's raucous 1925 poem "The Mountain Whippoorwill," subtitled "How Hill-Billy Jim Won the Great Fiddler's Prize," recounted how a young mountain fiddler defeated the reigning champion and associated the term "hillbilly" with fiddle music (although he did not label the music itself "hillbilly"). Benét well captured the exuberance of the fiddler contests, but his folksy allusions to by-then standard conventions about mountaineer laziness, poverty, and wildness also reflected a solidifying hillbilly stereotype that would soon be associated with the music and musicians.[13]

With its mix of satire and celebration ("never had a brother nor a whole pair of pants / But when I start to fiddle, why, yuh got to start to dance"), Benét's poem suggests the multiple possible readings of "hillbilly" that musicians, producers, journalists, and audiences would struggle over for the next four decades.[14] Early country performers may have used colorful names and stage personalities in their acts, but they did not intend to demean either the format or the sentiment of the music. Photographs of fiddling championships and early commercial musicians, even of known comedic entertainers such as John Carson, reveal men dressed in their Sunday best—with ties, coats and leather shoes (fig. 3.1). Although at times they played up their country her-

Figure 3.1
Early string-band musicians on the eve of commercial "discovery."
Left to right: Al Hopkins, John Hopkins, Tony Alderman, John Rector,
Uncle Am Stuart, and Fiddlin' John Carson; Old-Time Fiddlers'
Convention, Mountain City, Tennessee, 1925. Southern Folklife Collection,
Wilson Library, University of North Carolina at Chapel Hill, P-849.

Country Music and the Rise of "Ezra K. Hillbilly" in Interwar America

itage and performed boisterously, these musicians generally sought a degree of middle-class comfort and saw no advantage in parodying their rural and working-class status.

Producers and commentators on early commercial performers, however, assumed that the musicians and the music would have a rural, even bumpkinish, appearance, and described and costumed the performers accordingly. Thus, Ralph Peer, recollecting his first Atlanta recording session, described John Carson as "a white mountaineer who arrived for the recordings in overalls." The *Atlanta Journal* reported that Carson came to the 1914 convention "with many a pause to view the sights of the city," overlooking the fact that Carson had lived in a mill town bordering Atlanta since 1900 and was already a seasoned radio performer. The newspaper's description of Carson was typical of its "rustification" of all the performers at these festivals. One representative story described contestants arriving in town on "day coaches from hundreds of miles away, barefoot, with their Sunday shoes hung over their shoulders."[15] Peer and *Atlanta Journal* reporters may have truly believed this is how mountain people looked—or should look—or they may, as historian Charles Wolfe has argued, have felt that "the commercial appeal of this newly-discovered 'old time' music lay in its rustic, mountain quality." Whatever their origins, these images and themes would continue to mold producers, audiences, and even performers' conceptions of country music and musicians and would establish the cultural context in which the music came to be labeled "hillbilly."[16]

Constructing the Hillbilly Persona: Ralph Peer, George Hay, and John Lair

The complicated ambiguities of the term "hillbilly," and the convergence of outsider notions of a marketable primitive mountain culture and folk performers' own comedic string music tradition, are best reflected in the naming of the Hill Billies at the string band's self-initiated recording session in Okeh's New York City studio. Although the band members had all grown up in the mountains of northwestern North Carolina and southwestern Virginia, they were far from rustic rubes. Brothers Al and Joe Hopkins were the sons of a former North Carolina state legislator employed by the Census Bureau in Washington, D.C.; Alonzo "Tony" Alderman's father was a surveyor, civil engineer, and justice of the peace. Nonetheless, the term "hillbilly" was fresh in Al Hopkins's mind as he had been asked by his father just before the boys left for New York, "What d'you hillbillies think you can do up there?" Hence, when Peer asked bandleader Al Hopkins the name of his group, Hopkins's answer, "We're nothing but a bunch of hillbillies from North Carolina and Virginia. Call us anything," was clearly and self-consciously ironic. On the other hand, the word immediately appealed to Peer who had begun his career working for Columbia Records in Kansas City and, according to a later account, "was well acquainted with the Ozarks," and presumably, the derisive use of the term for the people of this mountain region.[17]

Tony Alderman's concerns about the group's name further reflect the term's ambiguous nature. He considered hillbilly "a fighting word," which connoted "a back-woods person who knew nothing at all about city life and who hadn't been to school much either." However, the band was persuaded to keep the name by old friend and fellow mountain musician (and commercial country music pioneer) Ernest "Pop" Stoneman who laughingly remarked: "you couldn't have ever got a better name." The band was a great hit in their first radio broadcast on station WRC in Washington, D.C. According to a contemporary magazine account, one listener who telephoned the station embraced the term as a label of cultural authenticity: "You-all cain't fool me," he is reported to have remarked "with a distinct Georgia drawl, . . . 'ah know where them boys come from. They's Hill Billies for suah. They ain't nobody kin play that music 'thout they is bawn in the hills and brung up thar.'" Nonetheless, Alderman remained worried about the name selection and the urban derision of rural life that it represented. As he recalled later: "I was afraid to go home as the country people played and sang this type of music, and hid their instruments at the sight of a city slicker. And now I had gone to New York and put their music on records and called it a bad name to boot. So I just didn't go home for four years."[18]

Not only did Peer readily embrace the "hillbilly" label for the music he recorded, but he also shaped the musicians' image to match his own preconceived notions of both the music and its likely audience. The first print illustration of the Hill Billies, for instance, was a pen and ink sketch modeled on a photograph that Tony Alderman had sent the record company of the band members as they wished to present themselves, respectable and modern musicians in suit coats, vests, and ties, sitting with their instruments in relaxed but formal positions (fig. 3.2). Within a year, however, the group's publicity photographs showed them in overalls and matching bandannas with hats askew, in full song, and outdoors rather than in a parlor setting (fig. 3.3). Although this image depicted the musicians as colorful yet still authentic country musicians, the same cannot be said of their 1927 film short *The Hill Billies*, which portrays the band "doing incredibly silly things and playing frenetically upon their respective instruments." Here, as in their vaudeville shows of the same years, the way the band allowed itself to be characterized helped break down the boundary between a well-intentioned celebration of a traditional culture and the farcical distortion of this culture.[19]

Figure 3.2
The Hill Billies as they chose to present themselves . . .
Talking Machine World, April 15, 1925, p. 50.

The two most influential country music radio programs of these early years, the *Grand Ole Opry* broadcast on Nashville station WSM and the slightly older *National Barn Dance* of Chicago station WLS, similarly transformed the public presentation of performers. Like Peer, George Dewey Hay, the self-named "Solemn Old Judge" who founded and directed the *Grand Ole Opry* from 1925 to 1956, reshaped the musicians' image into a more humorously rural one. For instance, he changed the name of "Dr. Humphrey Bate and His Augmented Orchestra" to "Dr. Bate's Possum Hunters" and renamed other groups "the Clod Hoppers," "the Fruit Jar Drinkers," and "the Gully Jumpers." These musicians originally wore suits and ties in the studio and their day jobs included insurance salesman, barber, and dispatcher. When the program was aired in front of a studio audience starting around 1928, however, the performers were required to wear country outfits of overalls and checked shirts and straw or crushed felt hats. As with the Hill Billies, later publicity pictures of the bands were shot in cornfields, outside of barns, or in other outdoor rural locations. Like the label "hillbilly," such costum-

Figure 3.3

. . . And as presented in publicity photographs by Ralph Peer
and Okeh Records. Al Hopkins and the Hill Billies, c. 1926.
Southern Folklife Collection, Wilson Library, University
of North Carolina at Chapel Hill, P-848.

ing not only caricaturized these performers, it also gave them a unique and
readily identifiable commercial identity clearly distinct from that of mainstream popular musicians.[20]

Perhaps the individual who most explicitly promoted a mountain (as op-
posed to simply a rural) image for country music was John Lair, a driving force
behind the WLS *National Barn Dance* (and later, the founder of the *Renfro
Valley Barn Dance*). Described in later publicity as "born a mountaineer,"
Lair was actually from Mount Vernon, Kentucky, close to the foothills of the
Cumberlands but in a part of the state more bluegrass than mountain. He was
responsible for establishing an entertainment pipeline between the upper
South and the *National Barn Dance*, encouraging a steady stream of musicians, including Homer ("Slim") Miller, Hartford Connecticut (Harty) Taylor, Karl Davis, Lily May Ledford, and Clyde ("Red") Foley to perform on the
show. More important, Lair constructed a distinctly mountain, and at times
even explicitly hillbilly, image for his performers and, to a degree, for the music as a whole. Like Hay, he rechristened individuals and groups with more

Country Music and the Rise of "Ezra K. Hillbilly" in Interwar America

colorful and rustic-sounding mountain names. Lair dubbed Harty Taylor and Carl Davis, previously known as "The Renfro Valley Boys," "The Cumberland Ridge Runners," and joined them with other performers he brought from Kentucky and elsewhere, inaccurately describing all as native mountaineers. He also brought Jean Meunich, a popular Chicago nightclub singer, to the *Barn Dance*, renamed her Linda Parker, "the Sunbonnet Girl," and featured her in checked gingham dresses and bonnets.[21]

Beyond name changes, Lair created an explicit stage and on-air persona for his performers that stressed their supposedly genuine mountain origins. In an early publicity still of the Cumberland Ridge Runners, Lair himself joined the group playing the jug, while other members wearing plaid shirts, boots, and felt hats strummed or bowed their instruments in front of a mountain log cabin, while in another shot of slightly later vintage, fiddler "Slim" Miller stretched out in front of the group, shoeless, his head resting in his hand. His increasingly common "lazy hillbilly" pose was meant to represent the group's authenticity in the same way as the dulcimer, banjo, and array of other instruments were meant to speak to the band's musical prowess and their inheritance of a folk music heritage (fig. 3.4). The radio copy Lair wrote for the band also emphasized the homespun mountain image he wished to project. A typical program of 1932 introduced the group with this folksy dialect:

> The boys an girls you're gonna hear durin these fifteen minits is the genuwine artickle—no frills and no furbelows—jest plain folks frum the hills of Kintuck an Tennessee whur they bin livin purty much the same lives that their foreparents lived—an most of the songs they know ar purty much the same ez they wuz when these same foreparents whistled an sung 'em while they wuz choppin Ameriky out of the Wilderness.[22]

As these lines suggest, Lair consistently sought to associate the musicians he managed, and country music in general, with a nostalgic portrait of the American past that emphasized a pure Anglo-Saxon cultural tradition and a rugged pioneer ancestry. To Lair, as to many others in the interwar years, this culture and its traditional values of independence and a strong sense of family and kin seemed most perfectly preserved in the southern Appalachians, where physical and social isolation had allowed it to survive long after it had been washed away elsewhere by the forces of modernity, urbanism, and industrialization. Lair portrayed himself as a protector and defender of this fast-disappearing traditional mountain culture, and he was indeed an important folksong and folklore collector who included performances of numerous traditional ballads on his radio programs. Furthermore, Lair himself never publicly used the term "hillbilly," denouncing it as a word attached to the music and musicians by tawdry commercial forces: "Hill billies in radio? They ain't no sich [*sic*] thing.

Figure 3.4.
Shoeless "Slim" Miller stretches out in an increasingly
standard "lazy hillbilly" pose in front of the rest of
the Cumberland Ridge Runners and John Lair, c. 1933
(left to right: Karl Davis, John Lair, Linda Parker,
Harty Taylor, "Red" Foley, Hugh Cross). John Lair Papers,
Southern Appalachian Archives, Berea College,
Berea, Kentucky, 083-030.

Mountaineers and folk from the hill country maybe, but no hill billies. . . . Tin Pan Alley hung this name on certain types of music and entertainers." And he took pains in the WLS promotional magazine *Stand By* to assure listeners that despite folksy stage personas, performers lead real-world, middle-class lives. For instance, the caption of a photograph of fiddler Lily May Ledford in street clothes in an urban setting described her looking "quite collegiate in a bright red sweater with a turn over collar, worn with a gray tweed skirt."[23]

Nonetheless, Lair did allow comical, even derisive, mountain imagery to be used in the construction and promotion of his musicians' public personae in the 1930s and 1940s. For example, he also featured Ledford in an ongoing advertising campaign for Pinex Cough Syrup that ran in *Stand By* from October 1936 to September 1937, titled "Lily May—The Mountain Gal." An early version of the roughly drawn comic strip recounts her upbringing in the hills of Kentucky. Lily May, her parents, and a fiddling mountaineer are all depicted barefoot and in rustic clothing, and the captions feature hackneyed hillbilly dialect (fig. 3.5). Other ads in the series featured men with exceedingly long beards and common hillbilly tropes of laziness and ignorance of modernity.[24] Harry Steele's 1936 article, "The Inside Story of the Hillbilly Business," offers even clearer evidence of Lair's association with the term and image of "hillbilly." Attempting to explain to an apparently perplexed Chicago-area audience the astounding success of country musicians, Steele revealed that country music on radio and recordings, personified by the character "Ezra K. Hillbilly," "rings the cash registers . . . to the tune of $25,000,000 a year." Steele then made his own contribution to the emerging stereotype: If all the "hillbillies employed in radio in 1934 . . . were laid end to end—they would be in the position they were most accustomed to before the lure of easy radio money brought them out of their cow pastures." "Ezra K. has become one of the most important figures in the entertainment world," he concluded; "the lazy lout of the mountains has been transformed into a potent factor in big business." Steele backed up his claims with testimony by "authentic" mountaineer John Lair. Described as "a native of the hills," Lair purportedly confirmed that "in his bailiwick the hillbilly is a lazy lout who gets off his back only when it's time to eat or to go down to get a fresh jug of corn at the spring house."[25]

George Hay of the *Grand Ole Opry* had a similarly ambiguous relation to the term and its pejorative overtones. Like Lair, he also rejected the label "hillbilly" as derogatory, writing in 1945, "We never use the word [hillbilly] because it was coined in derision. Furthermore, there is no such animal. . . . Intolerance has no place in our organization and is not allowed." Yet later in the same publication, he tones down his critique significantly, arguing that the term was "coined in mild derision as a gag, which we appreciate as such, but [which] . . . was not right for the Opry." And three years earlier, he had

Figure 3.5
National Barn Dance star Lily May Ledford presented
as a cartoon hillbilly. "Lily May, the Mountain Gal,"
Pinex Cough Syrup Advertisment, *Stand By*, October 10, 1936, 7.
John Lair Papers, Southern Appalachian Archives, Berea College,
Berea, Kentucky.

described the initial 1925 WSM barn dance program as the first of "our little informal, hill billy efforts." His varied responses reflect a certain ambivalence toward the term and an uncertainty regarding how strongly he needed to re-nounce the label. In addition, he intended his use of "hillbilly" in the last example to contrast the unpretentious and authentic folk quality of the music to the classical music programming that had immediately preceded the barn dance show. From this perspective, "hillbilly" connoted a celebration of the culture of the common people—the folk—and mirrored Hay's famous admonition to the *Grand Ole Opry* performers just before each show, "All right, let's keep it close to the ground tonight, boys."[26]

Early country music producers and promoters such as Lair and Hay may have denounced the hillbilly label "on the record" later in their careers, when the term faced increasing hostility in the country music industry, but they had played an important role in advancing a rural country image that helped legitimize both the use of the term and a humorous rustic conception of mountain folk and country musicians. They may have intended and recognized important differences between "mountain" and "hillbilly" and between a use of the hillbilly term and persona that celebrated southern folk culture and one that denigrated it. But writers like Harry Steele made no such distinctions, and the practices of Lair and Hay provided ready fodder for such distorted and mean-spirited portrayals of both southern mountain folk and folk music.

Like Lair and Hay, most record companies initially avoided the term "hillbilly," preferring instead labels such as "Favorite Mountain Ballads and Old Time Songs," "American Folk Music," and "Old Time Singing and Playing." Even well into the 1930s, musical folios of country musicians continued to feature similar titles, including "Home and Hill Country Ballads," "Songs of the Soil," and "Old Cabin Songs." But despite the recording industry's best efforts to limit the word's formal use, articles discussing the popularity of "hill-billy songs" and "Hilly-Billy numbers" appeared in the fall of 1925; *Variety* ran a front page story on "'Hill-Billy' Music" in December 1926; and the group "the Hill Billy Trio from Pickens County" recorded on station WSB in 1927. By 1929, when Al Hopkins's group that had first recorded under this label sought to preserve the uniqueness of their name by incorporating themselves as "The Original Hill Billies," even the major mail-order catalogs of Sears, Roebuck and Montgomery Ward had started to use the term as a tag phrase for some of their commercial country music selections. Within the next half decade, other record companies followed suit; Okeh in 1933, and Decca and Bluebird by 1935.[27]

By the mid-1930s, the term had become ubiquitous, and country music groups across the country were calling themselves hillbillies. At least nineteen groups used some version of hillbilly in their name, including the Hollywood Hillbillies, the Oudeans Hill Billy Boys ("the favorites of the Pacific North West" according to a 1935 songbook), and "Pappy" Cheshire and his Hill Billy Champions. In addition, numerous groups adopted (or at least accepted) related evocative terms such as "mountaineers," "clod hoppers," and "ridge runners." Dozens of songs of the 1930s featured "hillbilly" in their titles, including "Little Hill-Billy Heart Throb," "There's a Hill-Billy Heaven in the Mountains," and "Hill Billy Wedding in June." Many of these songs intentionally sought to divorce the term from its negative connotations, using "hillbilly" to indicate that the song was a country rather than a popular music selection or to evoke romantic notions of the southern mountains.[28]

But in other cases, such as the Ranch Boys' "Hill Billy Family," the songs played on an instantly recognizable backward hillbilly stereotype: "We're the haziest and craziest, and just about the laziest, Bunch of Hilly Billies you will ever want to see, / We're the roughest and greenest, And surely not the cleanest, We don't even know our A-B-C." This song is an example of a number of supposedly comical songs written in these years by professional songwriters about the strange ways of mountaineers. Some, such as "My Hillbilly Rose" and "You're Still a Hill Billy to Me," drew directly on the mountain stereotype itself, finding humor in contrasting the poverty and backwardness of the mountains with the wealth and sophistication of the city or in painting a portrait of a grotesquely mannish mountain girl. Other novelty songs such as "Since Yussel Learned to Yodel (He's a Yiddishe Mountaineer)" and "He's a Hillbilly Gaucho (with a Rhumba Beat)" freely mixed the hillbilly caricature with well-known parodies of other ethnic groups. Despite the differences between "Hill Billy Wedding in June" and the latter novelty numbers, all these songs reflected the blending of a genuine interest in supposedly authentic American folk culture in the Depression years and the desire to cash in on the vogue for all things mountain. As the comical musical quartet the Hoosier Hot Shots sang on the *National Barn Dance* in 1935, "They've invaded all the cities / With their pretty corn fed ditties / And they've got the population all in tears . . . Them hillbillies are mountain Williams now."[29]

"Hillbillies" and Their Audiences: Contrasting Conceptions of the Image from Coast to Coast

Perhaps the clearest example of the spread of "hillbilly" was the creation of the Beverly Hill Billies in the spring of 1930. The brainchild of radio station manager Glen Rice of KMPC Los Angeles, the Beverly Hill Billies were supposedly members of an authentic hillbilly community discovered by Rice while wandering lost through the Malibu mountains. In reality, they were local musicians Leo Mannes, Cyprian Paulette, and Tom Murray who were clandestinely recruited by Rice to portray genuine mountaineers. Rice carefully set up his audience for the ruse, announcing his plans to take a vacation in the mountains, disappearing from the air for several weeks, during which time radio announcers expressed concern for his well-being, and then reappearing with the incredible story of having discovered "Zeke Craddock," "Ezra Longnecker," and the other "Hill Billies" who had agreed to perform on the air. Dressed in hillbilly fashion and described by Rice as having just ridden into town on their mules, the band was an immediate success—so much so that the *Los Angeles Examiner* mused that if the residents of Los Angeles were divided into those who had seen the band perform and those who had not, "you'd find it pretty evenly balanced. If anything a little in favor of those who have seen [them]." All the members adopted "hillbilly" stage names such as "Zeke," "Lem," and "Hank," and an early publicity still shows them posed under a tree with plaid shirts, crumpled hats, and in one case, even a fake beard. Early newspaper accounts referred to the band as "Arkansas, Ozark boys," and Rice underscored this connection by twice flying boy yodelers from the Ozarks region to California to perform with their "cousins" from the Malibu mountains.[30]

Despite the heavy use of hillbilly terminology and imagery, the group's music was decidedly not the up-tempo fiddle tunes of the Hill Billies or Carter Family–style ballads but rather what would come to be called cowboy or western music. Typical of their repertoire was "When the Bloom is on the Sage," "Red River Valley," and "Strawberry Roan." The band's attire rapidly became increasingly cowboy-like, although they retained some hillbilly elements. No longer were they wearing strictly plaid shirts and suspenders, but they were not yet decked out in chaps, ten-gallon hats, and western shirts (fig. 3.6).

Figure 3.6
A blending of hillbilly ballyhoo and the "singing cowboy" sound.
The Beverly Hill Billies, c. 1934 (left to right: Hank Skillet, Mirandy,
Ezra Longnecker, Gus Mack, Elton Britt, Lem Giles, Jad Dees).
Southern Folklife Collection, Wilson Library, University of
North Carolina at Chapel Hill, P-199.

The strange case of the Beverly Hill Billies shows the expanding interest in country music by urban audiences nationwide and its growth into a full-fledged entertainment industry. By the mid-1930s, country performers such as Jimmie Rodgers, the Carter Family, and Gene Autry had produced million-selling records, the *National Barn Dance* and *Grand Ole Opry* were drawing overflow crowds and attracting millions of listeners nationwide, and Holly-wood was churning out dozens of "Singing Cowboy" westerns. Country music blossomed in these years for several reasons. In the hard economic times of the Depression years, the low-priced recordings and free radio broadcasts provided a cheap and readily available entertainment option to Americans in towns and cities as well as in far more remote locales. In addition, the migra-tion of tens of thousands of rural Americans to midwestern and western cities created a growing country music "subculture" of both performers and listen-ers. Country songs' imagery of personal independence, romantic landscapes, or a nostalgic past rooted in the traditional values of family, home, and faith appealed to these displaced Americans and thousands of others who felt psy-chologically adrift. In contrast to much of the popular music of the day that presented sugarcoated stories of blissful romances or material affluence, many country songs dealt forthrightly with economic and romantic hardship, daily struggle, and even death—the emotional issues of everyday life. Explaining this distinction between popular and country music, Columbia records talent scout Arthur Satherly wrote, "Whereas the sophisticated city person likes these humbug boy-girl love songs, with everything pretty-pretty, the mountaineer is a realist. His songs deal with loneliness, misery, death, murder." At the same time, although country music songs often addressed very real problems, their solutions were often an escape into a romanticized rural past, characterized not by the present-day reality for hundreds of thousands of rural Americans of tenancy and ruined crops, or even by actual farming itself, but rather by comforting rustic associations of "cabin homes . . . swimming holes . . . old gray mules, [and] coon dogs." Country music thus resonated with rural and working-class white Americans in a way that popular tunes often did not and provided daily sustenance to millions of listeners caught in the throes of the Great Depression.[31]

Most outside commentators of the day, however, firmly entrenched in a society that had long denigrated southern and rural working-class culture and people, were utterly incapable of understanding the emotional appeal of this music for its listeners and expressed astonishment at what they dis-missively referred to as the "hillbilly craze." Some were more amused than alarmed. An anonymous newspaper article from the early 1930s reporting on the apparent anomaly of "hillbilly music" being performed in New York, for example, quoted Walter O'Keefe, the director of the radio program *Magic*

Carpet Hour (and who later dubbed himself, "the Broadway Hillbilly"), who opined: "Broadway . . . has gone hillbilly and doesn't know it. The hillbillies once came from Pine Notch, Kentucky, and Dead Man's Gulch, Missouri, but now you find them in every hotcha cranny in this man's town." The ultimate sign of hillbilly music's acceptance, the author writes, was Rudy Vallee's staging of a barn dance on his *Fleischmann Hour* program. Despite the opposition of "song writers of Tin Pan Alley," the reporter concluded, America would hear "the mountain tunes of its fathers," for "this is hillbilly season!" Likewise, Harry Steele wrote of the emergence of "synthetic hillbillies" from Brooklyn and the Bronx whose singing "often is tinged with a slight European or Asiatic accent" and who dress in "the assumed hillbilly costumes of ten-gallon hat, high heeled boots, corduroy breeches and flaming flannel shirt."[32]

Yet Steele's observations also belie his and many commentators' underlying disdain for the music, its performers, and its audience. Defining "hillbilly" as a synonym for "debased," these writers easily fell back on long-established stereotypes of mountaineer ignorance, poverty, and slovenliness. Such a sneering attitude is evident in Steele's comment that in contrast to the outfits of phony urban performers, "for your private information the hillbilly at home is lucky if he has a pair of personal overalls." Arthur Smith, a phonograph salesman and author of a 1933 article in the music teacher's magazine *The Etude*, associated the qualities of baseness and mindlessness that he found in the music with his perception of its record buying and listening audience. "[T]he great, unnumbered, inarticulate multitude" of "the lowly native white folk of the South," he wrote, "live in a sort of subterranean musical world of their own," singing not proper folk melodies by Stephen Foster but songs about outlaws and prisons.[33]

The best example of this condescending attitude is the December 1926 front-page article by editor Abel Green of *Variety* that marked the first known use of the term "hill-billy music" in print. Green connected the music to a subgroup he labels "hillbilly" and describes as

> North Carolina or Tennessee and adjacent mountaineer type of illiterate white whose creed and allegiance are to the Bible, the chautauqua, and the phonograph. . . . The mountaineer is of "poor white trash" genera. The great majority, probably 95 percent, can neither read nor write English [and are] . . . [i]lliterate and ignorant, with the intelligence of morons.[34]

Despite the supposedly repellent nature of the music and the people, Green, like Peer, recognized the potential lucrativeness of this genre and was willing to hold his nose all the way to the bank. Green stressed that for record dealers, the "hill-billy craze" spelled a "bonanza" because "the ignoramuses buy as many as 15 records at one time of a single number" so that they can retreat to their "mountain perch" and not return to "the civilization such as is afforded by the nearest community center . . . for weeks." Yet, rather than reconsidering the music's merits in light of this popularity, Green only saw the high numbers of record sales as reconfirmation of his belief in the baseness of both the people and the music.[35]

A separate group that held an equally critical view of commercial country music but for different reasons was self-defined folklorists and folk performers. These folk music critics of "hillbilly" music varied widely, from *National Barn Dance* star Bradley Kincaid, who called his own selections "mountain music," and consistently denounced what he deemed "Hilly-Billy numbers" as "bum songs and jail songs," to John Jacob Niles, a highbrow interpreter of folk music who eschewed all aspects of commercial country music and performed in concert halls and before scholarly audiences. All were part of a widespread effort in the interwar years to promote "authentic" folk music and isolate it from commercially inspired and thus illegitimate "hillbilly" songs, and all falsely envisioned a primal and pure Anglo-Saxon-based folk music of the southern Appalachians, unsullied by market forces. Ironically, these efforts to artificially segregate "legitimate" and "illegitimate" folk music often were characterized by their own market-inspired contradictions. For example, Bascom Lamar Lunsford, long-time folk music collector and founder of the Mountain Dance and Folk Festival in Asheville, North Carolina, was such a cultural "purist" that he refused to allow square dancers in his festivals to wear even plaid shirts and cowboy hats—but he also co-wrote the classic "hillbilly" drinking song "Mountain Dew." Hollywood scriptwriter-turned-folklorist Jean Thomas, who helped found the American Folk Song Festival in Ashland, Kentucky, was downright deceitful. She rechristened "Blind Bill" Daley, an eastern Kentucky semiprofessional minstrel performer, "Jilson Setters," posed him in homespun clothing in front of rustic cabins, and presented him as an authentic Kentucky mountaineer from the remote backwoods.[36]

The use of "hillbilly" as shorthand for kitsch, banality, and crass commercialism by music industry personnel and folklorists led a few musicians and producers to denounce the term and to seek an alternative label and image. Late in his life, talent scout Arthur "Uncle Art" Satherly reported that as early as 1918 he resented the music being called "Hillbilly 'vulgarly.'" Bill and Earl Bolick, who formed the Blue Sky Boys, one of the leading singing groups of the 1930s, also resented the term "hillbilly music" and called their own music "folksongs." And songwriter Billy Hill so disliked the word that for a period in 1933 he published his songs under the name George Brown. Yet public disavowals were limited at least through the 1930s. Even Bill Bolick, earlier in his career, had reluctantly acquiesced to his sponsor's demand that he and his fellow band members accept the name the "Crazy Blue Ridge Hillbillies" (to help promote their sponsor Crazy Water Crystals) and dress in overalls, checked shirts, and straw hats because it was "cute"; in the hard years of the Depression, the assurance of a regular paycheck won out over personal control of his group's image. Others may have also disliked the label, but felt obligated to accept it at least for the moment.[37]

Despite some scholars' assertions that the term "hillbilly" was nearly universally rejected and resented by musicians and fans of country music alike, however, most country music enthusiasts had a decidedly ambivalent view of the term, in which awareness of the derision it evoked was mixed with personal and cultural pride. Atlanta musician George Daniell, when discussing his band, told friends (in words that closely mirrored Al Hopkins's famous line), "We're just a bunch of hillbillies," and differentiated his music from the "long hair" music of his wife's classical piano performances. Rosa Lee "Moonshine Kate" Carson expressed the same combination of dignity and embarrassment when she replied to her nephew's question why she and her father were not in the Country Music Hall of Fame: "Honey, we weren't country musicians. We were hillbillies." Likewise, Lulu Belle Wiseman (Stamey), a leading performer on the *National Barn Dance*, recalled that she was not upset that she and her colleagues were always called hillbillies, noting "I thought it was funny," although she added "but a lot of the acts resented it."[38]

The most intriguing example of the use of the term hillbilly, and one which belies the argument that the label was simply imposed on resentful musicians by industry producers and a derisive media, is the case of the string bands of the Finger Lakes region of upstate New York. These bands performed from the 1920s through the early 1950s and played predominantly "old time" quadrilles and fiddle tunes such as "Soldier's Joy" and "Sailor's Hornpipe" and old standards and minstrel numbers like "Irish Washerwoman" and "Turkey in the Straw." Using colorful names such as Ott's Woodchoppers, Hornellsville Hillbillies, and Woodhull's Old Tyme Masters, these performers incorporated an explicitly hillbilly stage persona, from their rube comedian costumes of funny hats, loud flannel shirts, and fake beards, to their use of props such as hay bales, whiskey jugs, and placards which read "We're not Bughouse, We Just Look that Way" (fig. 3.7). Like the Beverly Hill Billies, the musicians even adopted old-fashioned stage names such as "Pop," "Ezra," and "Zeke."[39]

Unlike the California musicians, the New York string bands were not pushed into marketing themselves as hillbillies by radio and phonograph industry producers interested in cashing in on an increasingly standardized na-

Figure 3.7
Hornellsville Hill Billys, 1932 (left to right:
Edwin Riopelli, Fay McChesney, Pete Madison,
Joseph Solan, Archie Thorpe, Lyle Miles).
Courtesy of Simon J. Bronner.

tional stereotype. When Floyd Woodhull formed his band in 1928, he had not
heard of Al Hopkins and the Hill Billies. His band's hillbilly costume and persona were not based on a southern hillbilly stereotype but on a highly localized conception. As Woodhull later recalled, "the hills of this area . . . that
was the image. . . . It was a farmer's image or a hillbilly image but not a hillbilly like you connect with moonshiners like you say Tennessee or something
like that." Indeed, the picture that appeared on one group's advertising card
of a rotund man and his lanky associate in a frock coat and with a short rec-
tangular beard is far removed from the usual conception of hillbillies (fig.
3.8). Underscoring the localized meaning of hillbilly, these images were a reference to the German ancestry of the Kouf family that made up the bulk of
this band and were based on the longtime vaudevillians (Lew) Fields and
(Joe) Weber and their "Dutch knockabout" act of German immigrants Meyer
and Mike that mixed rough physicality with tortured English.[40]

Country Music and the Rise of "Ezra K. Hillbilly" in Interwar America

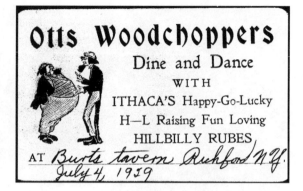

Figure 3.8
Personalizing the hillbilly:
The blending of German
vaudeville clowns and the
hillbilly label. Ott's
Woodchoppers, Advertising
Card, 1929. Courtesy
of Simon J. Bronner.

The New York string bands' incorporation of the hillbilly persona complicates our understanding of both the construction and meaning of "hillbilly" in interwar America. It also helps explain why such a potentially pejorative label and image spread so rapidly and was so quickly adopted at all cultural levels by musicians, promoters, and audience alike. The cases of Ott's Woodchoppers and the Hornellsville Hillbillies suggest that the term and image served as a negotiated space between contending concepts of urban and rural, modern and traditional, past and present. To many early country music performers and listeners, the term signified a strong rural tradition and a link to the land, basic values of home, family, and community, and a conception of self as one of the noble "plain folk" rather than as part of the indistinguishable urban masses or the cultural and economic elite. In a world of ever-increasing migration from farm to factory, economic uncertainty and disruption, and the uncontrollable forces of cultural and technological modernity, this music and term appealed to many Americans who nostalgically remembered their own or their families' rural roots, especially since they were now safely removed from the hardships of working the land. This was as true in the factory towns of central New York as in the industrializing South and Midwest. This is not to suggest that the word was somehow considered sacred or rarefied in the manner of "mother" or "home." "Hillbilly" always had an explicit humorous, even bufoonish connotation, but not one that unavoidably evoked derision or degradation.

At the same time, these men and women recognized that despite their removal from the farm, many born-and-bred urban Americans continued to perceive them as ignorant hicks—as hillbillies. Thus, by appropriating the term for themselves and actively engaging in a form of protective self-mockery —what folklorist Simon Bronner calls "a dialect-joke made visible"—they removed some of the word's stigma and defined their own identity. Playing "the hillbilly" helped performers and audience alike come to terms with the ambiguities in their own lives, simultaneously separating themselves from and connecting themselves to a rural ethnic and cultural tradition. This ambivalence is clear in the advertising card of Ott's Woodchoppers which announces both their professional status and musical prowess and celebrates the comedic and transgressive nature of their performance. And it is perfectly captured in the Hornellsville Hillbillies' self-description in the 1930s: "A Modern Up-To-Date Old-Time Band."[41]

The Triumph of "Cowboy" and the Demise of the "Hillbilly" Label

Despite the examples of the upstate New York string bands, by the mid-1930s, the vast majority of country music performers and supporters sought a new image that did not carry the increasingly negative connotations of the term hillbilly and the image of the mountaineer. Once again, the Beverly Hill Billies represented a broader trend, the general shift in country music from hillbilly and mountain to cowboy and western attire, songs, and personae. The introduction of cowboy imagery into country music was not a wholly new development. Eck Robertson, the first "Old-Time" fiddler commercially recorded, hailed from West Texas and dressed in cowboy attire for his audition, and a number of musicians in the 1920s, including Carson J. Robinson, Carl T. Sprague, and above all, Jimmie Rodgers, gained prominence singing cowboy songs and wearing exaggerated cowboy costumes. But not until the 1930s and the tremendous success of "Oklahoma's 'Singing Cowboy,'" Gene Autry, who moved from the *National Barn Dance* to an enormously successful career in Hollywood, did the cowboy persona envelop country music. Cowboy hats and boots became standard uniforms for country music performers throughout the United States and Canada, and "Red River Dave," "the Lonesome Cowboy," "the Girls of the Golden West," and countless others filled the radio airwaves, record stores, and mail order catalogs. The rise in Texas and elsewhere of "Western Swing" music with its mixture of blues, jazz, and traditional fiddle tunes, the growing importance of the Southwest as a seedbed for musicians and radio programming, and the increasing focus on the region by record companies such as Decca and Okeh, all reflected a steady move away from a mountain image and musical style.[42]

Several related factors underlay the abandonment of the "hillbilly" look and the widespread adoption of cowboy imagery in the mid- to late 1930s: ten-gallon hats, chaps, and pointed boots offered far greater romantic possibilities than did the traditional mountaineer costume; the string band and plaintive mountain ballad style sounded increasingly old fashioned and even alien to

modern audiences and performers; and in the searing psychological and economic environment of the Great Depression, the cowboy persona offered (in
the words of country music historian Bill Malone) "a reassuring symbol of independence and mastery" that doubtless provided great comfort to many
Americans struggling with financial hardship and personal and societal loss
of faith.[43] In the early twentieth century, the mythic mountaineer represented
these same qualities of individuality, independence, and stalwartness. But by
the mid-1930s, these more positive readings were being superseded by a growing derision toward, and increasingly negative image of, the southern mountains and mountaineers. A national audience, exposed on a regular basis to
stories of violent coal strikes in Kentucky and West Virginia, social depravity
and "aberrant" religious practices such as snake handling and speaking-
in-tongues, and a steady diet of increasingly degenerate hillbilly portrayals,
could no longer sustain a romantic and nostalgic sense of the mountains and
mountaineers. News reports on New Deal aid and construction programs
aimed at southern mountaineers administered by the Resettlement Administration, the Farm Security Administration, and the Tennessee Valley Authority also highlighted the region's wretched living conditions and portrayed
the southern mountains as a particularly depressed area within what President Franklin Roosevelt called "the Nation's No. 1 economic problem"—the
thirteen southern states. As audiences increasingly perceived the mountains
as a cultural site of backwardness and degradation, country musicians and listeners nationwide turned to an image that had been more consistently hero-
ically constructed by the popular media. As country music historian Douglas
Green observes succinctly, "no youngster in the thirties and forties ever wanted
to grow up to be a hillbilly, but thousands wanted to be cowboys." President
Franklin Roosevelt himself tapped into these same attitudes when he announced that "Home on the Range" was his favorite song.[44]

The cultural divide between hillbilly and cowboy was easily crossed because country music iconography had always occupied a middle ground between mountains and plains—a liminality perfectly illustrated by the almost
imperceptibly curved landscape on the cover of the 1940 songbook "Home &
Hill Country Ballads" (fig. 3.9). By the mid-1930s, then, country singers still
sang about cabins in the mountains, but they now referred to the Rockies not
the Cumberlands, and the Kentucky Ramblers of the *National Barn Dance*
became the Prairie Ramblers and backed up Patsy Montana (born Ruby
Blevins in Hot Springs, Arkansas). Whereas the 1930 to 1934 issues of the
WLS Family Album played up the mountain origins of the Cumberland
Ridge Runners and Bradley Kincaid, by 1936, the program was dominated by
publicity stills of cowboy groups such as Patsy Montana, Tumble Weed, and
Dollie and Millie, "the Girls of the Golden West." Kentucky fiddler Clifford

Figure 3.9
The liminal landscape of country music. "Home & Hill Country Ballads." Southern Folklife Collection, Wilson Library, University of North Carolina at Chapel Hill, FL-337.

Gross's career perfectly encapsulated this trend. In 1931, he moved to Fort Worth, Texas, and formed a string band called "The Kentucky Hillbillies." The band soon broke up but Gross found quick success, joining the very popular Light Crust Doughboys in 1933. In 1939, Gross returned to Louisville, Kentucky, and formed yet another band, but realizing the overwhelming trend in country music, he called his new group "Clifford Gross's Texas Cowboys."[45]

Despite the predominance by the end of the 1930s of cowboy costumes, imagery, and themes throughout country music, the term "hillbilly" remained into the 1950s the standard, if never wholly satisfactory, label for the genre. Decca's 1940 catalog cover prominently featured the term, although all the performers appear in coats and ties or cowboy hats and bandannas (including Clayton McMichen, an original member of the Skillet Lickers string band) (fig. 3.10). Influential country bands continued to use "hillbilly" in their names, including the Colorado Hillbillies and Wilbur Lee "Pappy" O'Daniel's Hillbilly Boys, formed in Dallas in 1935 to promote both O'Daniel's "Hillbilly Flour" and his high political aspirations. Radio-station-sponsored periodicals and country music fan magazines also widely used the term. Well into the postwar era, "fanzines" such as *Hillbilly & Western Hoedown* (Cincinnati, 1953–1966) and *Hillbilly and Cowboy Hit Parade* (1957–1961) continued to incorporate "hillbilly" not only in their titles but also throughout the publication (of-

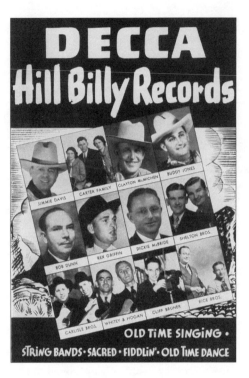

Figure 3.10
The persistence of "Hillbilly" into the
cowboy era of country music. Decca Hill
Billy Records catalog, May 2, 1940. Peter
Tamony Collection, 1890–1985, Western
Historical Manuscript Collection,
Columbia, Missouri.

ten mixed interchangeably with "cowboy," "western," "country," "country and western," and even "folk"). And at least some subscribers continued to embrace the term as well, using it to refer to both "hillbilly music" and to themselves as listeners. As one reader wrote, "[w]e enjoy it [*Hillbilly & Western Hoedown*] so much as it is the kind of magazine we hillbillys all enjoy." Proclaiming oneself a "hillbilly," therefore, as Bill Malone recalls from his youth in East Texas, was not labeling oneself a mountaineer but was instead an inclusive and positive (if often defensive) statement of one's musical taste and traditionally rural socio-cultural status.[46]

Since commercial country music's inception, "hillbilly" had always included denigrating connotations as part of a wide range of possible interpretations. Nonetheless, before the mid- to late 1930s, the novelty and relatively limited impact of the music on the whole of mass culture, the way the term and image fit easily into a grassroots comedic tradition, and, most significant, the absence of a standardized hillbilly icon combined to make the term acceptable to many musicians and fans alike. Promoters, musicians, and listeners all strove to disassociate the term from its negative stereotype and even from any connections to the southern mountains or southern mountain culture. "Bob Miller's Famous Hill-Billy Heart Throbs" 1934 songbook, for example, includes "Snow Capped Hills of Maine," "Sleepy Rio Grande," and "Harvest Time in Old New England" but not a single song featuring Appalachia or the Ozarks.[47]

Over the following decade, these circumstances changed dramatically. Country music became an increasingly powerful nationwide popular culture industry, particularly after the "breakout" years of World War II. Southern migrants seeking defense work in the industrial North and West and servicemen and women in military bases around the country introduced the music to thousands of new listeners and created a growing market in cities as disparate as Los Angeles, Detroit, and Baltimore for live performances, records, and jukebox selections. The traditional string band style and instrumentation was increasingly supplanted by electric guitars and drums. And the word and image of "hillbilly" became associated unequivocally with instantly recognizable cartoon figures. The popular press continued to belittle the music and its audience in articles such as "Hillbilly Boom," "Hillbilly Heaven," "Whoop-and-Holler Opera," and "Thar's Gold in Them Thar Hillbilly Tunes," but these mainstream accounts now drew heavily on the newly crystallized comical image of backward mountain folk. For example, describing phonograph company agents' initial efforts in the 1920s to discover local talent, one author gibed: "They found it in the raw: barefoot fiddlers who couldn't read a note but who could raise a voice on endless tunes, especially with the aid of corn liquor." The cover illustration of the article "Hillbilly Heaven" featured dozens of cartoon hillbillies running with kerosene lamps from hilltop cabins or driving wheezing jalopies to a country barn labeled "Grand Ole Opry." And as late as the 1950s, some record companies continued to use drawings of barefoot, corncob pipe-smoking hillbillies to advertise their musicians (figs. 3.11, 3.12).[48]

In the postwar years, country musicians and promoters, seeking to market their music to mainstream audiences and to be treated with respect by the recording and broadcasting industries, worked aggressively to repudiate the hillbilly label. Country songwriter Johnny Bond recalled that all his fellow musicians "agreed that the term [hillbilly] was an uncomplimentary put-down." Ernest Tubb, one of the leading country performers of the 1940s and perhaps the most influential musically, also fought hard to replace the hillbilly label, precisely because of its stereotyped connotations. He convinced his record label, Decca, to drop the name for the more amenable "country and western" (in 1948) and encouraged Judge Hay to stop using the term backstage and on the air at the Grand Ole Opry. As he explained to Hay: "a lot of people don't understand what hillbilly means; they think of somebody . . . out there in the hills, barefooted, with a long beard and making moonshine—they call them hillbilly. It looks like they think of our music as an in-

Figures 3.11, 3.12

Hillbilly iconography in postwar country music publicity.
Advertisements for Mercury Records and London Records,
Billboard, March 19, 1949, 39; June 3, 1950, 33.

ferior type of music." *Grand Ole Opry* star Roy Acuff took a similar tack, telling a reporter "We're not so wealthy or wise . . . but we're not ignorant and shouldn't be ridiculed." He also refused to participate in the 1940 Hollywood film *Grand Ole Opry* if the studio "put in a 'Snuffy Smith—sloshwocker' background"—a condition the studio eventually accepted. Acuff, Tubb, and other musicians were joined in this struggle by "Uncle Art" Satherly, the long time talent scout for Okeh and later Columbia Records, who discovered and recorded dozens of country music performers. A life-long champion of rural Americans and their culture, Satherly wrote late in life of his objection to the words "Hill Billy" and complained about being "stamped with the name Hill Billy Satherly" by others in the record industry who accused him of record-ing "trash." To Satherly, the term directly clashed with his sense of the dignity of the American farmer and his highly romanticized vision of rural people as "country folk . . . [the] tillers of the soil . . . our mainstay."[49]

Pressure from performers such as Tubb and Acuff and producers such as Satherly finally forced record companies and industry and popular press ac-counts to drop the term "hillbilly" in favor of the more positive and inclusive "country music." The new terminology was not universally adopted for over two decades, though; post–World War II hillbilly-titled songs including "Hill-billy Heaven" and "Hillbilly Fever" became hits, and country comedians in-cluding Homer and Jethro (Henry Haynes and Kenneth Burns) made lucra-tive careers out of using hillbilly costumes and humor to satirize city ways.[50] Nonetheless, by the 1960s, the efforts to eradicate the term "hillbilly" from the field of country music had largely succeeded, and only international hill-billy music fan club journals and newsletters continued to use the term.[51] The word appeared only occasionally by itself or linked to the new music of rock and roll, as in "rockabilly" music or in Elvis Presley's early nickname, "the Hillbilly cat." Certainly, Presley and other 1950s rockabilly singers in-cluding Jerry Lee Lewis and Carl Perkins shared with Fiddlin' John Carson, the Skillet Lickers, and the Hill Billies the same southern working-class back-ground, raucous performance style, and mixture of sincerity and humor in their music. And the term has made a comeback since the 1980s, defiantly embraced by self-defined "traditional" musicians such as Dwight Yoakam, Marty Stuart, and even BR 5-49 in order to differentiate their unadulterated "roots country" from the easy listening "Nashville Sound" of the 1970s or the "stadium country" of Garth Brooks and Brooks and Dunn. The label has thus come full circle; once used to denigrate base and commercial pabulum and distinguish it from "authentic" folk music, "hillbilly" now signifies this very authenticity.

Luke, Snuffy, & Abner

Hillbilly Cartoon Images in Depression-Era America

In the November 1934 issue of *Esquire* magazine, amid advertisements featuring dapper young men in evening wear and columns on the latest New York theater offerings, three barefoot and disheveled men with oversized beards and hats slouched on a rustic cabin porch behind an unkempt front yard, whiskey jugs at their sides. "Wonder if Maw's had her baby yet—I'm gettin' mighty hongry," one ponders as they languidly await the news (fig. 4.1). Thus began Paul Webb's cartoon series, eventually entitled *The Mountain Boys*, that ran monthly in *Esquire* until the late 1940s and sporadically thereafter until March 1958. *The Mountain Boys* was one of three cartoons/comic strips focused on hillbilly characters that debuted that same year. Webb's work, Billy DeBeck's transformation of his ongoing comic strip *Barney Google*, and Al Capp's new syndicated feature *Li'l Abner* were not only the first serialized cartoon images primarily depicting southern mountain folk but also some of the first featuring southern characters. Emerging within months of one another, all were an outgrowth of the same general mood of economic distress and decades-long expansion in both academic and popular interest in the rural folk in general, and mountaineers in particular, that fueled the national fascination with "hillbilly music."[1]

As did other media's use of the image, hillbilly comics and cartoons mirrored the complex mix of emotions and attitudes of Depression-era audiences. They reflected the widespread public fear of systemic economic and social collapse and daily reporting on the plight of the rural South. Yet these

deliberately exaggerated portraits of impoverished, but basically content, southern hill folk also provided cheering reassurance that rural poverty was not as bleak as it appeared in news accounts. From a cynical perspective, these comics and cartoons offered the pleasure of laughing at the misfortune of others, and even confirmation of the belief that the poor deserved their poverty because of innate laziness and ignorance. But they could also at times reflect a more sanguine vision of the durability of the American people and the American spirit in the face of adversity. To some readers, they could even be seen as populist celebrations of the hill folk, descendants of white Anglo-Saxon pioneers who preserved colonial life skills and values. From this perspective, hillbilly characters, who rejected a lifestyle driven by the pursuit of monetary gain and who cherished family, kin, and personal independence, might be seen as models of the traditional American values needed to save the nation from the twin threats of unfettered industrial urbanism and unregulated capitalism. While the hillbilly comics and cartoons of Webb, De-Beck, and Capp differed significantly in style, content, and the artist's perception of his subject, all exploited the varied and often contradictory dimensions of the popular fascination with mountain culture and the role of the mountain folk in modern America. In the process, they iconicized the pictorial hillbilly and fundamentally shaped all subsequent depictions and conceptions of the mountain people.

Paul Webb and *The Mountain Boys*

Through the words and (in)actions of his three nearly identical Tolliver brothers (Luke, Willy, and Jake), and their family and neighbors, Paul Webb presented endless variations on the standard tropes that defined hillbillies throughout popular culture: social isolation, physical torpor and laziness, unrefined sexuality, filth and animality, comical violence, and utter ignorance of modernity. Although all familiar ideas, Webb's portrayal was novel in the sense that such negative qualities were not offset by a correspondingly mythic vision of these folk as rugged pioneers, the inheritors of a proud Anglo-Saxon cultural heritage.[2]

Beyond his published artwork, the public record of Paul Webb's life is scant. Born in north-central Pennsylvania in 1902, he received professional art training at the Pennsylvania Academy of Fine Arts and in Europe. After several years as a freelance cartoonist for his regional newspaper and various national magazines, he began drawing his hillbillies for the *Saturday Evening Post* and soon thereafter for *Esquire*, his primary venue for the next two decades. Webb did not set foot in the southern mountain region until six months after he began *The Mountain Boys*, nor is there any evidence to suggest he had read much of the by-then voluminous literature on this population and region. Instead, he based his imagery solely on the popular conception of mountaineers in film and periodical literature as filtered through his own imagination. As he told a reporter much later, his artwork "didn't come from the Ozarks or anywhere else but out of my own head."[3]

At first glance, it seems strange that this cartoon series, peopled by slovenly laze-abouts and overflowing with rural animality, should have appeared in such a self-consciously sophisticated publication as *Esquire*. Itself an outgrowth of the Depression and first published in October 1933, *Esquire* was designed to appeal to what its editor Arnold Gingrich labeled the "neglected male," newly middle-class urbanites eager to acquire the products and knowledge of worldly modern living but hesitant about defining themselves primarily as consumers (traditionally conceived as a feminine realm). Brilliantly blending a woman's magazine format (mixing fiction, illustrations, and lifestyle features) with a male-oriented (and in many cases, outrightly misogynist) outlook, and "high brow" culture with "low brow" sex-driven cartoons and "pin-ups," *Esquire* sold 100,000 copies of its premier edition and reached a circulation of 750,000 by the spring of 1938.[4]

Webb's cartoons differed starkly not only from the advertisements and features on high culture in the magazine but also from the majority of other cartoons, most of which featured white middle- or upper-class urban men involved with seductive young women. Yet, they were not as anomalous as they might first appear. Like *Esquire* cartoons of urban working-class men and women, usually portrayed as European ethnics or African-Americans, Webb's work often featured an inordinate number of children and a general ignorance of modernity. Unlike working-class cartoon characters whose identity revolved around their labor and their place in the economic hierarchy, however, the Mountain Boys' identity stemmed from their total disconnection from the real world of work and the social power structure. In this regard, the most analogous *Esquire* cartoons of the 1930s and 1940s to *The Mountain Boys* were those of white men with comely women of color in South Pacific island huts, Eskimo igloos, or Arabian harems (fig. 4.2). Although not identical to these other cartoons that emphasized white male dominance over non-Western females and escape from familial and economic obligation, Webb's portrayal of rustic characters in a primitive setting, defined by the predominance of nature and their own physical urges, parallels these same ideas in cartoons of white men with enticing native women and clearly reflects the comparative exotic "other" status of the hillbilly.

Figure 4.2
"Then I threw a hammer through the time clock": A typical example of the dozens of *Esquire* cartoons showing white men escaping to primitive paradises beyond the world of work, bosses, and wives. Everett Shinn, *Esquire*, August 1934, 80. This artwork is copyright of its owner(s) (if applicable) and is used solely for historical and scholarly illustrative purposes.

Webb's cartoons also reflect *Esquire*'s overriding themes in its first years—conspicuous consumption, refined sexuality, and urbanity—precisely because *The Mountain Boys* represent a complete inversion of the *Esquire* ideal and exist in a realm wholly removed from the magazine's fantasy world. The fact that no specific locale or region is ever mentioned in the text heightens the sense that these characters live in a mythic land outside of time and space. Their isolation is so complete, that the boys wonder, in a 1935 cartoon, about the "rumor" that "Hoover ain't president no more" and later speculate about the "legend" that they have neighbors on the opposite side of a small copse of trees. Such an absolute disconnection results naturally in their utter ignorance of all things modern, from the proper use of soap bars ("Shucks—it tastes terrible" says one of the boys) to the safe operation of automobiles (a recurring visual trope was the boys crashing their ancient Model T).[5]

Because of their seclusion, the hillbillies exist in a state of animality and filth. Webb presents an absurd inversion of the proper social order, with barnyard animals eating and sleeping in the cabin, and the menfolk spending most of their time sitting, or more commonly lying, in the front yard, with a whiskey jug close at hand. Like George Washington Harris's *Sut Lovingood*, most of Webb's gags revolve around the seminaked body and bodily functions. Dozens of the cartoons feature jokes about Gran'pappy spending an inordinate amount of time in the outhouse, and male characters are invariably barefoot and often in their long underwear. Underwear, in particular, is a central signifier for Webb. For men and women, it simultaneously represents poverty and backwardness (he frequently portrayed men in flannel longjohns and women with underpants made from flour sacks); the sexualized body (reinforced by repeated references to new babies and excessive numbers of children); and uncleanliness and timelessness (as the once-a-year ritual of airing out or changing of underwear is one of the few ways the characters mark the passage of time) (fig. 4.3). The mountain folk's willingness to publicly display their underwear also represents their lack of social decorum and propriety, a theme exemplified by Webb's "Christmas" offering of 1939, showing the men in the family (including the baby) peeking through a door as "Gran'ma" tries on new underpants (fig. 4.4).

The fact that Webb frequently shows men in their underwear also underscores their laziness, which he contrasts with the drudgery of female characters. In one typical example during World War II, one of the boys laments that the army inspectors who turned down their mule as unfit for service overlooked the real workhorse on the farm: "too bad they didn't git a look at Gran'maw," he tells his brother as she strains to push a plow across a scrabbly field. Yet despite their constant toil, Webb's hillbilly women are perpetually pregnant and fertile—conditions defined solely as yet another onerous chore. From showing a father worrying that his twelve-year-old daughter will be an

Figure 4.3
The semiotics of underwear:
"Gawdamighty! Time flies—don't it?
There's Gran'pap gittin' his winter
underwear aired out already." Paul Webb,
Esquire, June 1936, 54. This artwork is
copyright of its owner(s) (if applicable)
and is used solely for historical and
scholarly illustrative purposes.

Figure 4.4
An utter lack of social decorum and
propriety: "Y'oughta see the ones we got
Gran'ma fer Xmas—they got lace on the
bottoms and buttons up the back." Paul
Webb, *Esquire*, December 1939, 81.
This artwork is copyright of its owner(s)
(if applicable) and is used solely for
historical and scholarly illustrative
purposes.

Figure 4.5
Webb's hillbilly women: A strange blend of drudgery and fecundity: "Oh—so that's it—another brat! Shecks—Ah was beginnin' to think you was a-goin' to be gone all day." Paul Webb, *Esquire*, September 1937, 38. This artwork is copyright of its owner(s) (if applicable) and is used solely for historical and scholarly illustrative purposes.

old maid to the appearance of infant "Oncle Rafe," the offspring of the brothers' grandmother, Webb presents both the women and, by extension, the men as almost supernaturally fecund. Gags abound about fathers who cannot remember which are their own children and which are their neighbors', and childbirth is portrayed as an event so commonplace that men see it as an inadequate reason for women to interrupt their unceasing toil (fig. 4.5).[6]

As well as representing through inversion the key themes of *Esquire* in its early years, Webb's cartoon was also a visual manifestation of a powerful new myth of southern society and culture that developed in the 1920s and 1930s, what historian George Tindall later labeled "the Benighted South," a society characterized by a degraded culture, oppressive economic and political institutions, staggering inequality, and widespread poverty. Challenging the long-standing view of an idyllic antebellum society of stately plantations and cultural sophistication, this reconceptualization was one result of a much broader struggle over the nature of modern America that was part of the shift from a country grounded in localized commerce and social relations to one characterized by mass production and consumption. Battles between "wets" and "drys," over whether or not women should smoke or "bob" their hair, and about the role of local and regional identity were all part of a general questioning of the proper place of rurality and traditional ways of life in an ever more urban and industrial nation.[7]

The key figure in this redefinition of the South was H. L. (Henry Louis) Mencken, *Baltimore Sun* columnist and editor of such influential magazines as *Smart Set* and *American Mercury*. In his many writings about southern society and culture, especially his hyperbolic critique "The Sahara of the Bozart," Mencken bemoaned the loss of the antebellum southern aristocracy during the Civil War and the subsequent emergence of a society dominated by "the poor white trash" in whose veins flowed "some of the worst blood of western Europe." The 1925 Scopes "monkey" trial in Dayton, Tennessee, in the hill country of the Cumberland Plateau, provided Mencken with a galvanizing opportunity to lampoon rural southerners, in general, and hill folk, in particular. To Mencken, the rural people living in the environs of Dayton were "gaping primates from the upland valleys," who "sweated freely and were not debauched by the refinements of the toilet."[8]

Mencken's simian references, suggesting that the hill people were not only uncivilized but also evolutionarily less advanced than urban Americans, mirrored contemporary "scientific" studies of mountain backwardness, most notably Mandell Sherman and Thomas Henry's *Hollow Folk* (1933). A study of five communities in Virginia's Blue Ridge Mountains, its authors conceived of this work as an effort to trace "the human race on its long journey from primitive ways of living to a modern social order." Focusing especially on what they considered the least advanced community, Colvin Hollow, they describe a place of sheer animality and squalor, where a six-month-old infant, his face "covered with flies," lies on a "bed of dirty rags" that "had not been 'changed' since he was born." Although later scholars have challenged the preconceptions and methodology of this study, this supposedly scientific account reinforced widely accepted ideas of mountaineer wildness. It also matched similar literary portrayals of southern poor whites, both within and outside of the hill country, by such influential authors as William Faulkner, Thomas Wolfe, and above all, Erskine Caldwell.[9]

While Webb's unflattering picture of the hillbillies was generally less mean-spirited than that of Mencken, Caldwell, and some social scientists, on a few occasions he matched this darker and more morally debased portrait of mountain society. His November 1940 presidential election cartoon is one such example (fig. 4.6). The fact that the hill folk are lining up to vote in an outhouse is demeaning enough, but the gagline's reference to a "two-headed cousin" clearly suggests inbreeding (if not incest). Potentially even more offensive are Webb's few cartoons featuring the dog-faced man Uncle Baldo—presumably the product of a human-canine sexual encounter—who can tree a raccoon like a bloodhound and has spent time in a carnival show. Webb's

Hillbilly

exact intent in creating these cartoons remains unclear, but one might conclude that these drawings were intended to represent how little removed from outright animality these characters are. This conception of dangerously inbred and imbecilic mountain folk was increasingly common in 1930s public discourse, not only in *Hollow Folk* but also in popular medical periodicals. A 1936 article on an isolated Virginia mountain clan, for example, argued that inbreeding and incest had created a whole community of feebleminded men and women. The description of one family living in a "one-room hut" mirrors almost exactly Luke and his brothers: "In the room were three grown boys, all imbeciles, all illegitimate, one stretched out on a filthy bed in a drunken stupor. There was not a normal human being in the room." But whereas Webb portrays such a scene as ludicrously comical, author Jack Manne saw this situation as a social crisis requiring a drastic response. "In view of the present inadequacy of medical science in curing these mental ills," Manne concludes, "the only alternative seems to be the prevention of further propagation by sterilization."[10]

Figure 4.6

Intimations of inbreeding and social devolution:
"Lem Hawkins promised to bring his two-headed
cousin along . . . that's three votes right there."
Paul Webb, *Esquire*, November 1940, 56. This artwork
is copyright of its owner(s) (if applicable) and is used
solely for historical and scholarly illustrative purposes.

Luke, Snuffy, & Abner

Cartoons insinuating such animality would have surely brought howls of protest if aimed at other American subpopulations, even minority and impoverished ones, but no public outcry was evident in *Esquire*'s "letters-to-the-editor" section. Perhaps partly indicating readers' unwillingness to publicly discuss something as seemingly insignificant as cartoons, the silence also suggests that many readers, predominantly self-defined urban cosmopolitans, apparently viewed such images as exaggerated, but at heart, truthful portrayals of southern poor whites. Most seemed to share the view of one man who wrote to defend the depiction of southern impoverished whites in an Erskine Caldwell short story previously published in *Esquire* and who concluded, apparently without irony, "the poor whites seem happy enough in all their squalor, so we may as well leave matters as they are."[11]

The magazine's editors reinforced the sense that Webb's portrayal of mountaineers was factually based by positioning his cartoons next to writings by Jesse Stuart, a native of eastern Kentucky and an important interwar commentator on the Appalachian experience. A mainstay of *Esquire* in its early years, Stuart created loving descriptions of the men and women of the "eternal Kentucky hills" that stressed not only their rugged pioneer ways and their harmonious relationship with nature but also their lack of formal education, propensity for violence, unique cultural practices from moonshining to folk remedies, and isolation from modern civilization. The close association between Webb's cartoons and Stuart's short stories encouraged readers to see both as somewhat farfetched, but at their core, essentially accurate depictions of the same mountain folk.[12]

This sense of quasi plausibility and Webb's standard portrayal (with a few notable exceptions) of ignorant and hopelessly inept but basically gentle souls who calmly accept their fate made his work widely popular in the Depression years. Despite an endless series of floods, wind storms, fires, and man-made disasters, Luke and his kin calmly endure all the crises they face with, in the words of media scholar Jerry Williamson, "placid equanimity and resiliency" (fig. 4.7). In this regard, contemporary audiences could see them as models of human endurance and a heartening symbol that the nation too could survive the current economic and social upheaval.[13]

Webb's cartoons remained popular throughout World War II and into the postwar era, and he produced a successful line of advertiser-sponsored calendars featuring his artwork. His appeal began to wane by the late 1940s, however (a 1948 internal *Esquire* memorandum warned that the company would be "extremely fortunate to dispose of the 50,000 calendars" they had printed that year), and he had an increasingly icy relationship with David and Alfred Smart, the owner-publishers of the magazine who took over as editors in 1945. After an extended legal dispute with Webb, *Esquire*'s new management concluded in November 1948 that "Paul Webb has outlived his usefulness for *Esquire*" and

Figure 4.7
In the midst of the Depression, a calm resiliency and heartening endurance: "Ah reckon we'd better wake Paw up afore it starts rainin' ag'in—he's over thar onder that tree." Paul Webb, *Esquire*, October 1938, 53. This artwork is copyright of its owner(s) (if applicable) and is used solely for historical and scholarly illustrative purposes.

his cartoons were suspended shortly thereafter. Although Webb began to sporadically recontribute cartoons to the magazine in the early 1950s (after David Smart's death and Arnold Gingrich's resumption as editor), by the late 1950s, Gingrich and his editorial board decided Webb's hillbilly portrayals no longer resonated with the magazine's target audience of young men, and he was let go along with many other cartoonists and writers of his generation as the magazine prepared to help launch the "new journalism" of the 1960s.[14]

Billy DeBeck and *Snuffy Smith*

Unlike *The Mountain Boys* and Al Capp's *Li'l Abner* that were both created whole cloth in 1934, *Snuffy Smith* grew out of Billy DeBeck's fifteen-year-old and highly successful comic strip, *Barney Google*. Born in Chicago in 1890 and professionally trained at the Chicago Academy of Fine Arts, DeBeck had grown wealthy on the strength of Barney Google and his pathetic but lovable horse Spark Plug, his mastery of fantastical dialogue, and his involved and constantly changing exotic adventure continuities.[15] Thus, when the audience learned in the June 14, 1934, episode, that Barney Google had been named by "a hill-billy by the name of Google" the sole heir to an estate in the North Carolina mountains, little did they realize that this storyline would continue for the next decade or that Barney would eventually be supplanted almost entirely by the even more outrageous character Snuffy Smith.[16]

Far from merely an attempt to cash in on the current craze for all things mountain, the change in the strip's plot revealed DeBeck's passionate and abiding interest in literary portrayals of the people and culture of the southern mountains. Unlike Webb and Capp, DeBeck read dozens of nineteenth- and twentieth-century novels and nonfiction books about the hill folk and his debt to earlier fabricators of southern Appalachia and the mountaineer is obvious. He was strongly influenced by the works of Mary Murfree and George Washington Harris, and his copy of *Sut Lovingood* is liberally annotated and includes his preliminary sketches of Snuffy Smith. He also drew heavily on the language and spellings used by Harris and other southwestern humorists, freely mixing, as did they, genuine local expressions with ones he invented. Although DeBeck traveled through the mountains of Virginia and Kentucky and conversed with the local inhabitants, his fanciful plots and colorful phrasings show that he, like Webb, clearly based his imagery and humor primarily on these literary accounts rather than on the people and conditions themselves.[17]

DeBeck also relied on many of the same tropes and themes as his literary predecessors. In the early months of the mountain episodes, he portrayed the mountaineers as impoverished (Google's "estate" is nothing but a run down shack similar to other domiciles in the region); ignorant (Google expresses shock that there is no school or kindergarten); and culturally isolated (in a strip titled "Catching Up with History!," a mountain woman who serves as Barney's maid has never seen a movie but has heard that D. W. Griffith is planning to direct the new film *Birth of a Nation*). In his most dramatic panels, he presents his mountain man as an almost supernatural primitive force of potential violence that emerges spontaneously from the surrounding woods (fig. 4.8).[18]

Snuffy Smith, the stocky and ornery mountaineer who would soon dominate the strip, epitomizes these qualities. Ignorant of all things modern, he makes his meager living by moonshining and stealing chickens and horses and responds to all comers with the threat of his omnipresent squirrel rifle. He so threatens social decorum and stability that he is feared and despised even by his fellow mountaineers of Hootin' Holler who, DeBeck informs his readers, tarred and feathered him the last time he made an appearance (fig. 4.9). Smith is clearly drawn from earlier fictional and actual personages such as Davy Crockett, Sut Lovingood, and "Devil Anse" Hatfield. Warns his wife, Lowizie: "'twixt [his] drink an' deviltry, mos' folkses hev been keerful ter give him plenty elbow room." To this image of an insular, trigger-happy primitive,

DeBeck added the Webbian vision of absolute laziness. Snuffy is constantly seen prone or asleep, his whisky jug clearly suggesting his perpetual state of inebriation. Like Webb's, DeBeck's jokes often revolve around Snuffy's sleeping for days at a time, despite the constant activity and noise around him.[19]

As did both Webb and Capp, DeBeck emphasized the dramatic contrast between impossibly lazy, good-for-nothing hillbilly men and their horrendously overworked and socially subordinate wives and daughters. Represented primarily by long-suffering Lowizie, DeBeck's mountain women are so defined by their work, that they see domestic efforts as their life's sole purpose. Thus, Lowizie's every waking hour is consumed by cleaning the house, preparing meals, and tending the farm. Even when she stays at a fancy hotel, she cannot help but continue her housekeeping, no matter how pointless

Figure 4.10

Hillbilly woman as willing drudge. *Barney Google,*
"Lowizie Keeps Busy!" November 28, 1935.
© King Features. Reprinted with special permission
of King Features Syndicate.

it may be (fig. 4.10). DeBeck also continually portrayed Lowizie as utterly subservient to her husband. Although Snuffy orders her around, flirts with other
women, abandons her for months at a time, and offers her little affection, she
remains firmly committed to him, even taking the blame for his physical
abuse (fig. 4.11). After Snuffy has been away from home for several years while
serving in the army during World War II, she even urges the visiting Barney
Google to dress up in Snuffy's old clothes and chase her around with a stick
while she cries happily "*Yes, Paw!!* . . . sich purty mem'ries!!!" Such images fit
easily into a long tradition of accounts of destructive mountaineer patriarchy
that defined the region's backwardness by female subordination.[20]

Figure 4.11
Lowizie Smith as a symbol of accepting female
subservience. *Barney Google*, "The Pure Truth!"
April 9, 1935. © King Features. Reprinted with
special permission of King Features Syndicate.

Snuffy Smith may be immoral, violent, lazy, and abusive, but he also
represents the antielite attitudes, rugged independence, and physical prowess
of the mythic frontiersmen epitomized by Crockett and Boone. DeBeck often portrayed Snuffy as a symbol of the common man who rejects any pretensions of cultural refinement and taste. On a visit to Chicago, he refuses
to stay in the "Hotel Aristocrat" on the basis of its name alone. Instead, he
goes to a flophouse by the stockyards but still accuses the landlady of running
a "ristercrat hotel" because she tries to change the sheets after two weeks.
Clearly, these episodes are overlaid with conceptions of mountaineer filth,
but the theme of rebellion against class pretension is unmistakable. As a sym-

bol and defender of frontier democracy, Snuffy refuses to kowtow to judges, military officers, and other authority figures and prizes personal independence and cultural tradition over money. His consistent flaunting of social rules also makes him something of a sex symbol to female characters who thrill at his coarse individuality. "I dream of you every night," writes one female admirer in the strip, "your mountain ruggedness—your forceful personality—your scorn of society." In short, Snuffy is cut in the mold of the American folk hero, a point clearly understood by at least one contemporary writer, Lovell Thompson, who in 1937 called him "a hero with all of a hero's trappings." Although for Snuffy, Thompson argued, these trappings are "a broken-down Kentucky Colonel hat, a corn-cob pipe, and a rifle borrowed from James Fenimore Cooper" rather than "the owl and shield of Minerva," their meaning is nevertheless "Greek in their profundity and rigidity." Simultaneously whimsical and serious, Thompson's description of Snuffy as mythic hero recognizes how DeBeck constantly played upon and undercut the mountaineer myth, fully realizing the comic possibilities in the mutually supporting duality of noble mountaineer and semisavage hillbilly.[21]

A final component of Snuffy's personification of the mythic frontier folk hero is his unquestioned Anglo-Saxon or, at least, Northern European racial lineage. Of the three primary cartoonists of hillbillies, DeBeck emphasized most explicitly the "whiteness" of his characters by contrasting them directly with standard stereotypes of African-American characters. Whereas Webb never portrayed anyone but his hillbillies and Capp almost never included black figures, DeBeck continued his long-standing practice (mirroring that of many early-twentieth-century cartoonists) of showing black characters as servants of white America. As porters, maids, stablehands, and other manual laborers, these characters served as homely and slow-witted comic foils for sophisticated white characters and, in *Snuffy Smith*, even humble mountain folk. Whereas numerous characters in positions of status and authority (businessmen, bankers, judges, lawyers) commonly refer to Snuffy and his kin as "hill-billies," "yokey(s)," and, even on one occasion, "back-woods trash," black characters almost never call him anything other than "suh" or "boss." The most dramatic example of Snuffy's enacting his whiteness is the graphic and grotesque violence of his reaction to a black doorman's request that he vacate a private club (fig. 4.12). In panels such as this, DeBeck asserts unequivocally Snuffy's whiteness through his domination over African-American figures, a quality that is meant to mitigate the degrading aspects of his character and to reinforce his role as mythic hero.[22]

Although DeBeck's work partially reflected the "Benighted South" vision of Mencken, Caldwell, and (to a large degree) Webb, it perhaps represented

Figure 4.12
Snuffy Smith graphically enacting his whiteness. *Barney Google*, "Under Cover" (detail), February 18, 1937. © King Features. Reprinted with special permission of King Features Syndicate.

even more a more upbeat countervision of rural southerners, and mountaineers in particular, that trumpeted their independence and traditional ways of life. This viewpoint was advanced by a diverse group of observers, who questioned the consequences of an increasingly mechanized, prefabricated, and centralized modern America. To these intellectuals, writers, artists, and even government administrators—characterized collectively as Regionalists for their focus on culturally, ethnically, and geographically distinct subregions as the fundamental framework of American (indeed, human) society—recovery of the original promise of America required the rediscovery and celebration of "the folk." Whether defined as nineteenth-century pioneers who "broke the Plains" or present-day American Indians, ex-slaves, or midwestern farmers, to the Regionalists, "the folk" embodied the cultural values and the simple but honest lifeways essential to saving the nation from what Walter Lippmann called "the acids of modernity."[23]

Mountaineers played a central role in this cultural movement that emphasized the importance of oneness with the land and escape from the confinements of industrialized and urbanized life. Writing for an urbane middle-class readership in 1924, playwright Percy MacKaye articulated this conception of the promise of mountain society:

> Over there in the mountains are men who do not live in cages; a million Americans, who do not chase the dollar, who do not time-serve machines, who do not learn their manners from the movies or their culture from the beauty parlors. Shall we not then, hasten to civilize them—convert their dirty log-cabins into clean cement cages? Or shall we inquire whether they may have something to contribute to our brand-new civilization—something which of old we cherished but now perhaps have forgotten?[24]

The idea of the uniqueness and importance of mountain society and culture extended well beyond the Regionalist movement, particularly in an era of resurgent nativism and immigration restriction. Endlessly trumpeted as "100 percent Americans" of "pure Anglo-Saxon stock" who continued to live as had their ancestors centuries earlier, the people of the mountains were presented across the cultural spectrum as a sort of "Ur-folk." Southern mountaineers appeared everywhere in news stories of the late 1920s and early 1930s, from the efforts of communists and local balladeers like "Aunt" Molly Jackson to publicize the violent coal strikes in "bloody" Harlan County, to repeated stories about child brides and "superstitious" religious practices, to accounts of the numerous New Deal agencies active in the region, including the Resettlement Administration, Farm Security Administration, and the Tennessee Valley Authority.[25] This fascination with the southern mountains and its people extended to all forms of American "middlebrow" culture, from the plethora of interwar nonfiction books, magazine articles, and short stories focused on the people of the backwoods of Appalachia and the Ozarks, to the numerous folk music festivals produced between 1928 and 1934, featuring the supposedly pure Elizabethan folk-songs and ballads still sung in this isolated pocket of America.[26]

Although all these cultural formats purported to present the "real mountaineers," nearly all presented their subjects as romantic primitives utterly isolated from broader economic and social forces. To better define their subject as a people caught forever in the past, they underplayed or, more often, simply ignored the racial, social, and economic heterogeneity of the region and the impact of market forces on present-day mountain folk. At times, this distortion of reality was even more deliberate. Photographer Doris Ullmann encouraged her subjects to dress in their grandmothers' linsey-woolsey dresses, surrounded by antique spinning wheels and looms, and then exhibited these photographs as accurate depictions of contemporary mountain folk. These works also tended to present all southern mountain people and locales as interchangeable, most egregiously in the case of Charles Morrow Wilson's *Backwoods America*, a book about the people of the Ozarks but illustrated with photographs of the mountains of western North Carolina and eastern Tennessee. Cartoonists and filmmakers soon embraced this conflation of all southern mountain regions into a single mythic space.[27]

Clearly influenced by the regionalist vision, DeBeck's art reflected this same mix of celebration and distortion of mountaineers and mountain culture. On the one hand, he portrayed a more full-bodied and naturalistic vision of mountain society than did any of his peers. Unlike Webb and Capp, who based their texts on standard stereotypes of southern (as opposed to mountain) dialect from vaudeville and motion pictures, DeBeck used dozens of mountain expressions such as "plime-blank" (meaning "exactly") and "a lavish of" (meaning "a lot of") in his work. He even introduced his audience to unfamiliar mountain expressions by incorporating brief definitions of the terms in the text itself (fig. 4.13). He was far from a stickler for absolute accuracy in the use of dialect and freely blended his own expressions with authentic mountain sayings, inventing such famous neologisms as "discombooberated" (which has evolved into "discombobulated"), "time's-a-wastin'," "a leetle tetched in the haid," "bodacious," and "balls o' fire." Nonetheless, even the phrases he coined had the ring of truth to many readers who could not distinguish between the actual and invented phrases. A reporter in 1940,

Figure 4.13

DeBeck's incorporation of actual mountain expressions
in his strip. *Barney Google*, "Breaking Home Ties"
(detail), March 17, 1936. © King Features. Reprinted with
special permission of King Features Syndicate.

Luke, Snuffy, & Abner

for example, introduced a list of DeBeck's famous phrases from the strip as "hillbilly lingo (authentic and otherwise)."[28]

DeBeck's depictions of mountain society were also somewhat more accurate and sympathetic than either of his peers. His cabins, spinning wheels, and costumes were based on photographs and descriptions in texts on the southern mountains and were designed primarily to be illustrative of a plain but honorable lifestyle rather than distorted to present a demeaning portrait of a savage society. Unlike the typical depiction in cartoons and movies of a "still" made up of crazily shaped pipes and pressurized boilers, DeBeck portrayed a more accurate distillery, composed of oaken barrels connected by wooden tubes.[29] His graphically sophisticated panoramas of community folk cover an entire panel and reflect a vital and interactive community, where women bathe children, hang laundry, and share the latest gossip (fig. 4.14). In stark contrast to Webb, whose figures barely communicate, DeBeck's panels overflow with colorful dialogue and his characters seem to be genuinely listening to one another rather than merely delivering gag lines. Furthermore, DeBeck conveys genuine emotion and pathos in the budding relationships between his teenage mountain sweethearts, between Snuffy and Barney, and even between Snuffy and Lowizie.

Finally, DeBeck also differed from his peers in his recognition of the way mountain people and their culture were simultaneously appropriated and denigrated by the producers and consumers of popular culture. His storylines frequently addressed the distorted portrayal of mountain life in film, theater, and literature. In one such example, he illustrates the appeal of quaint folkways to a refined urban audience by showing the smartly dressed attendees of an overblown melodrama set in the mountains adopting the actors' colorful language in a form of verbal "slumming." In another episode, DeBeck shows a Hollywood studio secretly filming a feud between Snuffy and his sworn en-

emy without compensating the "actors." He even suggests the mountain folk's resentment toward outsider chroniclers of their supposedly exotic and quaint lifestyle. When a writer visits Snuffy Smith to gather material for a "hillbilly novel," Snuffy hides the man's true identity from his fellow townsfolk and warns him "I thort it best not to tell 'em you wuz one o' them 'writin' fellars' . . . you'd be low-downer'n a mole to 'em—."[30]

Yet DeBeck's critique of popular representations of the mountaineers and the verisimilitude of his vision of mountain life should not be overstated. DeBeck's primary focus as a cartoonist was always amusement rather than cultural edification, and he played a leading role in constructing a broad-based public conception of southern hill folk as cartoonish figures. He also was instrumental in freely blending Ozark and Appalachian settings into a single mythical geographic location. Although the strip was initially set in the North Carolina mountains, characters in an early episode refer to ordering store-bought clothes from the nearby big city of "Little Rock"—in reality, 600 plus miles to the west. A month later, Sairy Hopkins runs away from Hootin' Holler and after three days of wandering through the woods arrives in "Crystal Springs, Arkansas." Such geographic confusion suggest the willingness of both the creators of the hillbilly image and the reading public to accept the conflation of hundreds of miles of distance and two diverse cultures into a homogeneous fantasy mountain South—a process that would only accelerate in the work of Al Capp.[31]

Furthermore, for all his references to the exploitation of mountaineers by the media, DeBeck never even hinted at the large-scale economic and social changes in actual mountaineers' lives. Like Webb's and Capp's hillbillies, DeBeck's characters remained largely outside of the larger economic nexus beyond the immediate borders of their "hollers." He did not acknowl-

Figure 4.14

An example of DeBeck's tableaux vivants of a vital mountain community. *Barney Google*, "Hill-Billy Gossip!" July 3, 1934. © King Features. Reprinted with special permission of King Features Syndicate.

edge the presence of extractive industries such as coal mining or lumbering or the rise of textile mills that collectively were displacing thousands of people and radically transforming the lives of men and women throughout the southern mountains. Nor would the strip's readers gain any sense of the wave of wildcat strikes that were spreading throughout the region's mill towns in the 1930s. Nonetheless, unlike his peers, he did present (at least initially) a somewhat plausible mountain community, where both men and women work the land, raise families, and are socially and economically attached to one another.

Despite, or perhaps because DeBeck's portrayal of southern mountain life and society was more fully developed than that presented in nearly all other popular formats, it did not translate into increased popularity with audiences. To the contrary, his employer, King Features Syndicate, urged that the "atmosphere [he portrayed] so faithfully . . . be 'toned down.'" Fred Lasswell, who assisted DeBeck and replaced him after his death in 1942, recalled later that the "authentic mountain dialect" was "rather difficult for the average flatlander to read and understand." Even though DeBeck made concerted efforts to move away from mountain settings and dialect, the strip's popularity continued to decline. When Lasswell took over the strip in the early 1940s, Joe Connolly, head of the King Features Syndicate, told him: "Billy lost a lot of client papers and if the trend continues, we'll have to drop it." Connolly urged Lasswell to "[k]eep the same general look and flavor" initially and then "gradually inject your own ideas and your own characters." Lasswell did just this, dropping Barney Google almost entirely and adding new members of Snuffy's family and community. He also abandoned the authentic dialect, instead working to broaden his audience by following the dictum: "keep it folksy, with a country twang." And he largely abandoned long-running stories in favor of daily sight gags and one-liners. Ironically, although the strip increasingly focused on Snuffy Smith and his mountain environs and Barney Google all but disappeared, it said less and less about the hillbilly and his place in society, becoming instead a homespun vision of generic rustic America.[32]

Al Capp and *Li'l Abner*

Of all the cartoonists of hillbilly images whose work pervaded popular culture in the 1930s and after, Al Capp was by far the most successful and influential. At the height of its popularity in the 1940s and 1950s, *Li'l Abner* was carried by nearly 900 newspapers in the United States and another 100 abroad—a combined circulation of sixty million that helped make Capp the highest paid cartoonist of his day (estimated in 1947 at $250,000 annually).

Capp's cartoon appeared on the covers of *Life* and *Time*; launched the national phenomenon of Sadie Hawkins Day dances; spawned a Broadway musical, two films, and a theme park; and proved wildly popular with both average newspaper readers and the intellectual elite.[33] And yet despite (or, perhaps, because of) its vast popularity, *Li'l Abner* was the least focused of the major cartoons of its genre on the hillbilly image. Instead, Capp used his mountain village of Dogpatch as a fantastical setting for morality tales that exposed what he saw as humankind's venality and cruelty. Presenting a dizzying array of settings and themes, he mixed social and political satire with adventure stories and parodies of celebrities and current events. His cast of characters was equally varied, including the Yokums (Li'l Abner and his parents Mammy [Pansy] and Pappy [Lucifer]), Daisy Mae Scragg (Abner's comely decades-long pursuer), and a seemingly endless cavalcade of outrageous personas, including (just to list Dogpatch natives) the circuit-riding preacher Marryin' Sam, the impossibly vicious Scraggs clan, hulking Earthquake Mc-Goon, massively bearded Hairless Joe and his Indian sidekick Lonesome Polecat, and Moonshine McSwine and his filthy but stunning daughter Moonbeam. Indeed, *Li'l Abner* incorporates such a panoply of characters and ideas that it defies summary. Yet though Capp's storylines often wandered far afield, his hillbilly setting remained a central touchstone, serving both as a microcosm and a distorting carnival mirror of broader American society.[34]

The specifics of Capp's early life and the origins of *Li'l Abner* are hard to pin down, largely because Capp was always willing to embellish in the name of a good story. Nonetheless, some facts are known. Born Alfred Gerald Caplin on September 28, 1909, in New Haven, Connecticut, Capp had a working-class upbringing in this and other northeastern cities (including Bridgeport, Brooklyn, and Boston). His later recasting of his youth featured two central events: the loss of a leg in a trolley accident at the age of ten, and a teenage hitchhiking trip through the southern mountains with a boyhood friend. Capp and his syndicate, United Features, later treated the latter event as the inspiration for his cartoon strip, insisting that Abner and his family were based on actual mountain folk with whom Capp had spent time. However, both the brevity of the boys' journey from Boston to Memphis and Capp's limited mobility cast doubt on the likelihood of such an encounter.[35]

More likely sources of *Li'l Abner* were motion pictures set in southern Appalachia and the Ozarks, the novels of John Fox, Jr., that Capp read as a child, and especially a vaudeville show of country comedians that he saw in New York, probably in 1933. As Capp's wife later recalled:

[W]e went to a vaudeville theater in Columbus Circle. One of the performances was a hillbilly act. A group of four or five singers/

musicians/comedians were playing fiddles and Jews harps and doing a little soft shoe up on stage. They stood in a very wooden way with expressionless deadpan faces, and talked in monotones, with Southern accents. We thought they were just hilarious. We walked back to the apartment that evening, becoming more and more excited with the idea of a hillbilly comic strip.[36]

Whether this act directly inspired *Li'l Abner* or was simply one of many influences, Capp did include hillbilly characters in the first comic strip on which he worked, Ham Fisher's *Joe Palooka*. In a series of episodes that Capp produced in 1933 while Fisher was on vacation, Palooka ventures to the Kentucky mountains where he is forced at gunpoint into an unfair boxing match with the huge oafish hillman, Big Leviticus. Uncouth, violent, and nasty, Leviticus and his family resemble Capp's feuding characters the Scraggs more than the pure and good-hearted Yokums, but the episodes reflect plainly Capp's growing interest in the use of hillbilly characters. When Capp left Fisher's employ on unfriendly terms shortly after the episodes ran, he took his idea of a hillbilly strip with him. *Li'l Abner*'s beginnings were less than auspicious; only eight newspapers had subscribed to the strip by the time it first appeared on August 13, 1934. Yet its popularity grew so rapidly that just a year later 102 newspapers carried the cartoon.[37]

Li'l Abner's popularity reflected the increasing importance of newspaper comics pages, a trend that mirrored the growing influence of the entire mass-oriented entertainment industry in these years of economic hardship. By the early 1930s, American comics had become a national institution. Between 70 and 75 percent of newspaper readers in 1933 followed comics regularly and nearly every major newspaper in the country, 2300 in all, carried daily or Sunday comic sections. The two major Sunday comics supplements, the Hearst-owned *Comic Weekly* and the Chicago Tribune's *Metropolitan Sunday Newspaper*, reached nearly ten million households in the nation's major cities, making it the most expensive advertising in the world at between $16,000 and $17,000 per page. Comics were so lucrative that even in 1935, in the depths of the Depression, the comics industry grossed an estimated six to seven million dollars annually.[38]

Syndicates prominently publicized comics' growing importance. Proclaimed the Chicago Tribune–New York News Syndicate in 1935, "[c]omics are on the upgrade today! . . . May we suggest that owners and publishers cast the same calculating eye over the potential earnings of their prospective comics purchases as they do over circulation, advertising and gross earnings —for the funmakers are *seriously* involved in these figures?" The steady expansion of the number of comics and their overall circulation suggests just how much Depression-era Americans relied on humor, particularly forms that celebrated the simple ways and values of the common people, to cope with the economic crisis. Whether in the radio programs *Fibber McGee and Molly* or *Lum and Abner* (the latter set in the fictional mountain village of Pine Ridge, Arkansas), country music barndances, or Will Rogers's columns and stage shows, these depictions of the reassuringly plain ways of small-town folk proved enormously popular. Capp's storylines were less paeans to country values and lifeways than were these other examples, but they did, at least initially, extol the virtues of the common folk and represented a strongly felt class-consciousness and hostility toward the wealthy.[39]

In response to the comic strip audience's burgeoning interest in dramatic continuities, most of the strip's early plots brilliantly blended adventure stories and outlandish comedy. As Capp explained later in his career, "If a point of view can be called anything as neat as a formula, mine for writing *Li'l Abner* is to throw comedy characters into melodramatic situations and to show them solving their monstrous tribulations in a simple-minded way." Typical early episodes featured the Yokums' run-ins with bank robbers, kidnappers, wealthy heiresses, and mad scientists. Capp's portrayal of the community and environs of Dogpatch was equally fantastical and was never intended to be a realistic portrayal of mountain life and conditions. As he later said, "I don't want to draw things right. . . . I want to draw them so that they look vaguely like they're supposed to." Nonetheless, he was widely considered an authority on the southern mountains, despite his own disavowals and all evidence to the contrary. Commentators on his work participated in promoting Capp's expertise—even while they simultaneously denied it—by intimating that his portrayal in *Li'l Abner* was, in its totality, if not in its details, an accurate one. Thus, *New Yorker* profiler E. J. Kahn, Jr. stressed in 1947 that Capp's "brief exposure to the backwoods country" had been his "only first-hand knowledge" of the region "about which he is now nationally considered an expert," but in the next sentence argued that this short trip was enough for Capp to "assimilate the fundamentals of a whole way of life."[40]

The unreality of his depiction is evident in the Dogpatchers' exaggerated generic southern dialect and the mountains topped with pines rather than deciduous trees. Geographically, Dogpatch was part of a mythic South, a land where mountains border on bayous, where caves and caverns stretch for miles, and where a two-day's walk beginning in the Appalachian hills brings one to the southwestern desert. Although Capp initially situated Dogpatch in Kentucky, he later relocated the community to the Ozarks, a move never explained in the strip or commented on in the press. To an even greater extent than DeBeck, Capp thus conflated the vast array of southern landscapes, separated in some cases by thousands of miles, into a single mythic space.

Capp's portrait of southern mountain life was also unrealistic in the absence of such central aspects of southern culture as organized religion, the ongoing cultural and political impact of the Civil War, and above all, African Americans. The latter omission was largely a response to the mandate of all newspaper syndicates to avoid potentially controversial topics or editorial comment and reflected the deep-seated but erroneous popular perception that the southern mountains was a region historically void of blacks, racial animosity, and slavery. But Capp's exclusion of black characters also reflects the fact that the mountaineers in this strip took the place of their black counterparts in other comic strips and throughout Depression-era popular culture; they are the clownish buffoons, the country innocents in the big city, the servants of socially superior white employers, or, in the case of the murderous Scraggs, the violent savages who threaten social order.[41]

Capp delineated the Yokums' cultural and racial "otherness" most explicitly in the first several years of Li'l Abner. He paid little attention to his mountain locale and set nearly all of his initial episodes, and close to half of his sequences in the first several years, outside of Dogpatch, most often in New York City. The dominant theme of these scenarios is class and social conflict. Beginning with the second episode in which Abner is invited to New York by his nouveau-riche aunt, Beatrixe, Duchess of Bopshire (born Bessie Hunks), so that he can "enjoy all the advantages of wealth and luxury," Capp repeatedly contrasted the simple innocence and nonmaterialism of Abner and his family with the snobbishness, venality, and egotism of high society. Building upon the long-established tradition in graphic art that physiognomy reflects the inner person, Capp embodied Abner's moral purity through his good looks and strong physique. His manly appearance combined with his utter naiveté allow Abner to associate with high society, and in so doing, to visually "pass" as "white," in the same way that light-skinned African Americans in an age of legal racial discrimination were able to enter all-white establishments. Whiteness in both cases signified not only "proper" skin tone but also the potential for social assimilation in the "right" group. Abner is wooed by society women (attracted to the promise of raw sexuality associated with mountain folk), and many of the New York swells even admire his quaint dialect and lack of social graces, interpreting these qualities not as signs of ignorance and poverty but rather as an amiable lack of pretension (fig. 4.15).

But all other characters from Dogpatch exude their physical, cultural, and social "otherness" too blatantly to pass as respectable "white" members of the dominant class. When Abner's parents don formal evening wear for a party aboard Mrs. Sneerworthy's yacht, they are incapable of blending in, becoming instead absurd caricatures of Capp's already exaggerated representatives of the wealthiest class (fig. 4.16). Ostensibly, Capp's theme in this episode is the Yokums turning the tables on the pomposity of the elite. But

Figure 4.15
Li'l Abner unknowingly ingratiating himself to the New York swells. Al Capp, *Li'l Abner*, "We All Understand One Another," strip #16, 1934 (detail). Courtesy Capp Enterprises, Inc., and Denis Kitchen Art Agency www.deniskitchen.com

Figure 4.16
The Yokums as ludicrously attired simians. Al Capp, *Li'l Abner*, "From the Frying Pan into the Fire" (detail), February 5, 1936. Courtesy Capp Enterprises, Inc., and Denis Kitchen Art Agency www.deniskitchen.com

Luke, Snuffy, & Abner

Pappy and Mammy's ridiculous attire and simian poses make them appear even more ludicrous than the characters supposedly being mocked and accentuate their status as white "others." In the same way that other American illustrators portrayed groups they perceived as threats to the social and political order, such as late nineteenth-century Irish immigrants, urban blacks, and World War II Japanese soldiers, as subhuman apes, basing such imagery on supposedly scientific theories about the stages of human evolution, Capp's simianization of his characters drew on contemporary social-science literature of southern mountaineers' primitivism.[42]

As the yacht party story suggests, these early episodes often had an explicitly populist overtone with Abner or Mammy Yokum repeatedly defending the weak and vulnerable from would-be exploiters. In a 1935 episode, Mammy protects a young orphan girl who has inherited a fortune against two venal aunts intent on getting custody of the child. When the women abandon the girl after a judge rules that her money is to be placed in a trust fund, Mammy triumphantly boots one of them in the behind (fig. 4.17). Similarly, in 1938, Abner defends emaciated children from an unspeakably cruel couple, appropriately named the Vulchers, who run an orphanage. In these scenes, Capp presents the Yokums as the unmistakably good-hearted and righteous defenders of the downtrodden and oppressed.[43]

But Capp's populist sympathies had their limits, as exemplified by his extended parody of John Steinbeck's *Grapes of Wrath*. Between December 1939 and March 1940, Capp presented the Yokums undergoing an absurd mirror

Figure 4.17
Mammy Yokum, defender of the oppressed, gives a representative
of the venal elite her richly deserved comeuppance. Al Capp, *Li'l Abner*,
"Her Unsuppressed Desire" (detail), July 6, 1935. Courtesy Capp Enterprises,
Inc., and Denis Kitchen Art Agency www.deniskitchen.com

image of the Joads' desperate exodus. Although the Joads were from the Oklahoma plains, both stories represented the real plight of thousands of displaced families during these years. Traveling across the country in beat-up jalopies following the promise of migrant labor in the supposed "orange orchards" of Boston, the Dogpatchers stop at a mansion seeking food and shelter. In one of his most biting portraits of the callousness of the elite, Capp shows a group of obese and well-dressed people, "the Committee to Feed Starving Mountaineers," devouring caviar and lobster while shedding crocodile tears for the fate of their fellow citizens (fig. 4.18). When the Dogpatchers attempt to enjoy the sumptuous buffet, claiming rightly *Starving Mountaineers? Thass us Lady!,*" they are angrily driven away by their supposed benefactors. Once the Dogpatchers arrive in Boston and realize there are no orange orchards in snowy New England, the mayor rallies the citizenry to provide funds for them to return to their home and to repurchase their repossessed houses. By the story's end, the Dogpatchers have only broken even, with no respite from the hardship that drove them away and without the consciousness of universal brotherhood gained by the Joads. Although Capp presents his story as a critique of faux-philanthropy, he uses physical and emotional suffering only for comedic purposes rather than to build empathy for the downtrodden. His ultimate message is that while the poor need to be pitied, definitive uplift is impossible, for they remain ignorant, backward and uneducable.[44]

Figure 4.18
Capp as populist: A stinging critique of pseudo philanthropy.
Al Capp, *Li'l Abner*, "Outside, Looking In!" (detail), January 9, 1940.
Courtesy Capp Enterprises, Inc., and Denis Kitchen Art Agency
www.deniskitchen.com

Nevertheless, in a world of bewildering change and turmoil, the Yokums have a clear and abiding sense of "home" and "place," always returning gratefully to Dogpatch after their many adventures. Mammy Yokum perhaps best represents the unshakable loyalty to home and kin that all the Yokums and Daisy Mae share. Motivated solely by her desire to protect her family and community, Mammy alone among the Dogpatchers possesses an unalloyed common sense that can cut through the duplicity and confidence scams of city slickers, whether a rich young heiress seeking to get the best of Abner or a fast-talking lawyer scheming to gain control of Dogpatch. The Yokums' absolute devotion binds them together, protects them from the stream of wealthy but heartless and, ultimately, hollow men and women who parade through the strip, and distinguishes them from the countless average urban characters driven by an insatiable desire for riches. Even though the pursuit of money was one of the strip's recurring themes during the Depression, the Yokums have no interest in acquiring wealth and usually give it away when they do.

Daisy Mae's and the Yokums' fairness, loyalty, and nonmaterialism grow out of their isolation from the corrupting influence of "civilization" and mark these characters and their fellow Dogpatchers as the human embodiment of a primitive but pure natural world. In Li'l Abner and Daisy Mae, Capp presented a prelapsarian vision of pristine innocence and physical purity—a modern-day (and explicitly white Anglo-Saxon) Adam and Eve who symbolized the ideal American beauty (fig. 4.19). But all other inhabitants of Dog-

Figure 4.19

Daisy Mae Scragg : The mountain woman as archetype of American beauty. Al Capp, *Li'l Abner*, "Yo' Said It, Fella!" (detail), February 12, 1936. Courtesy Capp Enterprises, Inc., and Denis Kitchen Art Agency www.deniskitchen.com

patch are physically grotesque and little better than wild animals. They walk around barefoot and in rags, think only of sex and food, and are utterly ignorant of and confused by the modern world beyond their mystical realm. Embracing myriad stereotypes about mountaineer primitiveness, Capp based countless episodes on the Dogpatchers' supposed filth, sloth, sexual promiscuity, bestiality, and social and cultural backwardness. At times, his visual and textual variations on these standard tropes could be quite playful. For example, he depicted Daisy Mae heading to the old maid's home because she is already seventeen and not yet married, and showed a married couple, who represent "the very *cream* o' Dogpatch society," looking down their noses on Abner's wife-to-be because she is barefoot, whereas they have had a pair of shoes in their family for over twenty years! Even his portrayal of the ravishingly beautiful Moonbeam McSwine, who constantly scratches herself, spits tobacco, and prefers the company of pigs to humans, is more absurd than degrading.[45]

Most of Capp's humor about mountain poverty and primitiveness, however, was demeaning and abrasive and became increasingly so. A group of recurring characters, Abijah Gooch and the Scraggs trio, offer the best examples of the dark side of his vision of mountain life. Although Abijah appeared in the strip's first two weeks as a somewhat more ragged counterpart of Abner, by October 1936, he metamorphosed into an incredibly muscular specimen with a long flowing beard (undoubtedly a direct influence of Webb's cartoons), who wears only a ragged pair of pants held up with a rope belt. Readers later learn that Abijah has borrowed the pants from his father, who is waiting in the woodshed for him to return! As Coach McGargle (who recruits Abner and Abijah for his football team) drives the boys to campus, he wonders, "maybe it *isn't* such a bright idea t'bring 'em to civilization!" Capp presents the theme of these hillbillies as modern-day cavemen even more explicitly in a following scene, where Abijah, dressed only in Abner's leopard-spotted night shirt, ignites a dormitory chair (and eventually the entire building) in an effort to stay warm.[46]

If Abijah Gooch represents the mountaineer as hopelessly ignorant and impoverished, Romeo Scragg and his two hulking sons, Lem and Luke, symbolize the mountaineer as uncontrollably violent and evil. Capp later described them as "unsanitary, uncouth, unregenerate, unspeakable apes." In an ongoing blood feud that lasted for most of the strip's existence, the Scraggs repeatedly attempt to kill the Yokums by any means possible, destroying anyone and anything that stands in their way. Always the symbol of unmitigated violence and social chaos, the Scraggs became increasingly savage by the late 1930s and the years of World War II. In a 1938 sequence, their path across the countryside best resembles that of a deadly tornado, and their hideous grinning faces fill civilized society with dread anytime they appear (figs. 4.20,

Figures 4.20, 4.21
The Scraggs: Mountaineers as "unregenerate, unspeakable apes."
Al Capp, *Li'l Abner,* April 12, 1938; "Welcome Homicide," April 13, 1938.
Courtesy Capp Enterprises, Inc., and Denis Kitchen Art Agency
www.deniskitchen.com

4.21). The Scraggs' hulking bodies and brutality were mirrored in countless other bit characters from the mountains whose sole purpose was to signify brute savagery. Capp freely used simian imagery and references in his depictions of Dogpatchers, at times even taking the logical leap to imply that these figures were less than human (fig. 4.22). Collectively, these images reinforced popular perceptions of the ignorance and innate violence of southern mountaineers and kept alive notions of regional social devolution first proposed by anthropologist Ellen Churchill Semple in 1901.[47]

Capp's contrasting of the simple innocence of Li'l Abner and his family with the subhuman savagery of the Scraggs and others reflects his funda-

Figure 4.22

Dogpatchers presented as subhuman brutes.

Al Capp, *Li'l Abner*, no title (detail), October 6, 1944.

Courtesy Capp Enterprises, Inc., and Denis Kitchen Art Agency

www.deniskitchen.com

mental understanding, to an even greater degree than DeBeck, of the inherent contradictions within the mountaineer/hillbilly duality and the satirical possibilities of merging concepts of plain but honest modern-day pioneers with notions of racial, physical, and cultural "otherness." The growing presence of barbaric characters in *Li'l Abner* during World War II also reflected both the savage fighting and manichean mentality of these years and Capp's accelerating shift away from presenting Dogpatch as an even remotely realistic mountain community and toward a pure fantasy realm of sexually charged grotesques and monsters. This trend reached its climax by the end of 1946, when Capp sent Li'l Abner to "Lower Slobbovia" (his version of the

Soviet Union) and nearly forced him to marry Lena the Hyena, an unspeakably hideous creature.

Although *Li'l Abner* continued for another thirty-one years, most aficionados consider the 1940s and 1950s the strip's golden era. In these years, the hillbilly component, never as central to the strip as it was for Webb and DeBeck, became less and less important as Capp populated his strip with all manner of fantastical creatures and the Dogpatchers became entangled in plots involving the cold war and atomic testing. In 1948, Abner and his fellow mountaineers participated in killing off the impossibly selfless Schmoos (creatures imbued with such goodness that they willingly allow themselves to be eaten in order to bring pleasure to their captors) on the grounds that allowing the spread of such an unmitigated boon would destroy the American work and consumption ethic. Thus, Dogpatch, once a possible antidote for the evils of modern civilization, increasingly became nothing more than a stand-in for the greed, corruption, and brutality that Capp believed characterized American society.[48]

Beyond the Comics Pages

Although these three cartoons lost some of their immediate cultural saliency in the years after World War II and both comic strips' focus on mountaineer settings and society diminished, Webb, DeBeck, and Capp's cartoon creations had a profound and abiding influence not only on national and regional conceptions of the media hillbilly but also on public perceptions of the actual mountain folk on which these images were supposedly based. Webb's hillbillies, in particular, penetrated deeply into American culture especially during World War II. In a strange variant of the practice of painting nude and near-nude women on fighter and bomber planes (many based directly on *Esquire*'s "Petty" and "Varga" girl foldout pictorials), for example, the crews of several coast guard and naval vessels adopted Webb's characters as insignia.[49] Through the auspices of the Brown and Bigelow advertising agency, Webb's cartoons were also used to promote a wide array of products. The Electric Auto-Lite Company, for example, featured his characters in a series of advertisements for their spark plugs in the early 1940s and even mailed a free paperback collection of *The Mountain Boys* cartoons to service men. Webb's iconography especially had a major impact on Hollywood's hillbillies. He transformed and iconicized the image of film hillbillies, previously an uncertain blend of lumberjack, sharecropper, and yeoman farmer, so that the terms "Esquire-style" and "Webb-like" came to evoke an instantly recognizable image of the hillbilly on film and throughout popular culture.[50]

Webb's influence even extended to college and high school students in the southern Appalachian region. *The Mountain Boys* arguably was the inspiration for the character "Dan'l Boone Yoseff" that students at Appalachian State Teachers College (now Appalachian State University) in Boone, North Carolina, created in 1942. They included the long-bearded, tall-hatted, corncob pipe-smoking mountaineer as a member of that year's freshman class and even pictured him on the yearbook cover as a self-mocking commentary on the broader world's image of southern mountaineers.[51] The hillbilly icon adopted in the late 1930s by the high school students at Asheville (North Carolina) High School for the cover of their annual, *The Hillbilly*, was even more directly based on Webb's imagery, from his long squirrel rifle, to his whiskey jug, bare feet, and slouched pose (fig. 4.23). As these examples make clear, by the later interwar era, Webb's image had become, nationally and locally, *the* standard image of the cartoon hillbilly and would remain so well into the postwar era.

Capp's hillbilly imagery was not as influential as Webb's, at least through the end of World War II, but his creation of Sadie Hawkins Day, on which Dogpatch women have the right to marry any man they can capture by whatever outrageous means, became a national phenomenon. Beginning on college campuses in the late 1930s, the practice of dressing in costumes inspired

Figure 4.23
Webb's influence in the southern mountains: The further evolution of *The Hillbilly* (and the hillbilly); *The Hillbilly*, 1946 yearbook, Lee H. Edwards High School, Asheville, North Carolina. Courtesy North Carolina Collection, Pack Memorial Public Library, Asheville, North Carolina, and Asheville High School.

by the comic strip and participating in chasing contests and dances soon spread to high schools, social clubs, and factories. Much of the appeal of Sadie Hawkins festivities' stemmed from the opportunity to challenge prevailing norms of decorum and feminine deference, but it also reinforced the widespread belief in the connection between impoverished southern mountaineers and aggressive and aberrant sexuality.[52]

The angry reactions of some southern mountaineers and their self-defined champions offer further evidence of the lasting influence of these images. John Lair of the *Renfro Valley Barn Dance* undoubtedly spoke for many in the region who found the cartoons demeaning. In a 1951 letter to the advertising executive in charge of publicity for his radio show's major sponsor (General Foods), in which he critiqued the far milder cartoons the agency had proffered to promote his programs, Lair stressed "the extreme dislike that is so often expressed for Esquire's 'Mountain Boys' and Al Capp's caricature monstrosities." Slightly less directly, native Kentuckian Harriete Arnow expressed her hostility toward the cartoon stereotypes in her epic 1954 novel *The Dollmaker* that traces the painful migration of Gertie Nevels and her family from the Kentucky hills to Detroit during World War II. In one scene, Gertie slaps her son for laughing at a Webb-like cartoon of an absurdly caricatured "barefooted and sun bonneted" hillbilly crone driving a bony mule. "It isn't funny" she snaps, thinking how the cartoon rudely parodies her husband's mother, who has been forced to single-handedly tend her Kentucky farmstead while her sons are all off at war.[53]

If we have only indirect and chronologically later demonstrations of the response of southern mountain people to these hillbilly cartoons, there is more evidence of their deep ambivalence toward the term itself. As musician Tony Alderman's reaction to the label discussed earlier, in chapter 3, makes clear, to many in the southern mountains this was a "fighting word," intended by urbanites to demean the backwoods inhabitants of the Ozarks and the Appalachians. Folklorist Vance Randolph claimed that one man murdered another over the use of the term in 1934, the very year the hillbilly cartoons and comic strips began. Howard Odum noted in 1936 its use as a slur against southern mountain migrant laborers in midwestern industrial cities, and Arnow's book is peppered with examples of hostile Detroit natives who spit out the word at Gertie Nevels and her children as if it were "a vile thing to be spewed out quickly." A 1944 article titled "Don't Call Me Hillbilly" explained that to the "native-born mountaineer," the word "smacks of ridicule" and "carries a stigma that sullies [his] pride."[54]

Yet other individuals from the southern mountains openly embraced the term. Despite acknowledging the ways outsiders had distorted the image of the Ozark hill folk, Vance Randolph consistently referred to them as "hill-billies," even publishing in 1943 a collection of anecdotes titled *Funny Stories about Hillbillies*. Likewise, Anthony Gish entitled his 1937 *Esquire* article "Yes, I'm a Hillbilly" and celebrated the independence, ruggedness, and male dominance of his Missouri Ozarks backcountry lifestyle. Roy Lee Harmon, West Virginia's poet laureate, insisted that the verses in his *Hillbilly Ballads* (1938) reflected the pioneer spirit of the Appalachian backwoodsman. The term "bears no stigma," he argued, but rather denotes "a person born and reared among our beloved mountains . . . where hardy Anglo-Saxons have built a modern and important commonwealth in what was once a wilderness."[55]

A third reaction by native hill folk, best articulated by Lucille Morris in her 1937 article "Good Ol' Hillbilly . . . ," was a somewhat reluctant acceptance of the term, recognizing that although it reflected urban derision, it also represented the way the unique folk culture of the Ozarks (and, by extension, the Appalachians) had captured the imagination of the urban middle-class and was stimulating the local tourist industry, a much-needed development in a depressed agricultural economy. Morris observed shrewdly that local resentment toward outsider's condescension "drifted away when being a hillbilly became good box-office." "Now," she continued, "we push our split-bonnet back . . . smooth out the creases in our store-boughten calico dress and coyly say 'Jest call me hillbilly.'" To Morris, this change in attitude also reflected the rediscovery of the region's folk heritage by a younger generation of Ozarkers, who had once been ashamed of the customs and dialect of their backwoods elders. "[B]ehind all the cheap crudities that are being dragged out by the exploiters of hillbillyism," Morris concluded, "there is an ancient and significant foundation." Ironically, therefore, the national mass media's distortions of genuine hill folk led some local inhabitants to recognize anew the value of skills and customs passed down through generations of hill country farmers and artisans.[56]

Such a wide array of local reactions to "hillbilly" reveals once again the fluidity of meaning of the word and image, and the way different audiences and individuals struggled to redefine and reconceptualize the term. The cartoons and comic strips that began in 1934 played a major role in this ongoing process. Influencing a far larger and more diverse audience than those who listened to country music, the works of Webb, DeBeck, and Capp changed the dominant definition of the mountaineer from genuine threat and danger to harmless, if aberrant, comical transgression. They also solidified an instantly recognizable graphic image of this new American stereotype. At the same time, their work retained the ambiguities inherent in this cultural construction by unifying derogatory conceptions of backwardness, ignorance, and savagery with positive ideas of ruggedness, independence, and devotion to family and home. In so doing, these cartoonists redefined this cultural form in ways that responded to the psychic needs of Americans enduring depression and war and looking back longingly to an imagined simpler time and place.

chapter**five**

Hollywood's Hillbilly in
Mid-Twentieth-Century America

Nowhere can one better see the comic reconceptualization of the media southern mountaineer in the period between the end of the First World War and the aftermath of the second than in motion pictures, the dominant medium of this era. Mountain characters appeared during these years, in which America seesawed between economic boom and collapse and international isolation and war, in nearly every possible film genre: action thrillers, pseudo-documentaries, social problem exposés, epic dramas, musicals, B-movie comedies, animated cartoons, and even government propaganda. Heavily influenced by both earlier mountaineer portrayals in silent films and the new conceptions and popularity of hillbilly images in other media, the hillbilly's constructed identity was marked as always by both ambiguity and a remarkable capacity to adapt to changing social perspectives and conditions. Despite the movie-going public's growing weariness of ignorant moonshiner and feudist stereotypes as early as the mid-1910s, these portrayals remained dominant well into the 1920s. Then, as the savage mountaineer persona increasingly lost credibility near the end of the decade, it was gradually supplanted by the new concept of the hillbilly, a comically backward yokel. This image reached its zenith in the mid- to late 1930s and held sway through the end of World War II, riding the same crest of glorification of the common folk and fascination with regional life and culture (particularly of the southern mountains) as had country musicians and cartoonists. By the end of a long and bloody war fought as much against ideologies of racial and ethnic hierarchy

and determinism as against Nazi Germany and Japan, by-then hoary stereotypes of barefoot and long-bearded feuding hillbillies came increasingly under attack. But the image was simply reinvented once again, this time in the
guise of rustic but domesticated Ma and Pa Kettle. In the enormously popular Kettle films, the hillbilly persona represented a cracked mirror image of
postwar attitudes about the sanctity of the child-focused nuclear family and
the new, and for many, unsettling, suburban and consumerist American society. When, by the mid-1950s, these films too had run their course, the image and the region they more broadly represented faded from view—waiting
to be rediscovered and reinvented anew.

The Fading Threat: The Dangerous Mountaineer in Post-World War I Film

Although a few comic films that spoofed the hundreds of pre–World War I
cookie-cutter feud-and-moonshine melodramas began to appear as early as
1911, the vast majority of 1920s mountaineer films continued to revolve around
these hackneyed plots. The theme of ignorant savagery was clear from their
titles: *Seeds of Vengeance* (1920), *Wolf Law* (1922), *The Valley of Hate* (1924),
and *Souls Aflame* (1928)—the latter described in *Variety* as "a convincing picturization of a half-civilized semi-barbarous folk." An early script for the 1925
drama *Thunder Mountain* suggests just how barbarous these characters were.
The fifth scene introduces "a wild, half-naked man," who tills the soil with a
"hand made plough of ancient type," and who calls his children to dinner by
throwing rocks into the underbrush. Even when filmmakers moved beyond
the theme of mountain savagery, they still presented the region's people as
culturally aberrant. *Mountain Madness* (1920) interwove "mountain bandits
and cold-blooded sheriffs" with quarreling lovers caught in West Virginia
mountain mists and "overtaken by a species of 'mountain madness,'" whereas
The Wives of the Prophet (1926) focused on a Virginia mountaineer sect that
annually chooses virgin partners for a supposedly divine seer.[1]

Even though feuding and moonshining remained common themes of
films about the mountains throughout the century, by the end of World War
I, the genre had been so thoroughly exploited that critics and exhibitors alike
routinely condemned these predictable plots and character types. Typical
was the reviewer of the new Tom Mix film, *The Feud*, who cautioned theater
owners in 1919: "This title will not sell readily. It is trite and suggestive of a
theme badly overworked." The sharp postwar decline in the number of films
that featured contemporary mountain characters and settings is further evidence of the growing reaction against these standard melodramas. Whereas
studios released 138 such films between 1915 and 1919, they produced only 84

over the following decade and only 37 between 1930 and 1939. The growing length of films and their escalating costs probably played a role in this decline, but more significant was the genre's diminishing credibility with audiences. Urban movie-goers had evidently lost interest and faith in the believability of shootouts between mountain clans or between justice officials and outlaws (although these plots became central to westerns). Yet Hollywood's belief that for the movie-going public, the southern mountain folk continued to be synonymous with primitive savagery and cultural ignorance remained unassailable. A more in-depth study of three distinct mountain films of the 1920s reveals this prevailing public perception of southern mountain folk, as well as the slow appearance of the hillbilly stereotype that would emerge full force in the following decade.[2]

Tol'able David (1921) remains one of the most lucrative and influential films about mountaineers ever produced. It garnered rave reviews from theater owners and critics nationwide ("Beyond the shadow of a doubt, the greatest picture of mountain life ever made" trumpeted one Illinois exhibitor), was voted best picture of 1922 by *Photoplay Magazine* readers, and made a star of its young leading man Richard Barthelmess. Based on a short story by Joseph Hergesheimer, the drama featured the coming of age of sixteen-year-old David Kinemon (Barthelmess), who is forced to defend his home and his budding sweetheart, Esther, from three brutish mountain savages on the run from the law in West Virginia. After the most vicious of these thugs maims David's older brother and indirectly causes their father to suffer a fatal stroke, David heads off to face down the assailants, despite his mother's desperate efforts to stop him. In a horrific and epic battle, David proves his manhood by killing the savage mountaineers and saving Esther.[3]

The film's box office success stemmed not only from its melodramatic storyline but also from the belief that because it avoided shopworn plots and was filmed on location in the uplands of Highland County, Virginia, it must be an accurate representation of the people and conditions throughout the contemporary southern mountains. Barthelmess and director Henry King played an important role in promoting this perception of authenticity, inviting newspaper reporters to join them in what one typical press account called the "[v]ery wilds of Virginia," "midst a primitiveness hardly believable." Although both King and Barthelmess stressed to reporters that this was "not a story of a feud or moonshiners" and that they wanted to capture "the real atmosphere of the Virginia mountains," they also exploited the feud myth to lend credibility to their venture. Evidently, they believed that the public saw feuding as such an integral aspect of mountain culture and identity that they would have to introduce this myth in order for their film to be believable. Thus, King discussed with reporters the "causes and sensational results [of family feuds]" and claimed that his crew had been stopped on their way to their filming site by a gang of armed men in pursuit of a rival "clan." This simultaneous rejection and embrace of the feuding myth was perfectly captured in a *Louisville Herald* review that noted that the film, though melodramatic, reveals "the 'eye for an eye' creed of the mountain feudist" and "appears to be life as the story writers have taught us to believe life is in the mountains of Kentucky and Virginia."[4]

While Barthelmess was the star of the film and the focus of most media attention, reviewers gave nearly equal attention to the main villain in the film, Luke Hatburn—a name clearly meant to evoke the Hatfields of feuding legend—who was played by Ernest Torrence (fig. 5.1). Taking his place in a long line of film mountaineer savages, Hatburn is a brutish giant, described in the opening titles as a man "whose peculiar humor it was to destroy whatever he encountered." More than living up to this introduction, Hatburn over the course of the film kills the family dog, maims David's brother by hitting him in the back with a rock and then stomping on his head, steals the U.S. mail, and nearly rapes Esther. Torrence's performance seemed so true to life that one reviewer marveled "it is so realistic that it fairly becomes painful to the audience." Torrence's character, agreed film critic Heywood Broun, "has been pretty generally awarded the heavyweight, blood-curdling championship for the present season." The film thus brilliantly combined both sides

Figure 5.1
The archetypal mountain ogre: Ernest Torrence as Luke Hatburn in *Tol'able David* (1922). Courtesy of the Academy of Motion Picture Arts and Sciences.

Figure 5.2

Agrarian purity meets mountain savagery:
Luke Hatburn (Ernest Torrence) and David Kinemon
(Richard Barthelmess) in a death struggle in *Tol'able David* (1922).
Courtesy of the Academy of Motion Picture Arts and Sciences.

of the mountaineer's mythic identity. Whereas David symbolized agrarian
purity and righteousness, uncorrupted by the modern industrial world and
the horrors of the Great War, Luke and his family represented unadulterated
evil and a culture and mentality so primitive and retrogressive that civilization's very survival demanded its extermination. In the final fight to the death
between the hulking Goliath and the diminutive David (fig. 5.2), these two
sides of the mythic mountaineer persona are unified as David achieves the
level of wanton savagery necessary to defeat his opponent and emerge tri-
umphant.[5]

While encapsulating all the elements of the savage hillbilly persona,
Tol'able David did not use the term "hillbilly" anywhere in the film or in its
advertising nor did it appear in any of the film reviews. But by 1924, the word
had become sufficiently familiar that it was used in the title of a film clearly
designed to cash in on *Tol'able David*'s success. *The Hill Billy* (1924), starring
Jack Pickford (Mary Pickford's younger brother), was the second film to incorporate the label in its title.[6] As in *Tol'able David*, the heroic young lad is

Figure 5.3
Jed McCoy (Jack Pickford) taunted by hunch-shouldered
hillbilly "type" in *The Hill Billy* (1924). Courtesy of the
Academy of Motion Picture Arts and Sciences.

initiated into manhood by killing a mountain monster who has murdered his
father. Although the star and his director, George Hill, tried to enliven the
storyline by giving Pickford's character a pet bear, only the title was truly
novel and a *Photoplay* reviewer complained that the well-worn plot "has been
done often—and, at times, better." Yet *The Hill Billy* may also have broken
new ground in its portrayal of a subsidiary figure as a slack-jawed, hunch-
shouldered, one-gallused ignorant hillbilly (fig. 5.3). Within a little over a
decade, this character would become a standard "type" in most Hollywood
films of the mountains. Because so few of the mountain films of the early
1920s remain, it is unclear if *The Hill Billy* marked the first film appearance
of this character type, but it does show the image was already forming by the
mid-1920s.[7]

Perhaps in response to this film or simply because of the term's broad-
ening cultural acceptance, by mid-decade, "hillbilly" variants began appearing in other films and film commentary, in some cases replacing previous
synonyms for poor white southerners. An early script for *Sun-Up* (1925), for
example, described the mountain characters as "scattered untamed Ameri-

cans called WHITE TRASH." The final title list six months later, however, labeled them "'Hill Billies' living in defiant seclusion in their sullen hills of the South." Some of the film's reviewers also adopted the term for both the characters and the real-life people they represented. One reviewer argued that the script lines, implying that the hill folk think that the war in France is taking place just on the other side of the mountains, were superfluous but concluded that they "serve probably to plant more firmly in the minds of those viewing the picture the exact mental and educational status of the average hillbilly." Such references clearly indicate the term's growing popularity as a label that struck a balance between the offensiveness of "white trash" and the romanticism of "mountaineers."[8]

Despite the rise of the "hillbilly" label and the emergence of a more exclusively comical conception of the southern mountain people, the stereotype of the brutish and ignorant mountaineer continued to appear in motion pictures of the late 1920s. One of the most significant of these films was *Stark Love* (1927). Although unsuccessful in its own time—after a brief run in American theaters, it disappeared until a sole remaining copy was discovered in the 1960s in the Czechoslovakian Film Archives—the film, the views of its writer and director, Karl Brown, and the reaction of reviewers and reporters perfectly reflect the unquestioned public conception of the degradation of contemporary mountain life.[9]

A long-time Hollywood cameraman who had made his reputation filming the epic landscapes of *The Covered Wagon*, a 1923 hit about the winning of the West, Brown was fascinated by what he conceived to be the uncloistered sexuality and near-savagery of frontier America. He was enthralled with missionary Lucy Furman's 1922 *Atlantic Monthly* account of the isolated and primitive lives of Kentucky hill folk, which was later published as *The Quare Women*. He was also strongly affected by Horace Kephart's *Our Southern Highlanders*, an informed and influential but highly romanticized adventure tale of the people and culture of the Tennessee and North Carolina mountains. Kephart himself helped Brown locate the film's site and frequented the movie set, consulting on the native culture.[10]

Given Brown's preconceptions and influences, it is not surprising that the major themes of *Stark Love* are the same ones stressed in nearly all cultural representations of the southern mountains since at least the turn of the century. The opening title introduces the characters in the by-now standard fashion as "an isolated and primitive people, descendants of the British pioneers." Scenes of their crude lives, from beating clothes clean and cooking over a large open hearth, to skinning a wild boar, punctuate the film. All of this work is conducted by women and the film highlights the totality of male domination. "[T]heir law of the wilderness," the second title card reads, "is

Figure 5.4

Mountain woman as slave: Rob Warwick's mother
(Adeline Queen) tends the fire in *Stark Love* (1927). Courtesy
of the Academy of Motion Picture Arts and Sciences.

expressed in the cruel principle MAN IS THE ABSOLUTE RULER—WOMAN IS THE
WORKING SLAVE." Brown repeatedly emphasized the laziness and drunkenness of the men and the drudgery of women's lives; the protagonist's mother
is driven to an early grave from overwork and excessive childbearing (fig. 5.4).
Unlike cartoonists DeBeck, Webb, and Capp, who meant their images to be
funny, Brown intended his work to be a damning (if lurid) critique of premodern rurality. Closely related to the theme of abusive patriarchy was the
idea that most fired Brown's imagination: the unrestrained carnality of the log
cabin. As he told his wife excitedly before he pitched his idea to producer
Jesse Lasky of Paramount:

> We know all about the outside of these [log] cabins, but not the inside.
> . . . how do you suppose these people live . . . when they are cribbed,
> cabined and confined [in winter and spring] . . . for weeks or months
> on end in a wooden prison from which there is no escape? And what
> do you suppose the older children think when a new life is started in
> their very presence, where they can see and hear and know what is
> happening?[11]

This mystery of the one-room cabin is at the very heart of *Stark Love*. As in *The Hill Billy* and other earlier coming-of-age films, a young mountain lad (here Rob Warwick, played by Forrest James) who longs to escape his mountain fastness must first defeat a more powerful adversary—the living symbol of degraded backwardness and savagery. But unlike its predecessors, in *Stark Love* the boy's nemesis, who stands between him and his childhood sweetheart, Barbara Allen (played by Helen Mundy), is his own father. After the elder Warwick has "married" (essentially acquired with her father's permission) Barbara Allen after his own exhausted wife has died, he attempts to have sex with his new "bride" against her will (fig. 5.5). Brown's themes of isolation, primitiveness, and male power come together in the penultimate scene of near rape, in which Rob attacks his father and is thrown out the cabin door and into a swollen river by the much stronger man. Chopping her way through the bolted cabin door after threatening to kill the old man with her axe, Barbara saves Rob from the raging river and then floats them both to safety. The film ends with Rob and Barbara, free at last from their mountain shackles, walking hand in hand toward the salvation offered by the valley town shimmering in the distance.

Despite the film's standard "escape from the mountains" ending, Brown

Figure 5.5
Patriarchy challenged: Barbara Allen (Helen Mundy) glowers at her new "husband" James Warwick (Silas Miracle) in a scene before his attempted rape of her in *Stark Love* (1927). Courtesy of the Academy of Motion Picture Arts and Sciences.

claimed his was a unique documentary-style film that moved beyond clichéd hillbilly storylines. As he told Horace Kephart: "I want to show these people as they are. As they *really* are. As human beings, not caricatures." In reality, however, Brown knew almost nothing about mountain culture and society and his entire project was designed to present his subjects *not* as they actually were but as he devoutly wished them to be. His unintentionally hilarious account of the making of the film reveals the depths of his ignorance. Setting out to find "the benighted people of the darkest recesses of the Great Smoky Mountains," he headed first to New Orleans! Journalists there directed him next to Berea, Kentucky, where local officials at Berea College were, predictably, decidedly uninterested in (as he himself later put it) "helping movies exploit mountain people." He then bumbled his way from Nashville to Knoxville to Asheville, in each case being assured by hotel clerks, bell boys, and newsmen that the type of people he sought were all in the environs of the next town. Finally, in an Asheville bookstore, he discovered *Our Southern Highlanders* and, eventually, its author.[12]

Firmly wedded to his preconception of a dangerously secluded and backward culture, Brown deliberately distorted the reality of mountain life and manipulated his actors. For his setting, which he later presented as a typical contemporary mountain community, he chose a site high in the Snowbird Mountains of Graham County, North Carolina, where there stood a few abandoned cabins that would soon be under water after the completion of Santeelah Dam. Furthermore, he intentionally filmed his sequences out of order and in short, unconnected segments to keep his local cast from recognizing the offensive nature of his portrayal of their lives. He later justified his "trickery" by explaining that the men were all "lazy, drunken, good-for-nothings" and the native people "were like children . . . in their implicit obedience." How else could one treat such people, who "have never seen a railroad train, automobile . . . or a telephone," Brown implicitly argued, but by telling them only what they needed to know in order to act out the scene? Finally, although Brown claimed that nearly all the members of his cast were Graham County natives, all four of his leading actors were outsiders. The two men who played Rob and Barbara's fathers were Kentuckians, and Forrest James and Helen Mundy were both from Knoxville, James a local football player and Mundy a thoroughly modern high school student.[13]

Despite their awareness that Brown had contrived his scenes and manipulated and misrepresented his actors, reporters and reviewers nonetheless presented the movie as a realistic portrayal of southern mountain life and people. One reviewer labeled the film "a picturization of the actual life and customs of the most primitive people of America." The *Motion Picture News* went even further. Comparing the film to the three recent and highly influential documentaries *Nanook of the North* (1922), *Grass* (1925), and *Moana* (1926), the newspaper pronounced *Stark Love* "as important sociologically and scientifically as the illustrious trinity which preceded it." Thus, a completely fabricated story, springing from the overactive imagination of a director who could barely locate the Appalachian mountains on a national map, was presented as an anthropologically valuable study of a primitive native race. Nonetheless, such supposed scientific bona fides were not enough to save the film from box office failure. Despite rave reviews in the film industry press, Paramount promoted the film only half-heartedly, and after a brief national release, it was withdrawn and the prints melted to recover their silver content.[14]

Films such as *Stark Love* and *Sun-Up* reflected seemingly contradictory aspects of 1920s American culture. On the one hand, their focus on "100 percent Americans," living as their colonial ancestors had, reflected the virulent nativism of this era—years marked by the passage of the National Origins Act (1924), the reemergence of the Ku Klux Klan, and the execution of Sacco and Vanzetti. They also reflected the demands of Protestant missionary associations to focus relief and education efforts on the benighted hill folk rather than on Asian or African "heathens." As one of the title cards for *Sun-Up* read: "America spends millions in China teaching them about their white God. . . . [but] [w]hat's the government doin' about some poor Americans—wandering in darkness in our own mountains back here." While these films celebrated the southern mountaineers as being worthy of uplift, however, they also presented them as ignorant, backward, and retrograde in their treatment of women and their life habits. This perspective mirrored not only dozens of popular press accounts on hopelessly primitive mountain folk but also the denunciation of rural and small-town Americans, in general, by prominent writers such as H. L. Mencken and Sinclair Lewis. As in other media and previous eras, film representations of southern mountaineers in the 1920s served both those who wanted to promote and to condemn nonurban American society.[15]

The Slow Rise to Dominance of the Comic Hillbilly

Stark Love's failure further indicated that by the late 1920s, audience interest in serious melodramas about the southern mountain people was dramatically declining. Reviewers and exhibitors now rejected any hint of the standard mountaineer plot line and themes as sure-fire failure. As feuding and moonshining became delegitimized as credible storylines and the standard Hollywood action genre shifted to cowboys and Indians in western settings, these themes increasingly became the purview of comedians. Their films, paralleling trends in the music business, helped to gradually redefine mountain life and culture as a site of comedic excess outside of socioeconomic reality rather than a serious social problem.

One of the earliest extant films featuring the new comedic hillbilly is Buster Keaton's 1923 silent spoof *Our Hospitality*, a take-off on the famed Hatfield-McCoy conflict and a parody of the standard Kentucky feud melodrama. Keaton plays Willie McKay, a young man spirited away by his mother to New York City as a child in order to escape the family's feud with the rival Canfield clan. When he learns he has inherited his father's estate, he is sure that a palatial plantation awaits him and, despite his aunt's warnings, heads into the Blue Ridge Mountains to claim his prize. Of course, the grand estate turns out to be (as in DeBeck's comic strip) only a run-down cabin. Keaton spends the rest of the film avoiding becoming the victim of the Canfields' "hospitality."

Our Hospitality shows the hillbilly image still in an early state of development. Unlike later hillbilly films and images that were set in the present day, Keaton's film is explicitly placed in the early nineteenth century (long before the actual Hatfield-McCoy conflict began in the 1870s) and does not suggest that such family feuds still exist in the contemporary mountains. Indeed, the fairy-tale-like title card of the Prologue underscores this distancing intent: "Once upon a time in certain sections of the United States there were feuds that ran from generation to generation." The feuding Canfields are portrayed not as impoverished and wild hill folk but as aristocrats of the planter class who live in a stately mansion, thus suggesting that the idea of warring hillbillies grew out of earlier conceptions of the prevalence of dueling between members of the southern elite (fig. 5.6). Finally, given the hillbilly image's exclusively comical quality by the late 1930s, it is interesting that some reviewers still had trouble finding the humor in an image of family battles to the death. Wrote one: "We have our doubts whether a 'take-off' of the Southern feud story could ever be made consistently humorous—because of its melodramatic character."[16]

Despite some reviewers' concerns, films in which the feud and moonshine plot was played strictly for laughs proliferated over the next decade. After the advent of sound in 1927, a growing array of film and vaudeville comedians starred in movies—mostly twenty-minute shorts rather than full-length features—in which ornery mountaineers were presented strictly as foils for their slapstick escapades. Nonetheless, the film hillbilly was still forming as late as the 1930s; films such as Laurel and Hardy's *Them Thar Hills* (1934) did not yet incorporate expected stereotypes of laziness, drunkenness, and filth.[17]

Kentucky Kernels (1934), starring Bert Wheeler and Robert Woolsey, il-

Figure 5.6
Feudists as aristocrats: Willie McKay (Buster Keaton)
warily shakes hands with the rival Canfields in *Our Hospitality* (1923).
Courtesy of the Academy of Motion Picture Arts and Sciences.

lustrates the continuing evolution of the hillbilly stereotype in these early
films. Presenting a hodgepodge of southern and western "types," the film liberally borrowed from earlier mountaineer plots and routines. In a replay of
hackneyed plot devices, Wheeler and Woolsey's characters come to the "feud
country" after they learn that the child they are guarding has recently inherited a Kentucky estate. In a scene that exactly mimics one from *Our Hospitality*, aristocratic men seated around a dining table suddenly fire off their
guns when they mistake a popped champagne cork for a rifle shot. As in
Keaton's film, the leaders of the feuding Wakefields are a southern plantation
family, but the other men in the "clan" are dressed in a variety of rustic costumes from plaid shirts and slouch hats to cowboy hats and string ties. In the
ensuing battle, described by one paper as "something like civil war," their rivals are more explicitly presented as stereotypical mountaineers (they are first
shown congregated around a moonshine still outside a log cabin), but they,
too, are costumed more like lumberjacks (with plaid shirts and high-top
boots) than like the stereotypical hillbillies to come. The word "hillbilly" is
not used anywhere in the film or the script, except for a reference to "a hill-

billy quartette" of musicians. *Kentucky Kernels* thus marked a further transitional stage in the evolving hillbilly image; although comically violent, the characters are not yet slothful and unhygienic.[18]

By *Kentucky Moonshine* (1938), the next hillbilly comedy set in the Bluegrass state, however, the iconic lazy, overbearded, and overhatted hillbilly had been undeniably established. Starring the Ritz Brothers—who made over a dozen "B" comedies between the mid-1930s and 1943 and were an equally zany but less ingenious version of the Marx Brothers—the film fully exploited the newly iconicized hillbilly image. The script, promotional materials, and film reviews all freely employed the term. The script referred to a "typical lazy hillbilly scene" as if the meaning were so well known that it hardly needed explication. This new cultural currency of "hillbilly" was, of course, partly a result of the adoption of the term and image by the promoters and performers of commercial country music, and the growing national fascination with the southern mountains as a site of an authentic folk culture but also social degradation, political unrest, and economic desperation. More directly, it was a response to the hillbilly comics and cartoons of DeBeck, Capp, and above all, Paul Webb. *Kentucky Moonshine*'s debt to Webb's work is obvious: a line of dialogue describes a run-down cabin that "looks like a fugitive from *Esquire*," and the Ritz Brothers pretend to be natives of the Kentucky hill town of "Coma" by costuming themselves as the living embodiment of "The Mountain Boys" (fig. 5.7). Producer Darryl Zanuck even tried to hire Paul Webb to do the movie's advertising posters.[19]

The screenwriters and actors did make a limited attempt to comment on the constructed nature of this image. For instance, the plot portrayed the Ritz Brothers as down-on-their-luck New York performers who travel to the Kentucky hills to be "discovered" by a New York music radio show host, who tries to cash in on the hillbilly music craze by broadcasting live on location. The film also included a memorable exchange between the costumed Ritz men and the suspicious, rifle-bearing Hatfields. When the Ritz Brothers try to appease the hill men by assuring them "we're hillbillies," the clan patriarch asks warily "What in tarnation is a hillbilly?" But for the most part, the film reinforced rather than undercut mountaineer stereotypes. From the all-too-familiar feud between the Hatfields and the Slacks, to big-city reporters breezily asking the girlfriend of one of the brothers what it feels like to wear shoes and has she ever been a child bride, to song lyrics such as "Oh we're the Slacks from Coma / And you'll pardon our aroma," the film consistently presented mountaineers as absurdly degenerate.[20]

The almost universally favorable review of the film reveals how seemingly uncontroversial the hillbilly image had become by 1938 and how relatively novel it still seemed. The film was approved without cuts by the Mo-

Figure 5.7
The Ritz Brothers as Paul Webb's *Mountain Boys*
come to life in *Kentucky Moonshine* (1938). Courtesy of
the Academy of Motion Picture Arts and Sciences.

tion Picture Association of America's Production Code Administration (PCA)
and drew no fire from any of the private citizen review boards set up by such
groups as the Daughters of the American Republic or the National Council
of Jewish Women, all of whom deemed it a "hilarious and wholesome" production. Tellingly, the PCA checklist of potentially problematic character
portrayals included "Negro," "Italian," "Chinese," "Mexican," and "Other"
but no explicit category for southern whites, hill folk, mountaineers, or any
other similar label. Although the film included every imaginable cliché about
mountain folks' backwardness and social impropriety, *Time* called its presentation of "hillbilly doings" "typically untypical" and *Variety* predicted the
film would bring "uproarious laughter" and "piles of silver" to its exhibitors.
Granted, the Ritz Brothers' spoofs were rather tame put-downs compared to
some of the degrading portrayals in Webb's cartoons and *Stark Love*. But
would a film that presented an equally crude stereotype of African Americans

or another ethnic group have garnered the same enthusiastic reviews? The widespread protests by the African-American community against the portrayal of black characters in *Gone with the Wind* suggests that the whiteness of the characters allowed *Kentucky Moonshine* to be seen as merely a harmless parodying of a fictionalized people rather than an offensive portrayal of actual mountain folk.[21]

Although *Kentucky Moonshine* indicated a general trend in motion pictures and the broader culture toward a humorous reenvisioning of the population and the land, some Hollywood dramas between the early 1930s and the end of World War II continued to portray southern mountain folk as a potential social problem. *Spitfire* (1934) featured the twenty-five-year-old Katherine Hepburn in an intentionally serious performance as the "lying, stealing, singing, praying witch girl of the Ozarks," and Paramount presented the third filmed version of the John Fox, Jr., classic *The Trail of the Lonesome Pine* about the cultural chasm between mountain and city as the first Technicolor movie in 1936. Even *Sergeant York* (1941), for which Gary Cooper won the Oscar for best actor for his portrayal of Alvin York as a poor but devout (and in war time, extremely deadly) hardscrabble hill farmer turned World War I hero, devoted much attention to the poverty and social backwardness of the hill people.[22]

Perhaps the film that best represented the "mountains-as-social problem" film genre was *Mountain Justice*. A 1938 Warner Brothers release, the film was obviously but unofficially based on the case of Edith Maxwell, a young schoolteacher in Pound (Wise County), Virginia, which became a cause célèbre after a local all-male jury found her guilty of murdering her father, even though he had attacked her with a knife in a drunken fury. The Maxwell case received weeks of front-page headlines, and the National Woman's Party, which helped pay Maxwell's legal fees, turned her into a symbol of gender oppression. In most press accounts, however, the real target was not Maxwell's father or even the jury that had found her guilty, but a backward-looking and generalized "mountain culture" that enforced absolute male authority.[23]

Mountain Justice played up these same themes of a degenerate mountain culture: the unhealthy conditions of the hill folk and their fierce opposition to modern medicine; the horrors of a patriarchal society; and the enforcement of an archaic "Hill Billy Justice" (the original title of the film), that is little more than mob rule. The film's most dramatic scenes vividly illustrate this supposed mountain savagery. Early on, Jeff Harkins (played by Robert Barrat) lashes his daughter Ruth (acted by Josephine Hutchinson) with an enormous bullwhip for disobeying his orders to marry an unsavory mountain man (fig. 5.8). In the ensuing struggle, she accidentally kills him in self-

Figure 5.8

Jeff Harkins (Robert Barrat) hulking over the prostrate
body of his daughter Ruth (Josephine Hutchinson) in
a graphic promotional still for *Mountain Justice* (1938).
Courtesy of the Academy of Motion Picture Arts and Sciences.
MOUNTAIN JUSTICE © 1937 Turner Entertainment Co.
An AOL Time-Warner Company. All Rights Reserved.

defense and is later put on trial and found guilty of murder. In the film's
penultimate scene, an angry mob of townspeople, outraged by what they consider Ruth's lenient punishment (twenty-five years in a state penitentiary),
and wearing Ku Klux Klan–like sacks over their heads, attempt to lynch her.
Only some tricky subterfuge and the kindness of a neighboring governor
(bearing a striking resemblance to Franklin Roosevelt) who refuses to extradite
her saves Ruth from certain death at the hands of these mountain fanatics.[24]

The "Mountain Justice" press book hammered home these themes of
"fanaticism and intolerance." Advertising copy beckoned movie-goers to
"learn the facts about 'America's Savage Million'" and to discover "the last
barbaric outpost of 20th century America . . . [where there exist] mysterious
communities of child brides, lash law, witch craft and mountain loves!" The

studio also provided exhibitors with lobby exploitation ideas such as making a display of children's clothing, dolls, and "other childish trifles" with the caption *"The trousseau of the bride-to-be in 'Mountain Justice'"* or displaying a sign proclaiming *"This is what mountaineers use to mete out justice in 'Mountain Justice'"* next to an arrangement of rifles, whips, and nooses.[25]

Perhaps because of the sensationalistic promotional campaign, critical reaction to Mountain Justice was largely negative. Some reviewers praised it—one called it a film made with "unholy skill and authentic power"—and most women's groups who reviewed it found it a distasteful but convincing portrayal of mountain society, describing it as a "graphic and honest presentation" and "starkly realistic." But most reviewers, recalling countless similar films from the past three decades, deemed it an overblown melodrama that rehashed mountaineer stereotypes. Variety called it a "lurid and unconvincing" story that "seems to contain every hill country cliché known to man." Another critic dismissed the film as "stirring and unbelievable tripe." "Doubtless the theory behind such an outspoken portrayal of mountaineers," the author continued, "is that mountaineers seldom if ever attend movies." Although this attitude clearly reflected the majority opinion in the national press and in Hollywood, Warner Brothers studio executives were actually so concerned about "mountaineers" (particularly those involved in the Maxwell case) viewing the film and possibly suing for libel, they did not release the motion picture in the state of Virginia or in Bristol, Tennessee. Such precautions may have avoided potential lawsuits, but they could not boost the film's popularity and it lasted only a few weeks in movie houses nationwide. Such a reception suggests the growing rejection of recycled mountain stereotypes in serious drama and the renewed fading interest in the mountains as a problem region.[26]

One final example of this era of a serious film treatment of the mountaineer, one that portrayed hill people as both potential problem and solution, was the government documentary Valley of the Tennessee (1944)—one of over thirty documentaries produced by the Office of War Information (OWI) and intended for an overseas audience. These films were meant to challenge the propaganda efforts of the Axis powers by showing, in the words of OWI director Elmer Davis, "the power and strength of the United States" and that American war aims "will conduce to the eventual good of the entire world." They were also designed to counter Hollywood's common portrayal of a frivolous, violent, and immoral society. In contrast, many of the OWI documentaries promoted a vision of a plain and virtuous people, constructing a more humane world by harnessing the powers of modern science and technology. In this spirit, Valley of the Tennessee extolled the social and economic benefits resulting from the Tennessee Valley Authority (TVA) hydroelectric dam-building projects and scientific agriculture programs. It promoted the same vision of a denuded land and seemingly defeated people being rejuvenated through systematic social planning and modern science that suffuses Pare Lorentz's influential documentary, *The River* (1937), and *Democracy on the March*, TVA Chairman David Lilienthal's popular 1944 book on the TVA "miracle."[27]

To a far greater extent than either of these works, however, *Valley of the Tennessee* presents the backwardness and destructive individualism of upland farmers, rather than capital interests or monopolistic private power companies, as the enemies of social and environmental progress. Unshaven, slouch-hatted, and shuffling slowly through the dust, these men are, according to the narration, almost incapable of conceiving any alternative future other than "poverty, ignorance [and] drudgery" after "years of isolation . . . and bigotry." Director Alexander Hammid portrayed the initial unwillingness of most farmers to participate in the government program as not only self-destructive but also immoral. He juxtaposed two neighbors: a "good" farmer (Henry Clark), who reluctantly agrees to adopt scientific practices such as contour farming and spreading phosphate fertilizers, and a "bad" farmer (Horace Higgins), who lives in a ramshackle shack with his bedraggled family and refuses to participate in these efforts. In the end, even Higgins is won over as he sees the dramatic improvements in Clark's crop yield and quality of life thanks to the new methods. As Higgins signs up to participate in the program, the narrator concludes that he has finally learned the lesson "that the individual through the cooperation with others, becomes a more important individual." The film closes with scenes of a glorious future made possible by modern collectivism combined with scientific planning and heroic engineering: a passenger airline flying over gleaming new dams; Henry Clark's family, now well dressed and fed, comfortably ensconced in a white clapboard house; and his children playing joyfully in front of the new dam that has made it all possible.[28]

In stark contrast to earlier films such as *Mountain Justice* and *Stark Love*, in which only individuals are able to escape the degenerate mountain culture while the culture itself remains stagnant and unchanged, *Valley of the Tennessee* posits the potential economic and social revitalization of the entire region through modern technology and "voluntary" federal intervention. Absent, however, is an earlier Regionalist conception of the cultural richness of the southern mountain folk. Nor is there any sense that such dramatic transformation might have significant individual and societal costs. Instead, the "hillbilly" farmer Horace Higgins represents only a reactionary roadblock to the headlong rush toward affluence and "progress," one that needs to be removed for the good of the region, the nation, and indeed, the world.

The Hillbilly Stereotype at High Tide—1937–1945

With their Appalachian setting and dramatic subjects, *Mountain Justice* and *Valley of the Tennessee* were clearly the exception that proved the rule of the gravitational shift beginning around 1936 in movie house portrayals of mountain people from Appalachia to the Ozarks and from serious social drama to musical comedy and rustic farce—a transition that paralleled the celebration of "the folk" at a time of anti-fascism and New Deal populism. Although the total number of films set in the southern mountains or based on the hill folk declined dramatically in each successive decade after 1920, the percentage of comic portrayals within this genre steadily grew, from 14 percent of 1920s films, to 42 percent of the 1930s movies, to 63 percent of 1940s films. The Ozark setting of nearly all these comic films reflected not only the long time association between the region and parodic portrayals of mountaineer but also the increasingly troubled portrayal of Appalachia in national press accounts. As the southeastern mountains became defined as a land of violent coal strikes, human suffering, and, more positively, as the site of large-scale government works programs, it grew more difficult for national film audiences to maintain their conception of the region as a land beyond the realm of social and economic reality. Conversely, it was far easier for film producers and viewers to define the Ozarks, which lacked similar large-scale extractive industries and government programs, as a mythic space inhabited by outlandishly caricatured men and women.[29]

The most immediate cause of the new filmic emphasis on the Ozarks, however, was that it was the home of nearly all of the rural humorists from the vaudeville stage and network radio who collectively starred in these productions. Bob Burns, a native of Van Buren, Arkansas, and the star of four films for Paramount between 1937 and 1940, dubbed himself "the Arkansas Traveller" and was best known for his "invention" of a musical contraption he called a "bazooka" (a name later applied to the similar-looking World War II anti-tank weapon). Chester Lauck and Norris Goff—the stars of the radio program *Lum and Abner* that ran an astonishing twenty-four years (1931–1955) and a half-dozen films based on these characters—both grew up in Mena, Arkansas and set their Jot 'Em Down general store in the mythical Ozark hill town of Pine Ridge. Frank, Leon, and June Weaver, better known as the Weaver Brothers and Elviry, came from Springfield, Missouri, and had been the preeminent "rube" vaudevillians of the 1910s and 1920s. Blending country humor and music with folksy morality tales, they starred in twelve films between 1930 and 1943. Of the leading rural clowns of films of this era, only

Judy Canova, "the hillbilly canary," who starred in at least seventeen films between 1940 and 1955, was not from the Ozarks.[30]

These performers' leap to the big screen was a result not only of the vogue for all things hillbilly in the mid- to late 1930s but also of the advent of the "B movie"—highly formulaic low-budget films produced by lower tier studios such as Republic Pictures, as well as larger film companies including Paramount and Columbia, and intended to be the bottom half of a double-feature presentation. Searching for a way to offset the cost of big-budget productions and recognizing that the vast and still expanding film audience (estimated to be 75 million a week by 1940 and 100 million per week by 1946 —an astonishing two-thirds of the national population) increasingly demanded an entire afternoon's or evening's entertainment, studios developed the double-feature in the mid-1930s, as a means of giving the audience twice the entertainment with a minimal increase in production costs. By 1936, double-bills were a staple of 85 percent of all movie houses, and lower tier studios such as Republic Pictures and Monogram were producing almost exclusively "B" films. The majority of these, including gangster and crime dramas and romantic serials, were mainly aimed at the expanding urban audience. Republic and similar studios produced the hillbilly and rural musical comedies discussed here, however, primarily for the rural and small-town market, which steadily supported this genre from the mid-1930s into the mid-1950s.[31]

Many of these films featured little more than cartoon hillbillies brought to life such as those in *Kentucky Moonshine*. The Bob Burns vehicles *Mountain Music* (1937) and *Comin' round the Mountain* (1940) and the Weaver Brothers and Elviry's first film, *Swing Your Lady* (1937), were merely a collection of stereotypes in the style of Paul Webb, featuring what *Comin' Round the Mountain* touted as "the only surviving species of the genus homus hillbillicus Americanious." Held together by the flimsiest of plots and featuring rube comedy and countrified (but not authentic "country") music, these films cataloged hillbilly isolation, slovenliness, and laziness. In *Mountain Music,* Burns plays an "afflicted" hillbilly boy, who disgraces his family by working and shaving; in both Burns' films the setting is the town of "Monotony." All three of these films overflowed with images of tattered clothes, scraggly beards, bare feet, and shotguns (fig. 5.9). Not surprisingly, most film critics dismissed these movies as bland and superficial ("a mild, pale hillbilly concoction" wrote *Variety* about *Comin' round the Mountain*) and ridiculed the crude sets and costumes. Yet a few, like Bosley Crowther of the *New York Times*, found the genre to be "freakish fun" that offered a fascinating insight into genuine Americana.[32]

The fad for such live-action hillbilly cartoons, however, was short-lived

Figure 5.9
Shotguns, scruffy beards, and cornpone humor:
Bob Burns gives away his sister at a shotgun wedding in
Mountain Music (1938). Courtesy of the Academy of
Motion Picture Arts and Sciences.

because such characterizations offered little room for plot and character development. Burns and the Weavers soon abandoned outright hillbilly caricatures, although their later films, such as Burns's *The Arkansas Traveller*
(1938) and *I'm from Missouri* (1939) and the Weavers' *Down in Arkansaw*
(1938), *In Old Missouri* (1940), *Arkansas Judge* (1941), and *Shepherd of the
Ozarks* (1942), continued to feature the Ozarkian regional identity. Judy
Canova's *Joan of Ozark* (1942) also featured the regional label, but, except for
a brief opening scene of Canova in a plaid shirt, jeans, and pigtails and brandishing a squirrel rifle, the plot and setting (involving Canova helping capture a Nazi spy ring) had little to do with the hills.

In contrast to the negative and stereotyped images of their "hillbilly"
genre predecessors, these films celebrated the simple values, sincerity, and
goodness of the "plain folk" and featured plots in which the hayseed protago-

Hillbilly

162

nists overcome symbolic representations of the evils of modern urban America: pretentious big-city snobs, exploitive businessmen, and corrupt politicians. Like Carl Sandburg's poetic paean *The People, Yes!* (1936), Granville Hicks's Popular Front manifesto *I Like America* (1938), the Regionalist art of Thomas Hart Benton and Grant Wood, and John Steinbeck's *Grapes of Wrath* (1939), these storylines reflected a general celebration of the common people in American culture of these years. Far less sophisticated or influential than any of these works or even Frank Capra's film trilogy praising the "little man" at war with vested interests, the films of the Weavers, Burns, and Canova nonetheless represented the same spirit of democratic populism and national affirmation at a time when America faced the twin threats of the spread of fascism abroad and the ongoing Depression at home. Cosmopolitan reviewers and audiences continued to dismiss these low-budget homespun comedies and melodramas as excessively corny, but they attracted a dependable rural and small-town audience throughout the World War II era. As one astute reviewer wrote about the Weavers' *Mountain Rhythm*: "sophisticated audiences in big cities, or college towns . . . will probably laugh in the wrong places" but "[f]olks out in the wide open spaces and in those places where they are still called 'folks' without pretense are going to like this picture."[33]

Perhaps another explanation for the briefness of the appeal of live-action hillbilly movies was that in terms of fully exploiting the stereotype of lazy, slovenly, and violent rustic oafs, they could not begin to compete with the string of animated cartoons of hillbilly caricatures that were a semiregular feature of all the major animation studios in the 1930s and war years. Directed by such famed animators as Fritz Freleng and Tex Avery, these cartoons mixed an array of sight gags with familiar Webb-like hillbillies. All included country music images and soundtracks, and above all, the central plot motif of the family feud, in which the animators pitted one group of hill folks against their identical-looking rivals and both against naively pacifist outsiders.

Avery's prototypical *A Feud There Was* (1938) opens on a decrepit mountain cabin where a half-dozen hillbillies doze noisily, interrupting their slumber only to perform before a radio station microphone that magically descends from the ceiling. When their song is over, they instantly fall back to sleep. When the inevitable feud begins, the combatants blast away at each other with all manner of absurd weaponry (including a rifle with multiple triggers and a howitzer that turns a pig and chicken into ham steak and fried eggs). Their mutual hostility is exceeded only by their sheer contempt for Egghead, a predecessor of Elmer Fudd, who tries to persuade both sides to put "an end to this meaningless massacre." His reward for his troubles is a huge fistfight with both clans. But even after Egghead emerges victorious and walks off screen, he is shot by a silhouetted mountaineer in the "theater audience," thus presenting hillbillies as irredeemably violent. An absurd exaggeration drawn from other cartoon stereotypes of the era, A Feud There Was nonetheless linked these representations to actual mountain folk by showing human characters as opposed to the barnyard animals featured in otherwise similar cartoons. It also began with a deliberately misnamed "Ripley's Believe It or Else" segment about an actual champion hog-caller from Arkansas, depicted as almost identical to the hillbilly characters of the cartoon. In this way, cartoonists linked in the public mind the fantasy "hillbilly" and the actual inhabitants of the southern hill country.[34]

Ma and Pa Kettle and the Domestication of the Hillbilly, 1945–1957

On the eve of World War II, the instantly recognizable Webb-like hillbilly stereotype featured in these animated shorts and in Bob Burns's and the Weavers' vehicles was widely considered an exaggeration of an actual social community or, more commonly, as an "absurd but harmless" caricature, as one women's group described the characters in Mountain Music. By the end of the war, however, opposition to what was increasingly viewed as an offensive image was mounting. As hundreds of thousands of southern Appalachians and Ozarkers poured into midwestern and Mid-Atlantic cities to work in war-production factories and enlisted in the military to fight in Europe and the Pacific, critics came more and more to question the popular conception of a region wholly removed from social and economic reality and to see ethnically and racially based stereotypes such as these as increasingly untenable. One can see this change in attitude most clearly in critiques of the most influential hillbilly presentation of the immediate postwar era, the cartoon musical sketch "The Martins and the Coys" in Make Mine Music, a 1946 Walt Disney compilation of ten animated musical numbers. The sketch offered a standard presentation of a feud between two clans of lazy, drunken hillbillies living in blissful squalor (fig. 5.10). The battle between these "reckless mountain boys" (as the accompanying song lyrics labeled them) is so extreme that all are killed in the hail of bullets, except for a single teenager from each clan. Inevitably, they marry, and after the obligatory hoe-down scene, take to fighting again and "carry[ing] on the feud just like before" to the delight of their deceased relatives who look down from heavenly clouds.[35]

Make Mine Music was generally not well received by either the public or the critics who groaned about the treacly and overly folksy tone of many of the selections. No sketch drew more heated criticism than "The Martins and the Coys." James Agee in The Nation found it "infinitely insulting" and The

Figure 5.10

The Martins take a drunken respite from their feuding in
"The Martins and the Coys" from Disney's *Make Mine Music* (1946).
Courtesy of the Academy of Motion Picture Arts and Sciences
and Disney Enterprises. © Disney Enterprises, Inc.

Commonweal deemed the sketch "tasteless." Recognizing the "white other"
nature of the stereotype, many critics offered explicitly racialized critiques,
comparing the cartoon to similar stereotyped portrayals of African Americans.
The "hillbilly ballad," observed the *Time* reviewer, would "offend those who
think such caricatures as insulting as the hush-mah-mouf kind of comic contempt for the Negroes." Manny Farber in the *New Republic* equated the cartoon's design, based on "a phony popular attitude about hillbillies," with the
equally "embarrassing" cartoon from the same film of Willie the Whale
singing "Short'nin' Bread" while a pod of porpoises "aping revival-meeting
Negroes" keep time. Long a staple of Hollywood comedies, in the aftermath
of the Holocaust and the "Double V" campaign for victory against fascism
abroad and racism at home, such blatant racial and ethnic stereotypes, including, to a degree, those of white southern mountaineers, were becoming
increasingly unacceptable to film reviewers and, to a lesser extent, to the
movie-going public.[36]

The comically unwashed, ill-mannered, and absurdly dangerous film hillbilly did not disappear altogether after World War II. Although representations of comic or benighted hill folk (and other poor southern whites) appeared less regularly on the Broadway stage than they had in the early 1920s and mid-1930s, noncommercial theater productions continued to feature comic hillbilly plays. Webb-like caricatures also appear in such early postwar films as *Murder, He Says* (1945, featuring Fred MacMurray and Marjorie Main), *Comin' round the Mountain* (1951, starring Bud Abbott and Lou Costello), *Feudin' Fools* (1952, with Leo Gorcey and the Bowery Boys), and in the successful 1959 film version of the hit Broadway musical *Li'l Abner*.[37] These low-budget, highly formulaic films offered few new twists on the standard caricature, although *Comin' round the Mountain* did feature nightclub singer Dorothy Shay, the self-titled "Park Avenue Hillbillie." In the film as in her stage performances, Shay combined New York sophistication with novelty numbers capitalizing on hillbilly stereotypes, such as "Feudin', Fightin' and Fussin'" and "(You'll Be Just) Another Notch on Father's Shotgun (Effen You Don't Marry Me)" (fig. 5.11). Despite such somewhat innovative attempts to revive the genre, these films seemed increasingly stale and out of step with contemporary American viewpoints. As the degraded cartoon

Figure 5.11
Dorothy Shay, "the Park Avenue Hillbillie," in a publicity still from *Comin' round the Mountain* (1951) starring Abbott and Costello. Courtesy of the Academy of Motion Picture Arts and Sciences.

hillbilly gradually lost favor with critics and audiences alike in the postwar years, however, the presentation of such primitive people in film transmogrified into the softer and more appealing conceptions of actors Percy Kilbride and Marjorie Main, who as Ma and Pa Kettle achieved astounding success through the 1950s. Blending unkempt and anti-modern characters with ancient slapstick routines, the Kettle films previewed the further domestication of the hillbilly in the medium of postwar television.

The Kettles first appeared as subsidiary characters in the 1947 film *The Egg and I*, based on Betty MacDonald's 1945 best seller about a middle-class housewife forced to adjust to her new life on an Olympic Mountains egg farm in Washington State. MacDonald's Maw and Paw Kettle and their fifteen children are more or less direct descendants, somewhat cleaned up and civilized, of Sut Lovingood's bedraggled and overflowing family from George Washington Harris's *Sut Lovingood: Tales* of 1867. Like Harris's clan, MacDonald's Kettles exude a slovenly and lethargic yet fecund backcountry ethos, heedless of middle-class rules of social propriety. Maw, "a mountainously fat woman in a very dirty housedress," is perpetually adjusting herself beneath her clothes and propounds the motto "I itch—so I scratch—so what!" Similarly, Paw, with his "tremendous flowing mustache generously dotted with crumbs" and clothed in "several layers of dirty underwear and sweaters" is characterized by his laziness, filth, and his constant "borrowing" [my quotation marks] from his neighbors, the narrator, and her husband. But MacDonald does not present her characters as utterly degraded or squalid, making them a step removed from the live-action and animated film hillbillies of the previous decade. Though they live simply, the Kettles are not desperately impoverished. They are essentially likable folk, affectionate to each other and their neighbors, and indispensable in helping the female narrator of the story adapt to the lack of urban amenities in her new environment.[38]

The film-version Kettles were even more toned down and appealing. Skillfully acted by Main and Kilbride (both of whom had long specialized in rustic roles), the movie Kettles exhibited an unpolished charm, even while Ma bellows for the children in a voice likened to "shifting gears, a stone crusher, a coffee grinder." Although the ostensible leads, Fred MacMurray and Claudette Colbert, received praise, critics reserved their strongest plaudits for Main and Kilbride. Most reviewers acknowledged that the rustic duo were most responsible for the film's great success ($5.5 million in ticket revenues).[39]

Recognizing their potential goldmine, Universal studio executives, led by producer Leonard Goldstein, quickly featured the couple in their own highly successful movie, *Ma and Pa Kettle* (1949), followed by eleven other films released from 1950 through 1957. Although critics lambasted the films' slapstick routines and corny puns, they also were forced to reluctantly acknowledge their appeal with rural and small-town audiences and even with supposedly more sophisticated urban moviegoers. "[T]he laughter almost rocked the foundations" marveled one reviewer, commenting on the reaction to *Ma and Pa Kettle Back on the Farm* (1951, the third film of the series) at a midtown New York theater.[40]

Upper-end "B" movies filmed in three weeks for $400,000 or less, the Kettle films perfectly exemplified Goldstein's approach: produce a large number of inexpensive pictures that might not educate or inspire but that "make money at the box office." And make money they did, earning an astounding $8 million for the first three films in the series alone and an estimated $35 million for the entire run. It was widely rumored that along with the "Francis the Talking Mule" series, the Kettles brought Universal-International back from the brink of bankruptcy. Constantly reiterating his mantra that "nobody likes my pictures but the public," Goldstein boasted that theater exhibitors gave the Kettle series not the Academy Award but the far more valuable "four [H]ershey bars" award.[41]

What accounted for the "Ma and Pa Kettle" phenomenon? First, like all hillbilly characters, the Kettles elicited a mixture of ridicule and empathy. On the one hand, audiences could laugh at these ignorant and bumbling country folk, horribly out of place in the fast-paced urbanized world in which they frequently found themselves, including vacations in New York (1950), Paris (1953), and Hawaii (1955). The plot of the original *Ma and Pa Kettle* of 1949, for example, involves the Kettles winning a fully automated "prefabricated model house of the future" and Pa doing battle with the new gadgets. Yet, the films' appeal also stemmed from many viewers' own unfamiliarity and unease with an increasingly mechanized and standardized postwar America and the films' flattering portrait of the Kettles' basic goodness and honesty in the face of urban con artists, snobs, and busybody bureaucrats. Percy Kilbride contended that the characters were so popular because "anybody, even the lowliest bum, can feel superior to the Kettles"; but Leonard Goldstein understood the dual-edged nature of his films' popularity: "[M]aybe people feel a little superior and maybe at the same time they recognize a lot of things about themselves," he commented in 1953. "That identification, whether the customer admits it to himself or not, counts as much as acceptance."[42]

Despite the usually absurd plots and outlandish actions and attitudes, the genuine humanity of the Kettles and their vast brood always shone through (fig. 5.12). Ma Kettle may have been capable of brandishing a shotgun to drive away local authorities trying to repossess her house (*Ma and Pa Kettle*, 1949), and she may have bristled at an imperious social worker trying to teach her the import of "hygiene" (*Ma and Pa Kettle Back on the Farm*, 1951), but she

Figure 5.12

Capturing the essence of 1950s family values:
Ma and Pa Kettle (Marjorie Main and Percy Kilbride)
and their enormous brood in a publicity still from
Ma and Pa Kettle Back on the Farm (1950). Courtesy
of the Academy of Motion Picture Arts and Sciences.

loved her husband and family and always lent a helping hand to a neighbor
in need. Similarly, the audience could both feel superior to Pa's ignorance of
modern conveniences in *Ma and Pa Kettle* and admire his nonmaterialism
and common-sense reaction to winning a "dream house" rather than his
more modest original goal: "Don't need a new house" he drawls, . . . "Do
need a new tobacco pouch."

The modern suburban "dream house" plot suggests another reason for
the films' popularity: their commentary, however indirect, on contemporary
social issues. Beneath the zany storylines and throwback characterizations,
the Kettle films were perfectly in step with early postwar social values and
concerns. The Kettles' loving relationship with their seemingly endless string
of offspring matched a general societal trend toward earlier marriages, more
children, and a focus on the nuclear family (as opposed to multigenerational
kin networks of the past). The Kettles also served as stand-ins for millions of

Americans confronting for the first time the bewildering new world of sub-urbanization, consumer abundance, and leisure travel. Doubtless many view-ers both felt superior to and identified with frumpy Ma who, in *Ma and Pa Kettle on the Town* (1950), is coifed in the latest fashion at the Lushun Dee Paris Beauty Salon in New York and then returns to her hotel room to soak her feet in a wooden bucket, or with Pa in *Ma and Pa Kettle on Vacation* (1953) as he tries to negotiate his way around the streets and social circles of Paris. The Kettle films even offhandedly alluded to atomic and cold war anxieties. In *Ma and Pa Kettle Back on the Farm* (1951), Pa is irradiated by uranium, and in *Ma and Pa Kettle on Vacation*, he gets mixed up with an international spy ring. The blending of farce and hominess, ancient comedy routines and cur-rent social concerns, helps explain the Kettles' resonance at a time of cultural and socioeconomic transformation from the shortages of the Depression and war years to the modern consumerist culture of the postwar era.

Finally, Main's and Kilbride's Kettles remained so popular for so long be-cause they firmly avoided the earlier hillbilly label, persona, and characteri-zations. Three of the first four episodes are set in cosmopolitan or suburban locales far removed from the rugged mountain setting of *The Egg and I*, and even the occasional rural settings in later films were more apt to be middle-American small towns or county fairs than the isolated backwoods. Goldstein and his lead actors rejected any hint of the traditional moonshining and feud-ing plots. Pa's tattered clothing and the Kettles' large family were the only links to their disreputable film predecessors, and both played an increasingly limited role as the series wore on. One reviewer noted the ever-more generic nature of the Kettles' humor and how little it had to do with their original characterization. Most scenes in the later Kettle films, the critic noted, "are totally unrelated to their numerous progeny, or, for that matter, to anything else specifically kettle-esque. . . . They are gags, situations, and routines that Mack Sennett dredged up in his boyhood from the even then dead era of medicine shows and wheel burlesque." Indeed, the one film that featured tra-ditional hillbilly characterizations, *The Kettles of the Ozarks* (1957), in which Ma and her children visit her shiftless cousin Sedge on his Ozark farm, was made when the series was in decline and after Percy Kilbride's withdrawal. Here, Ma Kettle represents social order and cleanliness and Sedge symbol-izes the Kettles' rough and rustic beginnings. Ironically, the return to stan-dard hillbilly tropes and storylines revealed the creative dead-end the writers and producers had reached. The series ended one year later.[43]

The move away from the hillbilly character in the Kettle films mirrored a general receding of this image in postwar American culture and con-sciousness that would persist until the early 1960s. The suburbanization of the Kettles also reflected a similar commodification and domestication of the southern mountain identity and culture beginning in the World War II years. Typical of this new attitude was the June 1942 special issue of *House & Garden* dedicated to the colorful folk customs and crafts of "Our Southern Highlands" and promoting mass-manufactured household furnishings and accessories loosely based on mountain patterns and forms in what the magazine later labeled the "new and entirely different American style . . . Southern Highland Provincial." Whereas wartime accounts in *National Geographic* still focused on the poverty and simplicity of the southern mountains, although explicitly rejecting the stereotype of widespread degeneracy, postwar articles emphasized accommodations and travel fun and discussed socioeconomic conditions only in passing if at all. No longer a dangerous wilderness or home to an aberrant, impoverished, and hostile people, the southern mountains were thus reconceptualized in the pages of 1940s travel and adventure magazines as a picturesque and safe region of friendly folk artisans suitable for middle-class vacationing.[44]

As the mountains came to be seen in this new light, the hillbilly faded from view in motion pictures and across the cultural spectrum. Not until the 1960s, in response to the unprecedented migration of poor Appalachians to midwestern and Mid-Atlantic cities and the launching of the War on Poverty programs, would the hillbilly reclaim its place in the cultural spotlight, primarily, in the dominant media of postwar America—television.

chapter six

The Hillbilly in the Living Room
Television Representations, 1952–1971

In the late 1950s and early 1960s, imagery and press accounts associated with the southern mountains and their people appeared to a degree unequaled since the 1930s. Presented in all forms of media, these images were most prominently featured on television both in news reports and documentaries, and most commonly, in a steady stream of highly successful and influential situation comedies. In an era when television's vast reach and the three networks' near total control of the airwaves created a national "common culture" to a degree unmatched before or since, televised images played a central role in shaping public perceptions of American society and values, in general, and of the southern mountain people, in particular.

The depiction of "the hillbilly" on television offered a domesticated version of our familiar persona, one shorn of much of its surface debasement and slovenliness. Partly this transformation of the hillbilly was simply a response to the strict content limitations of postwar television, resulting from (or justified by) the uniquely personal nature of the medium and its viewing space. The sanitized hillbilly was also, in part, a reflection of the formulaic nature of television sitcoms and the need for characters that audiences would welcome back week after week. Although it is easy to dismiss these programs as simply base and escapist entertainment aimed at unsophisticated rural and small-town audiences, television shows featuring hillbilly characters and settings also reflected contemporary social concerns about southern mountain people and conditions, and more generally, the possibilities and limitations of postwar America. In the late 1950s, fears of hillbilly "invasions" of mid-western cities prompted press accounts of backward and degenerate men and women who despite their "superior" racial heritage threatened the comity of the industrial heartland. The early 1960s saw the rediscovery of Appalachia as a site of an endemic "pocket of poverty" in a (supposedly) otherwise affluent society. Yet, as in the past, the region's people were also held up as the in-heritors of an uncorrupted culture and value system who challenged modern urbanity and pointed out the spiritual and ethical costs of materialist "pro-gress." These programs were also a response to the racial battle lines of the day. At a time when the Civil Rights movement was exposing the ugliness of southern white racism, these shows depicted a bucolic and lily-white south-ern landscape and celebrated the homespun goodness of southern whites, and by extension, America as a whole. *The Real McCoys*, *The Andy Griffith Show*, and *The Beverly Hillbillies* never made this connection to national headlines explicit. Nonetheless, press accounts about impoverished moun-taineers and the political and cultural maelstrom of the Civil Rights move-ment formed the historical context in which these shows were viewed and in-terpreted by a national television audience.

Early Television Incarnations and the Image of the Urban Hillbilly "Invader"

The earliest examples of the televised hillbilly image were mostly highly de-rivative representations of still earlier vaudeville, radio, and film characteri-zations. In the 1952 episode of *My Hero* simply entitled "Hillbilly," Robert (Bob) Cummings plays a real estate agent who gets mixed up in a formulaic Kentucky feud complete with shoot-out scenes and an amorous mountain girl named Lulubelle Hartfield. Jack Benny used a similarly hackneyed stereotype in a 1958 episode of his program. In a flashback scene, he portrayed his supposed Arkansas beginnings as country fiddler "Zeke Benny and his Ozark Hillbillies." Dressed in longjohns, overalls, and a straw boater, Benny interspersed performances of commercial country tunes such as "You Are My Sunshine" with comedy routines about child brides and ignorant hicks who stomp the ground like a horse when they count to four.[1]

Benny's show was one of at least four situation comedies and variety shows to use hillbilly characters and imagery between October 1957 and April 1958. The most interesting of these portrayals was on *The Bob Cummings Show*, in which Cummings generally played a suave and comfortably middle-class fashion photographer. In "Bob Goes Hillbilly," however, Cummings and his sister dress as ragged, gap-toothed yokels in an effort to teach his nephew,

Chuck (who is trying to impress his snobby date), a lesson about the unacceptability of social hierarchy. Laughing stupidly while milking a piglet, Cummings sends the debutante screaming from the house. In the end, Bob moralizes to Chuck and the viewing audience that "any romance based on class distinctions doesn't stand a chance." "Not in a democracy like this" pipes in his sister. Thus, the show discredited class divisions and upheld the widely shared belief in American "classlessness" by reinforcing long-established stereotypes of the poverty, stupidity, and slovenliness of hill folk. Interestingly, the writer and producer of the show was none other than Paul Henning, who had a hand in nearly all the presentations of television hillbillies and brought the image to the very heart of American culture four years later with *The Beverly Hillbillies*.[2]

More than just the ease of reusing hackneyed stereotypes accounts for the surge of televised hillbilly images in 1957 and 1958. It also reflected a historical moment when national press accounts articulated long-growing tensions over the large-scale influx of southern hill folk to midwestern and Mid-Atlantic cities. The migration of over three million southern Appalachians in the three decades after the start of World War II—part of the much larger southern diaspora of at least eleven million people, black and white, who relocated to the North and West in the years between 1910 and 1970—is one of the largest population movements in American history. Appalachian outmigration began in earnest around the turn of the century and continued fairly steadily over the next four decades. Although the number of migrants grew significantly in the Depression years, it mushroomed in the early 1940s, with the boom in industrial war production work, and again rose dramatically in the 1950s. Largely in response to the widespread mechanization of the coal mines and the rise of natural gas as an alternative to coal, millions of southern Appalachians fled the mass unemployment of the coal fields for midwestern cities such as Cincinnati, Chicago, Detroit, and smaller towns throughout southern Ohio and Indiana where a strong economy and foreign immigration restrictions made jobs fairly plentiful.[3]

Free from the institutionalized racism faced by their southern black counterparts, the majority of Appalachian migrants were able to find employment and to slowly improve their economic situations. Yet the perception of southern white migrants as an inassimilable and unwanted population was widespread in the postwar Midwest. Job listings that announced "No Southerners need apply" and restaurant owners who refused to serve "hillbillies" were not uncommon. Southern Appalachians were branded with a variety of derogatory labels, including "WASPs" (White Appalachian Southern Protestants), "SAMs" (Southern Appalachian Migrants), "ridgerunners," "briar-hoppers," and most universally, "hillbillies." "Hillbilly" in this context was unequivocally a derisive slur and the incoming mountain folk became the butt of jokes of varying levels of crassness. "Know the reason for building the Brent Spence bridge (spanning the Ohio River at Cincinnati) with two levels?" went one local quip. "So that all of the hillbillies leaving Ohio can take off their shoes and pass them below to their cousins leaving Kentucky for Ohio." More mean-spirited was the oft-told joke of the 1950s that there were now only forty-eight states because "all of Kentucky moved to Ohio, and Ohio went to hell." Perhaps the clearest example of widespread midwestern opposition toward the Appalachian migrants is provided by the results of a 1951 Wayne State University survey of Detroit residents that asked respondents to identify "undesirable people" who were "not good to have in the city." "Poor southern whites" and "hillbillies" were identified by 21 percent of those surveyed, second only to "criminals" and "gangsters" and well ahead of "drifters," "negroes," and "foreigners."[4]

A growing regional concern in midwestern cities since at least the 1930s, the southern migrant "problem" was first announced on a national stage in a series of late 1950s articles in nationally circulated social commentary magazines. The whiteness of these urban poor was the authors' primary concern, and James Maxwell's "Down from the Hills and into the Slums" (1956) presented its subject in explicitly racialized terms. After opening with a quote from an Indianapolis resident fearful of an uncivilized and dangerously independent population, Maxwell then informs his presumably shocked readers that this group was not Puerto Ricans or Mexicans but "white Anglo-Saxon Protestants," a group "usually considered to be the most favored in American society." Heavily reliant on information from antagonistic law enforcement officials, Maxwell quotes a police officer who accused the newcomers of a wide variety of crimes, including "shootings, child neglect, rape ... [and] incest." Although he stresses the difficulties migrants face, Maxwell generally portrays them as a backward people badly out of sync with urban ways and mores.[5]

The most infamous example of such fear mongering was Albert Votaw's February 1958 *Harper's* article "The Hillbillies Invade Chicago." "The cities' toughest integration problem has nothing to do with Negroes" reads the lead —rather "it involves a small army of white Protestant, Early American migrants from the South—who are usually proud, poor, primitive, and fast with a knife." What follows is a steady stream of negative, even vicious, characterizations of "Southern 'hillbillies,'" who Votaw contradictorily describes as "apathetic but bumptious." Relying, like Maxwell, on police sources, Votaw claims the newcomers are "clannish, proud, disorderly, [and] untamed to urban ways." They have "fecund wives and numerous children," their "housekeeping is easy to the point of disorder," and "their habits—with respect to such matters as incest and statutory rape—are clearly at variance with urban legal requirements." He also cites what he considered a brutal but accurate *Chicago Sunday Tribune* editorial that compared the arrival of "Southern hillbilly migrants" to "a plague of locusts" and described them as having "the lowest standard of living and moral code (if any), the biggest capacity for liquor, and the most savage tactics when drunk, which is most of the time." Although they should be "the prototype of what the 'superior' American should be," laments Votaw, "on the streets of Chicago they seem to be the American dream gone berserk."[6]

Many native-born whites in downtown Chicago, Detroit, and other midwestern cities were aggravated by the newcomers' southern dialect, taste for loud country music and alcohol in "hillbilly taverns," commitment to tightly knit kin-networks, and tendency to gather on stoops and fix their cars at curbsides (practices stemming from a combination of financial limitations and the preservation of rural ways). They saw these social mores and conduct as the cause of—rather than, in reality, symptomatic of—the deterioration of long-established neighborhoods. Yet the fact that one of Votaw's subheads is "A Disgrace to Their Race?" suggests that the greatest concern about these migrants was not simply their poverty or social customs, but that they were impoverished whites at a time when many middle-class whites felt that only blacks and other minorities were "supposed" to be poor. Northern whites, who had long associated poverty, laziness, drunkenness, and violence with blacks and other people of color, now found such racial demarcations threatened by what they saw as similar habits among Protestant Anglo-Saxons living in (in a racially freighted label) "hillbilly jungle[s]." The southern migrants, Votaw lamented, "confound all notions of racial, religious, and cultural purity." The only hope, he proffered, was if the few who had previously lived in southern cities would quickly assimilate, thus encouraging their unruly brethren to follow suit.[7]

Votaw's harangue drew a few angry responses by readers, including a Michigan reader who compared the migrants to their ancestors who had defeated the British at King's Mountain and Cowpens during the Revolutionary War. To this respondent, the migrants' refusal to cooperate with government and police authorities and to maintain their distinct identity represented a properly stubborn independence worth celebrating. These letters to the editor reveal the continuing resonance of the rugged mountaineer myth as a counterimage to the degenerate hillbilly. They also indicated a potential audience for a more positive portrayal of Appalachian migrants. *The Real McCoys*, the first rural situation comedy on network television and one of the most successful, offered such a softened vision of southern hill migrants.[8]

The Real McCoys – Romanticizing the Joads

First aired in the fall of 1957, *The Real McCoys* told the story of a West Virginia farm family seeking a better life in California's San Fernando Valley. It offered an updated and rosier story of southern agrarian migrants than either Votaw and his colleagues or *The Grapes of Wrath*—one that acknowledged American economic hardship in the midst of affluence but argued that it was eventually surmountable solely through personal initiative. Like the famous scenes from *The Grapes of Wrath* (and later, *The Beverly Hillbillies*), the pilot episode opens with a multigenerational family of southern migrants riding the California roadways in a decrepit old jalopy. The family reflects conceptions of extended kin networks among mountain families and of mountain women's lifelong fecundity. Alongside "strapping mountain boy" Luke McCoy (Richard Crenna) and his twenty-year-old wife Kate sit Luke's seven-year-old brother Little Luke, twelve-year-old sister "Aunt Hassie," and Grampa McCoy, "an authentic . . . grizzled specimen of the species hillbilly" (fig. 6.1). Like the Joads,

Figure 6.1
Affable Grampa surrounded by his rustic clan in a publicity still from *The Real McCoys*. (Left to right, back row: Kate McCoy [Kathleen Nolan], Grampa Amos McCoy [Walter Brennan], Luke McCoy [Richard Crenna]; front: Little Luke [Michael Winkelman], Aunt Hassie [Lydia Reed].) Courtesy of Walter Brennan Collection, Dickinson Research Center, National Cowboy & Western Heritage Museum, Oklahoma City, OK.

a highway patrolman stops the McCoys. Unlike the contempt and hostility that the Joads face, however, here the friendly policeman simply wants to return a spare tire that has fallen off the back of their car and to wish them "Good luck." When the McCoys reach their destination, they pull up to a rundown but workable ranch they have inherited from a relative rather than a squalid migrant labor camp.[9]

More similar to the *Grapes of Wrath* was the lead characters' constant economic struggle. Director Hy Averback argued the show's popularity stemmed from its "premise of being able to fight poverty," but it was a fight that the McCoys usually lost. When in an episode in the third season, for instance, a salesman assures them that television sets are now so inexpensive that "[a]ny family with an average income can afford them," Luke replies glumly "If our income ever gets average, we'll be back to see you." Although they do buy a television by episode's end, the themes of "doing without" and slow and unsteady economic advancement that were present throughout the program's six-year run contrasted dramatically with the dominant motif in late 1950s family sitcoms of comfortable suburban affluence. Such a backdrop of economic hardship also suggested that poverty or near-poverty were simply part of the McCoys' "mountain culture."[10]

Cantankerous and old-fashioned but lovable Grampa, played by long-time character actor Walter Brennan, was the undisputed star of the show and the epitome of the backward mountaineer opposed to all things modern from "pipe water" and daily baths to buying a newer car and opening a bank account. "There's only really one rule," summarized Averback about the nature of the scripts, "that whatever it is, Grandpa is against it." Yet despite his curmudgeonly outlook, Grampa also represented a strong work ethic, a dignified poverty, and a basic horse sense derived from years of working the land. When he is denied a bank loan for the farm, Grampa challenges the loan officer's overreliance on bureaucratic methods and "scientific" surveys. "Can figures tell you how good that soil is? Can figures tell you how easy a plow cuts through the fields without nickin' your blade on any stones. . . . You don't see a farm with your heart," he scolds the young banker, "ya see it with your fountain pen!" Hardly unique to portrayals of mountain folk, this mix of ignorance of modern life and knowledge of the land and basic human nature was a staple of representations of rural folk since the days of Brother Jonathan and was at the heart of all the rural sitcoms of the 1960s.[11]

Other than in Grampa's personality, however, the characters' mountaineer status was generally understated, except in a few episodes such as "Little Luke's Education" in which Little Luke is called a "dumb hillbilly" by classmates or "The Talk of the Town" in which he helps hide Grampa's illiteracy by drawing a series of pictures for him to "read" before a public gathering. The McCoys dressed and acted like a typical farm family (at least as envisioned by Hollywood producers) and most of the plots, like other sitcoms of the time, were designed to provide humorous but didactic moral lessons on the importance of family, hard work, and integrity. Both in publicity and scripts, the producers tried to distance the backwardness and humble status of the television McCoys from contemporary mountaineers. In a promotional tour of West Virginia, Brennan posed with a cocked shotgun in front of a log cabin but was careful to distinguish his character on the show from the local residents he met "in a tiny McCoy-like community." "Grandpa is a throwback," he explained to the *TV Guide* reporter. "These McCoys are pretty modern-thinking people. Not much real connection at all." Likewise, in a 1961 episode titled "Back to West Virginny," the McCoy clan returns home to celebrate Great Grandma's 100th birthday. Proud of all they have accomplished in California and expecting to find their relatives still awash in poverty, they are shocked to discover their kinfolk living in comfortably middle-class houses complete with ice-making refrigerators, wall to wall linoleum, and television sets, all thanks to their jobs in the new box-making factory.[12]

This storyline also explores the limits of such progress and the sort of Faustian bargain the McCoys' relatives have made. In the subsequent episode, when all of Grampa's relatives are fired after Grampa refuses to sell to the box company a key plot of land that Great Grandma wishes to hold on to for nostalgic reasons, he tries to comfort his kin by assuring them that "McCoys are people o' the soil" and that they can all go back to farming. Yet to Grampa's relatives, Jed and Myra, such a return to the land is impossible after one has been exposed to "the finer things in life." "Linoleum becomes a habit" sighs Myra; "If I have ta give up eatin' them TV dinners I swear I think I'd die" adds Jed. The writers' highlighting of even then debased household goods as symbols of modern living and the loss of a rural ethic offers a limited questioning of the "costs" of progress. The storyline comments on (albeit in an offhand manner) the exploitation of the land and people of Appalachia by extractive industries and reflected a growing environmental awareness and concern about the ecological costs of industrial capitalism and never-ending economic growth. In the end, however, this conflict between industrially driven consumerism and a pastoral ethic is finessed: Grampa agrees to sell the land to the box company, and the factory owner agrees to relocate Great Grandma's house to the top of the knob, where she can look out over the whole valley (although there is no mention of the fact that it will probably be choked with smoke!). The show thus both raised questions about the price of progress and resolved the issue in a way that ultimately upheld the primacy of mass consumerism and industrial development.[13]

Writers Irving and Norman Pincus found that 1950s network television executives were initially very wary about airing a rural-based situation comedy, and only ABC, the smallest and least successful of the networks, was willing to take a chance on such an untested product. *The Real McCoys*'s dramatic success (the eighth highest-rated show of the 1958 season, the fifth highest of the 1960 season, and never out of the top twenty from 1958 through 1961) illustrated the vast potential for other rural-based programming—a lesson network executives quickly took to heart. The show also had a more specific influence on the pastoral comedies that followed. Paul Henning, who wrote a few of the series' episodes, directly borrowed the show's opening for *The Beverly Hillbillies*, and two of its main writers, Jim Fritzell and Everett Greenbaum (who penned the West Virginia episodes described above), went on to write many episodes for the next highly successful rural comedy, *The Andy Griffith Show*, that debuted in 1960.[14]

String Bands, Rock-Throwing Crazies, and the War on Poverty:

Mountaineers on *The Andy Griffith Show*

The Andy Griffith Show remains one of the most successful shows in television history. It stayed in the top ten during its 1960 to 1968 run, was the top-ranked program of 1967, and has never been off the air since its inception. Mountain folk were only occasional characters in the program's first two years and the show generally celebrated the simple pleasures and tribulations of small-town life. But the show was always linked, at least indirectly, to hillbilly imagery. The fictitious town of Mayberry was based on Griffith's hometown of Mount Airy, North Carolina, close by the Virginia border on the edge of the Blue Ridge Mountains, and Griffith had risen to fame playing rural rubes—he launched his career in 1953 with a yokel stand-up routine "What It Was Was Football" and had had great success portraying hick private Will Stockdale in *No Time for Sergeants* on Broadway, television, and film between 1955 and 1958. His original stage persona was so intertwined with the stereotypical hillbilly that his first agent described him, to Griffith's chagrin, as "a real Li'l Abner!"[15]

Usually rough-mannered and slightly unkempt older men, the few hill folk represented in the show's first two seasons served as unsophisticated and slightly antagonistic country cousins to Sheriff Andy Taylor (Griffith) and the Mayberry townsfolk, themselves perceived as bumpkins in the eyes of most urban outsiders. Symbols of stubbornness, ignorance, and distrust of modern science and technology, the mountaineer characters tended to oppose any efforts to improve their lot in life. In a 1962 episode, for example, mountain farmer Rafe Hollister refuses to get a tetanus shot until Andy, using reverse psychology, sings the song he will perform at Rafe's funeral. Somewhat more frequently, the show incorporated standard mountaineer tropes such as moonshining (a theme used six times in the first four seasons) and feuding. In "A Feud Is a Feud" (1960), in a plot based loosely on both Romeo and Juliet and the love affair between Roseanna McCoy and Johnse Hatfield of the famed feuding families, two mountain farmers carry on a senseless feud, the origins of which neither can recall, and forbid their children to marry one another. Although both men make a pretense of wanting to kill the other, each is afraid to risk his life to accomplish the task. Here the older generation of mountaineers are presented as incompetently violent rubes, but their far-less-stereotyped children represent the capacity of such people to bridge the gap between an archaic and wrong-headed "mountain culture" and an idealized contemporary America.[16]

Beginning in March 1963, the show began to feature recurring characters who exemplified separate but related strands of the mythic mountaineer persona. Briscoe Darling (played by Denver Pyle) and his family represent the footloose musical mountaineer, who can be traced back to the Cumberland Ridge Runners, the Hillbillies string band, and even the Arkansas Traveler. Symbols of an outmoded but authentic mountain culture, the Darlings are superstitious, undereducated, slow-talking or mute (a running gag was that none of the four Darling boys ever said a word except when singing), and comfortably self-sufficient. But their primary function on the show was to provide musical entertainment. In actuality, the Darling sons were the Missouri Ozarks string band the Dillards and wrote many of the songs they performed on the program (fig. 6.2).

Music is central to the Darlings' way of life, a point driven home by family patriarch Briscoe. "You got time to breathe, you got time for music" he tells Andy in one episode. Although clearly presented as comical throwbacks, this is not a demeaning portrait of Webb-like hillbillies but one that celebrated a genuine indigenous folk music. The Darlings mention many laughably titled songs such as "Never Hit Your Grandma with a Big Stick," but the songs they actually played were either songs the Dillards had composed or traditional southern folk tunes like "Boil Them Cabbage Down" and "There Is a Time for Love and Laughter." The family always seems somewhat ill at ease during their periodic visits to Mayberry and even pose a potential threat to the townsfolk (Briscoe kidnaps Andy's Aunt Bee in one episode and brings her back to his cabin in an effort to convince her to marry him). But Sheriff Taylor appreciates their authentic mountain mannerisms and culture, and the feeling is mutual. "[T]hat haircut of yourn [sic] may be city-style," Briscoe warmly tells Taylor, "but your heart was shaped in a bowl."[17]

Figure 6.2

"You got time to breathe, you got time for music":
The Darlings as the epitome of dour musical
mountaineers in *The Andy Griffith Show* (1963–1964).
Courtesy of TAGSRWC Archives.

If the Darlings represent the slightly reckless musical mountaineers, Ernest T. Bass symbolizes the deranged mountain man, so wild that even his fellow hill folk consider him a threat. "Oh he's a pestilence," explains Briscoe Darling's son-in-law when Andy asks where he can be located, "and a pestilence will find you." As portrayed by Howard Morris, Bass is a half-savage who has a simian-like gait and shrieks like a chimpanzee. His trademark is throwing rocks and bricks through windows (fig. 6.3). Like Sut Lovingood before him, he is a "natural man" who constantly boasts of his physical prowess, once noting proudly that he was able to carry a mule five miles on his back. "I'm a little mean," Bass acknowledges sheepishly, "but I make up for it by being real healthy." Although he continually tries to fit into society and social institutions—different episodes portray his effort to join the army, to mingle at a formal reception, and to gain a primary-school education—his every encounter with civilization inevitably proves disastrous and each episode closes with Sheriff Taylor hastening him back to the mountains hoping he will not return. Although Bass is ostensibly a comedic character, potential violence

always underlies his eccentricity, and the distance between this characterization and the outwardly vicious Hatburns of *Tol'able David*, the Scraggs of
Li'l Abner, or even the mountain savages of *Deliverance* is not that great.[18]

The timing of these "mountaineer" episodes suggests that they were not
simply randomly selected storylines but were shaped by and reflected their
historical context. The Darlings and Ernest T. Bass appeared in eight episodes between March 1963 and December 1964, but only in one additional
show thereafter, and no mountaineer characters appeared on the show after
October 1966. Part of the explanation for this brief surge in mountaineer portrayals was undoubtedly the phenomenal success of *The Beverly Hillbillies*.
But like that show, the Darling and Bass episodes were also a response to the
sudden reemergence of the southern mountain region and people in the national consciousness and the conception of Appalachia as a distinct "problem
region." These developments were in turn part of a general rediscovery of
poverty in America in the early 1960s, a troubling realization that challenged
the widespread faith among the middle classes of a classless society and an
ever-improving quality of life.

Appalachia first reappeared on the national radar during the West Virginia Democratic presidential primary of 1960, in which candidate Senator John Kennedy made poverty and hunger in that state major themes of his campaign. One of Kennedy's first acts once elected was to implement emergency relief legislation for West Virginia. He also supported the establishment of the Area Development Administration (ADA) to provide development loans and grants for "depressed areas," including portions of certain Appalachian states. However, the ADA programs were generally underfunded and poorly administered, and Kennedy's commitment to either a regional or a national anti-poverty program was limited. Nor did he or many others yet conceive of the whole of the southeastern mountains as "Appalachia," a homogeneous "problem region" within a prosperous nation. Both these conceptions would change between 1962 and early 1963 with the publication of three influential books. *The Southern Appalachian Region—A Survey*, a collection of scholarly essays, presented Appalachia as a unified but troubled region. Harry Caudill's *Night Comes to the Cumberlands* (subtitled *A Biography of a Depressed Region*) traced its history of economic exploitation and defined Appalachia as a ravaged land with a battered people. Finally, Michael Harrington's *The Other America*, the most influential of the three, called for decisive action to respond to the forty to fifty million seemingly invisible Americans living in poverty, "maimed in body and spirit" and experiencing "needless suffering in the most advanced society in the world." Both Appalachia and Appalachian migrants ("urban hillbillies") were a central focus of his book, and Harrington presented the region as the locus of white poverty in America, equivalent to the Black poor of the nation's inner cities. The year 1962 closed with the CBS News documentary "Christmas in Appalachia" that movingly contrasted the ideal of Yuletide plenty with the "wretched" poverty of the remote Appalachian hollers.[19]

These works led Kennedy and his economic advisers to focus new attention on the issue of poverty in America and Appalachia, eventually leading under President Lyndon Johnson to a declaration of "unconditional war on poverty," the formation of the Office of Economic Opportunity, and the establishment of the Appalachian Regional Commission. Although the anti-poverty programs in Appalachia were flawed and poorly administered, the hill folk played a central symbolic role in the media's coverage of the War on Poverty, particularly in the turning point year of 1964, offering proof that poverty was a problem facing the entire nation and not just inner-city minorities. To illustrate the need for the Appalachian Regional Development Act he introduced that year, President Johnson made a well-publicized trip to eastern Kentucky in April, briefly shaking hands with impoverished locals on the front stoop of a ramshackle cabin. And nearly every major general-circulation magazine and newspaper featured articles on "the plight of the hill people," punctuated by the faces of dirty, ill-clothed, and malnourished men, women, and children living in tarpaper shacks.[20]

Television comedies like *The Andy Griffith Show* and *The Beverly Hillbillies* that featured mountaineer characters reflected the national media fascination with this "white other"—an isolated population outside mainstream American society. But they also served as a palliative for these disturbing images, providing a far more upbeat portrayal than did the news media of plain but comfortable folk, who were upright, self-assured, and imbued with a strong cultural tradition. Such images lessened the sense of the deep failure of the American economic system and its inability to prevent seemingly intractable poverty. They also tacitly reinforced the widespread belief that the mountain people were trapped in a "culture of poverty," but redefined it from a crippling cycle of degeneracy and dysfunction to a lifestyle choice of a people who valued leisure pursuits over material advancement.

The War on Poverty and the Appalachian poor were, of course, never directly mentioned on these programs or in any of the press accounts about these shows. Nor do I mean to argue that these shows were intentionally created to counter depictions like "Christmas in Appalachia" or even with the War on Poverty in mind. As always, the primary goal of television producers and network executives was to maximize profits by attracting the widest possible audience. But the historical context of the rediscovery of Appalachia and the War on Poverty did make these programs resonate with large sectors of the American public and therefore contributed to their popularity. Presenting poverty as a self-imposed lifestyle rather than the direct result of economic exploitation and local political corruption, these shows minimized the plight of many southern mountain folk (and by extension, the poor, in general) and weakened public sentiment for emergency federal intervention and assistance.

Redefining the Hillbilly and Reshaping Television: Paul Henning and *The Beverly Hillbillies*

The Beverly Hillbillies was another situation comedy whose popularity stemmed partly from the way it played off of fear and fascination with southern mountaineers much in the news. Like *The Real McCoys* and *The Andy Griffith Show, The Beverly Hillbillies* gained a broad audience and earned high ratings for much of its eight-year run (1962–1970) on CBS. But unlike its predecessors, *The Beverly Hillbillies* was more than simply a highly successful rural situation comedy that featured mountaineer characters. Instead, the show became a flash point for a national debate about the nature of television programming and the political possibilities of popular culture. By redefining the hillbilly stereotype, the show also offered an often overlooked and at-times trenchant critique of postwar American culture and value systems. The program's astounding success reshaped network television, as the show became a catalyst for the wave of rural sitcoms that swept over the airwaves in the 1960s.

As the show's popular theme song reiterated each week, *The Beverly Hillbillies* told the story of a family of Ozark mountaineers—Jed Clampett (played by Buddy Ebsen), Granny (Irene Ryan), Elly May (Donna Douglas), and Jethro (Max Baer)—who become millionaires after discovering oil in a swampy section of their land and then move into a Beverly Hills mansion (fig. 6.4).[21] The show was the work of Paul Henning, one of the most influential producers in the history of television. As the writer and producer of *The Bob Cummings Show*, occasional writer for *The Real McCoys* and *The Andy Griffith Show*, creator, writer, and producer of *The Beverly Hillbillies* and *Petticoat Junction* (1963–1970, CBS), and executive producer of *Green Acres* (1965–1971, CBS), Henning influenced nearly every program with a contemporary rural setting on television between 1955 and 1970. Born in Inde-

Figure 6.4
Mountaineers amid the Vulgarians: The Clampetts pull into Beverly Hills (left to right, bottom): Jed (Buddy Ebsen), Jethro Bodine (Max Baer); top: Elly May (Donna Douglas), Duke, Granny (Irene Ryan). Courtesy of Paul Henning Collection.

pendence, Missouri, in 1911, Henning began professionally in the early 1930s as a singer and jack-of-all-trades for radio station KMBC in Kansas City and went on to write for radio, film, and television, including *Fibber McGee and Molly*, *The Rudy Vallee Show*, *Burns and Allen*, and *The Bob Cummings Show*. Throughout his career, Henning exhibited a fascination with hillbilly characterizations, an interest he traced back to his teenage encounters with Ozark hill folk during hiking trips around a Boy Scout camp in Noel, Missouri, on the Arkansas-Oklahoma border. "I just sort of fell in love with the whole picture down there," he later recalled, "[a]nd the people were so kind and gracious. . . . It was a wonderful experience . . . that made a lasting impression on me.[22]

Henning acknowledged other media influences as well, including "religiously" listening to Bob Burns's monologues on the *Kraft Music Hall* starring Bing Crosby and attending a production of *Tobacco Road* in Kansas City, which he thought was "hilarious" but that had a setting that was "so depressing." Curiously, Henning failed to mention other clear media influences, including the overloaded jalopy from *The Grapes of Wrath* (and later *The Real McCoys*), the *Ma and Pa Kettle* films, and above all, Al Capp's *Li'l Abner*. Not only were Jethro, Elly May, and Granny clearly drawn from Abner, Daisy Mae, and Mammy Yokum (a connection made by several reviewers when the show first aired), Henning also featured scenes directly based on episodes in Capp's comic strip, including Jethro with his twin sister Jethrine, and Jethro attending elementary school in a ridiculously undersized school boy's uniform. Although Henning reconceptualized the hillbilly in important ways, his characters were thoroughly grounded in imagery of the past half-century.[23]

Regardless of the earlier media influences on his characters, the actual idea for the show came together in two places. First, in 1959, having just visited Abraham Lincoln's Kentucky homestead and whizzing along the highway, Henning wondered aloud "what reaction Abraham Lincoln might have had if he . . . suddenly found himself seated in the car with us." The idea stayed in the back of his mind until he read a news account of people in "a remote section of the Ozarks" who "actually . . . [tried] to stop the building of a road" because, Henning surmised, "a lot of them made their living moonshining and they didn't want 'fereners,' as they called them, coming in." Thus, for Henning, like Paul Webb before him, the mountain folk were not only a backward people living a century or more in the past, but they also stood in opposition to the dominant culture's notions of progress. Bringing such people into the heart of modern, cosmopolitan America would provide a comical study in cultural contrast, and it would also allow him to "escape the week-to-week depressive setting of the backwoods thing" as in *Tobacco Road*.[24]

The show's second germination point was a late 1961 lunch meeting at the famous Brown Derby restaurant in Los Angeles between Henning and President Al Simon and Board Chairman Martin Rasohoff of Filmways Television. Filmways represented the new breed of independent production companies that were coming to dominate network television production. Simon had been urging Henning to write a rural-based comedy for Filmways for several years, even offering to buy the television rights to Ma and Pa Kettle. When he and Rasohoff finally heard Henning's ideas, they offered immediate support. In the wake of hearings by the Senate Subcommittee on Juvenile Delinquency on the deleterious social effects of television violence, Simon thought "the cycle was right for fun" and that Henning's show "was going to be the best thing that hit television in a long, long while." Rasohoff pledged $100,000 on the spot before he had even lined up a sponsor.[25]

The reception from the networks, however, was not as warm. ABC passed when the show was first offered, and although CBS was more interested, it provided little advertising and assigned the program to what Henning and Simon deemed the "TV purgatory" of nine o'clock Wednesday night opposite NBC's highly rated *Perry Como Show*. Circumventing the network's limited promotion, Filmways launched a promotional media blitz that aired in eighty-five cities to an estimated thirty-five million viewers. Henning also carefully controlled the public image of his lead actors in an effort to maintain their believability. In contrast to the actors and producers of *The Real McCoys* who distanced their characterizations from actual mountain people, Henning sought to present his actors as credible mountaineers, as outlined in a June 28, 1962 memorandum:

> I would prefer that Buddy Ebsen, Irene Ryan, Donna Douglas and Max Baer *cease to exist as themselves*. The dissemination and publication of personal biographies . . . and so-called squibs, blurbs, plants in columns and photographic layouts of them at home *are to be discouraged by every means at our disposal!* NO STORY IS BETTER THAN THE WRONG STORY! . . . and a wrong story is one that damages the television image of our hillbilly characters.[26]

He also stressed that publicity layouts of his stars Buddy Ebsen on his yacht or Max Baer at a nightclub were "not conducive to believing in the characters," and he instructed his actors "to slant comments to 'the credibility of the show' and 'the basic integrity' of the roles they played."[27]

The result of this barrage of carefully controlled publicity was phenomenal ratings from the very first broadcast, watched by an estimated 50 percent of television viewers at the time. The show became the top-rated show by the end of its first month, was the highest rated show of the 1962 and 1963 television seasons, and never fell from the top twenty until its final years. Furthermore, the show boasts the highest rated half-hour individual episode in television history and eight individual episodes among the fifty highest. Not only a huge success in America, *The Beverly Hillbillies* also gained large followings in England, Holland, and Japan, becoming a truly international phenomenon. Concluded one British commentator, "More people in the world today know *The Beverly Hillbillies*, it is safe to assert, than know President Johnson or even the Pope."[28]

In stark contrast to its high ratings, initial press reaction was overwhelmingly negative. Most reviewers found the plots inane, and the gags, mistaken interpretations, and corny word play embarrassing (asked in an early episode if Jethro went to Eton as a boy, Jed replies, "If I knew Jethro, he went to eatin' when he was a baby"). "[A]n esthetic regression, mindless, stupid, a striking demonstration of cultural Neanderthalism" wrote one critic. *Variety* called it "painful to sit through. . . . strictly out of Dogpatch and Li'l Abner, minus the virtues of the Al Cappisms." "At no time," continued the reviewer, "does it give the viewer credit for even a smattering of intelligence. . . even the hillbillies should take umbrage."[29]

The idea that the show was perhaps the opening salvo of a lowbrow assault that would further debase American culture explains many critics' vitriol. They shared the outlook of Federal Communications Commission (FCC) chairman Newton Minow, who had blasted the medium a year earlier as "a vast wasteland" of "mayhem, violence, sadism, [and] murder" as well as "formula comedies about totally unbelievable families."[30] To these reviewers, *The Beverly Hillbillies* was further proof of the destructive vapidity of television and an attack on "legitimate" culture at a time when President Kennedy's "Camelot" seemed to be initiating a "heady cultural ferment" in the nation. As one astute commentator summarized the show's critical reaction: "Gone is the cheerful belief that with President Kennedy, Newton Minow, and Leonard Bernstein . . . at the helm, a mass cultural awakening had taken and is taking place. Thirty-six million people! How could they do this to us?"[31] Several commentators drew the connection to Minow's warning. Richard Warren Lewis in the *Saturday Evening Post* wrote the show is "dedicated to the proposition that . . . Minow's wasteland was really a cornfield," while Bob Hope quipped at the National Association of Broadcasters' reception that "Newton Minow's needlings have led our great industry up the path to the *Beverly Hillbillies*—an outhouse in the vast wasteland." Replied Irene Ryan in self-defense, "All I can say is that . . . millions of folks have moved that outhouse *inside* their homes." Yet like earlier disparagers of country music and the Ma and Pa Kettle films, the show's critics interpreted its vast popularity simply as confirmation of its baseness.[32]

Several factors help explain the show's unprecedented success. First, particularly in its first few seasons, the show was well crafted and genuinely funny. Ebsen and Ryan were both skillful entertainers who played their roles to perfection, director Richard Whorf had strong credentials in television and the Shakespearean stage, and Henning was a consummate professional who worked an exhausting schedule. Henning claimed that the show was so well received that they had to abandon the idea of filming before a live audience because "the laughter was so loud. . . . They laughed right through lines." Even critic Gilbert Seldes, although opposed to what he saw as the show's "encouragement to ignorance," nevertheless had to admit that "[t]he single simple, and to some people outrageous, fact is that *The Beverly Hillbillies* is funny."[33]

Second, much of what made the show humorous was the way Henning intentionally and successfully redefined the meaning and image of the hillbilly, making it more broadly appealing and innocuous. Most obviously, this sanitizing of the hillbillies was the result of making them millionaires and moving them out of the hills and into luxurious Beverly Hills. But Henning also actively tried to clean up and desexualize his characters, both to respond to the restrictive social mores of network television (a medium in which married couples had to be shown sleeping in separate beds well into the 1960s) and to remove the stigma of filth and debasement that defined earlier hillbilly characterizations. In a 1971 interview, Filmways Television president Al Simon summed up the dramatic conceptual change the show had achieved. Before *The Beverly Hillbillies*, he observed, "the word 'hillbillies' brought to mind the picture of dirty, unkempt people wearing long beards, inhabiting dilapidated shacks with outhouses out back." But because of his show, he claimed, "the word has a new meaning all over America. Now, it denotes charming, delightful, wonderful, clean, wholesome people."[34]

As Simon stated, the show did move dramatically, although incompletely, away from the standard hillbilly stereotype. The first time the audience sees Jed Clampett, he rushes in the door of his bare-bones Ozark cabin and immediately washes his hands. Long flowing beards and outhouses never appeared on the show nor did family feuds or shootouts with law enforcement agents. And although moonshining remained a common trope, drunkenness of the hillbilly characters did not. The Clampett clan dressed in jeans, linen blouses, and plaid shirts, but except for Jed's signature tattered slouch hat, their attire was clean and untorn. The alluring physiques of Elly May and Jethro played on standard conceptions of the innate sexuality of mountaineers and lines about Elly May's voluptuous body peppered the early episodes, but both characters were consistently portrayed as either impossibly sexually incompetent or naïve. Likewise, potential threat and violence remained latent in all the characters (in the common display of rifles, Jethro's lunacy, Elly May's menagerie of animals, and particularly Granny's quick temper), but the Clampetts also exuded an abiding neighborly warmth and a deep empathy for those they felt were less fortunate than themselves. Finally, in an era of a growing generation gap and challenges to parental authority, Jed is an undisputed but benevolent patriarch, and Elly May and Jethro almost always immediately follow their elders' orders.[35]

Henning also bridged the standard cultural division between the noble mountaineer and the hillbilly buffoon by merging the two into the same family. While Jethro's absolute ignorance of modernity was little removed from portrayals of Li'l Abner, Jed, like Grampa McCoy before him, symbolized the rugged, independent, and commonsensical mountain man who had a clear sense of himself and his culture. This mixture of traditional rural values and hillbilly buffoonery was perfectly captured by the 1963 *Saturday Evening Post* cover by photographer Allan Grant, showing Jed and Granny in the role of the tight-lipped couple from Grant Wood's famed 1930 masterpiece *American Gothic* while foolishly grinning Jethro and bosomy Elly May peer around either side of them (fig. 6.5). As Grant recognized, the show's hillbilly characterizations never entirely abandoned earlier meanings and indeed exploited more bawdy and degenerate stereotypes. But the show did expand the potential meaning of "hillbilly" and made it less of a slur nationally.

Figure 6.5
The blending of rural integrity and hillbilly ignorance: The Clampetts as updated *American Gothic*. Allan Grant, cover photograph, *Saturday Evening Post*, February 2, 1963. ©1963 SEPS: Licensed by Curtis Publishing, Indianapolis, IN. All rights reserved. www.curtispublishing.com

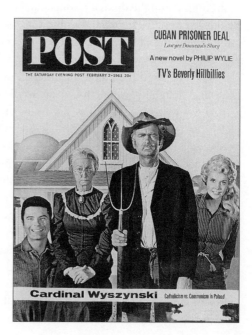

Third, the show's popularity stemmed from its capacity, like much of popular culture, to offer escapism and security in an uncertain world. The early 1960s were an era of social and political turmoil as the Civil Rights movement at home and the cold war abroad convulsed the nation. In the show's first week, newspaper headlines focused on the riot sparked by James Meredith's attempt to enroll at the University of Mississippi, church burnings in Georgia, the shooting of an East German who tried to scale the Berlin Wall, and a continuing deadlock at the Geneva disarmament talks. In such an uncertain and frightening time, *The Beverly Hillbillies*, and situation comedies, in general, offered the comfort of a totally known universe. As director Richard Whorf explained, "[y]ou know that no one will be killed, no one will have a brain tumor." The program continued to provide psychic sanctuary for millions, as the nation continued to be shaken by a steady stream of unsettling social and political crises, none more devastating than the assassination of President Kennedy in November 1963. Perhaps this explanation of the show as emotional balm in an atmosphere of uncertainty helps account for the phenomenal ratings (44 percent of all possible television viewers and a 65 percent share of the actual viewing audience) garnered by the show's otherwise unnoteworthy January 8, 1964, episode in which Granny mistakes a kangaroo for a giant jackrabbit—the highest ratings of any half-hour of programming in the history of television.[36]

Yet to argue *The Beverly Hillbillies* offered mere "escape" says little. As historian Lawrence Levine rightly reminds us, the potential for escapism lies in all forms of expressive culture; what matters most is not the mere fact of escapism but "to know from what and towards what we are escaping." To a far greater degree than either of its immediate predecessors, the show mixed its corny jokes and absurd characterizations with a deft mixture of social reflection and criticism. In the tradition of most producers of popular fare, Henning routinely denied this deeper interpretation of the show's significance. "Our only message is—have fun" he told the press. "Why go into deep analysis about it?" he scoffed on another occasion. "It's just escape, a lotta laughs, solid entertainment. . . . Viewers like 'em, and that's that." Cast members, however, understood the show's message was something more than belly laughs. Ebsen suggested that it was a reaction against a throwaway society, while Ryan claimed it represented "one of the last folk traditions in America, the lives and culture of the hill people." Although both interpretations were valid, the show's deeper significance, and the key to its success, lay in the way it both upheld and challenged the "American dream," blending a celebration of wealth and a lifestyle of leisure with a sustained critique of affluence, modernity, and "progress."[37]

On the one hand, the show reveled in the wealth, status, and leisure of the Hollywood elite and exploited California's popularity in the public imagination. Beyond an updating of the Joads' saga, the Clampetts' relocation mirrored the transplanting of millions of Americans during and after World War II to "the Golden State," a demographic shift that made California the most populous state in the union by the early 1960s. Likewise, their instant-millionaire status offered an exaggerated reflection of the relatively rapid prosperity attained by many Americans in the early 1960s, who had risen from Depression-era hardship to suburban ranch homes. Like their attitudes toward the Kettles a decade earlier, audiences could both laugh at and sympathize with the Clampetts' confusion about the proper use of what to them were new appliances and conveniences. In one early episode, Jed asks why the "electric meat grinder"—a kitchen disposal—does not work properly and believes he can use a telephone simply by shouting into it while it lies on its cradle. Despite the hillbillies' ignorance, viewers recognized in Jed and Granny's misunderstandings reflections of their own efforts to adjust to the new commodified culture.[38]

On the other hand, the values and actions of the Clampetts consistently called this dream of conspicuous consumption into question. Granny, the family member who is most ill at ease with her new surroundings, finds Beverly Hills a horrific place "full of the laziest, greasiest, unfriendliest mess o' people I ever laid my eyes on!"[39] With intentional irony, Henning employs the very words historically used to represent "hillbillies" to denounce the snobbish and idle Beverly Hills elite. Whereas her Ozark neighbors prized her skills as a cook, housekeeper, distiller, herbalist, and meteorologist, in Beverly Hills, Granny is considered at best eccentric, and at worst, a menace. And well should she be, for she is the character who most often exposes the vapidness and uselessness of the lifestyles of Beverly Hills, and by extension, of much of comfortably affluent American society. When Jethro complains of the lack of taste of a piece of wax fruit and Jed surmises that perhaps it is not meant to be eaten, Granny thunders:

> That's the trouble with this mis'uble place, y' ain't s'posed t' do
> nothin'! Ain't s'posed t' keep cows er pigs er chickens . . . ain't s'posed
> t' plow up th' ground an' plant corn er rye er 'falfa . . . ain't s'posed t'
> fire up th' still an' make a little moonshine whiskey! Anser me this—
> what kin y' do'in Beverly Hills?[40]

Like all the Clampetts, Granny may be ignorant of all things modern, but she has a clear sense of self and her rural heritage.[41]

Like Granny but without her hot temper, Jed Clampett also epitomizes a traditional rural value system based on an unswerving commitment to family and kin, a deep moral integrity in his dealings with all others, and a rock-solid horse sense. These traits allow him to either defeat or win over the steady stream of corporate and petty scam artists who weekly threaten his fortune. Like Sut Lovingood and Snuffy Smith before him, Jed also symbolizes egalitarian democracy, treating everyone he encounters with decency and kindness and acknowledging no legitimate distinctions of class or status. In an early episode, after his banker's assistant, Miss Jane Hathaway (Nancy Kulp), expresses shame for the way she has surreptitiously tried to spirit the Clampetts out of town, Jed replies: "The way I look at it, ain't nobody got a right to be ashamed of nobody else. Good Lord made us all," he sermonizes, "and if we's good enough for him we sure ought to be good enough for each other."[42]

Such values stem from his humble mountain background symbolized by his rustic log cabin home, to Jed as much a spiritual as a physical place. In the pilot episode, after an oil company has purchased Jed's land for $25 million, he asks his cousin Pearl (Jethro's mother) if he really should move to California. She responds incredulously:

> Jed, how can you even ask? Look around you! You're eight miles from the nearest neighbor! You're overrun with skunks, possums, coons and bobcats! You got kerosene lamps for light . . . a wood stove to cook on winter and summer . . . (indicates jug) you're drinkin' homemade moonshine . . . (picks up soap) washin' with homemade lye soap . . . and your bathroom is fifty feet from the house! And you ask should you move!

Jed ponders her words a minute and then replies: "Yeah—I guess you're right. A man'd be a dang fool to leave all this!" Clearly, his answer is meant to be seen as comically absurd, reflecting a stunning isolation from and ignorance of modern conveniences. Yet in a world of ever-increasing social and individual disruption, it just as certainly reflects an unshakeable sense of home and belonging. Despite his new riches, Jed refuses to change himself or his way of life. He continues to dress in his plain clothes, eat regional cuisine, and drive his ancient rattletrap of a truck. In contrast, his ludicrous relative Jethro repeatedly tries to embrace the new consumerist California lifestyle, always with disastrous results.[43]

In stark contrast to Jed's loyalty, honesty, and integrity and Granny's tenaciousness, the world beyond the Clampett household is peopled almost exclusively by money-grubbers, snobs, con artists, and sycophants. The show's main antagonist, Jed's banker Milburn Drysdale (Raymond Bailey), combines many of these qualities. He is a man so miserly and so desperate to keep the Clampetts as his main depositors that he is willing to go to any lengths to keep them happy no matter how much he must humiliate and degrade himself to do so. Numerous episodes feature him wearing ridiculous costumes or at the beck and call of Elly May's menagerie of "critters." His wife Margaret (Harriet MacGibbon), a vain and petty snob, is a hypochondriac who dotes on her poodle and considers the Clampetts uncouth barbarians who humiliate her in the eyes of high society. Even Jane Hathaway, the least caricatured character on the show and the one who graciously explains modern ways of living to the Clampetts, is nonetheless an often pathetic dilettante, incapable of leaving her job despite her abusive boss. Many other one-time characters try to bilk the Clampetts out of their millions by taking advantage of their naivete. The program therefore presents modern America, at least superficially, as venal, boorish, materialistic, and, ultimately, ethically and spiritually hollow.

A few insightful commentators recognized the deeper implications of the show's underlying message. Writer Arnold Hano understood that despite its awful puns and corny plots, the show did provide at least a "twitting of shallowness and pretentiousness." He also appreciated that the show embodied a rejection of urbanity and "a return to . . . natural ways," which he argued should have resonated with the "culture cult" who condemned the show as they "streamed from the cities, in search of Thoreau and Rousseau." Writing in the more self-consciously intellectual *Saturday Review*, Robert Lewis Shayon was more forthright in his defense of the show's social significance. To Shayon, the program was a "challenge to our money oriented value system" in striking contrast with the "pleasurable Eden" of most television programming. He acknowledged the show's "vaudeville patter" but argued that its corniness did not negate "the abrasiveness of . . . [its] moral values" and their critical import. "Valid social criticism with a top-ten Nielsen is an absolute rarity in television," Shayon concluded. "This is the true measure of success of 'Beverly Hillbillies'—first of its kind."[44]

Despite his perceptive commentary, Shayon badly underestimated the program's staying power. He felt the show's moral standards were so "heretical" the program could not endure, since they required the audience to "reexamine our own standards and discover their hollowness." What he failed to recognize, however, was that the power of the show's social critique was simultaneously made possible and undermined by the impossible ignorance and child-like naivete of the characters and the absurd storylines. Because the Clampetts and their chief antagonists, the Drysdales, are cartoonish caricatures, their distance from reality is too great for them to serve either as compelling models of noncompetitiveness and nonmaterialism (in the case of the Clampetts) or as legitimate symbols of moneyed power. For all the show's surface repudiation of the Beverly Hills lifestyle, the Clampetts never leave this den of hedonism and greed for longer than a few weeks nor do they reshape their social environment in any meaningful way. Instead, they remain strangers in a strange land with little sense of purpose, no longer working the land yet unwilling to become part of or to transform the commercial society around them. In the end, as Hal Himmelstein notes, the message of the *Beverly Hillbillies* is "quite cynical," "admiring but ultimately discounting basic human values" connected to a mythical rural American past that theoretically lives on in the southern mountains and "condemning yet tacitly accepting" the leisure and status world of Beverly Hills.[45]

One final and less savory possible reason for the show's popularity was its treatment of race relations and the southern past. Like *The Andy Griffith Show* (and indeed, nearly all early 1960s situation comedies), the program presented a nearly all-white world with African-American characters only appearing in a handful of episodes. Both programs also presented positive portrayals of southern small-town and rural folk that explicitly offset news coverage that consistently presented real-life southerners as villains. As a nearly pacifist small-town southern sheriff who refuses to wear a gun and who forces his trigger-happy deputy to keep his single bullet for his own revolver in his shirt pocket, Andy Griffith's character offered a studied contrast to racist violent southern sheriffs such as Jim Clark of Selma, Alabama, and "Bull" Connor of Birmingham, who were widely portrayed in early 1960s news media as the personification of southern white "massive resistance" to the Civil Rights movement. Promoting, in the words of one of its screenwriters, Bill Idelson, "man's *humanity* to man rather than man's inhumanity to man," the show offered a romanticized image of a benign southern past free of social tensions, a placidity largely made possible through the whitewashing of blacks from the southern landscape.[46] Going well beyond this portrayal of a deracialized and peaceful South, *The Beverly Hillbillies* portrayed not only humble but proud southerners but also self-avowed neo-Confederates, who saluted the rebel flag and cheered Jefferson Davis as the greatest president who ever lived. Although Granny is the most adamant in her allegiance to the Old South, even in one episode proudly donning a Confederate uniform, all the Clampetts at least implicitly embraced their Confederate heritage (fig. 6.6). In the episode "The South Rises Again," Granny mistakes actors playing Confederate soldiers in a Civil War movie for defenders against an actual Union army invasion and convinces Elly May, Jethro, and even Mr. Drysdale to join the fray. She even shoots and captures the actor playing General Grant (but then later shares a canteen of moonshine with him). Of course, the show presented such actions and beliefs as further evidence of the Clampetts' literalism (their inability to recognize the difference between real and pretend people) and their ridiculously anachronistic worldview. But at a time when the evening news almost daily featured civil rights activists being taunted and

Figure 6.6
Neo-Confederates in the midst of the Civil Rights era:
Granny dons a rebel uniform and prepares to do
battle with the hated Yankees in a 1967 scene from
The Beverly Hillbillies. Courtesy of Paul Henning Collection.

harassed by southern whites bearing rebel flags and promoting Confederate heroes, the show's association of neo-Confederacy with other positive traditional values espoused by Jed and his kin must have proven popular with those viewers who advocated the perpetuation of racial segregation.[47]

The fact that a disproportionate number of the show's fans lived in rural, small-town or southern locales and that American Research Bureau's "arbitron" ratings for selected urban markets reveal that the show did not reach consistent top-five status for most cities until the spring of 1963, also suggest that the show was somewhat more popular with viewers in the South than those in the North and West. Furthermore, some researchers have challenged the accuracy of the Nielsen ratings from this era, arguing that they overcounted rural and small-town viewers and undercounted urban African-Americans viewers, few of whom, these researchers conclude, watched *The Beverly Hillbillies* and other rural-oriented programming that featured all-white casts. On the other hand, both Irene Ryan and Paul Henning claimed, perhaps defensively, that blacks were some of the show's earliest and most eager viewers; Henning later noted that during a sequence filmed at Los Angeles airport, "the people who greeted us, you know, like old friends were . . .

the sky caps and . . . the black people. They were the first to enthusiastically embrace the show." Regardless of the accuracy of this assessment or of the Nielsen ratings, however, *The Beverly Hillbillies'* indisputable popularity with a broad swath of Americans cannot be divorced from its promotion and defense, however unspoken, of historical segregationists at a time of widespread racial struggle.[48]

The immediate and ongoing success of *The Beverly Hillbillies* and, to a lesser extent, that of *The Andy Griffith Show*, helped reshape the look of network television and CBS in particular. They so dominated the television world in the early 1960s that in March of 1964, *TV Guide* featured these shows on its cover in two consecutive weeks. Henning's success led CBS to offer him a contract for a new program of his choosing with the unprecedented arrangement of not first requiring a pilot. *Petticoat Junction*, his new show about the small farming community of Hooterville, premiered in 1963 and was the fourth highest-rated show of that season. Two years later, Henning collaborated on and was the executive producer of yet another CBS rural comedy, *Green Acres*. Indeed, the airwaves became saturated with rural situation comedies in the mode (but without the explicit hillbilly characterizations) of *The Beverly Hillbillies*. By 1966, CBS was airing five highly successful rural-based situation comedies—*The Beverly Hillbillies*, *Petticoat Junction*, *Green Acres*, *The Andy Griffith Show*, and *Gomer Pyle, U.S.M.C.* (a spin-off of the last)—and rode to network dominance on the backs of these programs.[49]

The Beverly Hillbillies phenomenon, coupled with the spate of news accounts surrounding Appalachia and the War on Poverty, spawned a new vogue for hillbilly iconography. Much of this imagery was related to the show itself; CBS launched a $500,000 merchandizing campaign and the Clampetts appeared in television and print advertising for Kellogg's corn flakes and Winston cigarettes and even in federal government public service announcements (fig. 6.7).[50] Another striking example of this trend was the initial promotional campaign for Pepsi Corporation's Mountain Dew, a soft drink high in sugar, caffeine, and calories. Its name a long-time synonym for moonshine whisky, the company chose to further advertise the product's potency and southeastern origins by embracing an explicitly hillbilly advertisement campaign. Between 1965 and 1968, many of these print and broadcast advertisements included a bearded, barefoot cartoon "spokesman" named "Willy the Hillbilly" (fig. 6.8). Advertisements featured slogans such as "Ya-hoo Mountain Dew . . . It'll Tickle Yore Innards" and "ther's a bang in ever' bottle!" Radio promotions used hoary comedic exchanges between ignorant and slovenly rustics ("Shecks, Sary Lou," the character "Clem" says to a mountain girl in one such spot, "I ain't never kissed *no one* 'ceptin' mah pet pig").

Figure 6.7
The hillbilly phenomenon: Ebsen and Ryan participate in an Internal Revenue Service tax filing promotion. Courtesy of Paul Henning Collection.

Figure 6.8
Hillbilly as spokesman: "Willy the Hillbilly" and friends advertise the potency of Mountain Dew. 1966 Mountain Dew Bottler catalog. Courtesy of Pepsi-Cola North America. © Pepsi-Cola North America.

The label even showed a picture of a hillbilly shooting at another emerging from an outhouse![51]

Although the Mountain Dew campaign ran through 1968, the cultural centrality of *The Beverly Hillbillies* was shorter lived. By the mid-1960s, the show's ratings had leveled off and the outrage that the show had caused had dissipated. As Judith Crist summed up in *TV Guide's* 1966 review: "[t]he Great Debate is over." She argued that the war between those who saw the show as proof of the "12-year-old mentality of the wanderers in the wasteland" and those who defended the program's social criticism had waned as it had settled into predictable comedy routines. Beyond changes in the show itself, however, the intellectual subtext behind the critics' apoplectic reaction—a belief in properly discrete levels of culture and the cultural and educational possibilities of television—no longer seemed as pressing a few years later. The sense that television should or could be anything more that a purveyor of strictly commercial entertainment did not long outlast Newton Minow's reign at the FCC (he resigned in 1963), and the rise of Pop Art, the new journalism, and stadium-sized audiences for rock-and-roll concerts further broke down the long-crumbling barriers between different cultural "brow-levels."[52]

As Crist's review suggests, *The Beverly Hillbillies* became considerably less significant in the second half of the decade. The show moved away from explicit themes of cultural conflict and increasingly focused on Jethro's absurd ignorance or ridiculous plots featuring the shenanigans of Elly May's animals or people dressed as animals. In an effort to keep the show at least somewhat fresh, Henning sent the Clampetts to England, Washington, D.C., New York, and briefly back to the Ozarks—where four episodes were filmed in the ersatz mountaineer heritage village of Silver Dollar City—but none of these new settings recaptured the show's original potency.

Beyond indicating Henning's difficulty in coming up with new concepts after more than 150 episodes, the program's increasingly outlandish storylines also reflected broader social and cultural transformations. As the escalation of the Vietnam War and increasing radicalization of the Civil Rights movement divided Americans and energized a wide variety of protest movements and subsequent countermovements, television became dominated by escapist situation-comedies—a trend encouraged by the success of *The Beverly Hillbillies.* Many of these half-hour comedies were either set in rural or small-town locales or, in the case of *Bewitched, The Munsters, The Addams Family,* and even *I Dream of Jeanie,* were bizarre fantasies about outgroups like the Clampetts living by their own code of conduct in the midst of "normal" society.[53] *The Beverly Hillbillies* did not avoid the societal unrest of the late 1960s altogether. Numerous episodes alluded to social developments from the student movement and the counterculture (the antiwar movement was conspicuously absent) to the interest in Eastern mysticism to the women's movement to environmentalism (in one episode, the Clampetts travel to Washington to present the president with their $95 million fortune to combat air pollution). The thrust of these protest movement-related episodes was generally to belittle these efforts as childish fads led by cartoonish radicals— ersatz hillbillies—who were as confused and absurd as the Clampetts themselves.[54]

Yet the tone of these programs was not the outright condemnation of many cultural conservatives and political leaders of the day but rather bemusement at the silliness of such challenges to the status quo, including the burgeoning drug culture. In the episode "Robin Hood and the Sheriff," for example, a group of stereotypical hippies choose to follow Jethro as their new leader primarily because he and his family seem to know of an exciting new hallucinogen, which is, in reality, a "traditional" southern recipe for crayfish. Their eyes grow wide with anticipation as Granny tells them "I'm going down to the lake to smoke some crawdads. But first I need a little pot." Half a decade earlier Granny would have denounced the hippies' hedonistic lifestyle, but here she is used to derive humor from double entendres. The episode thus reflects how far the show had moved from its original concepts of culture clash and ethical critique. Whereas the Clampetts were once emblematic of both rustic farce and bedrock American virtue, they now increasingly stood only for the former.[55]

"Everything with a Tree"—The Great Purge of 1970–1971

By the end of the 1960s, the "hillbilly vogue" seemingly had reached its end. The country lost interest in Appalachia as a "problem region," the War on Poverty was increasingly billed as a disastrous waste of money and resources, and rural poverty once again faded from public consciousness. Appreciating this trend, Mountain Dew dropped its hillbilly advertising campaign in 1969. On television, the ratings for most rural comedies, the *Beverly Hillbillies* included, fell so dramatically that only *Mayberry R.F.D.* (a sequel to *The Andy Griffith Show*) was in the top ten shows of the 1969–1970 season and none remained in the top twenty-five-rated shows by the following year.[56] Nonetheless, rural-based shows remained popular with millions of Americans, and CBS remained the number one network. New CBS president Bob Wood, however, realized that the network was faring poorly with most big city viewers and saw that the audience for the network's rural-based shows was now composed almost exclusively of children, the elderly, older blue-collar workers, and folks in rural and small-town locales—all told, the least desirable viewer demographics for attracting advertisers.[57] CBS had also gained such a reputation for rural programming that, according to a perhaps apocryphal story Buddy Ebsen recounted years later, network head William Paley's wife was greeted by her friends at a posh New York restaurant as "the wife of the owner of the hillbilly network." Thus, with Paley's full backing, Wood made a move beginning in the spring of 1970 to purge every rural-based program from the CBS lineup. As *Green Acres*'s regular Pat Buttram lamented: "they cancelled everything with a tree—including *Lassie*." By 1971, CBS had made the "turn toward relevance" and was broadcasting programs featuring young people with "sixties values" such as *All in the Family, The Mary Tyler Moore Show*, and, a year later, *M*A*S*H*.[58] Although the passing of the Clampetts from the airwaves did not denote the end of the mountaineer persona in the mass media, it did mark the last explicitly labeled "hillbilly" characters on twentieth-century television, and the end of the unification of the two halves of the hillbilly/mountaineer mythos—the stalwart democrat and the sexually charged fool (or monster)—that Henning had achieved.

How did southern mountain folk react to the televised hillbilly? Little more than sporadic anecdotal evidence exists of contemporary interpretations of these images, both because most hill folk had little access to avenues of public expression that could reach beyond their immediate community and because editorial directors paid attention to aggregate data on viewership and their demographics but rarely considered public reaction to televised images—particularly those they deemed noncontroversial—worthy of their time and attention. In 1963, *TV Guide* did recruit an Ozark hill man (labeled a "real hillbilly") to judge the show (he deemed it "a good, funny pergr'm" [*sic*]) and published a few subsequent letters to the editor, including one from an Arkansas reader who defended the "high-camp comedy" of Henning's programs. But, in the main, public reaction in large-circulation magazines and newspapers was scant.[59]

Opposing published reactions by two prominent Appalachians, however, offer some sense of the diversity of local reaction and the ongoing ambivalence this image inspired. To James Branscome, the director of the anti-strip-mining organization Save Our Kentucky, the CBS rural comedies *The Beverly Hillbillies, Green Acres*, and *Hee Haw*, aired back-to-back on Tuesday evenings, were the cultural equivalent of the coal industry's exploitation of the Appalachian land and people, "the most effective effort ever exerted by a nation to belittle, demean, and otherwise destroy a minority people within its boundaries." Similar portrayals of other minority groups, he continued, would generate "an immediate public outcry." But no opposition is heard regarding these offensive images because "America agrees: hillbilly ain't beautiful." Mack Morriss, an eastern Tennessee correspondent and radio commentator, offered a more nuanced interpretation:

> We alternately seem to swing, as a regional group, from one image to another in the eyes of much of the rest of the nation. . . . Sometimes we are a proud, fiercely independent people . . . naive perhaps but appealing types, whether we wear a coonskin cap or the slouch hat of Jed Clampett. Then, again, we find ourselves shorn of the phony glamour and we're not the Beverly Hillbillies but just hillbillies—poor, ignorant, shiftless, degenerate, substandard citizens. . . . This swing from one extreme to the other occurs with remarkable regularity . . . and is enough to set up a sort of schizophrenia—as a matter of fact, I think it has, in us and in the rest of the country regarding us—which may explain the popularity of the "Beverly Hillbillies."[60]

As Morriss realized, *The Beverly Hillbillies*, and to some degree all sitcom mountain folk, resonated with audiences precisely because these shows captured the dialectical relationship between the noble mountaineer and the farcical and base hillbilly at a time when real mountaineers were much in the news. When, by the end of the 1960s, the mountain people faded from public consciousness and the Clampetts became only caricatures and no longer the descendants of Crockett and Boone, they lost this inherently polyvalent meaning and, thus, much of their popularity.

From *Deliverance* to Cyberspace
The Continuing Relevance of "Hillbilly" in Contemporary America

If *The Beverly Hillbillies* marked the last appearance of the hillbilly label in the title of a major mass media production, it certainly did not represent the disappearance of the word and image altogether. Indeed, "hillbilly" continued to be a vital actor on the American cultural stage throughout the last three decades of the twentieth century, long after similar stereotypes for other racial and ethnic groups had become unacceptable. The cartoonized hillbilly perfected by Webb and Capp faded and the term and image met with increased opposition by a newly politicized cadre of activists in the southern mountains and midwestern cities. But the label was also reappropriated by many others as a battle cry of regional and cultural identity. To tell this full story would require several more chapters, but one can at least trace the overall contours of the diminished yet continuing relevance of the hillbilly in late twentieth-century America.

The year following the demise of *The Beverly Hillbillies*, 1972, brought two of the most influential mountaineer characterizations of the postwar era: the television drama *The Waltons* (based on Earl Hamner, Jr.'s loosely autobiographical account of his upbringing in Schuyler, Virginia) and the film *Deliverance* (adapted from James Dickey's best-selling 1970 novel and directed by John Boorman). *The Waltons*, another highly successful (1972–1980) CBS rural-based program, escaped the network's general purge of all things country because it had the strong backing of CBS founder and Chairman William Paley, who saw it as a "prestige" program that could attract a younger generation as well as CBS's traditional older viewers. The hour-long show presented noble, hard-working Virginia Blue Ridge mountain folk, steeped in traditional rural values and safely ensconced in the Depression era, the last great moment of national mountaineer resonance. Many Americans connected deeply with *The Waltons*, eager to embrace storylines that celebrated simple virtues and in which, in the words of one reviewer, all tensions "are resolved through understanding, love and growth of the family." But it simply could not compete in the public imagination with the mountaineers of *Deliverance*, retarded and crippled misfits and savage sodomizers of the North Georgia wilderness who terrorize a foursome of Atlanta canoeists (Ed Gentry, Lewis Medlock, Drew Ballinger, and Bobby Trippe) out to "do" the Cahulawassee River in northern Georgia before the entire region is flooded with the completion of a hydroelectric dam.[1]

Indisputably the most influential film of the modern era in shaping national perceptions of southern mountaineers and rural life in general, *Deliverance*'s portrayal of degenerate, imbecilic, and sexually voracious predators bred fear into several generations of Americans. As film scholar Pat Arnow only partly facetiously argued in 1991, the film "is still the greatest incentive for many non-Southerners to stay on the Interstate." Daniel Roper of the *North Georgia Journal* described its devastating local effect even more succinctly: "*Deliverance* did for them [North Georgians] what *Jaws* . . . did for sharks." Living on as cultural metaphor long after its theater showings, the film was repeatedly parodied on the nightly talk shows and *Saturday Night Live* and was the subject of countless cartoons and jokes. The film's infamous scenes of sodomy at gunpoint and of a retarded albino boy lustily playing his banjo became such instantly recognizable shorthand for demeaning references to rural poor whites that comedians needed to say only "squeal like a pig" (the command of one of the rapists to his suburbanite victim) or hum the opening notes of the film's guitar-banjo duet to gain an immediate visceral reaction from a studio audience.[2]

Given this singularly degrading connotation meant to evoke the unquestioned superiority of modern urbanity, it is not surprising that James Dickey's far more ambiguous interpretation in his novel of the mountaineers and the price of "progress" was later often forgotten. Through the words of Lewis Medlock, a survivalist enthusiast who is propelled by disgust with the flaccidity and meaninglessness of modern middle-class life and fear of civilization's devolution in the aftermath of nuclear annihilation, Dickey suggests that there "may be something important in the hills," a way of life that will be wiped out with the coming of the new dam. To Lewis (and Dickey), the mountain folk's very backwardness and social isolation has allowed them to retain a physical and mental toughness and to preserve a code of commitment to family and kin that has long ago been lost in the rush to a commodified existence. Telling Ed the story of how he and a friend became hurt and lost on a hunting trip and were rescued by a moonshiner and his son, Lewis praises the "values" passed down from father to son which led the boy to seek them out and bring them to safety. Despite the fact that they are both "ignorant and full of superstition and bloodshed and murder and liquor and hookworm and ghosts and early deaths," he concludes, "I admire the men that it [the culture] makes, and that make it."[3]

Lewis's story and much of the novel is loosely based on events from Dickey's life, particularly his canoeing trips on the Coosawattee River in the North Georgia wilderness with his friends, Al Braselton and Lewis King, and their encounters with the mountain folks who lived near its banks. On one such river run, Dickey and his party wrecked their canoe and were rescued by a teenage boy, Lucas Gentry, and his father Ira. Once convinced that the outsiders were not revenue agents, the Gentrys brought them to their rustic country house where they offered them cool water, sugarcane, and jars of moonshine.[4] Though Lewis's tale alludes to this real-life event marked by wary hospitality, Dickey centers the novel on the savagery that he believed this culture produces, particularly the brutal homosexual rape of Bobby Trippe. Dickey presents this action not as an aberration but a pattern of mountaineer behavior, for Ed thinks as his captors tie him to a tree just before they assault Bobby, "they must have done this before; it was not a technique they would just have thought of for the occasion." The mountain men's actions are so inhuman and committed with "such disregard for another person's body" that Ed's only chance to survive the ordeal is to transform himself into an animal, bare-handedly scale a sheer cliff wall, and then track down and kill the man who he presumes to be the surviving rapist.[5]

This equation of mountain folk with unadulterated savagery was made even more explicit in the film, directed by John Boorman and shot on location in Rabun County, Georgia, in the summer of 1971. Dickey always intended the book to be made into a film and wrote the screenplay, but he soon discovered, in the words of his son Christopher, who served as a stand-in on the film set that summer, "how little he'd have to say about the way his book was made into his movie."[6] Although Dickey devoted much of the first third of the novel and the nineteen opening scenes of his screenplay to an extended critique of modern urban life and the raping of the virgin land in the name of progress, Warner Brothers executives and Boorman were exclusively interested in producing a heart-pounding adventure tale of struggle and survival and cut nearly Dickey's entire opening sequence, including Lewis's qualified defense of mountaineer values.[7]

Boorman included voiceovers in the film's brief initial sequence that implicitly question the benefits of middle-class life and industrial development, but in all that follows, he consistently emphasized the social devolution of the mountain people and their utter separation from civilization. For example, in the novel, the serene guitar-strumming Drew Ballinger momentarily bridges the cultural divide between urban and mountain by playing a duet of the romantically traditional "Wildwood Flower" with an albino mountain boy banjoist. He stands so close to the boy that at one point they "put the instruments together and leaned close to each other," causing Ed to see in their union "something rare and unrepeatable."[8] By contrast, in the film, Drew (played by actor Ronny Cox) and the boy (played by Billy Redden, a local fifteen-year-old special education student whose head was shaved and skin powdered for the part) play the more raucous and more recent bluegrass number "Dueling Banjos" and they are separated by a high porch. Boorman also included scenes not in the novel, including a glimpse through a tattered curtain of a local mountain woman (played by Mrs. Andy Webb) cradling her sickly child (Webb's retarded granddaughter), the half-darkness of their sitting room accentuating the sense that she is too shameful to be presented in public. Christopher Dickey recognized even at the time how "terribly vulnerable" these people were and the distastefulness of these scenes. "Of course Hollywood paid these people and treated them as gently as it knew how to do," he wrote later, "but it was hard to get over the feeling as the lights went on and the cameras rolled that souls were being stolen here."[9]

It was, of course, the rape scene that would forever after be synonymous with the movie, and here too the film accentuated the idea of the mountaineers' utter degeneracy. The two unnamed rapists, played by Wild West shootout show veteran Herbert "Cowboy" Coward and local actor Bill McKinney, were later boastfully described in the film's press book as, respectively, "one of the scurviest villains in screen history" and "a degenerate character of no redeeming virtue, whose very presence in the wilderness seems to spoil what nature has accomplished." Graphic enough in the novel, the scene was made even more egregious by the addition of the "squeal like a pig" line and the squealing noises by a terrified Bobby (played by Ned Beatty), transforming the scene's meaning from homosexual rape into a substitute for bestiality. Sickened by the experience of having had to straddle (in his capacity as stand-in) the log over which Bobby is sodomized and then watch take after take, Christopher Dickey angrily telephoned his father and warned how the gruesome rape scene threatened to take over the movie. Although James Dickey continued to insist the scene was necessary because he "had to put the moral weight of murder on the suburbanites," his son rightly prophesized that "it was becoming what the movie was about, it was the thing everybody was going to remember. 'Squeal like a pig!' not Lewis's survivalism, not the climb

Hillbilly

Figure E.1

The only good hillbilly . . . : One unnamed mountaineer (Herbert "Cowboy" Coward) gawks in disbelief as his rapist companion (Bill McKinney) is shot through the back and dies violently in a scene from the filming of *Deliverance*. *Deliverance* © 1972 Warner Bros. Inc. All Rights Reserved.

up the cliff, not Ed's conquest of his own fear. It was all going to be about butt fucking." Such a brutal act made murder seem not only justified but also necessary, and the film explicitly portrays Lewis (Burt Reynolds) shooting the rapist through the back with an arrow and the man's shocked expression as he sees the blood smeared projectile protruding from his chest just before he dies violently (fig. E.1). James Dickey reacted electrically to the scene when he watched its New York premiere. Known for his outrageous antics and drunken public appearances, he is said to have shouted out in the crowded theater, "Kill the son of a bitch!" at the moment Lewis aims his fatal arrow and then "Hot damn" once the arrow found its mark.[10]

Initial reaction to the film outside Rabun County was generally positive, celebrating its gut-wrenching action and innovative cinematography. Both the novel (that sold 1.8 million copies by its eighth printing in 1973) and the film (that grossed $6.5 million in its first year) were a great success at home and internationally, and the film received nearly universally positive reviews (Stephen Farber of the *New York Times* called it "the most stunning piece of moviemaking released this year"). Georgia boosters fervently hoped the film would help promote the beauty of North Georgia and encourage tourist dollars, and dozens of local dignitaries, including Governor Jimmy Carter, attended the film's August 1972 premiere at the Memorial Arts Center in Atlanta. Carter tried to convince himself that the film would benefit his home state, even as the scenes became successively more disturbing. "This is good for Georgia" he commented to Dickey's friend Al Braselton, adding after a pause, "I hope."[11]

The reaction in the North Georgia mountains was less uncertain but, surprisingly, not simply one of angry repudiation. Rabun Country residents interviewed in 1973, who had been in the film or who had helped serve the cast and crew, were clearly uncomfortable with the "rough" and "vulgarish" scenes and the decision to film mentally retarded children. Resentment grew even while the film was being made. As word of how the mountaineers were being portrayed spread, Christopher Dickey, who was staying with his family in a low-budget motel and had more contact with the local residents acting or working on the set than did Boorman and the lead actors staying in chalets at a nearby golf resort, began to fear for his safety. Shaped by a century of media depictions of brutally violent mountaineers, he worried that some "real mountain men" with "real guns" might "teach some of these movie people a lesson." Frank Rickman, who had served as a local jack-of-all-trades and consultant to Boorman and the film crew and, more important, had been responsible for adding the pig squeals to the rape scene, also felt strong local animosity. He later acknowledged that after the film's release, "It was open season on me."[12] Yet Rickman felt the film had been a positive experience and many others agreed. Most residents who had been involved in the film said they enjoyed their brush with Hollywood glamour and the much-needed income it provided. Some even felt the film revealed truths about life in Rabun County that "should have been revealed forty or fifty years ago." Like Rickman, many also felt the film had generated positive outside interest in the region, encouraging studios to shoot other films in the area and helping launch a booming rafting and canoeing business on the Chattooga River.[13]

But there was a price paid for such interest, as they soon discovered. The thousands of suburbanites who flocked to the river in search of white water thrills also left behind mounds of garbage and created headaches for the local water safety patrol. Many exhibited what the press came to call "the Deliverance syndrome"—the same lack of respect and reverence for the river that the characters in the film had displayed. To the shame of local guides, some even would make pig squeals when they reached the section of the river where the rape scene had been filmed, almost willing nature to retaliate. In some cases it did. Seventeen people drowned on the river between 1972 and 1975 (most with excessive blood-alcohol levels), until new regulations were imposed when the river was officially designated Wild and Scenic in 1974.[14]

Deliverance not only shaped conceptions of mountaineers for decades to come, but it also helped launch a slew of adventure and horror novels and films, all premised on the fatal encounter of modern suburbanites rashly and disrespectfully penetrating raw nature and meeting a bloody end. *Texas Chainsaw Massacre* (1974), *The Hills Have Eyes* (1977), *The Evil Dead* (1983), *The Evil Dead II* (1986), *Pumpkinhead* (1988), and even the independently made surprise blockbuster *The Blair Witch Project* (1999) all stem more or less directly from *Deliverance*. The film's success also encouraged film studios to produce dozens of movies featuring moonshine-running southern rural outlaws that found a steady market in small-town and drive-in theaters in the mid-1970s, although a more direct inspiration for these films (and the cleaned up televised *Dukes of Hazzard* that followed them) was Robert Mitchum's 1958 drama *Thunder Road*. Though featuring high-powered cars and squealing car chases, it was the first film since *The Moonshiner* of 1904 to look at moonshining from inside the culture and the underlying story was of plain but forthright Luke Doolin (Mitchum) and his mountain family struggling to preserve what the film presents as a traditional craft in the face of northern organized crime interests. In the end, Doolin dies a hero's death on the highway, fighting to preserve a way of life that is clearly destined to disappear.[15]

The wave of southern good old boy films that followed in the next two decades, however, had none of the economic undertones and cultural pathos of Mitchum's work or the critique of modernity of *Deliverance*. Instead, they were unambiguous celebrations of male hedonism (almost always at the expense of women), of fighting and beating the corrupt and inept "system," and of the joys of watching vehicles and buildings destroyed. Films such as *Moonrunners* (1974), *Hot Summer in Barefoot County* (1974), *Moonshine County Express* (1976), and *Bad Georgia Road* (1977) freely blended hillbilly, redneck, and cracker iconography, presenting a fantastic South where mountains bordered on swamps, and cities and factories were nowhere to be seen.[16]

The sheer number of these movies and their steady popularity reflected the degree to which the image of the southern poor white permeated both popular and political culture in these years, as large numbers of working-class men and women across the South and throughout the nation began to embrace formerly unequivocally derogatory terms for poor and working-class southerners and rural folk, in general — including "redneck," "cracker," and "hillbilly" — as signifiers of racial and cultural pride. The plethora of country music songs in these years featuring "redneck" in the title (such as Johnny Russell's "Rednecks, White Socks, and Blue Ribbon Beer" (1973) and Vern Oxford's "Redneck! (The Redneck National Anthem)" [1976]) both reflected and encouraged this ideological transformation. Although rarely described so explicitly, this development was part of a general counterreaction to the social upheavals of the Civil Rights movement, counterculture, and women's movement of the late 1960s and early 1970s. Appropriating the "identity-consciousness" of these movements, but for the most part rejecting their political agendas, millions of the white working class (overwhelmingly men but including some women) struggled to reconceptualize these terms as positive markers of "whiteness" and industriousness. In so doing, they positioned themselves in opposition to both the growing cultural and economic power of middle- and upper-middle-class managers and bureaucrats and what they perceived to be a welfare-dependent and largely minority underclass.[17]

The election of Jimmy Carter as president in 1976 intensified the spread of redneck terminology and iconography. A wealthy peanut farmer and politician from southern Georgia who ran as a political outsider and man-of-the-people, Carter was ridiculed by some Washington insiders as an uncouth southern good old boy—a belief promulgated by the antics of his beer-drinking, garrulous brother Billy. Columnist Carl Rowan denounced those "self-styled intellectuals and socialites" who thought Carter a "Georgia Yokel" about to "impose a bunch of hillbillies, cornpone idiots and drawling numbskulls on the nation's capital." Yet Carter's presidency also legitimized the redneck label among many white middle-class southerners, who adopted the term, dressed in fancy Levis and boots, and drank regional beer in newly fashionable "honky tonks," leading social commentator Paul Hemphill to dub this social phenomenon "redneck chic."[18]

Although no comparable "hillbilly chic" arose among the urban middle classes, the continuing transformation of the term "hillbilly" in the 1970s mirrored the evolution of "redneck" in intriguing ways. Like "redneck," "hillbilly" was increasingly appropriated by southern mountaineers, both in their native region and in midwestern cities, as a marker of racial and class pride. But, unlike redneck, the term carried a strong regional specificity, representing not only southern whiteness and working-class status but also a pride in the independence and resistance of a mountain-identity. Nor was it as exclusively a signifier of male identity as was "redneck." Kathy Kahn's *Hillbilly Women* (1977) celebrated the lives of working-class mountain women, who told not only of their poverty and brutal working conditions but also of ethnic and cultural identity and self-esteem. "I'm proud to be a hillbilly," avows one of Kahn's interviewees, Donna Redmond, adding "And if you don't like the way I talk, then, damn it, go home!" Similarly, an older generation of southern mountain folk, most of whom had long since departed the region or moved to urban centers, also adopted the term in self-published autobiographies with titles such as *Call Me Hillbilly* and *By Gum, I Made It!—An Ozark Arkie's Hillbilly Boyhood*. Less explicitly class-conscious than the women in Kahn's book, these men and women nevertheless used the freighted term to signify their difficult but rewarding childhoods on farms and small towns in the southern mountains and their proud connections to a fast-disappearing way of life.[19]

Even as some southern mountain folk embraced the word, however, a new generation of activists and scholars began to fervently denounce the term "hillbilly" and the negative connotations it held in the popular media. As we have seen, local people had resented and resisted the label "hillbilly" since its origins, but the mid-1970s marked the first time the usage of "hillbilly" was systematically challenged and attacked. These efforts emerged from three overlapping yet distinct social and cultural movements. First, environmental, labor, and social welfare activists in eastern Kentucky and the surrounding area, active in or inspired by the examples of the many national social movements of the 1960s and 1970s, aggressively resisted further environmental and economic exploitation of the land and people by the mining industry, the U.S. Forest Service, and highway and home builders. Their actions on a variety of fronts began to break down the hillbilly myth of mountain folk as lazy and uneducated wards of the state or as passive victims. Second, a new generation of Appalachian scholars launched the field of Appalachian studies. Largely motivated by a desire to combat what they saw as egregious negative stereotyping in the broader culture, they promoted the scholarly study of the cultural, social, and economic nature of Appalachia and its history. Although often more influential regionally than in the national discourse, their work weakened the notion that the southern mountains and their people somehow existed outside the realm of social and economic reality. Third, urban Appalachian activists throughout midwestern cities, and particularly in Cincinnati, formed advocacy organizations in the mid-1970s to promote the social welfare of these communities and to promote Appalachian identity and culture. Efforts by the Urban Appalachian Council and Appal-PAC in Cincinnati, for instance, led to the November 1992 passage by the Cincinnati City Council of a human rights ordinance expressly protecting the civil rights of Appalachian Americans—the only ordinance of its kind in the nation. Although in all cases these Appalachian activists and scholars' primary objective was to reform local political and social institutions and to improve conditions at the grass roots, whether in Kentucky coal mines, Virginia school districts, or community centers in Cincinnati and Dayton, their actions and writings also helped to delegitimize the hillbilly stereotype in the minds of the broader public.[20]

Nonetheless, although the "hillbilly" label appeared far less frequently in commercialized popular culture than it had in the past, hillbilly imagery continued to crop up in the 1980s and 1990s in both the national media and in more localized events. *The Dukes of Hazzard* (CBS, 1979–1985), based on the 1974 film *Moonrunners* (itself drawn largely from *Thunder Road*), was adapted for television after the great success of Burt Reynold's 1977 *Smokey and the Bandit* car chase film and its many reincarnations. One of the highest-rated shows of the early 1980s, *Dukes* drew on the name of the actual eastern Kentucky mining town of Hazard for its mythical locale of Hazzard County and featured such typical hillbilly stereotypes as scantily clad bosomy women, a grizzled but lovable old moonshiner named Uncle Jesse (played by Denver Pyle in an updating of his Briscoe Darling role), and even an occasional outhouse joke. But the biggest star of the show (at least in terms of the amount of viewer fan mail received) was a Day-Glo orange souped-up 1969 Dodge Charger named "the General Lee." The producers were careful, however, to avoid the increasingly controversial label "hillbilly" in their scripts and promotional materials and to situate the show in a vaguely defined southern landscape.[21]

In the late 1980s, the hillbilly stereotype reemerged with a vengeance during the campaign and presidency of Bill Clinton from Arkansas—a state long associated by the mass media and in the public mind with hillbillies. Despite his status as a Rhodes scholar and Yale Law School graduate, urban sophisticates and the press lampooned Clinton and his associates as uncultured hillbillies to a far greater degree than they had Jimmy Carter. Writing in the *Washington Post* during the 1992 presidential campaign, Joel Achenbach tried to humorously express the dread felt by campaign workers (as well as much of the press corps) who traveled to Clinton headquarters in Little Rock—"a place that for all they knew had the lowest teeth-to-people ratio of any state" and where "the state song would be "Dueling Banjos!" References to *Deliverance, The Beverly Hillbillies*, and other popular culture hillbilly representations also appeared in a 1992 *Saturday Night Live* sketch lampooning that year's presidential debates. Moderator Sam Donaldson (played by Kevin Nealon) characterizes Clinton (Phil Hartman) as "the governor of a small backwoods state with a population of drunken hillbillies . . . [and] buxom under aged girls in cutoff denims" who cavort "in front of Jethro . . . while corncob-pipe-smoking, shotgun-toting grannies fire indiscriminately at runaway hogs."[22]

Such media hillbilly allusions continued into Clinton's presidency, effortlessly called upon by cartoonists to represent the seemingly endless series of scandals that tarred his administration (fig. E.2). These images also reinforced Clinton's public persona, promulgated by the press, on late-night talk shows, and by his critics, as a man of boundless animal appetites for caloric food and younger women. And when his sexual liaisons with White House intern Monica Lewinsky proved such assessments valid, a street protester calling for his resignation denounced him with a placard labeling him an "Ozark Caligula," merging the mountain locale long associated with supposedly libidinous backwoods folk with imperial excess and depravity (even though Clinton's hometown of Hope and adult home of Little Rock were far away from the Ozarks).[23]

Despite the brief resurgence of Clinton-related hillbilly cartoons and

"SAY, MR. PRESIDENT, WASN'T IT SOMEWHERE ALONG ABOUT HERE THAT THEY SHOT THE LOVE SCENE FROM 'DELIVERANCE'?!..."

Figure E.2

Cartoonists effortlessly linked President Clinton
with standard media hillbilly imagery. Doug Marlette,
March 23, 1994. © Tribune Media Services, Inc.
All Rights Reserved. Reprinted with permission.

punch lines in the mid-1990s, the commercial hillbilly seemed to be a slowly
dying image as the twentieth-century ended. A mid-1990s excursion through
heavily touristed portions of the southern Appalachians, for instance, produced few examples of businesses still using the familiar hillbilly label or
iconography—a motor home campground being one of the few exceptions
to the rule. Although a wide array of hillbilly novelty items (such as a dried
corncob marked "hillbilly toilet paper"), jokebooks, cookbooks, calendars,
T-shirts, and postcards continued to be sold, they were increasingly available
only in rundown souvenir stands and gift shops on the fringes of tourist
towns. Hill-Billy Village in Pigeon Forge, Tennessee, a few blocks away from
Dolly Parton's Disneyfied theme park Dollywood (described in a promotional brochure as "an atmosphere filled with rustic charm and mountain
lore") and less than an hour away from Great Smoky Mountains National
Park, is a case in point. When visited in 1995, this dilapidated store carried a
hodgepodge of gag gifts and softcore pornographic materials, and its highly
publicized "authentic" moonshine still turned out to be little more than a few
rusted pots from a federal raid decades earlier (fig. E.3). The hillbilly image
was more prevalent in tourist traps in the Missouri and Arkansas Ozarks than
in their southern Appalachian counterparts (perhaps because the burgeon-

Figure E.3
A fading commercial icon: The dilapidated
Hill-Billy Village souvenir store in Pigeon Forge,
Tennessee. Author's collection.

ing academic field of Appalachian Studies had no Ozark equivalent), but
even here it clearly lead a precarious existence, denounced as offensive and
demeaning by more and more southern mountaineers and increasingly out
of place in a society concerned with "political correctness" and multicultur-
alism. In this regard, a July 1999 *New Yorker* cartoon may well mark the last
gasp of the cartoon hillbilly, its liminal landscape and the figure's ghost-like
face indicating the decrystallization of this once instantly recognizable
mythic character and its disappearance from the national scene (fig. E.4).[24]

Yet such an assessment does not take into account the various, often contradictory, ways "hillbilly" continues to live on in the culture, in both commercialized and personal ways. A prime example of the former is the growing number of professional musicians who have associated themselves with
different elements of the hillbilly label and persona. Although many lesser-
known country performers never gave up the label, this trend began in
earnest with the success of eastern Kentuckian Dwight Yoakam's 1987 album *Hillbilly Deluxe*. Rejecting the "country" label as "a euphemism for

Figure E.4

The end of the line for the cartoon hillbilly? Harry Bliss,
New Yorker, July 26, 1999, 57. © The New Yorker Collection 1999
Harry Bliss from cartoonbank.com. All Rights Reserved.

nothing," Yoakam embraced the once reviled term, redefining country music as "hillbillies playing real loud." Following in Yoakam's footsteps, crossover country performers such as Steve Earle, Ronnie Milsap, the Judds, and
Marty Stuart (whose debut single was titled boldly "Hillbilly Rock") have
gained fame and fortune by positioning themselves as "hillbilly" inheritors of
a raucous yet proud musical and cultural heritage. Even British rock artists
the Kinks and Dire Straits's Mark Knopfler have released albums or formed
bands incorporating the hillbilly label. Still other bands and performers, who
blend musical forms spanning from punk to bluegrass, including the Kentucky Headhunters, Hasil Adkins, and Southern Culture on the Skids, have
embraced less the hillbilly label than the persona of the media-inspired
crazed mountaineer. Yet another distinct example of the reemergence of
"hillbilly" is the success of the Nashville band BR5-49. Drawing their name
from a standard *Hee Haw* sketch, these performers dress in the manner of
1940s and 1950s hillbilly groups and perform old hillbilly standards as well
as original songs such as "Little Ramona (Gone Hillbilly Nuts)." This diversity of musical approaches and presentations shows the multiple meanings

"hillbilly" still imbues and its continuing resonance with contemporary audiences.[25]

The Shriners' "Grand and Glorious Order of the Hillbilly Degree" offers a less explicitly commercial but far more outlandish example of the recent appropriation of the hillbilly persona. Founded in 1969 by Jim Harris of the El Hasa Shrine Temple in Ashland, Kentucky, this "sideline degree" (a combination of social club and charity within the Shriner organization) allows members the chance to dress in stereotypical "hillbilly" costumes and engage in mountaineer initiation ceremonies (including the imbibing of "corn likker") with the heartening knowledge that all proceeds from membership dues and the sale of memorabilia will be earmarked to assist burned and disabled children treated in Shriner hospitals. The Ashland "clan" grew rapidly after members paraded in their hillbilly costumes and rattletrap trucks complete with moonshine stills at the 1970 Imperial Shrine Convention. The organization soon included dozens of chapters nationwide, an official mascot, and a newsletter, the *Hillbilly News*. Then, in 1977, two other Kentucky "Hillbilly" shriners and coalminers, "Shady" Grady Kinney and "Dirty Ear" Howard Stratton, launched the Hillbilly Days Festival in Pikeville, Kentucky (the county seat where much of the Hatfield-McCoy conflict had been adjudicated nearly one hundred years earlier). Wearing overalls, cone-shaped felt hats, and oversized ties and coats festooned with buttons, and parading in their absurdly broken-down jalopies, the festival was a Rabelaiian outpouring of bad taste and vulgarity. But, in the eyes of its founders, it was also a celebration of mountain identity and pride, hosted by "born and bred hillbillies" who were "civilized, good common help your neighbor kind of people." Heavily promoted by the local tourism commission and the Pike County Chamber of Commerce, which advertised it in 1995 as "three days of the best in mountain music, dancing, crafts, food . . . and the famous Hillbilly Days Parade," the lucrative annual festival was celebrated for the twenty-sixth time in 2002 and continues to face only limited opposition in economically stressed Pike County. The Shriner's "Hillbilly Degree" sideline also remains strong, with 160 "clans" participating in the United States and Canada in 1999.[26]

But when in 1982, the Cincinnati chapter, headed by an Appalachian migrant, tried to host a similar parade in Cincinnati, they were accused by some Appalachian advocacy organizations of insulting and distasteful behavior that would reinforce negative hillbilly stereotypes, promulgated by the popular media and widely shared by the non-Appalachian community. To these advocates working for tens of thousands of Appalachian migrants trapped in rundown slums and limited to blue-collar jobs, the word "hillbilly" remained a "fighting word." As one local activist warned a *Cincinnati En-*

quirer reporter, "just try going up to an Appalachian at the General Motors assembly plant in Norwood . . . [use the term,] and watch what happens." The key factor, however, would not be the term itself but the "outsider" status of the speaker, for "hillbilly" had long been and remains an acceptable, even positive, label of inclusion for many poor whites of Appalachian heritage in inner-city Cincinnati, Chicago, Detroit, and other urban centers of migrant population. Although the Hillbilly clans did eventually hold their street parade, Mayor David Mann did not officially sanction it as originally planned. Thus, where the Shriners saw only a harmless chance to defy middle-class conventions, promote a mythic mountain heritage, and raise money for needy children, many Appalachians in Cincinnati viewed the event as yet another demeaning and destructive presentation of ignorant and drunken "hillbillies" that had real-life implications for the local Appalachian migrant community.[27]

Perhaps the clearest and most expansive example of the continuing relevance of "hillbilly" is its many manifestations in cyberspace. In the fall of 2002, over 6,330 Web sites on the Internet included the term in their title and over 192,000 Web pages used some form of the word hillbilly in their text. Many of these sites promote a wide array of musical groups, including the Hillbilly Hellcats, Hillbilly Holocaust, Hillbillies from Mars (despite the bizarre name, a San Francisco Bay Area contradance band), the Sierra Hillbillies (a group of California square dancers who dub themselves "the rowdiest square dancing club in America"), and even a rockabilly group from Málaga, Spain, called Mike Hillman and His Latin Hillbillies. In addition to music-related references and Web pages, dozens of other sites feature hillbilly jokes of varying levels of crassness or advertise products with this label from gag gifts (a site called "Hillbilly Headquarters" specializes in oversized and gapped "Billy Bob teeth") to a self-leveling lawn mower. The home page for *Hillbilly Hercules 2: Lost in New York City*, a bizarre video short, includes sound bites and clips from the movie in which the Greek demigod is relocated first to the West Virginia hills and then to Manhattan. On E-bay, the online auction house, one can purchase all manner of hillbilly memorabilia from *Beverly Hillbillies* songbooks and comic books, to Mountain Dew bottles and signs, to porcelain coffee cups and beer steins featuring hillbilly figurines and designs, to T-shirts and bumper stickers parodying the Tommy Hilfiger logo that feature a rebel flag and the words "Tommy Hillbilly." The Internet even includes several quasi-academic sites devoted to tracing the development of the poor white and hillbilly stereotypes.[28]

Finally, hundreds of individual users have designed home pages that use the label in strikingly different ways. Most Web page designers use "hillbilly" to signify either southern mountains' residency or origins or a simple life of good friends, family, and a closeness to nature. But other such Web pages range widely from the recently retired Hillbilly Redneck Rampage Page—a paean to southern white male hedonism with links to the Sons of the Confederacy, Playboy, Budweiser, NASCAR, and the National Rifle Association —to an issue of an online newsletter of Believers International that used the word to represent the value of humble religiosity and referred to Jesus Christ as "the greatest hillbilly that ever lived." This vast and diverse presence of "hillbilly" on the Internet offers compelling evidence that although the mass media stereotypical hillbilly may soon join little Black Sambo, the Chinese laundryman, and the Italian organ grinder as unacceptably offensive ethnic and racial stereotypes badly out of place in modern America, the hillbilly is still very much alive in the hearts and minds of millions of Americans throughout the country.

Such varied uses and interpretations reflect the image's remarkable longevity and persistence. Born in print in the first year of the century, the "hillbilly" has survived world wars, the Great Depression, the rise and fall of the cold war, the social revolutions of the 1960s, and the shift from radio to film to television to the Internet as the leading-edge medium of the age. It has endured because of its semantic and ideological malleableness—a changeability rooted in its core ambiguity as a representation of a "white other" that both celebrates and denigrates the American past and the folkways of the southern mountain folk.

This intrinsic duality has allowed the hillbilly's meaning to transform subtly but continuously throughout the century in order to reflect evolving social concerns. At the turn of the century, media producers' use of the hillbilly mirrored late-Victorian fears of the failure of social assimilation and the threat of rural folkways to the industrial urban social order. In the 1920s, as the nation became dominantly metropolitan and such fears dissipated, the hillbilly became increasingly a humorous persona associated with bumbling silent film comedians and fun-loving string band musicians. The hillbilly image/identity reached its apex during the Great Depression and blossomed across the cultural spectrum from novels to film to comic strips and cartoons. In an era of economic and social upheaval, the "hillbilly" represented both fears of societal collapse and devolution *and* a celebration of an indigenous American folk and folk culture. In the postwar years, the hillbilly's meaning evolved once again, used to represent a people and culture strangely out of sync with modernity but also to point out the moral and social costs of an increasingly automated and materialistic America. Finally, in the last decades of the twentieth century and into the next, although the hillbilly image in commercial popular culture waned dramatically, millions of Americans, especially southern hill folk both in and beyond the southern mountain region, continued to repudiate and embrace the label and identity, reflecting the fundamental ambiguity that has always characterized Americans' relationship to the hillbilly.

Such an understanding helps us recognize the permeability of the boundaries between folk, mass, and popular culture and complicates our conception of the nature and role of stereotypes and caricatures in American history and culture. Although media industries and commercial artists often control the production of these images and personas, they do not control their cultural meanings or uses. This outcome is the result of a continuous struggle between not only producers, promoters, and audiences but also within audiences and even within individuals. Far from merely inane "mass" images that are uniformly interpreted by brainless media consumers, therefore, this study suggests that national stereotypes are semantically and conceptually complex. They contain multiple possible layers of meaning that divulge as much about the "mainstream" culture as the groups and customs they ostensibly depict. Looking closely at the "hillbilly" image thus reveals the myriad ways Americans use popular culture to define personal and national identity and to help come to terms with the ambiguities in their own lives in a rapidly evolving society.

postscript

In the many years I have worked on this book, I have been repeatedly struck by the remarkable longevity of the media hillbilly, even in the face of increasingly vocal opposition to racial and ethnic stereotyping, including, to a degree, against rural and economically disadvantaged whites. Nothing better exhibits the persistence of the media's embrace of this image or better shows how its presentation and reception continue to evolve than the decision by CBS television in the fall of 2002 to bring back *The Beverly Hillbillies* as a "reality TV" program called *The Real Beverly Hillbillies*. Prompted by the stunning success of MTV's *The Osbournes*, the weekly "real-life" look into ex–heavy metal singer Ozzy Osbourne's bizarre but also strangely familiar nuclear family household, the network sought to cash in on both that show's peculiar appeal and the continuing popularity of the Clampett episodes (to which CBS conveniently owned the rights). Rather than having actors play the roles of poor mountaineers who magically become wealthy and relocate to posh Beverly Hills, the network planned to select a "multi-generational family of five or more—parents, children, and grandparents" from the southern mountains (casting agents were sent to "'mountainous, rural areas' of Arkansas, West Virginia, North Carolina, Tennessee, and Kentucky"), pay all their expenses to relocate to a mansion in southern California, and then document on film their experiences as they hire house servants, shop on Rodeo Drive, and dine in chic restaurants.[1]

Unlike in 1962, when the original show first aired, however, CBS programming executives realized that some might challenge the appropriateness of this concept and proactively tried to position both the show and their intentions in a positive light. Thus, CBS Vice President for Alternative Programming Ghen Maynard highlighted the show's comedic potential as "a great fish-out-of-water story" but was careful to stress that the audience would be laughing with and not at the real life cast that he envisioned to be "a family that's different from what most people know but still relatable, a family that loves each other a lot." The network also emphasized that the show's main developer was John "Dub" Cornett, a self-proclaimed "Appalachian American," who was raised in the town of Appalachia in Virginia's coal-mining region and who helped produce the old-time country music for the film *O Brother, Where Art Thou?* (whose soundtrack was a runaway best-seller). Acutely aware of mountain folk's sensitivity to the way they had long been caricatured, Cornett insisted that his intent was to mock not Appalachians but rather the Beverly Hills lifestyle. "We will accomplish the most," he told the press, "if we cast it well, with people who respect themselves but see the humor in themselves. We will end up with a piece that truly has, God forbid, social commentary, and maybe will enlighten, that it's not all barefoot hillbillies." Cornett thus tried to argue that the show would serve the same purpose as its progenitor, emphasizing the absurd excess of the Hollywood elite and the heartfelt values of plainspoken hill folk.[2]

Despite these efforts, the proposed show ran into a firestorm of opposition both in the southern mountains and beyond, reflecting many Americans' growing unwillingness to stand for long-accepted (or at least tolerated) stereotypes. Columnists, academics, local politicians, and political activists all lined up to express their shock that such a program was even being considered. "Please, say it ain't so" began one Kentucky journalist's article while a Raleigh, North Carolina, columnist mockingly pled, "Spare us the horror, sweet Jesus." Explicitly focusing on the racial identity of these "hillbillies," *National Review Online* senior writer Rod Dreher equated the program to a modern day "minstrel show," based on a plan to "ship the toothless poor white trash in from Appalachia, set them down amid immense luxury, and watch the dopes make inadvertent fools of themselves in front of the rich and the beautiful." Other detractors also stressed that such an idea for a television program would be dismissed out of hand for any other racial or ethnic group, mockingly suggesting the network's future shows could feature "a struggling black family from the Bronx" summering in the Hamptons or "orthodox Jewish college students" transferred to "Atlanta Baptist College." Most cuttingly, a Charleston, West Virginia, columnist suggested a program where a Hollywood television executive's family would be brought to West Virginia and forced to live "like ordinary, sensible West Virginians in this state where the largest private employer is Wal-Mart, where good jobs are scarce as hen's teeth and where businesses don't look kindly on us in part because of our image."[3]

Stung by the vituperative criticism, Cornett confided to a reporter for a Nashville alternative newspaper that although CBS might have a "different agenda," he planned to "trick the network into thinking that we were going to do something like *The Osbournes*" but instead offer a "really even-handed documentarian kind of approach." He also promised that he would "sink this ship in a heartbeat if this gets ugly or mean." But Dreher and many others found the very premise offensive and remained unconvinced. Rejecting out of hand Cornett's claims that his intent is to enlighten Americans, Dreher condemned his claims as "the weasel words of a phony trying to talk himself into taking the money he's being offered to help hold up a desperate Appalachian family to national ridicule." *New York Press* columnist Christopher Caldwell likewise sneered that "underneath his [Cornett's] platitudes it would be hard to express more contempt for the culture he fled."[4]

Yet confirming regional critics worst fears, Caldwell and other media reporters have also used the chance to question the show's motive to trot out demeaning stereotypes largely formed by earlier media depictions of the hillbilly as both monster and dirt-poor fool. For example, Caldwell argued the show could not possibly be realistic for the network would not dare show the mountaineer family as it really would be—rabidly Pentecostal, anti-semitic, violently homophobic, and interested only in sex and drugs. More in keeping with earlier comedic depictions, a story in *E! Online News* called on would-be applicants to "brush your tooth" and warned that "livestock" would not be counted as a member of the multigenerational family. The article also questioned the efficacy of CBS's hotline to field calls from applicants because there is "no word on how many members of the *Deliverance* set have phones."[5]

It is unclear at this point how this story will play out, but angry opposition in Appalachia is growing. While some vow simply not to watch the show or to shoot their television set if it airs, others have picketed the locations in Pikeville and Hazard, Kentucky, where CBS held casting-calls, and the Center for Rural Strategies, a nonprofit rural advocacy group based in Whitesburg, Kentucky, has undertaken a national ad campaign "to shame the network for perpetuating negative rural stereotypes." In response, forty-four members of Congress have signed an open letter to CBS president Leslie Moonves, expressing their "outrage" and demanding that development of "this offensive and distasteful show" be immediately halted. What happens to *The Real Beverly Hillbillies* may well be a bellwether for the mass media hillbilly. If all this pressure from protesters leads CBS to scrap their plans for the show, it may well mark the end of this century-old image. Or, less likely, perhaps the program will defy its critics' expectations and offer a sympathetic and even socially revealing view of both the costs and benefits of rural America's embrace of mainstream modernity, revealing yet again the malleability and continuing relevance of this image. Regardless of what happens to the mass media image, the hillbilly identity, with its multiplicity of racial, economic, gender, and cultural meanings, will undoubtedly live on, offering as it has for well over a century a means through which Americans can position themselves and "others" in a rapidly changing and increasingly diverse society.[6]

notes

JLP	John Lair Papers, Special Collections, Hutchins Library, Berea College, Berea, Kentucky
LAD	*Li'l Abner Dailies*
LGC	Leonard Goldstein Collection, Manuscript Collection 128, Special Collections, Margaret Herrick Library, Academy of Motion Picture Arts and Sciences, Beverly Hills, California
MF	Music Folios, John Edwards Memorial Foundation Collection, Wilson Library, University of North Carolina, Chapel Hill
MGMC	MGM Collection, Special Collections, Cinema-Television Library, Doheny Memorial Library, University of Southern California, Los Angeles
MPAA	Motion Picture Association of America Files, Margaret Herrick Library, Academy of Motion Picture Arts and Sciences, Beverly Hills, California
MPW	*Motion Picture World*
MS	Movie Scripts, Special Collections, Margaret Herrick Library, Academy of Motion Picture Arts and Sciences, Beverly Hills, California
PCA	Production Code Administration Files, Motion Picture Association of America Files, Margaret Herrick Library, Academy of Motion Picture Arts and Sciences, Beverly Hills, California
PF	Production Files, Margaret Herrick Library, Academy of Motion Picture Arts and Sciences, Beverly Hills, California
PTC	Peter Tamony Collection, Western Historical Manuscript Collection, Ellis Library, University of Missouri/State Historical Society of Missouri, Columbia
RBC	Richard Barthelmess Collection, Manuscript Collection 124, Special Collections, Margaret Herrick Library, Academy of Motion Picture Arts and Sciences, Beverly Hills, California
RKO	RKO Collection, Produced Scripts, Collection 003, Theater Arts Library/Special Collections, University Research Library, University of California, Los Angeles
RM	*The Real McCoys*
SFC	Southern Folklife Collection, Wilson Library, University of North Carolina, Chapel Hill
TBS	Turner Broadcasting System
TSS	Television Series Scripts, Theater Arts Library/Special Collections, University Research Library, University of California, Los Angeles

Introduction

1. A note on nomenclature. In recognition of the potentially derogatory nature of the labels I discuss and in order to avoid confusion, in nearly all cases, I will use the labels "hillbilly" and "mountaineer" to refer to the media depictions of the actual inhabitants of the southern mountains. I will refer to the people themselves as "(southern) mountain people," "(southern) mountain folk," or "hill people." The only exception will be when I cite an individual who chooses to describe him- or herself using one of the media labels I analyze.

2. The term is from Williamson, *Hillbillyland: What the Movies Did to the Mountains and What the Mountains Did to the Movies*. Educators, geographers, historians, and politicians have long debated the southern mountain region's exact physical boundaries. Briefly, as defined in this study, "Appalachia" is the mountainous district of the southeastern United States composed of three dominant landforms: the Greater Appalachian Valley, the Blue Ridge Mountains to its east, and the Cumberland Plateau and the Allegheny Mountains to its west. Under the much broader definition provided by the Appalachian Regional Commission (ARC) in 1998, the Appalachian region encompasses all or part of thirteen states and 406 counties, stretching from northeastern Mississippi to southwestern New York. "The Ozarks," consist of the Ouachita Mountains of western Arkansas and eastern Oklahoma, the Boston Mountains of west central Arkansas and the Ozark Plateau of northern Arkansas, southern Missouri, and the northeast corner of Oklahoma. For a more detailed description of the southern Appalachians (defined as "the Southern Highlands") see Campbell, *The Southern Highlander and his Homeland*, 10–18. See also Batteau, *The Invention of Appalachia*, 2–3, and Vance, "The Region: A New Survey," in Ford, *The Southern Appalachian Region—A Survey*, 1–3. On the Ozarks, see Blevins, *Hill Folks: A History of Arkansas Ozarkers and their Image*, 11–14.

3. For an introduction to the denigrating terms for southern poor whites, see Flynt, *Dixie's Forgotten People—The South's Poor Whites*, 8–9, and Charles Reagan Wilson's entry on "Crackers" and F. N. Boney's on "Rednecks" in Wilson and Ferris, eds., *Encyclopedia of Southern Culture*, 1132 and 1140–41, respectively. For a list of such terms for mountain people, see Randolph and Wilson, *Down in the Holler: A Gallery of Ozark Folk Speech*, 252. Patrick Huber has offered the best historical analysis of the evolution of these terms. See his "Rednecks and Woolhats, Hoosiers and Hillbillies: Working-Class Southern Whites, Language, and the Definition of Identity" and "A Short History of Redneck: The Fashioning of a Southern White Masculine Identity." For recent examples of the appropriation of white class slurs, see Wray and Newitz, eds., *White Trash—Race and Class in America*, and Hartigan, *Racial Situations: Class Predicaments of Whiteness in Detroit*.

4. On the social construction of whiteness in the United States and its manifestation in political, economic, and cultural practice, see Roediger, *The Wages of Whiteness: Race and the Making of the American Working Class* and *Towards the Abolition of Whiteness*, Saxton, *The Rise and Fall of the White Republic: Class, Politics and Mass Culture in Nineteenth-Century America*, Ignatiev, *How the Irish Became White*, and Jacobson, *Whiteness of a Different Color: European Immigrants and the Alchemy of Race*. Insightful monographs on white fascination with and attempted appropriation and subjugation of nonwhite culture and identity include Lott, *Love and Theft— Blackface Minstrelsy and the American Working Class*, Pieterse, *White on Black— Images of Africa and Blacks in Western Popular Culture*, Frankenberg, *White Women, Race Matters: The Social Construction of Whiteness*, Hale, *Making Whiteness: The Culture of Segregation in the South, 1890–1940*, and DeLoria, *Playing Indian*. See also Fishkin, "Interrogating 'Whiteness,' Complicating 'Blackness': Remapping American Culture."

5. For characteristic attacks on mass culture, see Bernard Rosenberg, "Mass Cul-

ture in America," in Rosenberg and White, eds., *Mass Culture: The Popular Arts in America*, 3–12, MacDonald, "Masscult and Midcult," and for a more recent example, Bloom, *The Closing of the American Mind*, especially 61–81. On the complexity and significance of popular culture, see Levine, "The Folklore of Industrial Society: Popular Culture and Its Audiences," Schudson, "The New Validation of Popular Culture: Sense and Sentimentality in Academia," and Lipsitz, "'This Ain't No Sideshow': Historians and Media Studies," and "Listening to Learn and Learning to Listen: Popular Culture, Cultural Theory, and American Studies."

6. My work builds on the firm foundation of earlier studies of the national construction of the image of the southern mountains (particularly "Appalachia") and the southern mountaineer. Seminal works include Shapiro, *Appalachia on Our Mind— The Southern Mountains and Mountaineers in the American Consciousness, 1870– 1920*, Williams, "The Southern Mountaineer in Fact and Fiction," Batteau, *The Invention of Appalachia*, Whisnant, *All That Is Native and Fine—The Politics of Culture in an American Region*, and Williamson, *Hillbillyland*. Other helpful scholarship includes McNeil, ed., *Appalachian Images in Folk and Popular Culture*, Becker, *Selling Tradition: Appalachia and the Construction of an American Folk, 1930–1940*, Walle, "Devolution and Evolution: Hillbillies and Cowboys as American Savages," Otto, "'Hillbilly Culture': The Appalachian Mountain Folk in History and Popular Culture," and Blevins, *Hill Folks*.

7. Richard Dyer, "Introduction," in Dyer, ed., *The Matter of Images—Essays on Representations*, 4.

Chapter 1

1. Morgan, *An American Icon—Brother Jonathan and American Identity*, 55–56; ibid., 23 ("mask of foolishness"). On the history of the Yankee, see Rourke, *American Humor: A Study of the National Character*, ch. 1, Blair, *Native American Humor*, 17–62, Blair and Hill, *America's Humor: From Poor Richard to Doonesbury*, 165–71, 180–86, and Bronner, *Old-Time Music Makers of New York State*, 57–59.

2. Morgan offers a careful study of the meanings and transformations of the Brother Jonathan figure. Johns's *American Genre Painting: The Politics of Everyday Life*, chs. 1–2, provides useful insights into the process of "typing" and the meaning of Yankee in the Jacksonian era.

3. Byrd actually wrote three accounts of this journey: a diary he wrote while on the expedition; a later so-called "secret history," which he wrote for the private amusement of his circle of Virginia friends; and a much expanded "official" text, intended for publication and broad circulation. Although written shortly after his completion of the survey, the "official" *History of the Dividing Line* was not published until 1841 and the "unofficial" *Secret History of the Dividing Line* did not appear in print until 1929. Both versions are presented side-by-side in *William Byrd's Histories of the Dividing Line Betwixt Virginia and North Carolina*. For a general discussion of Byrd and his account, see the introductions in this book by Adams and Boyd, v–xxii and xxiii–xxxix, respectively. See also Lynn, *Mark Twain and Southwestern Humor*, 3–22;

McIlwaine, *The Southern Poor-White—From Lubberland to Tobacco Road*, 3–15. On Byrd's comparison of Indians and frontier settlers, see Slotkin, *Regeneration through Violence—The Mythology of the American Frontier, 1600–1860*, 215–22.

4. *Histories of the Dividing Line*, 90–92. Interestingly, this passage does not appear in the *Secret History* version. Apparently, unlike his descriptions of sexual acts and joking asides about the physical attributes of the expedition party that he omitted from the official version, Byrd did not worry that his intended audience of colonial and European elites would find his description of the people of the North Carolina backwoods in the least bit offensive. Lynn even suggests that he used such characterizations to replace derogatory remarks about Virginians in the "secret history." See Lynn, *Mark Twain*, 14.

5. Charles Woodmason, *The Carolina Backcountry on the Eve of Revolution: The Journal and Other Writings of Charles Woodmason, Anglican Itinerant*, ed. Richard J. Hooker (Chapel Hill: University of North Carolina Press, 1953), 52, cited in Huber, "Rednecks and Woolhats, Hoosiers and Hillbillies: Working-Class Southern Whites, Language, and the Definition of Identity," 65–66.

6. "The Carolina Sand-Hillers." This story was evidently a reprint from the *Louisville (Ky.) Examiner*. I thank Joe Bauman for sharing a copy of this article with me. McIlwaine argues that such abolition-motivated portrayals of the plight of poor whites were common in antebellum northern periodicals and literature. See McIlwaine, *Southern Poor-White*, 32–39. For a thorough review of the southern poor white in literature and nonfiction accounts, see also McIlwaine; Cook, *From Tobacco Road to Route 66—The Southern Poor White in Fiction*, 3–4, and Huber, "Rednecks and Woolhats." Fascinating but dated accounts of the history and social status of this group include Buck, "The Poor Whites of the Ante-Bellum South," 41–54, and Hollander, "The Tradition of 'Poor Whites'." For more contemporary scholarship, see Newby, *Plain Folk in the New South—Social Change and Cultural Persistence 1880–1915*, Flynt, *Poor but Proud: Alabama's Poor Whites*, Jones, *The Dispossessed: America's Underclasses from the Civil War to the Present*, and Foley, *The White Scourge: Mexicans, Blacks, and Poor Whites in Texas Cotton Culture*.

7. Huber, "Rednecks and Woolhats," 68–71, 76–79; D. R. Hundley, *Social Relations in Our Southern States* (New York: 1860), 263–65, cited in Buck, "Poor Whites," 43, 45.

8. Boston *Daily Advertiser* correspondent quoted in *The Congressional Globe*, 39th Congress, 1st session (Washington D.C.: F & J Rives, 1866), 552, cited in Huber, "Rednecks and Woolhats," 76. For a wide variety of examples of nineteenth-century condemnations of "poor whites" and articulations of their separate racial status, see Huber, "Rednecks and Woolhats," 75–78, 88–91 and passim ch. 3.

9. Ibid., 91–92; Genovese, "'Rather Be a Nigger Than a Poor White Man': Slave Perceptions of Southern Yeomen and Poor Whites."

10. McIlwaine, *Southern Poor-White*, 48–50, 57–58; Cook, *From Tobacco Road to Route 66*, 6–7; Lynn, *Mark Twain*, 70–72, 77–78; Slotkin, *Regeneration through Violence*, 416–17 (literary analysis); Williamson, *Hillbillyland—What the Movies Did to the Mountains and What the Mountains Did to the Movies*, 34–35. Cohen and

Dillingham, eds., *Humor of the Old Southwest*, is a compendium of literary excerpts and useful biographical sketches.

11. Harris, *Sut Lovingood: Yarns Spun by a "Nat'ral Born Durn'd Fool,"* 24. See also Rickels, *George Washington Harris*, and Blair and Hill, *America's Humor*, 213–21. Williamson suggests that Lovingood should be seen not only as a hillbilly progenitor but also as part of the European tradition stretching back at least to the Medieval Ages of the fool with jackass ears and cockscomb, who holds up a mirror to reveal the vanity and hypocrisy of those in power. See Williamson, *Hillbillyland*, 21–27, 33–34.

12. On Harris's life and politics, see Rickels, *George Washington Harris*, 31–36, Lynn, *Mark Twain*, 131–32, and Day, "The Life of George Washington Harris"; Twain's review is cited in Caron and Inge, *Sut Lovingood's Nat'ral Born Yarnspinner*, 79. Edmund Wilson, Harris's most famous detractor, argued almost one hundred years after Twain in *Patriotic Gore* (1962) that Sut was nothing more than "a peasant squatting in his own filth" and that the collection of his stories was "the most repellent book of any literary merit in American literature." See republication of his review in Caron and Inge, *Sut Lovingood's*, 101, 100.

13. In sharp contrast, after World War II, illustrators consistently portrayed Sut as a stereotypical mountaineer, either a cartoon hillbilly or a strong and self-assured mountain man. My analysis of Sut's graphic depictors draws significantly on Inge's article "Sut and his Illustrators," which includes copies of all the illustrations discussed above.

14. *Virginia Gazette* (Richmond), November 11, 1780, cited in Hsiung, *Two Worlds in the Tennessee Mountains: Exploring the Origins of Appalachian Stereotypes*, 20.

15. Slotkin, *Regeneration through Violence*, 269. For a fascinating and detailed account of the historical development of the Boone myth, see Slotkin, especially chs. 9–10, 12–13. See also Faragher, *Daniel Boone: The Life and Legend of an American Pioneer*.

16. See Williamson, *Hillbillyland*, 278–79, 280; Hauck, "A Davy Crockett Filmography," 122–23. Popularly remembered as a "mountain man," in reality Crockett grew up in and represented south-central Tennessee, far from the Cumberlands or the Great Smoky Mountains to the east. On the life of David Crockett see Shackford, *Davy Crockett—The Man and the Legend*, and Williamson, *Hillbillyland*, 78–82. On cultural uses of the Crockett myth, see Hewitt, *Theatre USA—1668 to 1957*, 223–26, Lofaro, ed., *Davy Crockett*, and Lofaro and Cummings, eds., *Crockett at Two Hundred: New Perspectives on the Man and the Myth*.

17. Crockett's travels are discussed in Shackford, *Davy Crockett*, 212–13, Boone's in Faragher, *Daniel Boone*, ch. 8.

18. Examples of these early-nineteenth-century travelogues include James Kirke Paulding, *Letters from the South: Written during an Excursion in the Summer of 1816* (New York: James Eastburn & Company, 1817), Charles Fenno Hoffman, *A Winter in the West* (New York: Harper & Brothers, 1835), and Charles Lanman, *Letters from the Allegheny Mountains* (New York: G. P. Putnam's Sons, 1849), cited in Batteau, *Invention of Appalachia*, 30–32; Strother, "A Winter in the South," v. 16, 175–76. For background on Strother and his 1857 travels, see Eby, Jr., *"Porte Crayon": The Life of David Hunter Strother*, especially 93–94, and Hsiung, *Two Worlds*, 163–73.

19. Olmsted, *A Journey in the Back Country*, 275–78.

20. Batteau, *Invention of Appalachia*, 16–17, and Inscoe, "Olmsted in Appalachia: A Connecticut Yankee Encounters Slavery and Racism in the Southern Highlands, 1854."

21. Schoolcraft, *Scenes and Adventures in the Semi-Alpine Region of the Ozark Mountains of Missouri and Arkansas*, 235. Although this work was not printed until the 1850s, Schoolcraft had published parts of this work in 1819 and 1821. See Masterson, *Tall Tales of Arkansaw* (Boston: Chapman & Grimes Publishers, 1942), reprinted as *Arkansas Folklore—the Arkansas Traveller, Davey Crockett, and Other Legends*, 2, 306.

22. George William Featherstonhaugh, *Excursion through the Slave States from Washington on the Potomac, to the Frontier of Mexico* (New York, 1844), 87–88, cited in Williams, "The Bear State Image: Arkansas in the Nineteenth Century," 103; Frederick Gerstaecker, *Wild Sports in the Far West* (London: 1855); Charles Fenton Mercer Noland, *Pete Whetstone of Devil's Fork: Letters to the Spirit of the Times*, edited by Ted R. Worley and Eugene A. Nolte (Van Buren, Arkansas: 1957), and Thomas Bangs Thorpe, "The Big Bear of Arkansas," in William T. Porter, ed., *The Big Bear of Arkansas and Other Sketches, Illustrative of Characters and Incidents in the South and Southwest* (Philadelphia, 1845), 13–31. For a more detailed discussion, see Williams, "The Bear State Image," 103–5.

23. For a history of the contested usage of the term "Arkansas Traveller," see Masterson, *Arkansas Folklore*, 123–25, and Lancaster, "Bare Feet and Slow Trains," 90. On counterreactions to the state's negative image, see also Lancaster, 34–37, 98–101, Dale, "Arkansas: The Myth and the State," Dew, "'On a Slow Train through Arkansaw'—The Negative Image of Arkansas in the Early Twentieth Century," and Williams, "The Bear State Image," 99–111. I thank Jerry Williamson for bringing Lancaster's article to my attention.

24. Masterson notes twelve versions of the story and argues that Faulkner's is the oldest known example and thus, the most likely original form. See Masterson, *Arkansas Folklore*, 186–219. However, the image may have an even earlier origin. In a travel account of 1833 published in 1836, the writer describes his encounter with the owner of a small log house in the "fine, rolling, upland country" of the Ozarks. The settler "was sitting in front, dressed throughout in leather, and playing lustily on the fiddle." Unlike the squatter in the "Arkansas Traveller," the man is not dirty and surly, but a cheerful and stalwart frontiersman very much in the mold of Davy Crockett and with comparable physical prowess: "[t]all and athletic [he] combined the activity of the panther, the strength of the lion, with much of the silent, quick, and stealthy movements of the Indian." See "Letters from Arkansas," 25–26.

25. Brown, *"The Arkansas Traveller*: Southwest Humor on Canvas," 348–50, 372–73. This dialogue is a reprint of the text first published in 1859 by Edward Washbourne to accompany the "Arkansas Traveller" print by Leopold Grozelier. On the origins of the tale, also see Green, "Graphics #67: The Visual Arkansas Traveller," McNeil, "'By the Ozark Trail': The Image of the Ozarks in Popular and Folk Songs," and Mercer, "On the Track of 'the Arkansas Traveller,'" 709–11.

26. Masterson, *Arkansas Folklore*, 186. This 1876 version was based on a copy published in Little Rock of an antebellum (c. 1858–1860) original.

27. Brown, *"The Arkansas Traveller,"* 370.

28. The 1896 rendition begins: "The sun is setting over the plains. A belated horseman in coonskin cap, and well belted with pistol and bowie knife, rides up to a squatter cabin to ask a night's lodging. By the door of a rotting shanty sits a ragged man astride a barrel, slowly scraping out the notes you hear. There are children in the background and a slatternly woman stands on the threshold." See Mercer, "On the Track of 'the Arkansas Traveller,'" 707.

29. On the rise of the "new magazines" see Shapiro, *Appalachia on Our Mind— The Southern Mountains and Mountaineers in the American Consciousness, 1870–1920*, 6–7, Schneirov, *The Dream of a New Social Order—Popular Magazines in America, 1893–1914*, and Wilson, "The Rhetoric of Consumption: Mass-Market Magazines and the Demise of the Gentle Reader"; Shapiro, *Appalachia on Our Mind*, 4.

30. The term "local color movement" was a product of later writers and literary critics who saw in these disparate writings a unified body of literature, artistically limited, but nonetheless important to the development of turn-of-the-century realist literature and the establishment of a pluralistic national vision. For a detailed discussion of the significance of local color literature for Appalachia, see Shapiro, *Appalachia on Our Mind*, xiii–xiv, 3–18, and Williams, "The Southern Mountaineer in Fact and Fiction," 117–28. For examples of the genre, see Warfel and Orians, eds., *American Local-Color Stories*.

31. Shapiro, *Appalachia on Our Mind*, 18; Harney, "A Strange Land and a Peculiar People," 45–58.

32. For interpretations that challenge the realism of Murfree's portrayals, see Batteau, *Invention of Appalachia*, 39–41, Hsuing, *Two Worlds*, 179–82, Shapiro, *Appalachia on Our Mind*, 19, and Williams, "Southern Mountaineer," ch. 4. For a contrasting view, see Durwood Dunn, "Mary Noailles Murfree: A Reappraisal," 197–204. Regardless of the authenticity of her descriptions, Murfree's works were so popular that *In the Tennessee Mountains* was republished twenty-four times between 1884 and 1922. See Hsuing, *Two Worlds*, 176, and Shapiro, *Appalachia on Our Mind*, 19.

33. Allen, "Through Cumberland Gap on Horseback," 62; Harney, "Strange Land," 48, and Semple, "The Anglo-Saxons of the Kentucky Mountains: A Study in Anthropogeography," 151.

34. Allen, 55–56. Mountain folk were not the only social group that Kemble stereotyped. A leading political cartoonist from 1880 to the early 1930s for such magazines as *Collier's*, *Harper's*, *Leslie's Weekly*, and *Life*, as well as the illustrator of the inaugural edition of *Huckleberry Finn*, Kemble is best known as a delineator of African Americans. The titles of some of his collections such as *Kemble's Coons* and *A Pickaninny Calendar* indicate that these drawings were as broadly (and crudely) stereotyped as were his depictions of mountaineers. See "Edward Winsor Kemble," in Horn, ed., *The World Encyclopedia of Cartoons* v. 1: 332–33; and Holt, "*A Coon Alphabet* and the Comic Mask of Racial Prejudice," 307–18.

35. Warner, "Comments on Kentucky," 271. On depictions of mountain women in local color literature, see Shapiro, *Appalachia on Our Mind*, 22–26; Batteau, *Invention of Appalachia*, 49–56; Williams, "Southern Mountaineer," 153 and ch. 5 passim; and Miller, "The Mountain Woman in Fact and Fiction of the Early Twentieth Century."

36. Miller, *Revenuers and Moonshiners—Enforcing Federal Liquor Law in the Mountain South, 1865–1900*, and Holmes, "Moonshining and Collective Violence: Georgia, 1889–1895," 589–611.

37. The national press focused on the mountain region, despite the fact that nearly half of the forty-one Kentucky feuds reported in the *Louisville Courier-Journal* between 1874 and 1895 were outside the eastern mountain counties. See Waller, "Feuding in Appalachia—Evolution of a Cultural Stereotype," 354.

38. *Baltimore Sun* editorial quoted in Ashworth, "The Virginia Mountaineers," 188.

39. Waller, "Feuding," 347–76, and *Feud—Hatfields, McCoys, and Social Change in Appalachia—1860–1900*; Klotter, "Feuds in Appalachia: An Overview," 290–317, and McKinney, "Industrialization and Violence in Appalachia in the 1890's." Pearce, *Days of Darkness: The Feuds of Eastern Kentucky*, offers a popularized overview.

40. Crawford, *An American Vendetta: A Story of Barbarism in the United States*, 9. As Waller expounds in *Feud*, the two sides were divided far more along economic than kin lines—in a battle between market-oriented and traditionally-oriented forces. William Anderson ("Devil Anse") Hatfield and his associates were completely integrated into the expanding regional and national economy and both sides worked within the judicial system and the letter of the law as they perceived it to be. Furthermore, a variety of entrepreneurs in eastern Kentucky exploited the case in order to advance their economic interests by presenting Kentucky (where the McCoys resided) as a defender of law and order against "Devil Anse" Hatfield and his lawless backwoodsmen of West Virginia. On Crawford's negative preconceptions of the mountain folk that skewed his account, see Waller, *Feud*, 222–28.

41. Crawford, *Vendetta*, 8. Photographs of Hatfield in MacClintock, "The Kentucky Mountains and Their Feuds," 181; Williamson, *Hillbillyland*, 270–71.

42. On the enormous influence of John Fox, Jr., in shaping conceptions of the southern mountain people see Shapiro, *Appalachia on Our Mind*, 210–14; Waller, "Feuding," 362–63; Batteau, *Invention of Appalachia*, 64–74, 84–85; Titus, *John Fox, Jr.*, and Wilson, "The Felicitous Convergence of Mythmaking and Capital Accumulation: John Fox Jr. and the Formation of An(Other) Almost-White American Underclass."

43. Vincent, "A Retarded Frontier," 1; ibid., 15–16, 19; Warner, "Comments on Kentucky," 270.

44. Lynde, "The Moonshiner of Fact," 76–78.

45. Davis, "The 'Mountain Whites' of America," 426 ("moral looseness"); Wilds, "The Mountain Whites of the South," 921; Darlene Wilson, "Mythmaking and Capital Accumulation," 24–25 (Berea students' reaction to Fox). According to Darlene Wilson, Fox was also a great favorite of such highly influential men as Owen Wister,

Henry Cabot Lodge, and Theodore Roosevelt, who all shared his view of the mountaineers as the last frontiersmen. For early-twentieth-century examples of native mountaineer critiques of this stereotype, see Ashworth, "The Virginia Mountaineers," 196, and Johnson, "Life in the Kentucky Mountains. By a Mountaineer."

46. Berea College president William Goodell Frost's "Our Contemporary Ancestors in the Southern Mountains" of 1899 was the work that first named the land and people of the southern mountains "Appalachian America." Over the next two decades, educators, benevolence workers, social scientists, and nonfiction writers solidified the conception of Appalachia as a unique and distinct social and cultural entity. Among the most important of these writings were Semple, "The Anglo-Saxons of the Kentucky Mountains," Miles, *The Spirit of the Mountains*, Kephart, *Our Southern Highlanders—A Narrative of Adventure in the Southern Appalachians and a Study of Life among the Mountaineers*, and Campbell, *The Southern Highlander and His Homeland*.

47. Batteau, *Invention of Appalachia*, 63 ("Darkest Appalachia"). For overviews of early-twentieth-century nativism, see Higham, *Strangers in the Land—Patterns of American Nativism, 1860–1925*, chs. 4–7 passim, and Archdeacon, *Becoming American—An Ethnic History*, chs. 5–6. General overviews of Progressivism include Robert H. Weibe, *The Search for Order, 1877–1920*, Rodgers, "In Search of Progressivism," and Paul Boyer, *Urban Masses and Moral Order in America, 1820–1920*, pt. 4.

48. Semple, "The Anglo-Saxons of the Kentucky Mountains," 150; Wilson, *The Southern Mountaineers*, 161. Similarly, William Frost stressed in 1899 that while American families of the "more elegant circles" have "ceased to be prolific," men and women in the mountains were "still rearing vigorous children in numbers that would satisfy the patriarchs." "The possible value of such a population," he concludes, "is sufficiently evident." See Frost, "Our Contemporary Ancestors," 105.

49. "Poor White Trash," 579; John Fiske, *Old Virginia and Her Neighbors* (Boston: Houghton, Mifflin and Company, 1897), 2: 319–21, quoted in Shapiro, *Appalachia on Our Mind*, 94. For more on Fiske's significance, see also Shapiro, 92–98.

50. Johnston, "Romance and Tragedy of Kentucky Feuds," 111.

51. Klotter, "The Black South and White Appalachia," 62. On the historical development of the label "mountain white," see Klotter, "Black South," 54, 59–60, and Shapiro, *Appalachia on Our Mind*, 51–54.

52. William Goodell Frost, "New England in Kentucky," *Advance* (June 6, 1895): 1285, cited in Klotter, "Black South," 59.

53. Davis, "The 'Mountain Whites' of America," 423. Even though Davis condemns the degeneracy of "mountain whites," like Frost, she extols their faith and presents their potential as a religious bulwark in almost apocalyptic terms: "Who knows whether these people be not a reserve force that God will bring out of these mountains, saved by Christ, for the coming crisis of conflict, a stalwart band to stand with us in defense of Protestantism." See ibid., 423; Campbell, "Classification of Mountain Whites," 2.

54. Samuel Wilson, "The Southern Mountaineers," 24–25. Because this book was

first published in 1906, it is likely that Wilson repudiated the label as early as this date; ibid., 43.

55. Shapiro, *Appalachia on Our Mind*, 91.

Chapter 2

1. Cited in Ross, *Working-Class Hollywood: Silent Film and the Shaping of Class in America*, 45.

2. Green, "Hillbilly Music: Source and Symbol," 204. Green notes that "hill-folk" dates from the late seventeenth century and referred to Cameronian opponents of Charles II who fled first to the Scottish highlands and then to the American uplands. The term was thus one of reproach and social resistance that mirrored the later complex cultural meanings of "hillbilly." See also Huber, "Rednecks and Woolhats, Hoosiers and Hillbillies: Working-Class Southern Whites, Language, and the Definition of Identity," 103, Green, "Hillbilly Music," 204, and Otto, "Plain Folk, Lost Frontiersmen, and Hillbillies: The Southern Mountain Folk in History and Popular Culture"; Harben's novel is cited in Craigie and Hulbert, eds., *A Dictionary of American English—On Historical Principles*, v. 2: 1248.

3. Lovinggood, "Negro Seer: His Preparation and Mission," 163. A similar example of the use of "hillbilly" in African-American vernacular is the folk rhyme "I Would Rather Be a Negro Than a Poor White Man" that includes the verse "I'd druther be a Nigger, an' plow old Beck / Dan a white Hill Billy wid his long red neck." In Thomas W. Talley, *Negro Folk Rhymes* (New York: Macmillan, 1922), 42–43, cited in Folder: "Hillbilly Culture and Image," Box 3, AGP.

4. *Blue Ridge Country* (November/December 1992), 51 ('Camp Hillbilly' photograph). According to the magazine's following edition, the photograph is of men and women from Lewisburg, West Virginia, camping in the mountains of Greenbrier County, West Virginia. I thank Jerry Williamson for sharing this image with me.

5. Hawthorne, "Mountain Votes Spoil Huntington's Revenge," 2.

6. Hibler's text is cited in Masterson, *Arkansas Folklore—The Arkansas Traveller, Davey Crockett, and Other Legends*, 274–75; ibid., 275–76; For an overview of the "slow-train" genre see Masterson, *Arkansas Folklore*, 269–80 and W. K. McNeil's introduction to Jackson, *On a Slow Train through Arkansaw*, 11–13.

7. McNeil, Introduction to *Slow Train*, x-xi, 3, 7; Dew, "'On a Slow Train through Arkansaw'—The Negative Image of Arkansas in the Early Twentieth Century," 125–35, and Lancaster, "Bare Feet and Slow Trains," 39–41. On comparable constructions of African-American stereotypes, see Toll, *Blacking Up—the Minstrel Show in Nineteenth Century America*, Lott, *Love and Theft—Blackface Minstrelsy and the American Working Class*, and Hale, *Making Whiteness—The Culture of Segregation in the South, 1890–1940*, especially 151–68.

8. Masterson, *Arkansas Folklore*, 96; Hughes, *Three Years in Arkansaw*, 24–29; ibid., 14. One need only recall the infamous male rape scene from the 1972 film *Deliverance*, in which the mountaineer rapist demands that his victim "squeal like a pig,"

to recognize the power and longevity of this connection between hill people and sexual relations with swine.

9. Hughes, *Three Years in Arkansaw*, 8, 73, 79; ibid., 90–91.

10. Ibid., 76.

11. Ibid., 112–13; Masterson, *Arkansas Folklore*, 104.

12. Carr, "A List of Words from Northwest Arkansas," 416, 418 (italics in the original); *A Dictionary of American English*, 1248; Wentworth, *American Dialect Dictionary*, 292; Cassidy, ed., *Dictionary of American Regional English* v. 2, 1010.

13. On the turn-of-the-century economic transformation of Appalachia, see Eller, *Miners, Millhands and Mountaineers: The Modernization of the Appalachian South, 1880–1930*, and Hall et al., *Like a Family: The Making of a Southern Cotton Mill World*. On the criticism and defense of company towns and textile factories, see Shapiro, *Appalachia on Our Mind—The Southern Mountains and Mountaineers in the American Consciousness, 1870–1920*, 163–85, and Hall et al., *Like a Family*, 56–60. Representative contemporary examples critiquing and defending, respectively, the changes wrought by the cotton mills are Campbell, "From Mountain Cabin to Cotton Mill," 74–84, and Harriman, "Some Phases of the Southern Cotton Industry," 12.

14. Huber, "Rednecks and Woolhats," 115–19 (use of "redneck"). On the highly racialized political and social climate of turn-of-the-century America, see Kantrowitz, *Ben Tillman & the Reconstruction of White Supremacy*, ch. 6 and passim, Jacobsen, *Whiteness of a Different Color—European Immigrants and the Alchemy of Race*, ch. 2, and Hale, *Making Whiteness*. Regarding the potential relation between "hillbilly" and the reestablishment of white supremacy, it is worth noting that in his 1900 article discussed in n. 5, Hawthorne explicitly juxtaposes the voting power of "hillbillies" with the disenfranchisement of Georgian blacks.

15. Rose O'Neill, a native of Taney County, Missouri, in the heart of the Ozarks, told Randolph that she did not hear the term until after 1900, and a newspaperman in Mountain Home, Arkansas, claimed he never heard the term until 1906. See Randolph and Wilson, *Down in the Holler—A Gallery of Ozark Folk Speech*, 252. The term is also absent from an 1897 compendium of American argot, Barrere and Leland's *A Dictionary of Slang, Jargon and Cant*.

16. Audience-size estimation is from Koszarski, *An Evening's Entertainment: The Age of the Silent Feature Picture 1915–1928*, 25–26. Koszarski notes that due to the lack of records, paid admissions prior to 1922 cannot be reliably determined; Williamson, *Southern Mountaineers in Silent Films: Plot Synopses of Movies about Moonshining, Feuding, and Other Mountain Topics, 1904–1929*, 2; *Biograph Bulletins 1896–1908*, 229 ("most widely known . . ."); Williamson, *Southern Mountaineers*, 3–4. Although Williamson includes a number of categories (such as historical figures and coal mining) that are outside the purview of my more limited definition of hillbilly, even if one excludes one or more of these categories, the number of mountaineer films produced in these years is astonishing.

17. Williamson, *Southern Mountaineers*, 7–8. Williamson argues that his tally may even be low, given the motion picture trade papers' vague generalizations in their film synopses. See also his "Southern Mountaineers Filmography." For general in-

troductions to silent film of this era, see May, *Screening Out the Past—The Birth of Mass Culture and the Motion Picture Industry*, especially ch. 6, Ross, *Working-Class Hollywood*, 11–33, Everson, *American Silent Film*, and Koszarki, *An Evening's Entertainment*.

18. Williamson, *Southern Mountaineers*, 7–8.

19. Williamson counts eleven murders and over sixty-five assaults committed by women in the 476 films he studied. See Williamson, *Southern Mountaineers*, 7; *Biograph Bulletins 1908–1912*, 145 (*The Mountaineer's Honor*); As Williamson astutely argues, most "hillbilly gal silents . . . ended in traditional matri*money* [sic], with the former gals becoming 'ladies' because they accepted the weaker role and financial dependency." See Williamson, *Hillbillyland—What the Movies Did to the Mountains and What the Mountains Did to the Movies*, 234.

20. Discussions of the potentially transgressive nature of audience interpretations of media include Radway, *Reading the Romance—Women, Patriarchy and Popular Literature*, Jenkins, *Textual Poachers—Television Fans and Participatory Culture*, Fiske, *Reading the Popular*, and Levine, "The Folklore of Industrial Society: Popular Culture and Its Audiences." Two readings of the transgressive possibilities of early silent films are Hansen, *Babel and Babylon: Spectatorship in American Silent Film*, and Ross, "The Revolt of the Audience: Reconsidering Audiences and Reception during the Silent Era."

21. *Good Housekeeping* article quoted in Nye, *The Unembarrassed Muse—The Popular Arts in America*, 373. On film censorship efforts in this era, see ibid., 372–74, May, *Screening Out the Past*, 43–59, Grieveson, "Why the Audience Mattered in Chicago in 1907," 79–91, Ross, *Working-Class Hollywood*, 27–33, and Koszarki, *An Evening's Entertainment*, 198–210.

22. *Motion Picture World* 46:6 (October 9, 1920), cited in Williamson, *Southern Mountaineers*, 7.

23. On Griffith's racist portrayal of nonwhite characters, see Daniel Bernardi, "The Voice of Whiteness: D. W. Griffith's Biograph Films (1908–1913)," 104; ibid., 111–13. On Griffith's films, more generally, see Simmon, *The Films of D. W. Griffith*. Griffith's mountaineer films for Biograph (American Mutoscope and Biograph Company) are *The Feud and the Turkey: A Romance of the Kentucky Mountains* (1908), *The Mountaineer's Honor* (1909), *The Fugitive* (1910), *The Revenue Man and His Girl* (1911), *Love in the Hills* (1911), and *A Feud in the Kentucky Hills* (1912). In addition, Biograph released a number of mountain films prior to Griffith's arrival, including *The Moonshiners* (1904), *A Kentucky Feud* (1905), and *A Night of Terror* (1908). See Williamson, "Southern Mountaineers Filmography," *Biograph Bulletins 1896–1908*, 114–16, 228–29, 352–53, 410, and *Biograph Bulletins 1908–1912*, 145, 337, 347.

24. *Higginses vs. Judsons* (Lubin, 1911); *Secret Service Snitz* (Sterling, 1914); Arbuckle and Keaton starred in *Moonshine* (Paramount, 1918), Lloyd in *An Ozark Romance* (Pathe/Rolin, 1918). See Williamson, *Hillbillyland*, 38–39, 269–71; Williamson, "Southern Mountaineers Filmography."

25. On the multiple forms of similar racial stereotypes, see Toll, *Blacking Up*, Lott, *Love and Theft*, Curtis, *Apes and Angels: The Irishman in Victorian Caricature*. For a

thoughtful discussion of the power and malleability of racist stereotypes (in particular, simian portrayals of Japanese during World War II), see Dower, *War without Mercy—Race and Power in the Pacific War*, 302.

26. Williamson, *Southern Mountaineers*, 10, 2.

27. On changes in the film industry, see May, *Screening*, 62–66, 167–69, Williamson, *Southern Mountaineers*, 9–10, Ross, *Working-Class Hollywood*, 118–23; *A Moonshine Feud* (c. 1919), FTA.

28. S. T. Wilson, *The Southern Mountaineers*, 188; Deal, "'The Hill Billy' or 'American Mountaineer' . . . ," 1, 11, 4; None of arguably the three most influential nonfiction works on southern Appalachia written prior to 1920 include the term: Campbell's *The Southern Highlander and His Homeland*, Kephart's *Our Southern Highlanders*, or Miles's *The Spirit of the Mountains*.

29. It is interesting to speculate why the one pre–World War I film to use the term "hillbilly" had an Ozarks setting. Does this suggest that well-known satirical writings about this region made the term acceptable for Arkansas and Missouri mountain locales but not yet for the more romanticized and mythologized southern Appalachia? Such a connection between humorous literary accounts and Ozarks settings might indicate an essential comic component, however remote from the storyline, that was always inherent in the term "hillbilly" and its use.

30. Bradley, "Hobnobbing with Hillbillies," 95.

31. Ibid., 103.

32. Ibid., 100.

33. *The Hillbilly*, December 1914, no. 2, 1; ibid., January 1915, no. 3, 19–20.

34. Since the collection of this publication that I viewed was not a complete run, it is possible that the inaugural issue discussed the title's significance and that the hillbilly stereotype appeared prior to 1939; but it was not featured before 1935.

Chapter 3

1. Malone, *Singing Cowboys and Musical Mountaineers: Southern Culture and the Roots of Country Music*, 2, and Malone, *Don't Get above Your Raisin': Country Music and the Southern Working Class*, 16–22.

2. Country performers blended commercial musical products so seamlessly into their own work that the urban origins of such "folk" songs as Maybelle Carter's "Wildwood Flower" or Bradley Kincaid's "The Fatal Wedding" were often later forgotten. On the precommercial history of country music see Malone, *Singing Cowboys*, chs. 1–2, and *Country Music, USA*, ch. 1, Wiggins, *Fiddlin' Georgia Crazy—Fiddlin' John Carson, His Real World, and the World of His Songs*, ch. 1, Bronner, *Old-Time Music Makers of New York State*, 5–14 and passim, and Wilgus, "An Introduction to the Study of Hillbilly Music," 195–203.

3. Radio statistics from Malone, *Country Music*, 32, and Douglas, "Radio and Television," 903–4. On social and cultural changes of the 1920s, see Archdeacon, *Becoming American—An Ethnic History*, chs. 5–6, and Dumenil, *The Modern Temper—American Culture and Society in the 1920s*, especially ch. 4.

4. The first blues song Okeh recorded was Mamie Smith's "Crazy Blues" in February 1920. Peer first heard the term "race" used self-referentially by African Americans in Richmond, Virginia. See Porterfield, "Mr. Victor and Mr. Peer," 12; Malone, *Country Music*, 34–35; Crichton, "Thar's Gold in Them Hillbillies," 24. Although Peer deserves credit for conducting the first field recordings of this music, the first commercially recorded country music was made by southwestern fiddlers Eck Robertson and Henry Gilliland who came to New York in 1922 on their own initiative and asked the Victor Talking Machine Company to record their songs. The few sides they recorded sold well, but Victor failed to show much interest in such "base" folk music. See Porterfield, "Mr. Victor and Mr. Peer," 6–7, Malone, *Country Music*, 39–40, and Cohen, "Early Pioneers," 11–13.

5. On Peer's recording of Carson, see Crichton, "Thar's Gold," 24, and Green, "Hillbilly Music: Source and Symbol," 207–10. Some country music scholars argue that Carson was always scheduled to perform, and that Peer's role in the "launching" of commercial country music was less central than that of Polk Brockman, Okeh's Atlanta regional distributor, who recruited the musical groups to be recorded. Scholars also question whether Peer's words referred to the music itself or to the quality of the recording. See Peterson, *Creating Country Music: Fabricating Authenticity*, 17–20. Still, Peer's reaction to Carson's performance is strikingly similar to his view of Mamie Smith's first recording, which he later called "The most awful record ever made" but then quickly added "and it sold over a million copies." See Crichton, "Thar's Gold," 24.

6. Peer's quotation from a 1959 interview with Lillian Borgeson, cited in Peterson, *Creating*, 47. On Peer's role in recording early country musicians, see Porterfield, "Mr. Victor and Mr. Peer," 15–21, Green, "Hillbilly Music," 206–15, and Wolfe, "The Legend That Peer Built—Reappraising the Bristol Sessions," 3–5.

7. Folder: Catalogs and Promotional materials for Columbia, Vocalion, Victor, and Okeh records, JEMFC; Pugh, "Country Music Is Here to Stay?," 34; Pugh, research notes, in author's possession; Green, "Hillbilly Music," 221. I thank Mr. Pugh for generously sharing his notes for his at the time still-forthcoming article.

8. See Columbia Records catalog, September 1927, 9–10, in Folder: Columbia Record Catalogs, 1925, JEMFC; Porterfield, "Mr. Victor and Mr. Peer," 12 ("I invented . . ."). Except for DeFord Bailey, a black harmonica player who was one of the major attractions of the *Grand Ole Opry* between 1925 and 1941, no African-American performer gained a national reputation as a country performer until Charley Pride broke the unofficial color barrier in 1965. For a fuller account of Bailey's mixed experience on the program, see Morton and Wolfe, "DeFord Bailey: They Turned Me Loose to Root Hog or Die," 13–17.

9. Peterson, *Creating*, 249 n. 8 (dialect routines); J. E. Mainer and his Mountaineers were still performing their skit "Sambo and Liza" in 1965. See Daniel, "The National Barn Dance on Network Radio: The 1930s," 56, and Malone, *Country Music*, 8. On blackface comedians in country music, see Green, *Country Roots—The Origins of Country Music*, 71–78; Jordan, "Slo 'n' Easy Start Weakly Bull-A-Thon," 6; Wolfe, *A Good Natured Riot: The Birth of the Grand Ole Opry*, 225–30 ("Lasses & Honey").

10. Malone, *Country Music*, 4–5; Wolfe, "The White Man's Blues, 1922–40," 38–44. The brothers later dropped their lawsuit and signed with Victor Records, a rival label more interested in recording "white man's blues."

11. "Blue Bird—The World's Finest Low-Priced Hill Billy and Race Records" (October 1937), PTC. The Conqueror (Sears Roebuck) label offered a selection of "Cowboy, Race and Hill Country Records" (Fall 1941), King Records listed "Hillbilly, Novelty, Sepia, Blues" (July 1948), and Okeh Records advertised "Novelty Dance, Country Dance, Folk Song & Race" music (Oct. 1940). See Pugh, research notes, and Pugh, "Country Music," 38; Crichton, "Thar's Gold," 24.

12. Daniel, *Pickin' on Peachtree—A History of Country Music in Atlanta, Georgia*, 30 (farcical names); Campbell, "Fiddlers and Divas: Music and Culture in New South Atlanta, 1910–1925" (mocking "high art" pretensions); Daniel, *Pickin'*, 99 (Skillet Lickers' song names); Wiggins, *Fiddlin'*, 93, 104 (Fiddlin' John Carson).

13. Daniel, "George Daniell's Hill Billies: The Band That Named the Music?," 81; Green, "Hillbilly Music," 216; Wolfe, "The White Man's Blues," 40. "Hill Billie Blues" is listed in the 1925 Vocalion promotional catalog under the category "Comedy." See Folder: Vocalion-Promo, Catalogs & Info: Columbia, Victor, Vocalion, Okeh, JEMFC; "Hill Billie Blues" (Vocalion-14904); Benét, "The Mountain Whippoorwill," 635–39. On Benét's poem, see Wiggins, *Fiddlin'*, 88–92, and Green, "Hillbilly Music," 220. Wiggins argues that the poem is based directly on twenty-two-year-old Lowe Stokes's defeat of Fiddlin' John Carson's at the 1924 Georgia Old-Time Fiddler's Convention that Benét had read about in *Literary Digest*.

14. Benét, "The Mountain Whippoorwill," 635.

15. Crichton, "Thar's Gold," 24 ("white mountaineer"); Campbell, "Fiddlers and Divas" ("with many a pause"); Wiggins, *Fiddlin'*, 51–52 ("day coaches").

16. Wolfe, "The Legend," 4. Peer later used similar mountaineer stereotypes in describing his 1927 recording session with the Carter family in Bristol: "He [A. P. Carter] was dressed in overalls and the women they are country women from way back there —calico clothes on . . . They looked like hillbillies." Despite such claims and local legends that the Carters were barefoot and had never been in town before, the Carters had visited Bristol many times and, although plainly dressed, were certainly all shod. Wolfe, "The Legend," 4–5.

17. Green, "Hillbilly Music," 212–14; Crichton, "Thar's Gold," 27.

18. Letter from A. E. Alderman to Archie Green, May 6, 1961, 2, Folder: Tony Alderman—Correspondence; Box 3, AGP; "'Hill Billies' Capture WRC," *Radio Digest-Illustrated*, 6 March 1926, 5, hand-typed copy in Box 3, AGP; Alderman to Green, May 6, 1961, 3.

19. Green, "Farewell Tony," 232; Malone, *Singing Cowboys*, 77.

20. Peterson and DiMaggio. "The Early Opry: Its Hillbilly Image in Fact and Fancy," 43. These scholars found that the majority of performers on the show in its first years were middle class and lived in Nashville or in surrounding small towns; for photographs of "countrified" performers, see Hurst, *Nashville's Grand Ole Opry*, 84–86, and Kingsbury, *The Grand Ole Opry History of Country Music*, 24–29. For further analysis of Hay's role in the construction of the hillbilly image, see Peterson, *Creating*, 71–77, and Wolfe, *A Good Natured Riot*, 53–55.

21. WLS *Family Album*, 1933, 21, JEMFC ("born a mountaineer"); Hurst, "'Barn Dance' Days—Remembering the Stars of a Pioneering Chicago Radio Show" (reprint of article from *Chicago Tribune Sunday Magazine*, August 15, 1984, 11), Folder: Radio Station WLS "National Barn Dance," SFC; *WLS Family Album*, 1935, 42, SFC; Lair, "Renfro Valley—Then and Now—An Account of the Happenings in 'The Valley Where Time Stood Still,'" 32, JLP (name change of Renfro Valley Boys); Hurst, "'Barn Dance,'" 11.

22. Photograph of Lair playing the jug is from Photograph Collection, JEMFC (P-1092); "NBC—Farm and Home—8/15/32—Cumberland Ridge Runners," Folder: Cumberland Ridge Runners—Various Programs 1931–2, Box 1, JLP.

23. John Lair, "No Hill Billies in Radio," *WLS Weekly* 1 (March 16, 1935), 7, JLP; Photograph titled "Kentucky Gal," *Stand By*, November 21, 1936, p. 16, JLP. I thank Harry Rice for bringing this picture to my attention.

24. *Stand By*, October 10, 1936, p. 7, and passim 1936–1937, JLP. I thank Harry Rice for his insights and for providing me examples of these cartoons.

25. Steele, "The Inside Story of the Hillbilly Business," 20–21.

26. Hay, *A Story of the Grand Ole Opry*, 23, 41; "Song Favorites of the WSM Grand Ole Opry" (Chicago: M. M. Cole Publishing, 1942), 1, in Folder: Song Favorites of the WSM Grand Ole Opry, MF ("our little informal . . .); Peterson and DiMaggio, "The Early Opry," 41 ("All right . . . boys). The often-retold story of the naming of the show reflects Hay's deliberate cultural positioning. Dr. Walter Damrosch, the host of a radio program of operatic and symphonic music that immediately preceded Hay's show, closed his program one evening by playing a classical composition that mirrored the sound of a locomotive, informing the audience that he was making a one-time exception to his standing rule that "there is no place in the classics for realism." When Hay's turn on the air came, he played off these comments brilliantly, instructing harmonica player DeFord Bailey to play the train song "Pan American Blues" and then announcing to his audience that what would follow "would be nothing but *realism*" and that rather than grand opera, his program would be more like grand ole opry. See Jack Harris, "True Story of the Famous WSM GRAND OLE OPRY," *Rural Radio* 1, no. 2 (October 1938): 4, JEMFC; Malone, *Country Music*, 75; Kingsbury, *Grand Ole Opry*, 28–29.

27. Pugh, "Country Music," 33, 36; Pugh, research notes ("Favorite . . . Playing"); MF ("Home and Hill . . . Songs"); "What the Popularity of Hill-Billy Songs Means in Retail Profit Possibilities," *The Talking Machine World*, December 15, 1925, 177, and "Edison Cylinder Sales Gain in Rural Districts," *The Talking Machine World*, November 15, 1925, 186, both in Folder: "Footnotes and some unused materials since trip to UCLA, May 1963," Box 4, AGP; Abel Green, "'Hill-Billy' Music," 1; Daniel, *Pickin'*, 62 ("Hill Billy Trio"); "Tape to Charley Bowman and Archie Green, April 20, 1961," Folder: Tony Alderman/Tony's Interview, Box 3, AGP. Al Hopkins's group decided to seek the name change after seeing a rival band named The Ozark Hillbillies advertised on a New York theater marquee. See Green, "Hillbilly Music," 214. On the public use of "hillbilly" by recording companies, see Green, "Hillbilly Music," 221–22, and Pugh, "Country Music," 33–34.

28. Bands cited are from "New and Original Favorite Songs of Famous Hill Bil-

lies—Featured by Famous Hill Billy Groups of Radio, Stage and Screen" (FL 0464) and "'Pappy' Cheshire and his Hill Billy Champions—Mountain Songs, Home Songs, Western Songs, Cowboy Songs" (FL 0490), MF; description of the Oudeans Hill Boys from the former source; "Polly Jenkins and Her Plow Boys—Heart Throbs of the Hills" (New York: Bob Miller, Inc., 1937) (FL 0502), MF; "'Red River' Dave [McEnery] Songbook Book No. 1" (Stasny Music Corp. [1939?]) (FL 0529), MF. "Hill Billy Wedding in June" was originally recorded in 1941 and many times subsequently, most famously by Gene Autry. See Malone, *Singing Cowboys*, 91.

29. Clarence A. Stout, "Hill Billy Family" in *The Ranch Boys' Songs of the Plains* (Chicago: M. M. Cole Publishing Company, 1939) (FL 0517), "Songs of the Tennessee Ramblers Folio No. 1" (Portland: American Music, Inc., 1940) (FL 0617); "Drifting Pioneers' Song Folio No. 1" (Portland: American Music, Inc., 1939) (FL 0189); "Clarke's Comedy Song Folio" (Rialto Music Publishing Company, 1935) (FL 0143); "100 WLS Barn Dance Favorites—Pioneer Songs, Southern Songs, Cowboy Songs, Fiddle Tunes, Sacred Songs, Mountain Songs, Home Songs" (Chicago: M. M. Cole Publishing Company, 1935) (FL 0483): all from MF; Daniel, " The National Barn Dance on Network Radio: The 1930s," 52; The Hoosier Hot Shots, "Them Hill-Billies Are Mountain Williams Now," Rex 8744 (78A) Cavanaugh-Sanford-Mysels. I thank Adam Wilson for transcribing the lyrics for me. In my rather unscientific tabulation of published "hillbilly"-titled songs, I count nine up until 1940, twenty-five additional titles from 1940 through 1949, and thirty-six from 1949 through 1960. This does not include the countless other songs with "hill," "mountain," "mountaineer," or related terms in their titles. Sources include MF, *BMI General Index, BMI Performance Index*, 1941–1960, and Huber, "Rednecks and Woolhats," 153.

30. Griffis, "The Beverly Hill Billies," 7. See also Griffis, "The Charlie Quirk Story and the Beginning of the Beverly Hill Billies, 173–78, and Martin, "Zeke Manners, 'Hillbilly' Who Ruled Radio, Dies at 89."

31. Malone, *Country Music*, 93–101, and *Singing Cowboys*, 91–92, Grundy, "'We Always Tried to Be Good People': Respectability, Crazy Water Crystals, and Hillbilly Music on the Air, 1933–1935," Gregory, *American Exodus—The Dust Bowl Migration and Okie Culture in California*, ch. 8, and Peterson, *Creating*, part 3; Zolotow, "Hillbilly Boom," 38 (Satherly quote); Malone, *Don't Get above Your Raisin'*, 23.

32. "Hillbilly Songs Take U.S. by Storm—Even Broadway" [early 1930s?], WLS Scrapbook, 5, JEMFC; Steele, "The Inside Story," 21. Note that the costume Steele describes is a blend of cowboy and mountaineer elements, akin to that adopted by the Beverly Hill Billies in the early 1930s. Historian Gregory Waller notes that the 1934 Fox musical *Stand Up and Cheer* included a lavish song and dance number "Broadway Goes Hillbilly," in which chorus girls change from satin gowns into checked shirts and straw hats. See Waller, "Hillbilly Music and Will Rogers: Small-town Picture Shows in the 1930s," 164.

33. Steele, "The Inside Story," 21; Smith "'Hill Billy' Folk Music—A Little-Known American Type," 154.

34. Abel Green, "'Hill-Billy' Music," 3.

35. Ibid., 22.

36. See Malone, *Singing Cowboys*, 82–84, Wilgus, "Bradley Kincaid," in Malone and McCulloh, *Stars of Country Music*, 86–94 (Kincaid quotations), and Wolfe, "Take Me Back to Renfro Valley," 12 (Niles); Horstman, *Sing Your Heart Out, Country Boy*, 119 and *Ballad of a Mountain Man—The Story of Bascom Lamar Lunsford* (Lunsford); Wolfe, "Take Me Back," 9–10 (Thomas). On the folk music movement of the 1930s, see Whisnant, *All That Is Native and Fine—The Politics of Culture in an American Region*, 184–86 and passim ch. 3, Wolfe, "Take Me Back," 9–12, and Denisoff, *Great Day Coming: Folk Music and the American Left*.

37. Undated and unaddressed typed sheet signed "Art Satherly," ASP. See also "Hill Billy Info," *Music Business* (Sept. 1946), 20, ASP; Malone, *Country Music*, 129 ("folksongs"); Horstman, *Sing Your Heart Out*, 171 (Billy Hill); Grundy, "We Always Tried," 1604.

38. Daniel, "George Daniell's Hill Billies," 58 ("We're . . . hillbillies," "long hair"); Wiggins, *Fiddlin'*, xv ("Moonshine Kate" Carson quotation); Lightfoot, "Belle of the Barn Dance: Reminiscing with Lulu Belle Wiseman Stamey," 9.

39. Bronner, *Old-Time Music Makers*, 53–54, 64–66.

40. Ibid., 55; Fields and Fields, *From the Bowery to Broadway—Lew Fields and the Roots of American Popular Theater*.

41. Bronner, *Old-Time Music Makers*, 55, 88. Because the industrial town of Hornell, New York, the band was from had not been called Hornellsville since 1915, dubbing themselves the Hornellsville Hillbillies was intended, and recognized locally, as an inside joke akin to their rube stage personas—but one which also evoked a simpler rural past. See ibid., 85–86. For a broader discussion of the ambiguities of conceptions of rural domesticity in country music, see Malone, *Don't Get Above Your Raisin'*, ch. 3.

42. On the growth of cowboy imagery, see Malone, *Singing Cowboys*, 89–95, Peterson, *Creating*, ch. 6, Green, "The Singing Cowboy: An American Dream," and Oermann and Bufwack, "Patsy Montana and the Development of the Cowgirl Image."

43. Malone, *Country Music*, ch. 5, and *Singing Cowboys*, 91, 99–100.

44. On New Deal efforts in the southern mountains see Williams, *Appalachia: A History*, 291–306, and Batteau, *Invention of Appalachia*, 138–43; president's letter accompanying *The Report on Economic Conditions in the South* (1938), republished in Carlton and Coclanis, eds., *Confronting Southern Poverty in the Great Depression: The Report on Economic Conditions of the South with Related Documents*, 42. Douglas B. Green, "Gene Autry," in Malone and McCulloh, *Stars of Country Music*, 154.

45. Malone, *Singing Cowboys*, 94; *WLS Family Album*, 1930–1940, JEMFC; Wolfe, "Take Me Back," 23.

46. Malone, *Country Music*, 161. O'Daniel converted the popularity of his band's music and his own populist rhetoric into high elective office; two terms as governor of Texas from 1938 to 1942, and election to the U.S. Senate in 1941 (in a special election) and 1942; Pugh, "Country Music," 33; letter of Betty June Glasiner, *Hillbilly & Western Hoedown* 1 (December 1953): 5, JEMFC. Fan magazines included *Stand By* (WLS, Chicago, 1936–1938), *Rural Radio* (WSM, Nashville, 1938–1939), *Mountain Broadcast and Prairie Recorder* (Rialto and Dixie Music, New York, 1939–1947), and

National Hillbilly News (West Virginia, 1940–1952). Bill Malone, brochure notes, 3, *Smithsonian Collection of Classic Country Music* (Smithsonian P8–15640, 1981), and conversation with the author, March 3, 1996.

47. "Bob Miller's Famous Hill-Billy Heart Throbs" (New York: Bob Miller, Inc., 1934) (FL 0060), MF.

48. On country music in the war years, see Malone, *Country Music*, ch. 6; Zolotow, "Hillbilly Boom," Eddy, "Hillbilly Heaven," Antrim, "Whoop-and-Holler Opera," and Davidson, "Thar's Gold in Them Thar Hillbilly Tunes"; Antrim, 85 ("They found . . . liquor").

49. Copy of transcription of Ronnie Pugh's interview with Ernest Tubb, in author's possession (Bond and Tubb quotations). My thanks to Mr. Pugh for sharing this material; "Roy Acuff Not a Hillbilly Singer," *Columbus (Ga.) Ledger*, July 20, 1950, ASP; Unaddressed, undated, handwritten letter by Arthur Satherly ("Hill Billy Satherly"), ASP; Arthur Satherly to Mr. Thurston Mome [?], July 13, 1969 ("trash"), ASP; previously cited unaddressed Satherly letter ("country folk").

50. From the late 1930s to the 1960s, musicians, promoters, reporters, and audiences tried out various alternative labels including "western," "folk," "American folk," and "country & western." The record review columns in *Billboard* reflect not only this conflict of terminology but also a broader shift from considering the work as musical leftovers to recognizing it as a legitimate separate category that demanded its own billing. Country music first appeared in the magazine's review columns under the title "Hillbilly and Foreign Record Hits of the Month" (December 1941), a label replaced within one week by "Western and Race." During the 1940s, the column changed names repeatedly from "American Folk Records—Cowboy Songs, Hillbilly Tunes, Spirituals, Etc." (March 1942) to "American Folk Tunes—Cowboy and Hillbilly Tunes and Tunesters" (May 1944) to "Folk (Country & Western) Record Section—Folk Talent and Tunes" (June 1948) to "Most Played Juke Box (Country and Western) Records" (June 1949). Not until 1962 did the chart take its present name, changing once more from "Hot C & W Sides" to "Hot Country Singles." See *Billboard* 1940–1949; Pugh, "Country Music," 35–36, 38; on Homer and Jethro, see Malone, *Don't Get Above Your Raisin'*, 181.

51. Possibly incomplete runs of international fan publications I viewed in JEMFC that used the term include: *Friends of Hillbilly—Journal of Hillbilly & Cowboy Music* (published in Japanese, 1972–1974); *Hillbilly Hayride* (The Netherlands: Dutch Stickbuddy Club, 1962–1963); and *The Hillbilly-Folk Record Journal* (Essex and Kent, England: Hillbilly-Folk Record Collectors' Club, 1954–1957).

Chapter 4

1. On southern characters and settings in the comic strips, see Blackbeard, "Them Thar Hillbillies: Abner, Leviticus, Snuffy—a (Gasp!) Look at What Al Capp Unleashed," 3, 5, Inge, "Sut, Scarlet, and Their Comic Cousins: The South in the Comic Strip," 154, and Inge, "Comic Strips," 914–15.

2. See also the analysis of Webb's work in Batteau, *The Invention of Appalachia*, 127–32, and Williamson, *Hillbillyland*, 40–42.

3. Webb quote from article by Harry Neigher, *Bridgeport (Conn.) Herald*, n.d., n.p., EC. Webb also produced cartoons for *Life* and *Collier's*, a syndicated comic strip of his characters titled *The Mountain Boys* that ran for several years in the 1930s, and two collections of his cartoons in book form, *Comin' round the Mountain* (1938) and *'Keep Em Flyin'* (1942). See Falk, ed., *Who Was Who in American Art*, 664, Horn, ed., *The World Encyclopedia of Cartoons*. v.1, 402–3; v.2, 57, Harrison H. Smith, "'Mountain Boys' Won Fame for Artist" and "Paul Webb's Hilarious 'Mountain Boys,'" both from *Times-Leader, Evening News, Record* (Wilkes-Barre, PA), June 11, 1977, n.p., and June 18, 1977, n.p., respectively, EC. I thank Stephen Goddard for sharing these articles with me.

4. See Breazeale, "In Spite of Women: *Esquire* Magazine and the Construction of the Male Consumer," 1, 11–17, Merrill, *Esky: The Early Years at Esquire*, 13–30, and Gingrich, *Nothing But People: The Early Days at Esquire—A Personal History, 1928–1958*, 102–3. Circulation statistics are from Merrill, 46, 51.

5. *Esquire*, August 1935, 27; May 1940, 64; May 1936, 60; April 1936, 37, October 1936, 38, and February 1938, 38.

6. *Esquire*, January 1943, 52; August 1937, 38; February 1936, 92.

7. Tindall, "The Benighted South: Origins of a Modern Image," 284. On the struggles between forces of modernity and traditionalism in the 1920s, see Archdeacon, *Becoming American—An Ethnic History*, chs. 5–6, Coben, *Rebellion against Victorianism—The Impetus for Cultural Change in 1920s America*, and Dumenil, *The Modern Temper—American Culture and Society in the 1920s*. On the 1930s, consult Pells, *Radical Visions and American Dreams—Culture and Social Thought in the Depression*, and Susman, "The Culture of the Thirties," 150–83.

8. Mencken, "The Sahara of the Bozart," 143, 147; Mencken, "In Memoriam: W. J. B.," 65. For a detailed analysis of the cultural significance of "The Sahara of the Bozart," see Hobson, *Serpent in Eden: H. L. Mencken and the South*, especially 11–32. For other examples of Mencken's attacks on southern mountaineers, see "The Hills of Zion," "the Scopes Trial," and "Inquisition."

9. Sherman and Henry, *Hollow Folk*, 1, 27 [page references are to reprint edition]; see also Batteau, *Invention*, 96–97. Wolfe's *Look Homeward Angel* (1929), Faulkner's *As I Lay Dying* (1930), and Caldwell's *Tobacco Road* (1932) and *God's Little Acre* (1933) are only the most famous of the many novels featuring poor white characters published in the five years surrounding the publication of *Hollow Folk*. See McIlwaine, *The Southern Poor-White—From Lubberland to Tobacco Road*, and Cook, *From Tobacco Road to Route 66—The Southern Poor White in Fiction*.

10. *Esquire*, June 1943, 55, and January 1944, 107; Manne, "Mental Deficiency in a Closely Inbred Mountain Clan," 270, 279.

11. Letter to the editor by Edwin Ehrhardt, *Esquire*, December 1939, 6.

12. Webb's cartoon appeared on the page next to Stuart's writings ten times between 1936 and 1944. Stuart published thirty-six pieces in the magazine in these years and seventy-nine *Esquire* selections in his career. See Gingrich, *Nothing but People*, 307.

13. Williamson, *Hillbillyland*, 42.

14. A. L. Blinder to M. Davis, April 7, 1948, EC ("extremely fortunate"); Alfred Smart to Daniel Doran, November 23, 1948, EC ("outlived his usefulness"). I thank Stephen Goddard for making these materials available to me. For an overview of *Esquire* in the postwar years, see Howd, "Esquire."

15. DeBeck's introduction of Spark Plug in 1922 led to one of the first successful mass marketing campaigns of a cartoon character and even spawned a hit song by Billy Rose, "Barney Google," with its inescapable catch line "with your goo-goo-googly eyes." DeBeck nationalized many catch phrases, including "heebie jeebies," "horse feathers," and "sweet mama," a trend that continued in the later incarnation of the strip. The best source on DeBeck's personal and artistic background is Walker, *Barney Google and Snuffy Smith—75 Years of an American Legend*. See also Inge, "Sut Lovingood and Snuffy Smith," 69–76.

16. *Barney Google*, June 14, 1934, 15; Snuffy's usurpation was so complete that even the title of the comic strip changed from *Barney Google* to *Barney Google and Snuffy Smith* (on October 24, 1938) to *Snuffy Smith* (on May 11, 1942). Currently, the strip is entitled *Barney Google and Snuffy Smith*, although the former character almost never appears. [Unless otherwise noted, all references to the text and artwork of this comic strip come from the episodes published six days a week in the *Capital Times* (Madison, Wisconsin) between June 1, 1934, and February 1, 1946.]

17. Inge, "Sut Lovingood," 74–75.

18. *Barney Google*, June 17, 1934, n.p.; "Beyond His Knowledge!" June 21, 1934, 17; "Catching Up with History!" July 23, 1934, 11.

19. In a 1940 interview, DeBeck described his character as a "moonshining, horse- and chicken-thieving illiterate who does what he damn pleases," but added, "you can't help liking the little cuss." See "Barney Google's Birthday: He's 21 Now but Sadly Eclipsed by the Toughie Snuffy Smith"; *Barney Google*, "An Unpleasant Encounter!" November 28, 1934, 13.

20. *Barney Google*, September 1, 1944, 8. I found only one instance between 1934 and 1945 where Lowizie rebeled openly against Snuffy's philandering and autocracy (April 25, 1940, 24).

21. *Barney Google*, "Snuffy Loses Count!" November 26, 1935, 17; "Under His Own Steam!" December 16, 1935, 13; "Too Close for Comfort," April 12, 1938, 15; Thompson, "America's Day-Dream," 4.

22. DeBeck's most famous African-American character was Sunshine, Barney Google's pint-sized, simple-minded, and ever-loyal servant and jockey, whose favorite expression was "You sho am a smaht man, mistah Google." See Walker, *Barney Google and Snuffy Smith*, 86–87. For a fuller discussion of the nature and role of African-American stereotypes in comic strips and American and Western popular culture, see Jones, "From 'Under Cork' to Overcoming: Black Images in the Comics," Lott, *Love and Theft—Blackface Minstrelsy and the American Working Class*, and Pieterse, *White on Black—Images of Africa and Blacks in Western Popular Culture*.

23. Walter Lippmann, *A Preface to Morals* (New York, 1929), 19–20, quoted in Dorman, *Revolt of the Provinces: The Regionalist Movement in America, 1920–1945*, 24. Dorman's book offers the best overview of the entire movement. For an analysis of the

competing approaches of advocates of a regionally distinct folk culture and those touting a unified national culture, see Kammen, *Mystic Chords of Memory*, ch. 13.

24. Percy MacKaye, "Untamed America: A Comment on a Sojourn in the Kentucky Mountains," *Survey* 51 (January 1, 1924): 327; quoted in Shapiro, *Appalachia on Our Mind—The Southern Mountains and Mountaineers in the American Consciousness, 1870–1920*, 261. MacKaye waxed even more poetic about the potential of his plays based on the mountain folk to become "a conservation of spiritual wild nature" and the "unspoiled heritage of thought and untamed imagination" in "Poetic Drama in Kentucky's Mountains," 29.

25. Other regional federal projects—including the establishment of two national parks (Great Smoky Mountains National Park [1934] and Shenandoah National Park [1936]) and the construction of the Blue Ridge Parkway (begun in 1935)—also kept the region and its inhabitants much in the news. On the uneasy relationship in the 1930s between southern Appalachia, the national media, and the federal government, see Batteau, *Invention*, 92–94, 116–26, 133–43, and Perdue and Martin-Perdue, "Appalachian Fables and Facts: A Case Study of the Shenandoah National Park Removals."

26. Seventy-nine articles were published between 1920 and 1930 and an additional 114 from 1930 to the end of World War II. Magazine article totals cited include all pertinent articles in *The Reader's Guide of Periodical Literature* for these years and include articles in fifty-six separate publications. The most influential interwar nonfiction portrayals of the mountain folk were Sheppard, *Cabins in the Laurel*, Wilson, *Backwoods America*, and Randolph's *The Ozarks: An American Survival of Primitive Society* and *Ozark Mountain Folks*. In addition, two widely read works on mountain folk arts were Goodrich, *Mountain Homespun*, and Eaton, *Handicrafts of the Southern Highlands*. The four primary festivals were Bascom Lamar Lunsford's Mountain Dance and Folk Festival (Asheville, North Carolina), Jean Thomas's American Folk Song Festival (Ashland, Kentucky), Sarah Gertrude Knott's National Folk Festival (various locations), and Annabel Morris Buchanan's White Top Folk Festival (southwest Virginia). See Whisnant, "Finding the Way between the Old and the New: The Mountain Dance Folk Festival and Bascom Lamar Lunsford's Work as a Citizen" and *All That Is Native and Fine—The Politics of Culture in an American Region*, ch. 3, and Wolfe, "Take Me Back to Renfro Valley," 9–12.

27. On Doris Ulmann's practices, see the remembrance by her long-time traveling companion, John Jacob Niles, in Niles and Williams, *The Appalachian Photographs of Doris Ulmann* and Watkins, "Merchandising the Mountaineer—Photography, the Great Depression, and *Cabins in the Laurel*," 235; Watkins, 217 (mislabeled photographs).

28. Inge, "Sut Lovingood," 75; "Barney Google's Birthday," 60.

29. *Barney Google*, "A Suitor That Doesn't Suit," June 29, 1934, 15.

30. *Barney Google*, "A Feud That Pays," August 16, 1936; "Maintaining a Reputation," April 27, 1938, 16.

31. *Barney Google*, "Surprise Packages!" August 8, 1934, 13; "Out of the Woods!" September 9, 1934.

32. Scheinfeld, "A Portrait in Zowie!" 142–43 ("be toned down"); Lasswell, "Billy, Barney, Snuffy & Me,"17, 21.

33. Inge, "Al Capp's South: Appalachian Culture in *Li'l Abner*," 5, and McCoy, "The Art and Politics of Al Capp," 2 (in author's possession) (circulation estimates); Kahn, "Ooff!! (Sob!) Eep!! (Gulp!) Zowie—I," 54 (annual income estimation). The success of Capp's forays into other media was decidedly mixed. Although the Broadway show *Li'l Abner* opened in 1956 and was a smash hit, the musical film adaptation (Paramount, 1959) was less successful and its predecessor of the same name (Astor Pictures, 1940) bombed with both critics and movie audiences. Likewise, the theme park *Dogpatch USA* that opened outside of Harrison, Arkansas, in 1968 was struggling to stay afloat by the end of the 1970s and went out of business in 1993. See Price and Turner, "Abner Goes Hollywood; Gets Lost in Shuffle," Brown, "The Road to Hokum: Dogpatch, USA," and Russ, "Dogpatch, U.S.A." On Capp's appeal to the intelligentsia, see Steinbeck, "Introduction," to Al Capp, *The World of Li'l Abner*, 6, and McCoy, "Art and Politics of Al Capp," 3–4.

34. For a broader analysis of Capp and *Li'l Abner*, see Berger, *Li'l Abner—A Study in American Satire*, and Arnold, "Al, Abner, and Appalachia."

35. On Capp's childhood, see Schreiner, "The Storyteller," 7–8, and Capp, *My Well-Balanced Life on a Wooden Leg: Memoirs*. On Capp's southern expedition, see Schreiner, "Storyteller," 8; Inge, "Al Capp's South," 6. Capp provided a publicity sketch for a United Features 1937 press book (reproduced in *LAD:* 1, 6) that showed his supposed meeting with a hill boy on whom he based Li'l Abner. His brother, Elliott Caplin, however, calls Capp's later explanation that this was a preliminary research trip one more example of his "mythology" and argues that, like the historian of the Trojan War, "Alfred became his own Homer." See Caplin, *Al Capp Remembered*, 61–63.

36. An ardent moviegoer, young Capp likely viewed many of the dozens of films set in the southern mountains released between 1920 and 1934. As for literature, Capp not only read the novels of Fox but also old copies of *Harper's Monthly*, some of which may have included Murfree and Fox short stories and the mountaineer illustrations of E. W. Kemble. See Caplin, *Al Capp Remembered*, 7, 30–31, and Inge, "Al Capp's South," 8–10; Halberstadt, "Introduction," 4 (vaudeville show). Although she does not recall the name of the group, it was possibly "the Weaver Brothers and Elviry," the preeminent "rube" vaudevillians of the day. See McNeil, "Special issue on the Weaver Brothers and Elviry."

37. Schreiner, "Storyteller," 12; *Editor and Publisher*, August 17, 1935, 23.

38. "The Funny Papers," 45, 49; Berchtold, "Men of Comics," 35. A slightly earlier article reported that, of metropolitan newspaper readers, 68 percent of men, 72 percent of women, and 99 percent of children read the "*best* comics" [italics in original]. See Tarcher, "The Serious Side of the Comic-Strip," 4.

39. *Editor and Publisher*, April 27, 1935, 1 [italics in original]; On Depression-era American humor, see Levine, "American Culture and the Great Depression," and Linneman, "Will Rogers and the Great Depression."

40. Capp, "Innocents in Peril," 5; Kahn, "Ooff!! Zowie-I," 57 ("I don't want . . . "); Kahn, "Ooff!! (Sob!) Eep!! (Gulp!) Zowie-II," 48.

41. The syndicates' policy of avoiding controversial topics is best illustrated by the "Code of the Comics," stipulated in a 1949 *Catalog of Famous Artists and Writers* published by King Features Syndicate: "No blood, no torture, no horror, no controversial subjects such as religion, politics and race. Above all, is the important matter of taste. The comics must be clean. No suggestive posturing and no indecent costumes." Although Capp repeatedly violated most of these mandates, he did avoid the subjects of (organized) religion and race. On the "comic's code," see Reitberger and Fuchs, *Comics—Anatomy of a Mass Medium*, 146.

42. See Jacobson, *Whiteness of a Different Color*, Dower, *War without Mercy: Race and Power in the Pacific War*, and Curtis, *Apes and Angels: The Irishman in Victorian Caricature*.

43. *Li'l Abner*, "Any Takers," labeled July 5, 1935; reprinted in *LAD: 1*, 53; "Riot Call," labeled July 20, 1938; reprinted in *LAD: 4*, 103.

44. For interpretations of this sequence, see Schreiner, "1940: On the Road," 14, Arnold, "Abner Unpinned—Al Capp's *Li'l Abner*, 1940–1955," 422, and McCoy, "Art and Politics of Al Capp," 8–13.

45. *Li'l Abner*, "Journey's End!" undated; reprinted in *LAD: 6*, 60; and "The Dowager of Dogpatch," labeled November 4, 1938; reprinted in *LAD: 4*, 149.

46. *Li'l Abner*, "College, H'yar We Come!" labeled October 15, 1936; reprinted in *LAD: 2*, 135; "Abijah—Yo Said It!" labeled October 17, 1936; reprinted in *LAD: 2*, 136.

47. Reprinted in Schreiner, "1938: Soap and Slapstick," 6. The Scraggs bear an uncanny resemblance to the villainous Hatburns, a mountaineer trio who terrorize a peaceful town in the 1921 hit movie, *Tol'able David*. It is quite possible that young Alfred Caplin saw the original movie or its less successful 1930 remake; Semple, "The Anglo-Saxons of the Kentucky Mountains: A Study in Anthropogeography."

48. For an insightful account of *Li'l Abner* in the years of World War II and the early cold war, see Arnold, "Abner Unpinned."

49. *Esquire*, May 1943, 123; Webb, "Hillbillies in the Bigtime Feud." It is interesting to compare how the three artists responded to U.S. involvement in World War II. In Webb's cartoons, war mobilization advances around, and sometimes at the expense of, his hillbillies. The military conducts maneuvers on their land; drops bombs on the outhouse; and confiscates their moonshine as an explosive agent; but Luke and his brothers remain unflappably passive, too lazy to even turn around to see the tanks rolling by. In contrast, DeBeck had Snuffy Smith join the army in October 1940, and his adventures in uniform became the central theme of the strip. When Lasswell took over the comic strip in 1943, he had Snuffy (and Barney Google) travel with U.S. military forces to the Caribbean, North Africa, and the South Pacific. Snuffy even participated in (rather farcical) hand-to-hand combat against Japanese soldiers. Unlike either of his peers, Capp almost completely excluded any mention of the war in the strip and neither Li'l Abner nor any other Dogpatcher joined the military services. In an open letter to his readers in the July 4, 1942, episode, Capp explained that his decision to exclude direct war references was meant to keep Dogpatch a "peaceful, happy, free world . . . where a fella is free to be as wise or foolish as he pleases."

The world of *Li'l Abner*, however, was neither peaceful nor happy and became increasingly sadistic, violent, and sexually charged as the war progressed. On *Snuffy Smith* and the war, see Walker, *Barney Google and Snuffy Smith*, 124, and Lasswell, "Billy, Barney, Snuffy & Me," 20. On Capp and the war, see Arnold, "Abner Unpinned," 423–28, and Horn, "*Li'l Abner* in Wartime: The Mystery of the Dog That Didn't Bark in the Night."

50. For sample advertisements, see *Esquire*, April 1942, 139, June 1942, 123 (cartoon book mailed to servicemen), and May 1943, 123. The producers of *Kentucky Moonshine* (1938) referred specifically to "typical Esquire-type-hill-billies" as the model for their lead characters. See Folder 1781.8, "Moonshine over Kentucky Conference with Mr. Zanuk (on Temporary Script, Part I—December 4th Part II—December 8th)," December 8, 1937, 2, Box FX-PRS-290, FXC.

51. Williamson, *Hillbillyland*, 29. As Williamson explains, as a deliberate play on "yourself," "Yoseff" was "a sly piece of mirroring" showing that these middle-class students from the hill regions "knew they were the hillbillies in the structure of a larger power." See his discussion, 29–32.

52. On Sadie Hawkins Day's origins, see Schreiner, "1937: Sadie's First Run." For examples of its popularity, see "On Sadie Hawkins Day, Girls Chase Boys in 201 Colleges," and "Li'l Abner's Mad Capp," 60.

53. John Lair to Phil Bottfeld, January 30, 1951, 1, Folder 5, Box 17, JLP; Arnow, *The Dollmaker*, 501.

54. Randolph and Wilson, *Down in the Holler—A Gallery of Ozark Folk Speech*, 252; Odum, *Southern Regions of the United States*, 467; Arnow, *Dollmaker*, 147; Roberts, "Don't Call Me Hillbilly."

55. Randolph, "Ozark Anthology—An Introduction"; Randolph, *Funny Stories about Hillbillies*; Gish, "Yes, I'm a Hillbilly," Harmon, *Hillbilly Ballads*, n.p.

56. Morris, "Good Ol' Hillbilly . . . ," 188–89.

Chapter 5

1. I have benefited greatly from Jerry Williamson's definitive "Southern Mountaineers Filmography" and deeply appreciate his willingness to share his extensive research files and film library with me. I indicate below sources from his research files with [JW]. "Souls Aflame," *Variety*, July 18, 1928, p. 15 [JW]; "Scenario of Howdy Folks," Folder 356.5, Box FX-PRS, 811, FXC (*Thunder Mountain*); "'Mountain Madness,' August Release, Shows Moonshiners," *MPW*, August 21, 1920, 1052 [JW]; C. S. Sewell, "'The Wives of the Prophet'—Lee-Bradford," *MPW*, January 9, 1926, 137 [JW].

2. *MPW*, December 20, 1919, 1008, cited in Williamson, *Hillbillyland*, 295 (review of *The Feud*); figures on number of films released by decade are drawn from Williamson's filmography but exclude his listing of nonfiction educationals and films on coal mining and historical subjects.

3. Comments of Steve Farrar, Orpheum Theater (Harrisburg, IL), *MPW*, December 23, 1922, 768 ("Beyond the shadow . . .") [JW]; *Photoplay* poll cited in *Hill-*

billyland, 177–78. For an analysis that focuses on Barthelmess's role as a symbolic "mama's boy" redeemed through violence, see Williamson, *Hillbillyland*, 177–89.

4. "Barthelmess in Very Wilds of Virginia," source unknown (marked "Chicago"), August 28, [1921], Scrapbook 4, RBC (first three quotations); "Dick's Adventure in the Land of Mountaineers and Moonshine," *Motion Picture Post*, August, 1921, Scrapbook 4, pp. 1, 3, RBC (next three quotations); "Finds the Real Native Stock," *Baltimore Sun*, September 9, 1921, Scrapbook 4, p. 43, RBC ("causes . . ."); "Untitled," *Louisville Herald*, undated and unpaginated, Scrapbook 5, p. 73, RBC.

5. "Richard Barthelmess' Debut as Star in 'Tol'able David' Is a Great Success," [*Movietime?*] *Review*, January 7, 1922, Scrapbook 4, p. 87, RBC; Heywood Broun, "Poor Goliath!" *Image*, February 11, 1922, Scrapbook 4, RBC.

6. For a discussion of the first hillbilly-titled film, see pp. 64–65. Director John Ford produced a standard western originally titled *Hill Billy* in 1918, but it was either never released or its name was changed, possibly to *The Scarlet Drop*. See letter from Bill Wooten to Archie Green, 15 September 1963, Folder: John Ford, Box 3, AGP.

7. "The Hill Billy," *Photoplay*, June 1924, p. 65, PF; Jerry Williamson discovered a similar "ectomorph from the backwoods" in the 1926 comedy *Rainbow Riley*. See *Hillbillyland*, 38–39.

8. "Sun-Up by Lulu Vollmer, Dictated by Bela Sekley 2/12/1925," stamped "1514–Vault Copy," p. 1, Folder: "Sun-Up/1924," MGMC (synopsis); "Sun-Up/Continuity," dated "Feb. 24" and stamped "1514," p. 1, Folder: Sun-Up/1924, MGMC; "Final Title List," August 5, 1925, p. 2," Sun-Up/1924, MGMC ('Hill Billies'); "Sun-Up," signed "Fred." [*Variety?*], August 19, 1925, Folder: "Sun-Up/ Metro-Goldwyn/1925," PF.

9. *Stark Love* is in the Museum of Modern Art's film collection. I thank Jerry Williamson for allowing me to view his copy of this film and for sharing his research files on its production and reception with me. On the film's fortuitous rediscovery, see Brownlow's Introduction to "Hollywood in the Hills—The Making of 'Stark Love,'" 171, the first publication of Karl Brown's unpublished manuscript "The Paramount Story."

10. Ibid., 171; Brown, "Hollywood in the Hills," 177 (Furman's influence) and 184–92, 206, and 216–17 (Kephart's influence). I am indebted throughout this section to Williamson's analysis of the cultural politics of the film in *Hillbillyland*, 190–207.

11. *Stark Love* (1927, Paramount Famous Lasky Production); Brown, "Hollywood in the Hills," 174.

12. Brown, "Hollywood in the Hills," 189 ("I want to show . . . caricatures") (italics in original); ibid., 179, 182–84, 187. See also Williamson, *Hillbillyland*, 198–99.

13. On the film location, see Brown, "Hollywood in the Hills," 194–95, and Williamson, *Hillbillyland*, 197–98, 200; "Mountaineers in Picture," *New York Times*, August 29, 1926, sect. VII, p. 5 [JW] ("trickery" of shooting out of order); "Primitive Mountaineers Filmed in Native Nooks," *New York Times*, February 20, 1927, sect. VII, p. 6 [JW] (mountaineers as "lazy"; "like children"; "never seen a railroad train").

14. "Primitive Mountaineers," 6 [JW] ("picturization"); Paul Thompson, untitled and undated, *Motion Picture News*, Folder: Stark Love/Paramount/1927, PF; Brownlow, Introduction, 171.

15. Script for *Sun-Up*, dated February 11, 1925, Folder: Sun-Up/1924/MGM, MGMC.

16. *Our Hospitality* (1923, Metro Pictures/Buster Keaton Productions) and synopsis of the film in Wead and Lewis, *The Film Career of Buster Keaton*, 50–52; Laurence Reid, "Title," *Motion Picture News*, November 24, 1923, p. 2483, File: Our Hospitality/Metro/1923, PF.

17. Examples of early hillbilly-themed films starring leading comedy teams are: *The Feud* (1926, 20th Century–Fox) starring Van Bibber; *The Big Killing* (1928, Paramount) with Wallace Beery and Raymond Hatton; *Noisy Neighbors* (1929, Pathe) with the Quillan family; and *Them Thar Hills* (1934, MGM) with Stan Laurel and Oliver Hardy.

18. *London Chronicle*, March 9, 1935, Folder: Kentucky Kernels—publications and reviews—4, GSC ("something like"); Estimating Script, dated July 24, 1934, p. 31, Folder: Synopses, Kentucky Kernels, Box RKO-S-338, RKO, and Folder: Kentucky Kernels, Script 1, GSC. George Stevens was the film's director.

19. For a biographical sketch of the Ritz Brothers with filmography, see "The Ritz Brothers," in Parish and Leonard, eds., *The Funsters*, 528–39; M. M. Musselman and Jack Lait, Jr., "Kentucky Moonshine—a Skeleton Outline" (attached memo dated September 25, 1937), Folder 11A6.2.10, File: Kentucky Moonshine, Box FX-PRS-290 (hereafter, KM), FXC ("typical lazy"); *Kentucky Moonshine* (1938); Folder 1781.8, "Moonshine over Kentucky Conference with Mr. Zanuk (on Temporary Script, Part I—December 4th Part II—December 8th), December 8, 1937, p. 8, KM, FXC. As far as I can determine, Webb did not create the posters for *Kentucky Moonshine*, but he did produce the advertisements and opening credits for *Comin' round the Mountain* (1940, Paramount).

20. Plots revolving around the confusion between genuine mountaineers and urban performers pretending to be or mistaken for natives stretch back at least to *Where Broadway Meets the Mountains* (1912, American); Folder 1781.5, "Moonshine over Kentucky, typed material November 23, 1937," p. 33, KM, FXC ("tarnation"); Folder 1781.15, "Kentucky Moonshine, January 24, 1938, Shooting Final," p. 104, KM, FXC ("child bride"); *Kentucky Moonshine*, Plot Summary, April 12, 1938, MPAA ("Slacks from Coma").

21. File: Kentucky Moonshine/20th Century–Fox/1938, PCA (women's groups' reactions); "Kentucky Moonshine," *Time* (undated) and "Kentucky Moonshine," *Variety*, April 30, 1938 (Previews), both in File: Kentucky Moonshine/20th Century–Fox/1938, PCA. A typical PCA checklist of "problematic" ethnic characterizations appears in File: Arkansas Traveler/Paramount/1938, PCA.

22. Film advertisement copy, Microfiche: Spitfire/RKO/1934, PF; In 1941, Paramount also produced the third version of another "mountain classic," *Shepherd of the Hills*. On *Sergeant York*, see Williamson, *Hillbillyland*, 207–24.

23. Hatfield, "Mountain Justice: The Making of a Feminist Icon and a Cultural Scapegoat."

24. "Hill Billy Justice" is listed as the film's title in a letter from Will Hayes of the PCA to Harry Warner, March 11, 1936, File: Mountain Justice/Warners/1936 (hereafter, MJ), PCA.

25. Mountain Justice Press Book, p. 4, MJ, PF ("fanaticism"); ibid., p. 10 (Mat 402) ("savage million"); ibid., p. 12 ("last outpost"); ibid., p. 17 (exploitation lobby displays).

26. "Hutchinson Barrat Score in Grim Pic," *Hollywood Reporter*, May 6, 1937, MJ, PCA ("unholy skill"); reviews of California Federation of Business and Professional Women's Clubs ("graphic") and General Federation of Women's Clubs ("starkly"), both in MJ, PCA; *Variety*, May 19, 1937; [New York?] *Post*, cited in "Mountain Justice," *Hollywood Reporter*, June 1, 1937, MJ, PCA; Hatfield, "Mountain Justice," 39–40, 43. Hatfield notes that the studio also paid Edith Maxwell $10,500 for her secret endorsement of the film so that she would not criticize the film publicly.

27. Statement by Elmer Davis, House hearings, 78th Congress 2nd session, National War Agencies Appropriation bill for 1945, April 19, 1944, reprinted in MacCann, *The People's Films—A Political History of U.S. Government Motion Pictures*, 138. For background information on the film and the Motion Picture Bureau of the Office of War Information, see ibid., 118–51, *Documentary Film Classics—Produced by the United States Government*, 35, 38, and Barsam, *Nonfiction Film—A Critical History*, 216–19.

28. *Valley of the Tennessee* (American Scene Series, no. 7) (1940, Office of War Information, Overseas Branch). I am indebted to David Whisnant for sharing his copy of the film with me and for his insights into the film's significance. I have also been influenced by Batteau's interpretation of the film in *The Invention of Appalachia*, 140–41.

29. Statistics drawn from Williamson filmography. On conceptions and media portrayals of the Ozarks in the 1930s, see Blevins, *Hill Folks: A History of Arkansas Ozarkers and Their Image*, especially ch. 6.

30. For a general overview of these "hillbilly" comedians, see Austin, "The Real Beverly Hillbillies." On Bob Burns, see Lancaster, "Bare Feet and Slow Trains," 93–94; on Goff and Lauck, see Kesterson, "A Visit with Radio Humorist Chester Lauck (Lum Edwards)"; on the Weavers, see McNeil, ed., "Special Issue on the Weaver Brothers and Elviry"; on Judy Canova, see "Judy Canova," in Parish and Leonard, eds., *The Funsters*, 155–62.

31. Miller, *B Movies*, 29–31, and Flynn and McCarthy, "The Economic Imperative: Why Was the B Movie Necessary?"

32. Script for *Comin' round the Mountain*, dated March 15, 1940, File: Comin' round the Mountain (1940) (00314), MS ("only surviving"); *Variety*, August 8, 1940, File: Comin' round the Mountain/Paramount/1940 (hereafter, CRTM), PCA ("mild, pale"); "Comin' round the Mountain," *Variety*, August 14, 1940, CRTM, PCA (costume complaints); Crowther, "Comin' round the Mountain." *Swing Your Lady* also starred the then-unknown actor Humphrey Bogart, who later called this film the worst he had ever made.

33. "Mountain Rhythm—Corn a la Mode," *Motion Picture Herald*, December 12, 1942, File: Mountain Rhythm/Republic/1942, PF.

34. Similar animal-based cartoons include *I Like Mountain Music* (1933, Max Fleischer), *When I Yoo Hoo* (1936, Warner Brothers), *Naughty Neighbors* (1939, Warner Brothers), and *Comin' round the Mountain* (1940, Paramount/Famous). *A Feud There*

Was (1938, Warner Brothers), available on the videodisc *The Golden Age of Looney Tunes* (1992, Turner Entertainment Company), v. 3. See also Frierson, "The Image of the Hillbilly in Warner Bros. Cartoons of the Thirties."

35. Council of Federated Church Women, review of *Mountain Music*, File: Mountain Music/Paramount/1937, PF ("absurd"); *Make Mine Music* (Disney, 1946); lyrics from "The Martins and the Coys," Ted Weems and Al Cameron (1936). I thank Jerry Williamson for sharing a copy of the song lyrics with me and for allowing me to view his copy of the film.

36. Agee, "Films," 517; "Fun without Mickey," 73; "Make Mine Music," 98; Farber, "Make Mine Muzak," 769.

37. Examples of this genre of hillbilly plays include Albert, *Comin' round the Mountain (A Hillbilly Comedy in One Act)*; Braun, *Feudin' (A Hillbilly Comedy in One Act)*; and Oswalt, *Hillbilly High Jinks (A Rousing Hillbilly Comedy in One Act)*. The musical *Li'l Abner* was the first successful film adaptation of comic strip hillbillies. An earlier version of *Li'l Abner* (1940, Astor Pictures) was such a critical and box office bomb that Capp disavowed it. Billy DeBeck's main character did appear briefly in two 1942 Monogram Pictures low-budget comedies, *Snuffy Smith, Yardbird* and *Hillbilly Blitzkrieg*, but both had more to do with wartime espionage plots than mountain settings and neither fared well with reviewers or movie-goers.

38. MacDonald, *The Egg and I*, 112–13; ibid., 114; ibid., 117. As Jerry Williamson notes, the real "hillbillies" in MacDonald's book and the primary target of her blistering attacks are not the Kettles but the regional Indians. "The coast Indian is squat, bowlegged, swarthy, flat-faced, broad-nosed, dirty, diseased, ignorant and tricky," she writes in one typical example. "[The] more I saw of them the more I thought what an excellent thing it was to take that beautiful country away from them." See ibid., 210, 220, and Williamson, *Hillbillyland*, 55.

39. Liza Wilson and David McClure, "Ma and Pa Kettle—Hollywood Goldmine," *Collier's* December 8, 1951, in Scrapbook 4, p. 6, LGC; Parish and Leonard, "Marjorie Main," in *The Funsters*, 447.

40. *Exhibitor*, March 28, 1951, Scrapbook 2, LGC.

41. Paul Denis, "He Doesn't Want an Academy Award," *Daily Compass*, September 11, 1950, Scrapbook 5, LGC ("make money"); Wilson and McClure, "Ma and Pa Kettle," 23 ($400,000 average cost); ibid. ($8 million profit); Parish and Leonard, "Marjorie Main," 448 ($35 million net profit); "He Can Add," *Time*, April 28, 1952, 96, Scrapbook 5, LGC ("nobody likes"); Denis ("four hershey bars").

42. Wilson and McClure, "Ma and Pa Kettle," 23 ("lowliest bum"); Al Hine, "Million Dollar Kettle Drummer," *Esquire*, May 1953, 89, bound copy of magazine in LGC ("maybe people").

43. *Motion Picture Daily*, March 2, 1953, in File: Ma and Pa Kettle on Vacation/Universal/1952, PF.

44. "Southern Highlands—Special Issue"; "Our Southern Highlands Makes News To-day"; *National Geographic* articles include Simpich, "Land of a Million Smiles" and Borah, "Home Folk around Historic Cumberland Gap." Representative postwar articles promoting the Ozarks region as tourist mecca include Strong, "The Friendly

Ozarks," Bradshaw and Bradshaw, "The Ozarks," Anoe, "There's No Place Like the OZARKS," and Eddy, "Let's Go to the Ozarks." For contemporary tourist-oriented accounts of Appalachia, see Lagemann, "You'll Be Comin' round the Mountain," Holman, "The Great Smokies—America's Most Popular Park," Blassingame, "Smoky Mountain Holiday," and Harshaw, "South's Top Scenic Strip."

Chapter 6

1. "Hillbilly," *My Hero* (NBC, 1953), FTA; "The Hillbilly Show," *Jack Benny Program* (March 20, 1958, CBS), FTA. Benny also used a hillbilly sketch (a clear response to the huge popularity of *The Beverly Hillbillies*) in his show of October 30, 1964.

2. Other "hillbilly" episodes include "Hillbilly whiz," *You'll Never Get Rich* (October 1, 1957, CBS), and "Hug that Hillbilly," *Love That Jill* (March 17, 1958, NBC); "Bob Goes Hillbilly," *The Bob Cummings Show* (January 28, 1958, NBC). All programs viewed at FTA.

3. For Appalachian migration totals, see Philliber, "Urban Appalachians: Unknown and Unnoticed," in Philliber et al., eds., *The Invisible Minority: Urban Appalachians*, 2, and Jones, *The Dispossessed—America's Underclasses from the Civil War to the Present*, 227; The scope of this 1950s exodus is staggering. Fifteen percent of white Kentuckians and West Virginians left their respective states in this decade; in certain coal-dependent counties, the total out-migration reached almost 40 percent. See Jones, *Dispossessed*, 209, 212. On the Appalachian migration, see Jones, chs. 7–8, *Invisible Minority*, and James S. Brown and George A. Hillery, Jr., "The Great Migration, 1940–1960," in Ford, ed., *The Southern Appalachian Region—A Survey*, 54–78. For a thorough overview fleshed out by numerous biographical accounts, see Berry, *Southern Migrants, Northern Exiles*. Gregory, "The Southern Diaspora and the Urban Dispossessed: Demonstrating the Census Public Use Microdata Samples," provides a recent comparison of the postwar migration of black and white southerners.

4. As Gregory points out, in contrast to the widely shared notion of a people who continue to face endemic poverty, by 1970, southern-born migrants to the Great Lake states and California lagged only slightly behind other whites in average income and percentage of households below the poverty line. See Gregory, "The Southern Diaspora," 119–20; "Advertisement in Daily Requests 'No Southerners,'" *Michigan Chronicle*, May 1, 1943, p. 4, and George Henderson, "Southern Whites: A Neglected Urban Problem," *Journal of Secondary Education* 41 (March 1966): 11–14, cited in Jones, *Dispossessed*, 257 (job/restaurant bias); "Okies of the '60s," 31 (labels); Clyde B. McCoy and Virginia McCoy Watkins, "Stereotypes of Appalachian Migrants," in *Invisible Minority*, 21–23; Dale Nouse, "Detroiters Like City Just Fine, Survey Reveals," *Detroit Free Press*, date unknown, 1952, cited in Killian, *White Southerners*, 98.

5. Maxwell, "Down from the Hills and into the Slums," 27; ibid., 28.

6. Votaw, "The Hillbillies Invade Chicago," 64–66.

7. Ibid., 67; "'Murder Won't Out,' Paper Concludes after Investigation," *Uptown News*, May 21, 1957, cited in Guy, "The Media, the Police, and Southern White Migrant Identity in Chicago, 1955–1970," 333; Votaw, "Hillbillies Invade Chicago," 64.

For a broader discussion of reactions to southern migrants in Chicago and Detroit, see Guy, "The Media," and Hartigan, Jr., *Racial Situations*, especially 26–37, respectively.

8. William A. Garyls, *Harper's*, April 1958, 10.

9. "Episode #1" ("Californy Here We Come!"), *RM*, p.1, Box TV-539, Collection 081, TSS.

10. "A Mutual Admiration Society"; "The Television Set" (Episode 97), *RM*, December 3, 1959, p. 3, Box TV-211, TSS.

11. "Episode #1," p. 24, "The New Car" (Episode 43), Box TV-539, and "Money in the Bank" (Episode 145), *RM*, TSS; "Mutual Admiration," 7; "The Bank Loan" (Episode 55), *RM*, p. 34, Box TV-210, TSS.

12. "Little Luke's Education" (Episode 10), *RM*, described in Eisner and Krinsky, *Television Comedy Series—An Episode Guide to 153 TV Sitcoms in Syndication*, 695; "The Talk of the Town" (Episode 102), *RM*, Box TV-211, TSS; "This is the Real McCoy," 23; "Back to West Virginny," (Episode 147), *RM*, May 23, 1961, Box TV-212, TSS.

13. "Back to West Virginny" (Episode 147), *RM*, May 23, 1961, and "Fly Away Home" (Episode 148), *RM*, July 20, 1961, pp. 30–32, both Box TV-212, TSS. See also Magoc's analysis of the latter episode in "The Machine in the Wasteland," 27.

14. "This Is the Real McCoy," 22; Brooks and Marsh, *The Complete Directory to Prime Time Network and Cable TV Shows*, 119.

15. Williamson, *Hillbillyland: What the Movies Did to the Mountains and What the Mountains Did to the Movies*, 57–61, Brooks and Marsh, *Complete Directory*, 1261–64; Graham, *Framing the South: Hollywood, Television, and Race during the Civil Rights Struggle*, 101.

16. "The County Nurse" (Episode 56, originally aired March 19, 1962), AG, TBS; "A Feud is a Feud" (Episode 8, originally aired December 5, 1960), AG, TBS.

17. "Mountain Wedding" (Episode 94, originally aired April 29, 1963), AG, TBS. On described versus performed mountain music, I am indebted to Smith's unpublished paper, "'What It Was Was Real Mountain Music': The Authentic Treatment of Music in the *Andy Griffith Show*," 12, and to Jerry Williamson for sharing this paper with me. For a list of the Darlings' selections, see Harrison and Habeeb, *Inside Mayberry*, 151–52; "Briscoe Declares for Aunt Bee" (Episode 96, originally aired October 28, 1963), AG, TBS.

18. "Mountain Wedding"; "Ernest T. Bass Joins the Army" (Episode 99, originally aired October 14, 1963), "My Fair Ernest T. Bass" (Episode 113, originally aired February 3, 1964), "The Education of Ernest T. Bass" (Episode 133, originally aired October 12, 1964), all AG, TBS.

19. Brauer, "Kennedy, Johnson, and the War on Poverty," 101; Batteau, *The Invention of Appalachia*, 150 (first act); On the degree of Kennedy's early interest in Appalachia and poverty, see Brauer, "Kennedy, Johnson," 101–13, Batteau, *Invention*, ch. 8, Whisnant, *Modernizing the Mountaineer: People, Power, and Planning in Appalachia*, 93–94; On the influence of these three books, see Batteau, 153–57, and Brauer, 103; Harrington, *The Other America: Poverty in the United States*, 24, 186, 196.

20. On the failures of the War on Poverty in Appalachia, see Whisnant, *Modernizing*, chs. 4–6, and Glen, "The War on Poverty in Appalachia: A Preliminary Report."

On media coverage of Appalachia in these years, see Batteau, *Invention*, chs. 8–9, and Bowler, "'That Ribbon of Social Neglect': Appalachia and the Media in 1964."

21. The exact familial relationship between the four lead characters is more complex than most viewers realize. Elly May is widower Jed Clampett's daughter and Granny (whose given name is Daisy Moses) is his mother-in-law. Jethro Bodine is the son of Jed's first cousin Pearl, making Jethro and Elly May second cousins. For simplicity's sake, however, they were often called, and I will refer to them as, the Clampetts.

22. Cox, *The Beverly Hillbillies*, 97–101, author telephone interview with Paul Henning, June 3, 1997, transcript in author's possession; author interview with Henning.

23. Author interview with Henning.

24. Cox, *Beverly Hillbillies*, 3. Henning recounts the same story in his interview with Bob McClaster, September 4, 1997, AAT; McClaster interview with Henning, AAT. I am indebted to Andrew Cypiot for transcribing this interview for me.

25. Mark Alvey notes that by 1963, telefilm independents were responsible for 70 percent of televised programs. See Alvey, "The Independents: Rethinking the Television Studio System," 146; Lewis, "The Golden Hillbillies," 33; Cox, *Beverly Hillbillies*, 4.

26. Lewis, 34; ibid [Italics and capitalization in the original].

27. Ibid.

28. Ibid., 34; Brooks and Marsh, *Complete Directory*, 1262–65; Cox, *Beverly Hillbillies*, xvii. These records date back to when Nielsen established its current ratings system in 1960; Muggeridge, "Why Those Hillbillies Are Rampant in Britain," 26.

29. "Jethro Goes to School," *BH*, DEC; cited in Hano, "The G.A.P. Love the 'Hillbillies,'" 30; "Review," *Variety*, October 3, 1962, 35.

30. Newton Minow, speech before the thirty-ninth annual convention of the National Association of Broadcasters, May 9, 1961, reprinted in Watson, *The Expanding Vista—American Television in the Kennedy Years*, 22.

31. Gould, "TV: 'Beverly Hillbillys' [*sic*]," 63.

32. Hano, "G.A.P.," 30 ("legitimate"); Gould, "TV," 63 ("heady"); Hano, "G.A.P.," 30 ("cheerful belief"); Lewis, "Golden Hillbillies," 30; Davidson, "Fame Arrived in a Gray Wig, Glasses and Army Boots," 5 (Bob Hope quotation); ibid., 5.

33. Henning interview with McClaster, AAT; Seldes, "The Beverly Hillbillies," 66, 65.

34. Hobson, "The Grandpappy of All Gushers," 16.

35. "The Hillbillies of Beverly Hills," (Pilot Episode), *BH*, DEC; Lewis, "Golden Hillbillies," 32; Cox, *Beverly Hillbillies*, 18.

36. Headlines from *New York Times*, October 1, 1962, Hano, "G.A.P.," 120; Cox, *Beverly Hillbillies*, 194.

37. Robert Escarpit, *The Sociology of Literature*, Ernest Pick, trans., 2d edition (London, 1971), 91, cited in Levine, "The Folklore of Industrial Society: Popular Culture and Its Audiences," 1375; Hano, "G.A.P.," 120; Dern, "'Viewers Like 'Em, and That's That,'" 11; Hano, "G.A.P.," 120.

38. I am indebted to Farber's analysis in his *The Age of Great Dreams: America in the 1960s*, 52–54; "The Clampetts Meet Mrs. Drysdale" (Episode 4), *BH*, DEC.

39. Cited in Barnouw, *The Image Empire—A History of Broadcasting in the United States (v. 3—from 1953)*, 205.

40. *BH*, episode of October 31, 1962, cited in Hano, "G.A.P.," 122.

41. On Granny's culture war with affluent modernity, see also Marc, *Demographic Vistas—Television in American Culture*, ch. 2, and Himmelstein, *Television Myth and the American Mind*, 146–50.

42. "The Clampetts Meet Mrs. Drysdale."

43. Paul Henning, "The Beverly Hillbillies" (Pilot), dated December 7, 1961, Collection 081, Box TV-371, TSS. The line remained unchanged when the show aired. See "The Hillbillies of Beverly Hills," *BH*, DEC.

44. Hano, "G.A.P.," 123; Shayon, "Innocent Jeremiah," 32.

45. Shayon, "Innocent Jeremiah," 32; Himmelstein, *Television Myth*, 150. See also the analysis of Marc in *Demographic Vistas*, xvi, 54–58, and Farber, *Age of Great Dreams*, 55.

46. Harrison and Habeeb, *Inside Mayberry*, 8 (Idelson quote). On the conceptual relation between Sheriff Taylor and real-life southern sheriffs, see Graham, *Framing the South*, 154–60.

47. "The South Rises Again," *BH*, Episode 5000–186, Box TV-61, TSS.

48. For arbitron samples for urban markets, see the weekly syndication figures in *Variety*, November 1962 to October 1963. For assessments of the validity of Nielsen ratings, see Mayer, *About Television*, ch. 2. On underrepresentation of African-American viewers, see Brown, *Televi$ion—The Business behind the Box*, 60–61. Henning's comments are from McClaster interview, AAT.

49. *TV Guide*, March 14 and 21, 1964; "The Country Slicker"; Three of the top five programs of 1963 were rural-oriented programs (four if one counts *Bonanza*), and Henning's shows and *Andy Griffith* constituted four of the top twenty-one programs of 1965. CBS later added country music variety shows like *Hee Haw* (1969–1971) and the *Glen Campbell Goodtime Hour* (1969–1972) to its lineup; all ratings from Brooks and Marsh, *Complete Directory*, 1262–63.

50. Cox, *Beverly Hillbillies*, 26–27, 163–68.

51. Pepsi purchased the brand in 1964 from the Hartman Beverage Company of Knoxville, Tennessee. Collins, "Ya-hooo! A Marketing Coup"; "Abbreviated Mountain Dew Historical Reel, 1966–1996," produced by Batton, Barton, Durstine, and Osborn (BBDO), videocassette; "Kissin' Lesson" (Spot 2), Radio Advertising Scripts, 1966 Mountain Dew Bottler catalog. I thank Tom Bené and Jon Harris of Pepsi North America for graciously sharing these items with me.

52. Crist, "The Beverly Hillbillies."

53. Historian Susan Douglas has argued perceptively that despite their outlandish premises, many of these programs featuring women with supernatural powers were also reactions to the nascent feminist movement. See Douglas, *Where the Girls Are*, ch. 6. On general trends in 1960s television and sitcoms, see Bryant, "Situation Comedy of the Sixties: The Evolution of a Popular Genre," 118–39, Spigel and Curtin, eds.,

The Revolution Wasn't Televised—Sixties Television and Social Conflict, and Baughman, *The Republic of Mass Culture*, 100–107. For contemporary accounts, see Moss, "The New Comedy," 42–45, and Hano, "TV's Topmost: *This* Is America?"

54. These plots matched the conservative views of Irene Ryan and Buddy Ebsen, both of whom supported Ronald Reagan's presidential candidacy in 1968 and who denounced "hippies" as "the great conformists in the world," see Efron, "American Gothic—On Television and Off," 34.

55. "Robin Hood and the Sheriff," *BH*, TBS.

56. Bryant, "Situation Comedy of the Sixties," 133, Brooks and Marsh, *Complete Directory*, 1264–65.

57. So many children watched *The Beverly Hillbillies* that R. J. Reynolds, responding to federal legislation banning tobacco advertisements on programs for which at least 45 percent of the audience was minors, withdrew its sponsorship in 1967. See "Untitled," *New York Times*, May 10, 1967, 60.

58. Buddy Ebsen quoted in the *Los Angeles Times*, cited in "Putting the Clampett on 'Hilbillies'"; Buttram quotation is from Henning interview, AAT, and conversation with Stephen Cox; For an overview of the transformation at CBS, see Gitlin, "The Turn toward 'Relevance.'"

59. Richardson, Sr., "Junior Cobb of Three Brothers, Ark., Judges *The Beverly Hillbillies* (He's hill folks, himself)"; Dow, "Letter to the Editor."

60. Branscome, "Annihilating the Hillbilly: The Appalachians' Struggle with America's Institutions," 120–21. Mack Morriss quotation cited in Day, "Pride and Poverty: An Impressionistic View of the Family in the Cumberlands of Appalachia," 376.

Epilogue

1. Gitlin, "The Turn toward 'Relevance,'" 218–19; Roiphe, "Ma and Pa and John-Boy in Mythic America: *The Waltons*," 132.

2. Arnow, "The Hills Meet Hollywood—The *Now and Then* Guide to Selected Feature Films about Appalachia," 8–9; Hart, *James Dickey: The World as a Lie*, 513.

3. Dickey, *Deliverance*, 40; ibid., 48–49.

4. Dickey, *Summer of Deliverance*, 98–99. See also Hart, *James Dickey*, 250–51.

5. Dickey, *Deliverance*, 111; ibid., 112.

6. Dickey signed a contract with Warner Brothers to write the screenplay five months before the book was published. See Hart, *James Dickey*, 442. Dickey, *Summer*, 163. Though James Dickey wanted to play a major role in the making of the film, his bullying demeanor and constant interference so annoyed Boorman and the lead actors that he was rather unceremoniously ordered off the set. He was later allowed a small role as the local sheriff. A notorious self-aggrandizer, Dickey later falsely claimed repeatedly that he had been responsible for nearly everything in the movie from the acting and directing to writing the music. See Hart, *James Dickey*, chs. 25, 27, and Dickey, *Summer*, 167–68.

7. Dickey, *Summer*, 165. For a thoughtful discussion of the film as a commentary

on the destructive potentiality of city people and modernity, see Williamson, *Hillbillyland*, 155–67.

8. Dickey, *Deliverance*, 60.

9. Dickey, *Summer*, 170, and Graham, "Tale a Mixed Blessing for Rabun County," M4 (Redden). Boorman always intended to dub in the music and have Cox and Redden pretend to play their instruments, but Redden was so incapable of miming the fretwork that the filmmakers had to design a special shirt so that another boy could surreptitiously put his arms through the sleeves to "play" the chords. Thus, the decision to highlight the mountaineers' imbecility created the need to hide the other boy and precluded the side-by-side playing featured in the novel. See Taylor, Thomas, and Brunson, "'He Shouted Loud, "Hosanna, DELIVERANCE Will Come,"'" n.p.; ibid. (Webb and granddaughter); Dickey, *Summer*, 170.

10. Press book, *Deliverance* (Warner Brothers, 1972), PF; Dickey, *Summer*, 180; Hart, *James Dickey*, 508. On Dickey's destructive alcoholism and outlandish public excess, see Hart, *James Dickey*, and Dickey, *Summer*.

11. Hart, *James Dickey*, 455, 512 (sales statistics); press book, *Deliverance* (Farber quotation); Hart, *James Dickey*, 508–11.

12. Taylor, Thomas, and Brunson, "'He Shouted Loud,'" n.p.; Dickey, *Summer*, 180; Hart, *James Dickey*, 514.

13. Hart, *James Dickey*, 514; Taylor, Thomas, and Brunson, "'He Shouted Loud,'" n.p.

14. The number of rafters on the Chattooga tripled between 1972 (when 7600 floated down the river) and 1973 and reached 68,000 by 1989. See Graham, "Tale a Mixed Blessing," M4. On "the Deliverance syndrome" see Taylor, Thomas, and Brunson, "'He Shouted Loud,'" n.p., and Williamson, *Hillbillyland*, 162–63, 290.

15. Williamson, *Hillbillyland*, 124–31.

16. Ibid., 131–41.

17. Huber, "A Short History of Redneck: The Fashioning of a Southern White Masculine Identity," 158–60.

18. Carl Rowan, "Hillbilly Jokes Are an Insult," *San Francisco Examiner*, November 19, 1976, p. 36, PTC; Huber, "Short History," 158–59.

19. Kahn, *Hillbilly Women*, 180; Russell, *Call Me Hillbilly—A True Humorous Account of the Simple Life in the Smokies before the Tourists Came*, and Lawson, *By Gum, I Made It!—An Ozark Arkie's Hillbilly Boyhood*. Other examples include Silcox, *A Hillbilly Marine*, and Heath, *Hillbilly Homestead*.

20. Fisher, "The Grass Roots Speak Back," 203–14, and Fisher, ed., *Fighting Back in Appalachia: Traditions of Resistance and Change*; Obermiller, "Paving the Way—Urban Organizations and the Image of Appalachians," 251–66.

21. Brooks and Marsh, *The Complete Directory to Prime Time Network and Cable TV Shows*, 1267–69, Sackett, *Prime Time Hits—Television's Most Popular Network Programs*, 264–65.

22. Joel Achenbach, "Little Rock, Where Spin Meets Homespun," *Washington Post*, October 2, 1992, C1–2, cited in "The Hillbillies at the *New* Center of Civiliza-

tion," *AJ* 20 (Spring 1993): 259; reprinted in Cox, *The Beverly Hillbillies*, 143 (*Saturday Night Live* sketch).

23. Photograph by J. Emilio Flores, *New York Times*, September 15, 1998, A23.

24. I thank Paul Boyer for bringing this cartoon to my attention.

25. "Dwight Yoakam Says He Hasn't Changed, Country Music Has," Scripps-Howard News Service, December 9, 1993, CMF; Pam Lambert and Todd Gold, "Dwight Attitude," *People Magazine*, April 26, 1993, 48; and Jim Lewis, "Marty Stuart Earns Respect as a 'Hillbilly,'" *Chicago Sun-Times*, December 3, 1990, CMF. See also Williamson, *Hillbillyland*, 8. The Kinks released *Muswell Hillbillies* (RCA) in 1971, while Knopfler formed the group the Notting Hillbillies in 1990; BR5-49, *BR5-49* (Arista, 1996). The name BR5-49 is drawn from the phone number for Junior Samples's used car lot in his regular *Hee Haw* sketch.

26. Harris, *History — Grand & Glorious Order of the Hillbilly Degree*, "Here's How It Is in Pikeville," letter from Howard "Dirty Ear" Stratton to "Hillbilly Bob" (n.d., c. 1983), Williamson, *Hillbillyland*, 10–12. I am indebted to Jerry Williamson for sharing these documents with me; promotional card published by the Pike County Chamber of Commerce, c. April 1995; Hillbilly Days Web site (http://www.hillbillydays.com); "History: Grand & Glorious Order of the Hillbilly Degree," Webmaster's note (http://www.trowel.com/hillbilly99/history.htm) (1999 "clan" statistics). See also Brown, *Ghost Dancing on the Cracker Circuit: The Culture of Festivals in the American South*, ch. 3. Interestingly, Pikeville's festival was not the first such celebration of hillbilly identity and imagery in the southern mountains. Residents of Highlands, North Carolina, a fashionable community outside of Asheville, held the "Highlands Hillbilly Days" each August between 1951 and at least 1957. Like the Pikeville festival, participants dressed as hillbillies and participated in beauty contests, as well as the more traditional pursuits of wood chopping, square dancing, and ballad singing. See articles from these years in the *Asheville Citizen-Times*.

27. "Hillbilly Convention Drawing Criticism," *Cincinnati Enquirer*, October 12, 1982, C1–2, reprinted as "Fed Up in Cincinnati," in *AJ* 10 (Spring 1983), 225. See also Williamson, *Hillbillyland*, 13–14. On the use of "hillbilly" as an inclusive label, see Hartigan, Jr., "Name Calling: Objectifying 'Poor Whites' and 'White Trash' in Detroit," in Wray and Newitz, eds., *White Trash — Race and Class in America*, 41–56, and Hartigan, *Racial Situations: Class Predicaments of Whiteness in Detroit*, ch. 2.

28. http://www.rockabillyhall.com/HillHellcats.html (Hillbilly Hellcats); http://www.squank.net/albums/hh/hhalbm01.htm (Hillbilly Holocaust); http://www.instantharmony.com/HfM/ (Hillbillies from Mars); http://sierrahillbillies.homestead.com/files/Hillbillies_Main.htm (Sierra Hillbillies); www.angelfire.com/hi/MikeLatinHillbillies/ (Mike Hillman and Latin Hillbillies); www.hbhq.com/ (Hillbilly Headquarters); http://home.dti.net/pwilhelm/hh2/ (Hillbilly Hercules); http://www.ebay.com/ (E-bay links); http://xroads.virginia.edu/~MA97/price/open.htm ("White Trash: The Construction of an American Scapegoat"). All sites accessed December 4, 2002.

Postscript

1. de Moraes, "Gold in Them Thar 'Hillbillies'?"

2. "*Beverly Hillbillies* to Become Reality Show"; de Moraes, "Gold in Them Thar."

3. Kinney, "Reality Show Will Perpetuate Hillbilly Stereotype"; Rogers, "Shootin' for Some Crude"; Dreher, "Minstrel Show"; Pitts, Jr., "Reintarnation! Second 'Beverly Hillbillies' as Reality TV Not Funny"; Peyton, "First *Beverly Hillbillies* Bad Enough: 'Montani semper Stereotype' Strikes W. Va. Once Again."

4. Garrigan, "Bubba Goes to Hollywood"; Dreher, "Minstrel Show," Caldwell, "Hill of Beans—Reality Is Optional."

5. Caldwell, "Hill of Beans—Reality Is Optional"; "Must Hee-Haw TV."

6. Kinney, "Reality Show Will Perpetuate Hillbilly Stereotype"; Rogers, "Shootin' for Some Crude"; Abramson, "New 'Hillbillies' Sure to Take Swipe at South"; letter from Congressman Hal Rogers (and forty-three colleagues) to Leslie Moonves, March 12, 2003, Center for Rural Strategies Web site <http://www.ruralstrategies.org/campaign/cong.ltr.html>.

bibliography

Archival Sources

Academy of Motion Picture Arts and Sciences, Margaret Herrick Library, Beverly
    Hills, California
  Biography Files
  General Subject Files
  Movie Scripts
  Production Files
  Special Collections
    Richard Barthelmess Collection
    Leonard Goldstein Collection
    George Stevens Collection
    Motion Picture Association of America
    Production Code Administration Case Files
Academy of Television Arts and Sciences, North Hollywood, California
  Archive of American Television
    Andy Griffith Interview
    Paul Henning Interview
    Sheldon Leonard Interview
    Aaron Ruben Interview
Appalachian State University, William L. Eury Appalachian Collection, Boone,
    North Carolina
  Vertical Files

Mountain People
 Stereotypes
Berea College, Hutchins Library, Berea, Kentucky
 Special Collections
  John Lair Papers
Country Music Foundation, Nashville, Tennessee
 Country Music Journal and Fan Magazine Collection
 Arthur Satherly Papers
 Biographical Folders
East Tennessee State University, Archives of Appalachia, The Sherrod Library, Johnson City, Tennessee
 Thomas G. Burton-Ambrose N. Manning Collection
 Charles R. Gunter Jr. Collection
University of California, Los Angeles
 Theater Arts Library/Special Collections, University Research Library
  Twentieth Century–Fox Film Corporation Collection
   Produced Scripts: *Kentucky Moonshine; Thunder Mountain*
  RKO Pictures, Inc. Collection
   Produced Scripts
  Warner Brothers Collection
  Charles Isaacs Collection
  Television Series Scripts
   The Andy Griffith Show
   The Beverly Hillbillies
   The Real McCoys
   The Waltons
 Department of Special Collections, University Research Library
  Richard Wilson Papers
 Film and Television Archive, Archive Research and Study Center, Powell Library
University of Kansas, Spencer Museum of Art, Lawrence, Kansas
 The Esquire Collection
University of Kentucky Library, University Archives, Lexington
 Special Collections and Archives
  Kentucky Postcard Collection
  John Jacob Niles Collection
 Appalachian Collection
University of Missouri/State Historical Society of Missouri, Columbia
 Western Historical Manuscript Collection, Ellis Library
  Peter Tamony Collection
University of North Carolina-Chapel Hill, Southern Folklife Collection, Wilson Library
 John Edwards Memorial Foundation Collection
  Music Folios
  WLS Family Album, 1930–1957

Archie Green Papers
Photograph Collection
Music Catalogs
Biographical Folders
Periodical Collection
University of Southern California, Los Angeles
Cinema-Television Library, Doheny Memorial Library
Special Collections
Twentieth Century–Fox Collection
MGM Collection
Press Books

Primary Sources

Motion Pictures

LIVE-ACTION FILMS

Arkansas Judge: Republic Pictures, 1941.
The Cabin in the Cotton: First National Pictures, 1932.
Child Bride: Raymond Friedgen, 1952.
Comin' round the Mountain: Universal Pictures, 1951.
Deliverance: Warner Brothers, 1972.
The Egg and I: Universal Pictures, 1947.
Hills of Kentucky: Warner Brothers, 1927.
In Old Missouri: Republic Pictures, 1940.
Joan of Ozark: Republic Pictures, 1942.
A Kentucky Feud: Biograph, 1905.
Kentucky Kernels: RKO Radio Pictures, 1934.
Kentucky Moonshine: Twentieth Century-Fox Productions, 1938.
The Kettles in the Ozarks: Universal-International Pictures, 1955.
Li'l Abner: Triad Productions/Paramount, 1959.
Ma and Pa Kettle: Universal-International Pictures, 1949.
Ma and Pa Kettle Go to Town: Universal-International Pictures, 1949.
Ma and Pa Kettle Back on the Farm: Universal-International Pictures, 1951.
Make Mine Music: Walt Disney Studios, 1946.
A Moonshine Feud: 1919.
The Moonshiner: Biograph, 1904.
Mountain Justice: Warner Brothers, 1937.
Mountain Music: Paramount Pictures, 1937.
Murder, He Says!: Paramount Pictures, 1944.
Our Hospitality: Metro Corporation, 1923.
The Revenue Man and His Girl: Biograph Company, 1911.
Stark Love: Paramount Famous Lasky Production, 1927.

Swing Your Lady: Warner Brothers, 1937.

Thunder Road: DRM Productions, 1958.

Tobacco Road: Twentieth Century–Fox, 1941.

Tol'able David: Inspiration Pictures, Inc., 1921.

The Trail of the Lonesome Pine: Paramount Pictures, 1936.

Valley of the Tennessee: American Scene Series, no. 7, Office of War Information, Overseas Branch, 1940.

The Winter People: Nelson Entertainment, 1989.

ANIMATED SHORTS

Comin' round the Mountain: Paramount, 1949.

A Feud There Was: Warner Brothers, 1938.

Hillbilly Hare: Warner Brothers, 1950.

When I Yoo Hoo: Warner Brothers, 1936.

MUSICAL SHORTS

"The Hillbilly Grand Opera": Minoco Productions, 1941.

"The Hillbilly Hoosegow": Soundies Distribution Corporation, 1942.

"Hillbilly Love": Skibo-Educational Fox, 1935.

"Sadie Hawkins Day": Soundies Distribution Corporation, 1942.

Television Programming

SERIES

The Andy Griffith Show: Danny Thomas Productions, 1960–1968. Miscellaneous Episodes 1960–1968: viewed in syndication on Turner Broadcasting System.

The Beverly Hillbillies : Filmways Productions, 1962–1971. Miscellaneous Episodes 1962–1964: Diamond Entertainment Corporation, videocassettes; 1965–1970: viewed in syndication on Turner Broadcasting System.

INDIVIDUAL PROGRAMS AND ADVERTISEMENTS

Abbreviated Mountain Dew Historical Reel, 1966–1996. BBDO. videocassette.

The Beverly Hillbillies. (Pilot episode): aired September 26, 1962; FTA.

Bob Cummings Show. "Bob Goes Hillbilly"; (January 28, 1958), FTA.

Chimps. "A-feudin' and a fightin'"; Bing Crosby Entertainment, 1959; FTA.

Jack Benny Program. "The Hillbilly Show"; March 20, 1958, CBS; FTA.

——. "Hillbilly sketch"; October 30, 1964, NBC; FTA.

Love That Jill. "Hug that Hillbilly"; March 17, 1958, NBC; FTA.

McHale's Navy. "Hillbillies of PT 73"; June 6, 1963, ABC; FTA.

The Monkees. "Hillbilly Honeymoon: Double Barrel Shotgun Wedding"; October 23, 1967; FTA.

My Hero. "Hillbilly"; 1953, NBC, FTA.

You'll Never Get Rich. "Hillbilly Whiz": October 1, 1957, CBS; FTA.

Record Albums

Bare, Bobby, *Detroit City*. RCA Victor LSP 2776. 1963.

Hoosier Hotshots, The. "Them Hill-Billies Are Mountain Williams Now." Rex 8744 (78A) Cavanaugh-Sanford-Mysels (Library of Congress, Recorded Sound Collection).

Macon, Uncle Dave. "Hill Billie Blues." Vocalion-14904. 1925.

Shay, Dorothy. *Dorothy Shay Sings*. Columbia CL 6003. 1947.

Smithsonian Collection of Classic Country Music. Smithsonian P8–15640. 1981.

Yoakam, Dwight. *Hillbilly Deluxe*. Warner Brothers Records. 1987.

Newspapers, Magazines, and Continuous Publications

Appalachian Journal, 1972–1999.

Billboard, 1940–1954.

(Madison) Capital Times, 1934–1950.

Editor and Publisher, 1934–1945.

Esquire, 1934–1960.

The (Asheville High School) Hillbilly Literary Magazine; yearbook, 1914–1948.

Li'l Abner Dailies. Kitchen Sink Press. Volumes 1–26 (Al Capp's daily comic strips from 1934–1960).

TV Guide, 1955–1975.

Variety, 1960–1965.

WLS Family Album (National Barn Dance Fan magazine), 1930–1957.

Oral Interviews

Paul Henning. Telephone interview conducted by author, June 3, 1997. Transcript in author's possession.

Books and Articles

Abramson, Rudy. "New 'Hillbillies' Sure to Take Swipe at South." *Tucson Citizen*, December 9, 2002 (http://www.tucsoncitizen.com/opinion/12_9_02tv.html)

Adams, E. C. L. "The Carolina Wilderness." *Scribner's Magazine*, June 1931, 611–17.

Agee, James. "Films." *The Nation*, April 27, 1946, 516–17.

"Aid for Mountain Children." *Christian Science Monitor Weekly Magazine*, September 29, 1937, 12.

Albert, Ned. *Comin' round the Mountain (A Hillbilly Comedy in One Act)*. New York: Samuel French, 1938.

Allen, James Lane. "Mountain Passes of the Cumberlands." *Harper's*, September 1890, 561–76.

———. "Through Cumberland Gap on Horseback." *Harper's New Monthly Magazine*, June 1886, 561–76.

Alpert, Hollis. "The Golden Kettles." *Saturday Review*, March 28, 1953, 29–30.

"—And High Time! After 7 Years on the Air, the Beverly Hillbillies Pay Their First Visit to the Ozarks." *TV Guide*, August 23, 1969, 10–13.

Anoe, Pearl. "There's No Place like the OZARKS." *Americas*, May 1955, 10–15.

Antrim, Doron K. "Whoop-and-Holler Opera." *Collier's*, January 26, 1946, 18, 85.

"Appalachia: Myth and Reality: A Panel Discussion." *James Dickey Newsletter* 2, no. 1 (Fall) (1985): 11–16.

Armory, Cleveland. "Green Acres [Review]." *TV Guide*, November 27, 1965, 19.

———. "The Waltons [Review]." *TV Guide*, November 18, 1972, 49.

Armstrong, Anne W. "The Southern Mountaineers." *Yale Review*, n.s., 24, no. 3 (1935): 539–54.

Arnow, Harriette. *The Dollmaker*. 1954. Reprint, New York: Collier Books, 1970.

———. "The Gray Woman of Appalachia." *The Nation*, December 28, 1970, 684–87.

Ashworth, John H. "The Virginia Mountaineers." *South Atlantic Quarterly* 12 (July 1913): 193–211. Reprinted in *Appalachian Images in Folk and Popular Culture*, ed. W. K. McNeil, 187–203. Ann Arbor: UMI Research Press, 1989.

AuCoin, Bill. *Redneck*. Matteson, IL: Greatlakes Living Press, 1977.

"Backwoods Sparkin'." *Atlantic Monthly*, January 1937, 127–28.

Barker, Catharine S. *Yesterday Today*. Caldwell, ID: Caxton Printers, 1941.

"Barney Google's Birthday: He's 21 Now but Sadly Eclipsed by the Toughie Snuffy Smith." *Newsweek*, October 14, 1940, 59–60.

Barrere, Albert, and Charles Leland. *A Dictionary of Slang, Jargon and Cant*. London: George Bell and Sons, 1897.

Barry, Phillips. "Miscellaneous Notes." *American Speech*, August 2, 1927, 473.

Barton, Bruce. "Exercise Your Spirit—Don't Wrap It Up in Your Business and Let It Grow Flabby. Have a Pet Enthusiasm; It Will Keep You Young and Make You Happy." *Good Housekeeping*, September 1925, 23, 128–40.

Becker, Edwin J. "Made in the Land of Do Without." *American Mercury*, May 1954, 141–43.

Benét, Stephen Vincent. "The Mountain Whippoorwill—How Hill-Billy Jim Won the Great Fiddlers' Prize." *Century Magazine*, March 25, 1925, 635–39.

Berchtold, William E. "Men of Comics." *New Outlook*, April 1935, 34–40.

Bergren, Ellen H. "Pioneering Days in Appalachia." *Missionary Review of the World*, June 1939, 302–9.

"The Beverly . . . What?" *TV Guide*, January 18, 1964, 12–13.

"Beverly Hillbillies." *Variety*, October 3, 1962, 35.

"'Beverly Hillbillies' to Become Reality Show." Reuters. *CNN.com*, August 28, 2002 (http://www.cnn.com/2002/SHOWBIZ/TV/08/28/television.hillbillies.reut/index. html)

Biggs, Wallace R. "A Man Is Hanged." *American Mercury*, January 1940, 37–41.

Biograph Bulletins, 1908–1912. New York: Octagon Books, 1973.

Biograph Bulletins, 1896–1908. Los Angeles: Locare Research Group, 1971.

Blassingame, Wyatt. "Smoky Mountain Holiday." *American Magazine*, April 1956, 98–101.

Boleman-Herring, Elizabeth. "James Dickey: An Interview." *James Dickey Newsletter* 12, no. 2 (1996): 13–18.

Borah, Leo A. "Home Folk around Historic Cumberland Gap." *National Geographic Magazine*, November 1943, 741–68.

Botkin, B. A., ed. *A Treasury of American Folklore: Stories, Ballads, and Traditions of the People*. New York: Crown, 1944.

Braden, William, and Morton Kondracke. "What City Is Doing for Hill Folk." *Chicago Sun Times*, February 10, 1964, 4+.

Bradley, William A. "Hobnobbing with Hillbillies." *Harper's Monthly Magazine*, December 1915, 91–103.

Bradshaw, Henry, and Vera Bradshaw. "The Ozarks." *Better Homes and Gardens*, May 1952, 70–71, 238–44.

Branscome, James G. "Annihilating the Hillbilly: The Appalachian's Struggle with America's Institutions." In *The Failure and the Hope—Essays of Southern Churchmen*, ed. Will D. Campbell and James Y. Holloway, 120–39. Grand Rapids, MI: William B. Eerdmans, 1972.

Braun, Wilbur. *Feudin' (A Hillbilly Comedy in One Act)*. New York: Samuel French, 1948.

Brearkey, H. C. "Are Southerners Really Lazy?" *American Scholar* 18 (1949): 68–75.

Breckinridge, Mary. "The Corn-Bread Line." *Survey*, August 15, 1930, 422–23.

——. "Maternity in the Mountains." *North American Review*, December 1930, 765–68.

——. "Is Birth Control the Answer?" *Harper's Magazine*, July 1931, 157–63.

Breitigam, Gerald B. "Lifting Up the Mountains—Bringing a Knowledge of America to Pure-Blooded Americans." *Ladies' Home Journal*, July 1920, 45, 152.

Broun, Heywood. "Wham! and Pow!" *New Republic*, May 17, 1939, 44.

Brown, John Mason. "The Case against the Comics." *Saturday Review of Literature*, March 20, 1948, 31–32.

Brown, William P. "A Peculiar People." *Overland Monthly*, November 1888, 505–8.

Buck, P. H. "The Poor Whites of the Ante-Bellum South." *American Historical Review* 31 (1926): 41–54.

"Bull Market in Corn." *Time Magazine*, October 4, 1943, 33–34.

Burman, Ben Lucien. "That Good Old Mountain Justice." *Collier's Magazine*, July 25, 1953, 46–49.

Burt, Struthers. "The Wood Choppers of Nass." *Scribner's Magazine*, June 1936, 351–54.

Cable, Raymond M. "Fishbone College." *American Mercury*, May 1933, 117.

Caldwell, Christopher. "Hill of Beans—Reality Is Optional." *New York Press* 15, no. 36 (2002) (http://www.nypress.com/print.cfm?content_id=6971)

Caldwell, Mary F. "Change Comes to the Appalachian Mountaineer." *Current History* 31 (1930): 961–67.

"A Call to Combat Race Suicide." *Literary Digest*, November 22, 1924, 36.

"Camp Hillbilly" (photograph). *Blue Ridge Country*, November/December 1992.

Campbell, John C. "From Mountain Cabin to Cotton Mill." *Child Labor Bulletin*, May 1913, 74–84.

——. *The Southern Highlander and His Homeland*. New York: Russell Sage Foundation, 1921.

Campbell, Reverend Robert F. *Classification of Mountain Whites*. N.p.: Hampton Institute Press, 1901.

Canterbury, Edith. "Background Years." *Mountain Life and Work* 30 (1954): 11–12.

Caplin, Elliot. *Al Capp Remembered*. Bowling Green: Bowling Green State University Popular Press, 1994.

Capp, Al. "The Case for the Comics." *Saturday Review of Literature*, March 20, 1948, 31–32.

———. "There Is a Real Schmoo." *New Republic*, March 21, 1949, 14–15.

———. "It's Hideously True!! The Creator of Li'l Abner Tells Why His Hero Is (Sob!) Wed." *Life*, March 31, 1952, 100–108.

———. "Innocents in Peril." In *Al Capp, The World of Li'l Abner*. N.p.: Capp Enterprises, 1953.

———. *My Well-Balanced Life on a Wooden Leg: Memoirs*. Santa Barbara: John Daniel and Company, 1991.

"Capp's Cuts." *Time*, April 11, 1969, 67–68.

"The Carolina Sand-Hillers." *(Boston) Odd Fellow*, September 15, 1847, 193.

Carr, Joseph W. "A List of Words from Northwest Arkansas." *Dialect Notes* 2 (1900–1904): 416–420.

Cash, W. J. "Genesis of the Southern Cracker." *American Mercury*, May 1935, 105–8.

"Casting Agents in Search of 'The Real Beverly Hillbillies.'" Associate Press. *Concord Monitor Online*, September 20, 2002 (http://www.cmonitor.com/stories/a&e2002/hillbillysearch_o7y14y54_2002.shtml)

Caudill, Harry M. *Night Comes to the Cumberlands—A Biography of a Depressed Area*. Boston: Little, Brown and Company, 1963.

———. "The Mountaineers in the Affluent Society." *National Parks & Conservation Magazine*, July 1971, 17–20.

"The Causes of Feuds and Moonshining." *Literary Digest*, April 22, 1922, 35–36.

Chapman, Maristan. "The Mountain Man—An Unbiased View of Our Southern Highlanders." *Century Magazine*, February 1929, 505–11.

———. "American Speech—As Practised in the Southern Highlands." *Century Magazine*, March 1929, 617–23.

Churchill, Allen. "Tin Pan Alley's Git-tar Blues." *New York Times Magazine*, July 15, 1951, section 6, reprinted in *A History and Encyclopedia of Country, Western, and Gospel Music*, ed. Linnell Gentry, n.p. St.Clair Shores, MI: Scholarly Press, 1972.

Cleghorn, Reese. "Appalachia—Poverty, Beauty and Poverty." *New York Times Magazine*, April 25, 1965, 12–13, 124–27.

Coleman, McAlister, and Stephen Raushenbush. *Red Neck*. New York: Harrison Smith & Robert Haas, 1936.

Combs, Josiah H. *The Kentucky Highlanders from a Native Mountaineer Viewpoint*. Lexington: J. L. Richardson, 1913.

"Comics—1894–1934." *Editor and Publisher*, November 17, 1934, 26.

Cooper, James Fenimore. *The Last of the Mohicans; Narrative of 1757*. New York: P. F. Collier & Son, 19??.

"The Corn Is Green." *Newsweek*, December 3, 1962, 70.

"The Corn Is Still Green." *Time Magazine*, August 8, 1969, 59.

"Country Music Snaps Its Regional Bounds." *Business Week*, March 19, 1966, 96–98, 103.

"The Country Slicker." *Newsweek*, December 6, 1965, 97.

Craddock, Charles Egbert (Mary Noailles Murfree). "The Star in the Valley." *Atlantic Monthly*, November 1878, 532–43.

———. *In the Tennessee Mountains*. Boston: Houghton Mifflin, 1892.

Craigie, Sir William A., and James Hulbert, eds. *A Dictionary of American English: On Historical Principles*. Vol. 2. Chicago: University of Chicago Press, 1940.

Cralle, Walter O. "Social Change and Isolation in the Ozark Mountain Region of Missouri." *American Journal of Sociology* 41 (1936): 435–46.

Crawford, T. C. *An American Vendetta: A Story of Barbarism in the United States*. New York: Belford, Clarke, and Company, 1889.

Crichton, Kyle. "Thar's Gold in Them Hillbillies." *Collier's National Weekly*, April 30, 1938, 24, 27.

———. "Hillbilly Judy." *Collier's*, May 16, 1942, 17+.

Crist, Judith. "The Beverly Hillbillies." *TV Guide*, August 27, 1966, 1.

Crowther, Bosley. "Comin' round the Mountain." *New York Times*, September 26, 1940, 27:3.

Daley, Mary Dowling. "The Not So Beverly Hillbillies." *Commonweal*, March 13, 1970, 4–5.

Davenport, Walter. "Just a-settin'." *Collier's National Weekly*, July 30, 1927, 8–9, 28.

———. "Up an-gittin'." *Collier's National Weekly*, September 10, 1927, 19, 42–43.

Davidson, Bill. "Thar's Gold in Them Thar Hillbilly Tunes." *Collier's Magazine*, July 28, 1951, 34–35, 42–45.

Davidson, Muriel. "Fame Arrived in a Gray Wig, Glasses and Army Boots." *TV Guide*, September 7, 1963, 4–7.

Davidson, Theodore F. "The Carolina Mountaineer—The Highest Type of American Character." *First Annual Transactions of the Pen and Plate Club of Asheville, N.C.*, May 11, 1905, 1–11.

Davis, D. H. "Changing Role of the Kentucky Mountains and the Passing of the Kentucky Mountaineers." *Journal of Geography* 24 (February 1925): 41–52.

Davis, Mrs. S. M. "The 'Mountain Whites' of America." *Missionary Review of the World*, June 1895, 422–26.

Davis, Rebecca Harding. "By-Paths in the Mountains." *Harper's New Monthly Magazine* 61 (1880): 167–85, 353–69, 532–47.

Dawber, Rev. M. A. "The 'Forgotten Man' of the Mountains." *Missionary Review of the World*, April 1934, 177–79.

Dawley, Thomas R. "Our Southern Mountaineers: Removal the Remedy for the Evils that Isolation and Poverty Have Brought." *World's Work*, March 1910, 12704–714.

Deal, J. A. *"The Hillbilly" or "American Mountaineer."* Asheville, NC: Inland Press, c. 1915.

de Moraes, Lisa. "Gold in Them Thar 'Hillbillies'?" *Washington Post*, August 29, 2002, A1.

"A Defense of the Mountaineer." *Literary Digest*, April 20, 1912, 800–801.

Dern, Marian. "Viewers Like 'Em, and That's That." *TV Guide*, March 14, 1964, 10–13.

Dickey, Christopher. *Summer of Deliverance*. New York: Simon and Schuster, 1998.

Dickey, James. *Deliverance*. Boston: Houghton Mifflin, 1970.

Dingman, Helen H. "New Trails in Southern Highlands." *Missionary Review of the World*, September 1933, 437–41.

"Dogpatch in Semi-Nude." *Newsweek*, December 21, 1959, 92–93.

"Dogpatch Is Ready for Freddie—After 43 years, Al Capp Decides to Hang Up His Pen." *Time Magazine*, October 17, 1977, 78.

Douglas, Paul. "Strip-mined Landscape and Impoverished Souls." *Christian Century*, June 8, 1966, 753–54.

Dow, Jack. "Letter to the Editor." *TV Guide*, April 19, 1969, A-1.

"The Dream of a Shirt-Tail Boy Comes True." *Outlook and Independent*, July 28, 1920, 557–58.

Dreher, Rod. "Minstrel Show." *National Review Online*, August 30, 2002 (http://www.nationalreview.com/script/printpage.asp?ref=/dreher/dreher083002.asp)

Eaton, Allen H. *Handicrafts of the Southern Highlands*. New York: Russell Sage Foundation, 1937.

Eddy, Don. "Hillbilly Heaven." *American Magazine*, March 1952, 28–29, 119–23.

———. "Let's Go to the Ozarks." *American Magazine*, March 1954, 38–41, 92–97.

"The Editor's Forum: Hillbilly Music." *Mountain Life and Work* 35, no. 2 (1959): 34–42.

Efron, Edith. "American Gothic—On television and off." *TV Guide*, April 20, 1968, 32–34.

"Eliminate the Racial Slur!" *Christian Century*, June 10, 1964, 757–58.

Elliot, Lawrence. "Andy Griffith: Yokel Boy Makes Good." *Coronet*, October 1957, 105–10.

Ellison, Jerome. "The Plight of the Hill People." *Saturday Evening Post*, June 4, 1960, 43+.

Ernst, Harry W., and Charles H. Drake. "'Poor, Proud and Primitive' . . . —The Lost Appalachians." *The Nation*, May 30, 1959, 490–93.

Estabrook, Arthur H. "Is There a Mountain Problem?" *Mountain Life and Work*, July 1928, 5–13, 35–36.

———. "The Population of the Ozarks." *Mountain Life and Work*, April 1929, 2–3, 25–28.

Everts, Mrs. C. S. "Modern Methods Invading the Mountains." *Missionary Review of the World*, May 1917, 365–67.

Farber, Manny. "Make Mine Muzak." *New Republic*, May 27, 1946, 769.

Fetterman, John. "The People of Cumberland Gap." *National Geographic Magazine*, November 1971, 591–621.

"Forgotten Men: The Poor Whites." *U.S. News & World Report*, November 27, 1967, 76.

"Fortune Survey: VI: The Comic Strips." *Fortune*, April 1937, 190–91.

"The Founding of the Hindman Settlement School." *Outlook and Independent*, July 28, 1920, 558.

Fox, John, Jr. "A Mountain Europa." *Century Magazine*, September–October 1892, 760–75, 846–58.

———. "The Southern Mountaineer." *Scribner's Magazine*, April–May 1901, 387–99, 556–70. Reprinted in *Appalachian Images in Folk and Popular Culture*, ed. W. K. McNeil, 121–44. Ann Arbor: UMI Research Press, 1989.

———. "On Horseback to Kingdom Come." *Scribner's Magazine*, August 1910, 175–86.

———. "On the Trail of the Lonesome Pine." *Scribner's Magazine*, October 1910, 417–29.

French, Laurence. "When I Get Good and Ready." *Appalachian Journal* 16, no. 1 (1988): 62–70.

Frome, Michael. "Threats to Southern Appalachia." *National Parks & Conservation Magazine*, July 1971, 6–9.

Frost, William Goodell. "Our Contemporary Ancestors in the Southern Mountains." *Atlantic Monthly*, March 1899, 311–19. Reprinted in *Appalachian Images in Folk and Popular Culture*, ed. W. K. McNeil, 92–106. Ann Arbor: UMI Research Press, 1989.

———. "The Southern Mountaineers: Our Kindred of the Boone and Lincoln Type." *American Monthly Review of Reviews*, March 1900, 308–11.

———. "God's Plan for the Southern Mountains." *Biblical Review*, 1921, 405–25.

"Fun without Mickey." *Commonweal*, May 3, 1946, 72–73.

"FUNNIES: Colored Comic Strips in the Best Health at 40." *Newsweek*, December 1, 1934, 26–28.

"Funny Paper Advts." *Fortune*, April 1933, 98–99.

"The Funny Papers." *Fortune*, April 1933, 44–49+.

"Funny Strips: Cartoon-Drawing Is Big Business; Effects on Children Debated." *Literary Digest*, December 12, 1936, 18–19.

Garrigan, Liz Murray. "Bubba Goes to Hollywood." *Nashville Scene*, September 5–11, 2002 (http://www.nashscene.com/cgi-bin/textonly.cgi?story=This_Week:News: City_Limits)

Garyls, William A. "Letter to the Editor." *Harper's*, April 1958, 10.

Gavit, John Palmer. "Bootstrapping among the Pioneers." *Survey*, July 1, 1932, 304–6.

Gingrich, Arnold. *Nothing but People: The Early Days at Esquire—A Personal History, 1928–1958*. New York: Crown, 1971.

Gish, Anthony. "Yes, I'm a Hillbilly." *Esquire*, April 1937, 95, 128, 130.

Gitlin, Todd. "JOIN: Coal-Operatin' in Uptown." *Christian Century*, June 8, 1966, 754–58.

Gitlin, Todd, and Nancy Hollander. *Uptown—Poor Whites in Chicago*. New York: Harper & Row, 1970.

"Goat's Nest Neighbors: They Swap Food and Houn's for Photos." *Newsweek*, September 21, 1942, 47.

"The Gold Guitars." *Newsweek*, April 4, 1966, 96–97.

Goodrich, Frances Louise. *Mountain Homespun*. 1931. Reprint, Knoxville: University of Tennessee Press, 1989.

Goodwin, Fritz. "Right at Home with the Clampetts." *TV Guide*, November 10, 1962, 15–16, 18–19.

Gould, Jack. "TV: 'Beverly Hillbillys [*sic*].'" *New York Times*, November 2, 1962, 63.

"Grandpap's A-Makin'." *Atlantic Monthly*, October 1938, 551–52.

Grattan, C. Hartley. "Trouble in the Hills." *Scribner's Magazine*, November 1935, 290–94.

Green, Abel. "'Hill-Billy' Music." *Variety*, December 29, 1926, 1.

Greene, Laurence. "I Found a Hide-Out." *Saturday Evening Post*, June 2, 1951, 36–37+.

Haddix, Cecille, ed. *Who Speaks for Appalachia?* New York: Washington Square Press, 1975.

Halberstadt, Catherine Capp. "Introduction." In *Li'l Abner Dailies: Vol. 1 (1934–1936)*, 3–4. Princeton, WI: Kitchen Sink Press, 1988.

Hall, Mordaunt. "Primitive Mountaineers." *New York Times Film Review*, February 28, 1927, 22:3.

———. "Where Man Is Vile—'Stark Love' a Realistic Reproduction of Life of Mountaineers." *New York Times*, March 6, 1927, Sect. VII, p. 7.

Ham, Tom. "Close-Up of a Hillbilly Family." *American Mercury*, June 1941, 659–65.

Haney, William H. *The Mountain People of Kentucky: By a Kentucky Mountain Man.* Cincinnati: Robert Clarke, 1906.

Hano, Arnold. "The G.A.P. Love the 'Hillbillies.'" *New York Times Magazine*, November 17, 1963, 30, 120, 122–23.

———. "TV's Topmost—*This* Is America?" *New York Times Magazine*, December 26, 1965, 10–11+.

"The Happy Pappies of Handshoe Holler." *Time Magazine*, November 5, 1965, 38–39.

Harlow, Alvin F. "People of the Hills." *Saturday Evening Post*, March 2, 1935, 12–13+.

Harman, A. F. "Culture in the South." *Christian Science Monitor Weekly*, June 30, 1937, 1–2.

Harmon, Lee. *Hillbilly Ballads*. Beckley, WV: Beckley Newspaper Corporation, 1938.

Harmon, Ronald Lynd. "American Rustic: The Ozarks." *Travel*, August 1977, 42–45.

Harney, Will Wallace. "A Strange Land and a Peculiar People." *Lippincott's Magazine* (October 1873): 429–38. Reprinted in *Appalachian Images in Folk and Popular Culture*, ed. W. K. McNeil, ed., 45–58. Ann Arbor: UMI Research Press, 1989.

Harriman, Mrs. J. Borden. "Some Phases of the Southern Cotton Industry." *Harper's Weekly*, July 11, 1911, 12.

Harrington, Michael. *The Other America: Poverty in the United States*. New York: Macmillan, 1962.

Harris, Corra. "Behind the Times." *Saturday Evening Post*, September 15, 1928, 37+.

Harris, George Washington. *Sut Lovingood: Yarns Spun by a "Nat'ral Born Durn'd Fool."* New York: Dick & Fitzgerald, 1867. Reprint edited by M. Thomas Inge. New Haven: College and University Press, 1966.

Harris, Imperial Jim. *History—Grand & Glorious Order of the Hillbilly Degree*. Milford, OH: Hillbilly Press, 1982.

Harris, Jay S., ed. *TV Guide—The First 25 Years*. New York: Simon and Schuster, 1978.

Harshaw, Lou. "South's Top Scenic Strip." *Travel*, August 1956, 18–21.

Haselden, Kyle. "Mountain Movements." *Christian Century*, May 10, 1961, 582–83.

"Haute Couture—Hillbilly Style." *TV Guide*, March 9, 1963, 6–8.

Hawthorne, Julian. "Mountain Votes Spoil Huntington's Revenge." *The Journal*, April 23, 1900, 2.

Hay, George D. *A Story of the Grand Ole Opry*. Nashville: N.p., 1953.

Haynes, Henry "Homer," and Kenneth "Jethro" Burns. "From Moonshine to Martinis." *Journal of Country Music* 15–16 (1993–1994).

Heath, Evelyn. *Hillbilly Homestead*. New York: Exposition Press, 1965.

"Hillbilly Bus." *American Magazine*, March 1956, 54–55.

"Hillbilly TV Show Hits the Big Time." *Business Week*, March 10, 1956, 30–31.

Hine, Al. "Million Dollar Kettle Drummer." *Esquire*, May 1953, 88–89, 132.

Hobson, Dick. "The Grandpappy of All Gushers." *TV Guide*, April 24, 1971, 16–20.

Hogue, Wayman. "Ozark People." *Scribner's Magazine*, April 1931, 509–20.

Hollander, A. N. J. "The Tradition of 'Poor Whites.'" In *Culture in the South*, ed. William T. Couch, 403–31. Chapel Hill: University of North Carolina Press, 1935.

Holman, Ross L. "The Great Smokies—America's Most Popular Park." *Travel*, October 1948, 18–21, 33.

Holmes, S. J. "Will Birth Control Lead to Extinction?" *Scientific Monthly*, March 1932, 247–51.

Hughes, Marion. *Three Years in Arkansaw*. Chicago: M. A. Donohue & Company, 1905.

Hutchins, William J. "Introduction." *Mountain Life and Work*, April 1925, 1.

Jackson, Thomas W. *On a Slow Train through Arkansaw*. 1903. Reprint. Ed. W. K. McNeil. Lexington: University Press of Kentucky, 1985.

Janofsky, Michael. "Pessimism Retains Grip on Region Shaped by War on Poverty." *New York Times*, February 9, 1998, A-1, A-13.

Johnson, Samuel. "Life in the Kentucky Mountains. By a Mountaineer." *Independent* 65 (July 1908): 72–78. Reprinted in *Appalachian Images in Folk and Popular Culture*, ed. W. K. McNeil, 175–85. Ann Arbor: UMI Research Press, 1989.

Johnston, Josiah Stoddard. "Romance and Tragedy of Kentucky Feuds." *Cosmopolitan* 27, (September 1899): 551–58. Reprinted in *Appalachian Images in Folk and Popular Culture*, ed. W. K. McNeil, 107–19. Ann Arbor: UMI Research Press, 1989.

Jones, Howard Mumford. "The Southern Legend." *Scribner's Magazine*, May 1929, 538–42.

Jones, Ora L. *Peculiarities of the Appalachian Mountaineers*. Detroit: Harlo Press, 1967.

Jordan, Dick. "Slo 'n' Easy Start Weakly Bull-A-Thon." *Rural Radio*, March 1939, 6.

Kahn, E. J., Jr. "Ooff!! (Sob!) Eep!! (Gulp!) Zowie—I." *New Yorker*, November 29, 1947, 46–50+.

———. "Ooff!! (Sob!) Eep!! (Gulp!) Zowie—II." *New Yorker*, December 9, 1947, 48–59.

Kahn, Kathy. *Hillbilly Women.* New York: Doubleday Press, 1973.

Kennedy, Paul. "Minstrels of the Kentucky Hills." *Travel*, June 1942, 14–15, 39.

"The Kentucky Mountaineers." *Science*, April 6, 1928, 12.

Kephart, Horace. *Our Southern Highlanders—A Narrative of Adventure in the Southern Appalachians and a Study of Life among the Mountaineers.* 1913. Reprint, Knoxville: University of Tennessee Press, 1976.

Kernodle, Wayne. "Last of the Rugged Individualists." *Harper's Magazine*, January 1960, 46–51.

King, Nelson. "Hillbilly Music Leaves the Hills." *Good Housekeeping*, June 1954, 18.

"King of Corn." *Newsweek*, July 14, 1969, 94.

Kinney, Courtney. "Reality Show Will Perpetuate Hillbilly Stereotype." *Kentucky Post*, August 31, 2002 (http://www.kypost.com/2002/aug/31/kinney083102.html)

Kirkland, Winifred. "Mountain Mothers." *Ladies' Home Journal*, December 1920, 26–27, 193.

Krout, Maurice H. "Culture and Culture Change." *American Journal of Sociology* 38 (September 1932): 253–63.

Lagemann, John Kord. "You'll Be Comin' round the Mountain." *Collier's Magazine*, May 15, 1948, 84–89.

Lane, Rose Wilder. *Hill Billy.* New York: Harper & Brothers, 1926.

Lasswell, Fred. "Billy, Barney, Snuffy & Me." *Cartoonist PROfiles*, June 1994, 10–21.

Lawson, Marvin. *By Gum, I Made It!—An Ozark Arkie's Hillbilly Boyhood.* Branson, MO: Ozarks Mountaineer, 1977.

Leamy, Hugh. "Now Come All You Good People." *Collier's Magazine*, November 2, 1929, 20, 58–59.

Lee, Alfred. *Race Riot.* New York: Dryden Press, 1943.

"Leena the Unseena." *Newsweek*, July 1, 1946, 58.

Lessing, Bruno. "Humor-Laughter-'Comics.'" *Circulation*, April 1925, 12–13, 40–41.

"Letters from Arkansas." *American Monthly Magazine* n.s., 1 (1836): 25–26.

"Leviticus vs. Yokums." *Newsweek*, November 29, 1948, 58.

Lewis, Richard Warren. "The Golden Hillbillies." *Saturday Evening Post*, February 2 1963, 30–35.

"A Light in the Mountains." *Time Magazine*, October 16, 1950, 74–75.

"Li'l Abner's Mad Capp." *Newsweek*, November 24, 1947, 60–61.

"Li'l Abner—Broadway and Dogpatch." *Life*, January 14, 1957, 74–83.

Lilienthal, David E. *The Journals of David Lilienthal: The TVA Years 1939–1945.* New York: Harper & Row, 1964.

———. *TVA—Democracy on the March.* New York: Harper & Brothers, 1964.

Lovinggood, R. S. "Negro Seer: His Preparation and Mission." *African Methodist Episcopal Church Review* 24, no. 2 (1907): 156–72. Cited in *The African American Experience in Ohio, 1850–1920.* Web site (http:dbs.ohiohistory.org/africanam/)

Lowrie, Sarah D. "The Comic Strips." *Forum*, April 1928, 527–36.

"Luring the Poor Out of the Hills." *Business Week*, July 1, 1967, 74–78.

Lynde, Francis. "The Moonshiner of Fact." *Lippincott's Magazine* 57 (January 1896): 66–76. Reprinted in *Appalachian Images in Folk and Popular Culture*, ed. W. K. McNeil, 75–88. Ann Arbor: UMI Research Press, 1989.

MacClintock, S. S. "The Kentucky Mountains and Their Feuds." *American Journal of Sociology* 7 (1901): 1–28, 171–87.

MacDonald, Betty. *The Egg and I.* Philadelphia: J. B. Lippincott, 1945.

MacKaye, Marion Morse. "God, Humanity, and the Mountains." *Survey Graphic*, August 1946, 288–93, 302.

MacKaye, Percy. "Poetic Drama in Kentucky's Mountains." *Literary Digest*, January 26, 1924, 29–31.

———. *This Fine Pretty World: A Comedy of the Kentucky Mountains.* New York: Macmillan, 1924.

"Make Mine Music." *Time*, May 6, 1946, 98, 101.

Maloney, John. "Time Stood Still in the Smokies." *Saturday Evening Post*, April 27, 1946, 16–17+.

Maloney, Russell. "Li'l Abner's Capp: His Cartoon Characters Are America's Favorite Hillbillies." *Life*, June 24, 1946, 58–62+.

Manne, Jack. "Mental Deficiency in a Closely Inbred Mountain Clan." *Mental Hygiene*, April 1936, 269–79.

Marey, Stuart. "Pioneer of 1941." *American Magazine*, March 1941, 104.

Markham, R. H. "As Old as the Mountains." *Christian Science Monitor Weekly Magazine*, March 1, 1941, 12.

Martin, Roscoe. *TVA—The First Twenty Years—A Staff Report.* University, AL, and Knoxville, TN: University of Alabama Press and University of Tennessee Press, 1956.

Masters, Victor I. "The Mountaineer of the South." *Missionary Review of the World*, November 1919, 845–49.

Maxwell, James A. "Down from the Hills and into the Slums." *The Reporter*, December 13, 1956, 27–29.

McAdoo, Julia. "Where the Poor Are Rich." *American Mercury*, September 1955, 86–89.

McCord, David Frederick. "The Social Rise of the Comics." *American Mercury*, July 1935, 360–64.

McVey, Frank L. "Is There a Mountain Problem?" *Mountain Life and Work*, July 1935, 1–4.

Meek, Frederick M. "Sweet Land of Andy Gump." *Christian Century*, May 8, 1935, 605–7.

Mell, Mildred. "The Southern Poor White—Myth, Symbol, and Reality of a Nation." *Saturday Review of Literature*, January 23, 1943, 13–15.

Mencken, H. L. "The Sahara of the Bozart." In *Pejudices: Second Series*, 136–54. New York: Octagon Books, 1920.

———. "The Hills of Zion." In *Prejudices: Fifth Series*, 75–86. New York: Alfred A. Knopf, 1926.

———. "In Memoriam: W. J. B." In *Prejudices: Fifth Series*, 64–74. New York: Alfred A. Knopf, 1926.

———. "Inquisition." In *The Days of H. L. Mencken: Heathen Days*, 214–38. New York: Alfred A. Knopf, 1947.

———. "The Scopes Trial." In *The Impossible H. L. Mencken*, ed. Marion Elizabeth Rodgers, 560–611. New York: Doubleday, 1991.

Mercer, H. C. "On the Track of the Arkansas Traveler." *Century Magazine*, March 1896, 707–12.

Miles, Emma Beth. *The Spirit of the Mountains*. 1905. Reprint, Knoxville: University of Tennessee Press, 1975.

"Modernizing Elizabethans of To-day." *Literary Digest*, February 15, 1936, 17.

Morgan, Arthur E. *The Making of the TVA*. Buffalo: Prometheus Books, 1974.

Morris, Lucille. "Good Ol' Hillbilly . . ." *University Review—A Journal of the University of Kansas City* 4, no. 2 (1937): 188–90.

Moss, Sylvia. "The New Comedy." *Television Quarterly* 4 (1965): 42–45.

"Mountain Dew Bottler Catalog." Pepsi-Cola, 1966.

"The Mountain Whites." *Outlook and Independent*, May 17, 1922, 92, 94.

"Mountaineers in Picture." *New York Times*, August 29, 1926, Sect. VII, p. 5.

Muggeridge, Malcolm. "Why Those Hillbillies Are Rampant in Britain." *TV Guide*, March 6, 1965, 22–26.

"Must Hee-Haw TV." *E! Online News*, August 29, 2002 (http://entertainment.msn.com/news/eonline/082902_hee.asp)

"A Mutual Admiration Society." *TV Guide*, January 23, 1960, 6–7.

"My Neighbors and Myself—By a Country Doctor." *Ladies' Home Journal*, February 1928, 6–7, 58, 60, 62.

Newman, Thomas. "The Folk of Bloody Mountain." *Esquire*, January 1938, 68–69, 139.

Newton, Dwight. "High Flying Hillbillies." *San Francisco Examiner*, November 18, 1965, 33.

Niles, John Jacob. "Hill Billies." *Scribner's Magazine*, November 1927, 601–5.

———. "In Defense of the Backwoods." *Scribner's Magazine*, June 1928, 738–45.

———. "My Precarious Life in the Public Domain." *Atlantic Monthly*, December 1948, 129–31.

Niles, John Jacob, and Jonathan Williams. *The Appalachian Photographs of Doris Ulmann*. Highlands, NC: Jargon Society, 1971.

Nixon, Herman Clarence. *Forty Acres and Steel Mules*. Chapel Hill: University of North Carolina Press, 1938.

O'Connell, Mary Rebecca. "One Hundred Percent American." *Catholic World*, May 1930, 153–56.

Odum, Howard W. *Southern Regions of the United States*. Chapel Hill: University of North Carolina Press, 1936.

"The Okies—A National Problem." *Business Week*, February 10, 1940, 16–17.

"Okies of the '60s." *Time Magazine*, April 20, 1962, 31.

Olmsted, Frederick Law. *A Journey in the Back Country*. New York: Mason Brothers, 1863.

"On Sadie Hawkins Day, Girls Chase Boys in 201 Colleges." *Life*, December 11, 1939, 32–33.

"On the Cob." *Time Magazine*, November 30, 1962, 76.

Oswalt, Lovat. *Hillbilly High Jinks (A Rousing Hillbilly Comedy in One Act)*. Boston: Walter H. Baker, 1952.

"Our Southern Highlands Makes News To-day." *House and Garden*, November 1942, 48–51.

"A People Who 'Hanker Fer Larnin.'" *Literary Digest*, February 10, 1923, 34–35.

"Personal and Otherwise—the Embarrassing Truth about Davy Crockett, the Alamo, Yoknapatawpha County, and Other Dear Myths." *Harper's Magazine*, July 1955, 16–18.

Peyton, Dave. "First *Beverly Hillbillies* Bad Enough. 'Montani Semper Stereotype' Strikes W.Va. Once Again." *Charleston Daily Mail*, September 2, 2002, 4A.

Photiadis, John D., and Harry K. Schwarzweller, eds. *Change in Rural Appalachia— Implications for Action Programs*. Philadelphia: University of Pennsylvania Press, 1970.

"Pistol Packin' Mama." *Life*, October 11, 1943, reprinted in *A History and Encyclopedia of Country, Western, and Gospel Music*, ed. Linnell Gentry, n.p. St. Clair Shores, MI: Scholarly Press, 1972.

Pitts, Leonard, Jr. "Reintarnation! Second 'Beverly Hillbillies' as Reality TV Not Funny." *Charleston Gazette*, September 6, 2002, 4A.

Plumb, Charlie. "Inside the Funny Page." *Esquire*, April 1942, 57, 110–11.

"Poetic Drama in Kentucky's Mountains." *Literary Digest*, January 26, 1924, 29–30.

Politzer, Heinz. "From Little Nemo to Li'l Abner—Comic Strips as Present-Day American Folklore." *Commentary*, October 1949, 346–54.

Poole, Ernest. "The Nurse on Horseback—Has Brought New Life and Hope to the Kentucky Mountaineers." *Good Housekeeping*, June 1932, 38–37+.

"Poor White Trash." *Cornhill Magazine*, April 1882, 579–84.

Portis, Charles. "That New Sound from Nashville." *Saturday Evening Post*, February 12, 1966, 30–38.

Portor, Laura Spencer. "In Search of Local Color." *Harper's Magazine*, August– September 1922, 281–94, 451–66.

Powell, Levi W. *Who Are These Mountain People? An Intimate Historical Account of Southern Appalachia*. New York: Exposition Press, 1966.

Pridemore, Francis. "What Prohibition Has Done for the Mountaineers." *Outlook and Independent*, July 20, 1927, 884–85.

"Primitive Mountaineers Filmed in Native Nooks." *New York Times*, February 20, 1927, Sect. VII, p. 6.

"Putting the Clampett on 'Hillbillies.'" *Appalachian Journal* 21, no. 1 (1993): 22.

Quinn, Arthur Hobson. "New Notes and Old in the Drama: 1923–1924." *Scribner's Magazine* 76 (1924): 79–87.

R., of Tennessee. "A Week in the Great Smoky Mountains." *Southern Literary Messenger* 31 (August 1860): 117–31. Reprinted in *Appalachian Images in Folk and Popular Culture*, ed. W. K. McNeil, 23–44. Ann Arbor: UMI Research Press, 1989.

Raine, James Watt. *The Land of Saddle-Bags: A Study of the Mountain People of Ap-*

palachia. New York: Council of Women for Home Missions and Missionary Education Movement of the United States and Canada, 1924.

Ralph, Julian. "Our Appalachian Americans." *Harper's Magazine*, June 1903, 32–41.

Randolph, Vance. "The Ozark Dialect in Fiction." *American Speech*, March 1927, 283–89.

———. *The Ozarks: An American Survival of Primitive Society*. New York: Vanguard Press, 1931.

———. *Ozark Mountain Folks*. New York: Vanguard Press, 1932.

———. "Ozark Anthology—An Introduction." *University Review—A Journal of the University of Kansas City* 4, no. 2 (1937): 101–4.

———. *Funny Stories about Hillbillies*. Girard, KS: Haldeman-Julius Publications, 1944.

———. *Ozark Superstitions*. New York: Columbia University Press, 1947.

A Reminiscent History of the Ozarks Region. 1894. Reprint, Easley, SC: Southern Historical Press, 1978.

Reynolds, Horace. "I Hear America Singing." *American Mercury*, October 1944, 463–67.

Richardson, Don, Sr. "Junior Cobb of Three Brothers, Ark., Judges *The Beverly Hillbillies* (He's hill folks, himself)." *TV Guide*, July 16, 1963, 8–9.

Richardson, Eudora Ramsay. "Contented Though American." *Forum and Century* 89, no. 5 (1933): 263–67.

Roberts, A. W. "Don't Call Me Hillbilly." *Christian Science Monitor Weekly Magazine*, March 18, 1944, 4.

Roberts, Bruce, and Nancy Roberts. *Where Time Stood Still: A Portrait of Appalachia*. New York: Macmillan, 1970.

Rodell, Fred. "Everybody Reads the Comics." *Esquire*, March 1945, 50–51+.

Rogers, Dennis. "Shootin' for Some Crude." *Newsobserver.com*, September 4, 2002 (http://newsobserver.com/new...sts/v-print/story/1699351p-1717518c.html)

Roiphe, Anne. "The Waltons—Ma and Pa and John-Boy in Mythic America." *New York Times Magazine*, November 18, 1973, 40–41+.

Ross, Malcolm. *Machine Age in the Hills*. New York: Macmillan, 1933.

———. "My Neighbors Hold to Mountain Ways." *National Geographic Magazine*, June 1958, 856–80.

Russell, Gladys Trentham. *Call Me Hillbilly—A True Humorous Account of the Simple Life in the Smokies before the Tourists Came*. Rev. ed. Alcoa, TN: Russell Publishing Company, 1987.

"Sadie Hawkins at Yale." *Time*, November 11, 1940, 51.

Sauer, Carl O. "The Economic Problem of the Ozark Highland." *Scientific Monthly*, September 1920, 215–27.

Scheinfeld, Amram. "A Portrait in Zowie!" *Esquire*, November 1935, 78+.

Scherman, Robert. "Hillbilly Phenomenon." *Christian Science Monitor Weekly Magazine*, March 13, 1948, 10.

"The Schmoo's Return." *New Yorker*, October 26, 1963, 39–40.

Schoolcraft, Henry. *Scenes and Adventures in the Semi-Alpine Region of the Ozark*

Mountains of Missouri and Arkansas. Philadelphia: Lippincott, Grambo, and Company, 1863.

Schuyler, George. "Our White Folks." *American Mercury*, December 1927, 385–92.

Seitz, Don C. "Mountain Folks—Some Glimpses of the One Hundred Per Cent Americans in the Blue Ridge Country." *Outlook and Independent*, September 29, 1926, 146–47.

Seldes, Gilbert. *The Seven Lively Arts*. New York: Harper & Brothers, 1924.

——. "The Beverly Hillbillies." *TV Guide*, December 15, 1962. Reprinted in *TV Guide—The First 25 Years*, ed. Jay S. Harris, 65–66. New York: Simon and Schuster, 1978.

Semple, Ellen Churchill. "The Anglo-Saxons of the Kentucky Mountains: A Study in Anthropogeography." *Geographical Journal* 17 (June 1901). Reprinted in *Appalachian Images in Folk and Popular Culture*, ed. W. K. McNeil, 145–74. Ann Arbor: UMI Research Press, 1989.

Shanley, John. "TV: Simplicity Rescues One of Four Weekly Comedies." *New York Times*, October 1, 1962, 63.

Shaub, Earl L. "Tennessee's Vanishing Mountaineers." *Christian Science Monitor Weekly Magazine*, February 20, 1943, 8–9.

Shayon, Robert Lewis. "Innocent Jeremiah." *Saturday Review*, January 5, 1963, 32.

Sheppard, Muriel Earley. *Cabins in the Laurel*. Chapel Hill: University of North Carolina Press, 1935.

Sherman, Mandel, and Thomas R. Henry. *Hollow Folk*. 1933. Reprint, Berryville, VA: Virginia Book Company, 1973.

Sherwood, Herbert Francis. "Our New Racial Drama: Southern Mountaineers in the Textile Industry." *North American Review*, October 1922, 489–96.

Silcox, Segil Glenn. *A Hillbilly Marine*. N.p., 1977.

Simon, Charlie May. "Retreat to the Land—An Experience in Poverty." *Scribner's Magazine*, May 1933, 309–12.

Simpich, Frederick. "Land of a Million Smiles." *National Geographic Magazine*, May 1943, 589–623.

Smith, Arthur. "'Hill Billy' Folk Music—A Little-Known American Type." *The Etude*, March 1933, 154, 208.

Smith, Beverly, Jr. "The Change in the Mountains." *Saturday Evening Post*, March 28, 1964, 60–62.

Somerndike, J. M. "The Southern Mountaineers, Past, Present and Future." *Missionary Review of the World*, March 1928, 198–203.

"Southern Highlands—Special Issue." *House and Garden*, June 1942, 1–51.

"The Southern Highlands: A Short History." *National Parks & Conservation Magazine*, July 1971, 5.

Spaulding, Arthur W. *The Men of the Mountains*. Nashville: Southern Publishing Association, 1915.

"Special Hillbilly Issue." *Western Folklore*, July 1971.

"Sprightly Comics Really Middle-Aged." *Editor and Publisher*, July 21, 1934, 306–7.

"Stark Love." *Variety*, March 2, 1927.

"'Stark Love'—Interesting and Absorbing Drama of Primitive Life of Mountaineers, Acted by a Native Cast." *Moving Picture World*, March 19, 1927, 214.

Starr, Fred. *Of These Hills and Us.* Boston: Christopher Publishing House, 1958.

Staunton, Helen M. "Editors, Specialists Discuss the Comics." *Editor and Publisher*, November 22, 1947, 40.

Steele, Harry. "The Inside Story of the Hillbilly Business." *Radio Guide* (1936): 20–21, 42. Reprinted in *JEMF Quarterly* 10, pt. 2 (Summer 1974): 51–54.

Steinbeck, John. "Introduction." In *Al Capp, The World of Li'l Abner.* N.p.: Capp Enterprises, 1953.

Stepmann, Charles A. "What Is Wrong with TV—and with Us." *New York Times Magazine*, April 19, 1964, 13+.

Strong, Phil. "The Friendly Ozarks." *Holiday*, August 1951, 90–97+.

Strother, David Hunter. "A Winter in the South." *Harper's New Monthly Magazine* 15 (1857): 433–51; 594–606; 721–40; 16 (1858): 167–83; 721–36.

"The Subject Is Television." *TV Guide*, July 20, 1963, 15–27.

Swift, W. H. "The Campaign in North Carolina. The Mountain Whites—By One of Them." *Child Labor Bulletin*, May 1913, 96–104.

"Tain't Funny." *Time*, September 29, 1947, 79.

Tannenbaum, Frank. *Darker Phases of the South.* New York: Negro Universities Press, 1969.

Tarcher, J. D. "The Serious Side of the Comic-Strip." *Printer's Ink*, April 28, 1932, 3–6.

Taylor, Barbara, Mary Thomas, and Laurie Branson. "'He Shouted Loud, "Hosanna, DELIVERANCE Will Come".'" *Foxfire* 7, no. 4 (Winter 1973): Special Insert, n.p.

"There Are No 100% Americans." *Collier's Magazine*, July 26, 1941, 58.

These Are Our Lives (as Told by the People and Written by Members of the Federal Writer's Project of the Works Progress Administration in North Carolina, Tennessee, and Georgia). Chapel Hill: University of North Carolina Press, 1939.

"They Love Mountain Music." *Time Magazine*, May 7, 1956, 60.

"They're Still Single." *TV Guide*, February 27, 1965, 22–24.

"This Is the Real McCoy." *TV Guide*, August 2, 1958, 20–23.

Thomas, Jean. "The Changing Mountain Folk." *American Mercury*, July 1945, 43–49.

Thompson, Lovell. "America's Day-Dream." *Saturday Review of Literature*, November 13, 1937, 3–4, 16.

———. "How Serious Are the Comics." *Atlantic Monthly*, September 1942, 127–29.

Thompson, Samuel H. *The Highlanders of the South.* New York: Eaton & Mains, 1910.

Thornborough, Laura. "Americans the Twentieth Century Forgot." *Travel*, April 1928, 25–28, 42.

"Thousands Expected Here for 'Hillbilly Days.'" *Pike County News*, March 31, 1977, 1:1, 1:3.

Tommasini, Anthony. "Those Backwater Folks, Happily Dispensable." *New York Times*, March 28, 1998, A-13.

Trotter, Margaret. "Appalachia Speaking." *Mountain Life and Work*, October 1937, 25–27.

Tunley, Roul. "The Strange Case of West Virginia." *Saturday Evening Post*, February 6, 1960, 19–21, 64–66.

Ulmann, Doris (photographer). "The Mountaineers of Kentucky—A Series of Portrait Studies." *Scribner's Magazine*, June 1928, 675–81.

Vaughn, Marshall Everett. "Purpose of This Magazine." *Mountain Life and Work*, April 1925, 2–3.

Verde, Tom. "98 Moonshiners Add Drugs and Guns to the Recipe." *New York Times*, February 2, 1998, A-12.

Vincent, George E. "A Retarded Frontier." *American Journal of Sociology* 4, no. 1 (1898): 1–20.

Vlamos, James Frank. "The Sad Case of the Funnies." *American Mercury*, April 1941, 411–16.

Votaw, Albert N. "The Hillbillies Invade Chicago." *Harper's Magazine*, February 1958, 64–67.

Wallace, Henry A. "Racial Theories and the Genetic Basis for Democracy." *Science*, February 17, 1939, 140–43.

Warner, Charles Dudley. "On Horseback." *Atlantic Monthly*, July–October 1885, 88–100, 194–207, 388–98.

———. "Comments on Kentucky." *Harper's New Monthly Magazine*, January 1889, 255–71.

Watkins, Floyd C. *Yesterday in the Hills*. Chicago: Quadrangle Books, 1963.

Watterson, Henry. *Oddities in Southern Life and Character*. Boston: Houghton Mifflin, 1910.

Webb, Paul. "Hillbillies in the Bigtime Feud." *Esquire*, December 1943, 10.

Weller, Jack E. *Yesterday's People—Life in Contemporary Appalachia*. Lexington: University Press of Kentucky, 1965.

Wenrick, Lewis A. "Teaching the Mountaineers of Tennessee." *Missionary Review of the World*, October 1922, 811–12.

Wentworth, Harold. *American Dialect Dictionary*. New York: Thomas Y. Crowell, 1944.

"When Whites Migrate from the South." *U.S. News & World Report*, October 14, 1963, 70–73.

Whitney, Dwight. "It's about the Atavistic Urge." *TV Guide*, January 8, 1966, 16–19.

———. "The Simple Virtues Are Back in Style." *TV Guide*, April 28, 1973, 24–28.

Wiggam, Albert Edward. "The Rising Tide of Degeneracy—What Everybody Ought to Know about Eugenics." *World's Work*, November 1926, 25–33.

Wightman, Reverend Robert S. "The Southern Mountain Problem—A Study of the Efforts to Solve a Great Unfinished Task." *Missionary Review of the World*, February 1922, 120–26.

Wilds, Reverend J. T. "The Mountain Whites of the South." *Missionary Review of the World*, December 1895, 921–23.

William Byrd's Histories of the Dividing Line betwixt Virginia and North Carolina. New York: Dover Publications, 1967.

Williamson, Gladys Parker. "Living Memorials to Abraham Lincoln—Teaching Independence, Industry and Christian Service at Cumberland Gap." *Missionary Review of the World*, April 1923, 279–82.

Wilson, Charles Morrow. "Moonshiners." *Outlook and Independent*, December 19, 1928, 1350–52, 1381.

———. "Backwoods Morality." *Outlook and Independent*, January 9, 1929, 65–67, 80.

———. "Backhill Culture." *The Nation*, July 17, 1929, 63–65.

———. "Elizabethan America." *Atlantic Monthly*, August 1929, 238–44. Reprinted in *Appalachian Images in Folk and Popular Culture*, ed. W. K. McNeil, 205–14. Ann Arbor: UMI Research Press, 1989.

———. *Backwoods America*. Chapel Hill: University of North Carolina Press, 1934.

Wilson, Liza, and David McClure. "Ma and Pa Kettle—Hollywood Goldmine." *Collier's*, December 8, 1951, 22+.

Wilson, Samuel Tyndale. *The Southern Mountaineers*. New York: Literature Department—Presbyterian Home Missions, 1914.

Wobus, Paul A. "Experiences among Ozark Mountaineers." *Missionary Review of the World*, June 1939, 282–85.

Woodward, C. Vann. "Hillbilly Realism." *Southern Review* 4 (1938/1939): 676–81.

"Yokum Gold." *Newsweek*, July 21, 1947, 54.

Zolotow, Maurice. "Hillbilly Boom." *Saturday Evening Post*, February 12, 1944, 22–23+.

Secondary Sources

Published Materials (Books, Articles, Web-based Sources)

Alvey, Mark. "The Independents: Rethinking the Television Studio System." In *The Revolution Wasn't Televised—Sixties Television and Social Conflict*, ed. Lynn Spigel and Michael Curtin, 139–58. New York: Routledge, 1997.

Amossy, Ruth. "Commonplace Knowledge and Innovation." *SubStance* 62/63 (1990): 145–56.

Archdeacon, Thomas J. *Becoming American—An Ethnic History*. New York: Free Press, 1983.

Arnold, Edwin T. "Al, Abner, and Appalachia." *Appalachian Journal* 17, no. 3 (1990): 262–75.

———. "Abner Unpinned—Al Capp's Li'l Abner, 1940–1955." *Appalachian Journal* 24, no. 4 (1997): 420–36.

Arnow, Pat. "The Hills Meet Hollywood—The *Now and Then* Guide to Selected Feature Films about Appalachia." *Now and Then* 8, no. 3 (1991): 8–12.

Asbell, Bernard. "The Vanishing Hillbilly." *Saturday Evening Post*, September 23, 1961, 92–95.

Askins, Donald. "John Fox, Jr.: A Re-Appraisal; or, With Friends Like That, Who Needs Enemies." *Mountain Review*, Winter 1975, 15–16.

Austin, Wade. "The Real Beverly Hillbillies." *Southern Quarterly* 19, no. 3–4 (1981): 83–94.

Averill, Patricia. "Folk and Popular Elements in Modern Country Music." *Journal of Country Music* 5, no. 2 (1975): 43–54.

Balio, Tino, ed. *Hollywood in the Age of Television*. Boston: Unwin Hyman, 1990.

Banes, Ruth A. "Doris Ulmann and Her Mountain Folk." *Journal of American Culture* 8 (Spring 1985): 29–42.

Barnouw, Erik. *The Image Empire—A History of Broadcasting in the United States (v. 3—from 1953)*. New York: Oxford University Press, 1970.

———. *Documentary—A History of the Non-Fiction Film*. New York: Oxford University Press, 1993.

Baron, Robert, and Nicholas R. Spitzer, eds. *Public Folklore*. Washington, DC: Smithsonian Institution Press, 1992.

Barsam, Richard Meran. *Nonfiction Film—A Critical History*. New York: E. P. Dutton, 1973.

Bartlett, Richard. "Daniel Boone." In *The Reader's Companion to American History*, ed. Eric Foner and John Garraty, 122–23. Boston: Houghton Mifflin, 1991.

Batteau, Allen. "Appalachia and the Concept of Culture: A Theory of Shared Misunderstandings." *Appalachian Journal* 7, no. 1–2 (Autumn–Winter, 1979–1980): 9–31.

———. ed. *Appalachia and America—Autonomy and Regional Dependence*. Lexington: University Press of Kentucky, 1983.

———. *The Invention of Appalachia*. Tucson: University of Arizona Press, 1990.

Baughman, James L. *The Republic of Mass Culture—Journalism, Filmmaking, and Broadcasting in America since 1941*. Baltimore: Johns Hopkins University Press, 1992.

Baughman, Ronald. *Understanding James Dickey*. Columbia: University of South Carolina Press, 1985.

Becker, Jane S. *Selling Tradition: Appalachia and the Construction of an American Folk, 1930–1940*. Chapel Hill: University of North Carolina Press, 1998.

Belcher, Anndrena. "Relatively Strange—On the Set of *Next of Kin*." *Now and Then—The Appalachian Magazine*, Fall 1991, 22, 25–26.

Belton, John. *American Cinema/American Culture*. New York: McGraw-Hill, 1994.

Berger, Arthur Asa. *Li'l Abner—A Study in American Satire*. New York: Twayne, 1970.

Bernardi, Daniel, ed. *The Birth of Whiteness—Race and the Emergence of U.S. Cinema*. New Brunswick: Rutgers University Press, 1996.

———. "The Voice of Whiteness: D. W. Griffith's Biograph Films (1908–1913)." In *The Birth of Whiteness: Race and the Emergence of U.S. Cinema*, ed. Daniel Bernardi, 103–28. New Brunswick: Rutgers University Press, 1996.

Bertrand, Michael T. *Race, Rock, and Elvis*. Urbana: University of Illinois Press, 2000.

Billings, Dwight B., Gurney Norman, and Katherine Ledford, eds. *Confronting Appalachian Stereotypes—Back Talk from an American Region*. Lexington: University Press of Kentucky, 1999.

Billings, Dwight B., Mary Beth Pudup, and Altina L. Waller. "Taking Exception with Exceptionalism—The Emergence and Transformation of Historical Studies of Appalachia." In *Appalachia in the Making—The Mountain South in the Nine-

teenth Century, ed. Dwight B. Billings, Mary Beth Pudup, and Altina L. Waller, 1–24. Chapel Hill: University of North Carolina Press, 1995.

Biskind, Peter. *Seeing Is Believing—How Hollywood Taught Us to Stop Worrying and Love the Fifties*. New York: Pantheon Books, 1983.

Blackbeard, Bill. "Them Thar Hillbillies: Abner, Leviticus, Snuffy—a (Gasp!) Look at What Al Capp Unleashed." In *Li'l Abner Dailies: Vol. 3 (1937)*, 3–7. Princeton, WI: Kitchen Sink Press, 1988.

Blair, Walter. *Native American Humor (1800–1900)*. New York: American Book Company, 1937.

———. *Essays on American Humor—Blair through the Ages*. Madison: University of Wisconsin Press, 1993.

Blair, Walter, and Hamlin Hill. *America's Humor—From Poor Richard to Doonesbury*. New York: Oxford University Press, 1978.

Blevins, Brooks. *Hill Folks: A History of Arkansas Ozarkers and Their Image*. Chapel Hill: University of North Carolina Press, 2002.

Bloom, Alan. *The Closing of the American Mind*. New York: Simon and Schuster, 1987.

Bogart, Leo. *The Age of Television*. New York: Frederick Ungar, 1972.

Boskin, Joseph, and Joseph Dorinson. "Ethnic Humor: Subversion and Survival." *American Quarterly* 37, no. 1 (1985): 81–97.

Bowler, Betty Miller. "'That Ribbon of Social Neglect': Appalachia and the Media in 1964." *Appalachian Journal* 12, no. 3 (1985): 239–47.

Boyer, Paul. *Urban Masses and Moral Order in America, 1820–1920*. Cambridge: Harvard University Press, 1978.

Bradley, Donald S., Jacqueline Boles, and Christopher Jones. "From Mistress to Hooker: 40 Years of Cartoon Humor in Men's Magazines." *Qualitative Sociology* (September 1979): 42–62.

Brauer, Carl M. "Kennedy, Johnson, and the War on Poverty." *Journal of American History* 69 (June 1982): 98–119.

Breazeale, Kenon. "In Spite of Women: *Esquire* Magazine and the Construction of the Male Consumer." *SIGNS* 20, no. 1 (1994): 1–22.

Brodbeck, Arthur J., and David M. White. "How to Read Li'l Abner Intelligently." In *Mass Culture—The Popular Arts in America*, ed. Bernard Rosenberg and David M. White, 218–23. Glencoe, IL: Free Press, 1957.

Bronner, Simon J. *Old-Time Music Makers of New York State*. Syracuse: Syracuse University Press, 1987.

Brooks, Tim, and Earle Marsh. *The Complete Directory to Prime Time Network and Cable TV Shows—1946-Present*. 6th ed. New York: McGraw-Hill, 1982.

Brown, Charles T. *Music U.S.A.—America's Country and Western Tradition*. Englewood Cliffs, NJ: Prentice Hall, 1986.

Brown, James S. "An Appalachian Footnote to Toynbee's A Study of History." *Appalachian Journal* 6, no. 1 (1978): 29–32.

Brown, Karl. "Hollywood in the Hills—The Making of *Stark Love*." *Appalachian Journal* 18, no. 2 (1991): 170–220.

Brown, Lester. *Televi$ion—The Business behind the Box*. New York: Harcourt Brace Jovanovich, 1971.

Brown, Rodger. "The Road to Hokum: Dogpatch, U.S.A." *Southern Changes* (1994).

———. *Ghost Dancing on the Cracker Circuit: The Culture of Festivals in the American South*. Jackson: University Press of Mississippi, 1997.

Brown, Sarah. "*The Arkansas Traveller*: Southwest Humor on Canvas." *Arkansas Historical Quarterly* 46, no. 4 (1987): 348–75.

Brownlow, Kevin. *The War, the West, and the Wilderness*. New York: Alfred A. Knopf, 1979.

———. Introduction to "Hollywood in the Hills—The Making of *Stark Love*." *Appalachian Journal* 18, no. 2 (1991): 171–73.

Brundage, W. Fitzhugh. "Racial Violence, Lynchings, and Modernization in the Mountain South." In *Appalachians and Race: The Mountain South from Slavery to Segregation*, ed. John Inscoe, 302–16. Lexington: University Press of Kentucky, 2001.

Bryant, John. "Situation Comedy of the Sixties: The Evolution of a Popular Genre." *Studies in American Humor* n.s., 7 (1989): 118–39.

Cantwell, Robert. *When We Were Good: The Folk Revival*. Cambridge: Harvard University Press, 1996.

Carawan, Guy, and Candie Carawan. *Voices from the Mountains*. New York: Alfred A. Knopf, 1975.

Carlton, David L., and Peter A. Coclanis. *Confronting Southern Poverty in the Great Depression: The Report on Economic Conditions of the South with Related Documents*. The Bedford Series in History and Culture. Boston: Bedford Books, 1996.

Caron, James E., and M. Thomas Inge, eds. *Sut Lovingood's Nat'ral Born Yarnspinner: Essays on George Washington Harris*. Tuscaloosa: University of Alabama Press, 1996.

Carr, Patrick, ed. *The Illustrated History of Country Music*. Garden City, NY: Doubleday, 1979.

Cassidy, Frederic G., ed. *Dictionary of American Regional English*. Vol. 2. Cambridge: Belknap Press, 1991.

Castleman, Harry, and Walter J. Podrazik. *Watching TV—Four Decades of American Television*. New York: McGraw-Hill, 1982.

Chappell, Fred. "The Ninety-Ninth Foxfire Book." *Appalachian Journal* 11, no. 3 (1984): 260–67.

Chase, Allan. "Eugenics vs. Poor White Trash—The Great Pellagra Cover-Up." *Psychology Today*, February 1975, 83–86.

Ching, Barbara. *Wrong's What I Do Best: Hard Country Music and Contemporary Culture*. New York: Oxford University Press, 2001.

Clabough, Casey Howard. *Elements: The Novels of James Dickey*. Macon, GA: Mercer University Press, 2002.

Cobb, James C. "From Muskogee to Luckenbach: Country Music and the 'Southernization' of America." *Journal of Popular Culture* 16, no. 3 (1982): 81–91.

Coben, Stanley. *Rebellion against Victorianism—The Impetus for Cultural Change in 1920s America*. Cambridge: Oxford University Press, 1991.

Cohen, Henning, and William B. Dillingham. *Humor of the Old Southwest*. Athens: University of Georgia Press, 1994.

Cohen, Norman. "The Skillet Lickers: A Study of a Hillbilly String Band and Its Repertoire." *Journal of American Folklore* 78, no. 309 (1965): 229–44.

——. "Early Pioneers." In *Stars of Country Music—Uncle Dave Macon to Johnny Rodriguez*, ed. Bill C. Malone and Judith McCulloh, 11–13. Urbana: University of Illinois Press, 1975.

Coles, Robert. *Migrants, Sharecroppers, Mountaineers*. Boston: Little, Brown and Company, 1971.

——. *The South Goes North*. Boston: Little, Brown and Company, 1971.

Collins, Glenn. "Ya-hooo! A Marketing Coup—At 50, Mountain Dew Manages to Tickle Innards of Young Men." *New York Times Magazine*, May 30, 1995, C1+.

Coltman, Robert. "Sweethearts of the Hills: Women in Early Country Music." *JEMF Quarterly* 14, no. 52 (1978): 161–80.

Cook, Sylvia Jenkins. *From Tobacco Road to Route 66: The Southern Poor White in Fiction*. Chapel Hill: University of North Carolina Press, 1976.

Cooper, B. Lee. *Popular Music Perspectives: Ideas, Themes, and Patterns in Contemporary Lyrics*. Bowling Green: Bowling Green State University Popular Press, 1991.

Cox, John Harrington, ed. *Folk-Songs of the South*. Hatboro, PA: Folklore Associates, 1963.

Cox, Stephen. *The Beverly Hillbillies*. New York: HarperCollins, 1993.

"Culture Wars—David Hackett Fischer's *Albion's Seed*." *Appalachian Journal* 19, no. 2 (1992): 161–200.

Cumming, William P., ed. *The Discoveries of John Lederer*. Charlottesville: University of Virginia Press, 1958.

Cunningham, Rodger. "Eat Grits and Die; or, Cracker, Your Breed Ain't Hermeneutical." *Appalachian Journal* 17, no. 2 (1990): 176–82.

——. "Scotch-Irish and Others." *Appalachian Journal* 18, no. 1 (1990): 84–90.

——. "Signs of Civilization: The Trail of the Lonesome Pine as Colonial Narrative." *Journal of the Appalachian Studies Association* 2 (1990): 21–46.

Curtis, L. Perry, Jr. *Apes and Angels: The Irishman in Victorian Caricature*. Washington, DC: Smithsonian Institution Press, 1997.

Cusic, Don. "Comedy and Humor in Country Music." *Journal of American Culture* 16, no. 2 (1993): 45–50.

Dale, E. E. "Arkansas: The Myth and the State." *Arkansas Historical Quarterly* 12, no. 1 (1953): 8–29.

Daniel, Pete. *Standing at the Crossroads—Southern Life in the Twentieth Century*. New York: Hill and Wang, 1986.

——. *Lost Revolutions: The South in the 1950s*. Chapel Hill: University of North Carolina Press for Smithsonian National Museum of American History, Washington, DC, 2000.

Daniel, Wayne W. "George Daniell's Hill Billies: The Band That Named the Music?" *JEMF Quarterly* 19, no. 73 (1983): 81–84.

———. "The National Barn Dance on Network Radio: The 1930s." *Journal of Country Music* 9, no. 3 (1983): 47–62.

———. *Pickin' on Peachtree—A History of Country Music in Atlanta, Georgia*. Urbana: University of Illinois Press, 1990.

Davis, Lloyd. "When Country Wasn't Cool." *Southern Quarterly* 22, no. 3 (1984): 158–72.

Day, Donald. "The Life of George Washington Harris," *Tennessee Historical Quarterly* 6 (1947): 3–38. Reprinted in *Sut Lovingood's Nat'ral Born Yarnspinner: Essays on George Washington Harris*, ed. James E. Caron and M. Thomas Inge, 33–68. Tuscaloosa: University of Alabama Press, 1996.

Day, Ronnie. "Pride and Poverty: An Impressionistic View of the Family in the Cumberlands of Appalachia." In *Appalachia Inside Out—Culture and Custom*, ed. Robert J. Higgs, Ambrose N. Manning, and Jim Wayne Miller, 370–76. Knoxville: University of Tennessee Press, 1995.

DeLoria, Philip J. *Playing Indian*. New Haven: Yale University Press, 1998.

Denisoff, Serge. *Great Day Coming: Folk Music and the American Left*. Urbana: University of Illinois Press, 1971.

Dew, Lee A. "On a Slow Train through Arkansaw—The Negative Image of Arkansas in the Early Twentieth Century." *Arkansas Historical Quarterly* 35, no. 2 (1980): 125–35.

Documentary Film Classics—Produced by the United States Government. Washington, DC: National AudioVisual Center, 1980.

Dorman, Robert L. *Revolt of the Provinces: The Regionalist Movement in America*. Chapel Hill: University of North Carolina Press, 1993.

Dorson, Richard M. *American Folklore and the Historian*. Chicago: University of Chicago Press, 1971.

Douglas, Susan J. "Radio and Television." In *The Reader's Companion to American History*, ed. Eric Foner and John A. Garraty, 903–6. Boston: Houghton Mifflin, 1991.

———. *Where the Girls Are: Growing Up Female with the Mass Media*. New York: Three Rivers Press, 1994.

Dower, John W. *War without Mercy: Race and Power in the Pacific War*. New York: Pantheon Books, 1986.

Drake, Richard B. *A History of Appalachia*. Lexington: University Press of Kentucky, 2001.

Dumenil, Lynn. *The Modern Temper—American Culture and Society in the 1920s*. New York: Hill and Wang, 1995.

Dunn, Durwood. "Mary Noailles Murfree: A Reappraisal." *Appalachian Journal* 6, no. 3 (1979): 197–204.

Dyer, Richard. *The Matter of Images—Essays on Representations*. New York: Routledge, 1993.

Eby, Cecil D., Jr. *"Porte Crayon": The Life of David Hunter Strother*. Chapel Hill: University of North Carolina Press, 1960.

Eisner, Joel, and David Krinsky. *Television Comedy Series—An Episode Guide to 153 TV Sitcoms in Syndication.* Jefferson, NC: McFarland and Company, 1984.

Eller, Ronald D. *Miners, Millhands and Mountaineers: The Modernization of the Appalachian South, 1880–1930.* Knoxville: University of Tennessee Press, 1981.

Ely, Melvin Patrick. *The Adventures of Amos 'n' Andy—A Social History of an American Phenomenon.* New York: Free Press, 1991.

Everson, William K. *American Silent Film, A History of the American Film.* New York: Oxford University Press, 1978.

Falk, Paul Hastings, ed. *Who Was Who in American Art.* New York: Sound View Press, 1985.

Faragher, John Mack. *Daniel Boone: The Life and Legend of an American Pioneer.* New York: Holt, 1992.

Farber, David. *The Age of Great Dreams—America in the 1960s.* New York: Hill and Wang, 1994.

Fields, Armond, and L. Marc Fields. *From the Bowery to Broadway: Lew Fields and the Roots of American Popular Theater.* New York: Oxford University Press, 1993.

Fisher, Stephen L., ed. *Fighting Back in Appalachia—Traditions of Resistance and Change.* Philadelphia: Temple University Press, 1993.

Fisher, Stephen S. "The Grass Roots Speak Back." In *Confronting Appalachian Stereotypes—Back Talk from an American Region,* ed. Dwight B. Billings, Gurney Norman, and Katherine Ledford, 203–14. Lexington: University Press of Kentucky, 1999.

Fishkin, Shelley Fisher. "Interrogating 'Whiteness,' Complicating 'Blackness': Remapping American Culture." *American Quarterly* 47 (September 1995): 428–66.

Fiske, John. *Reading the Popular.* Boston: Unwin Hyman, 1989.

Flynn, Charles, and Todd McCarthy. "The Economic Imperative: Why Was the B Movie Necessary?" In *King of the Bs—Working within the Hollywood System,* ed. Todd McCarthy and Charles Flynn, 13–43. New York: E. P. Dutton, 1975.

Flynt, J. Wayne. *Dixie's Forgotten People—The South's Poor Whites.* Bloomington: Indiana University Press, 1979.

———. *Poor but Proud—Alabama's Poor Whites.* Tuscaloosa: University of Alabama Press, 1989.

Foley, Neil. *The White Scourge: Mexicans, Blacks, and Poor Whites in Texas Cotton Culture.* Berkeley: University of California Press, 1997.

Ford, Thomas R., ed. *The Southern Appalachian Region—A Survey.* Lexington: University Press of Kentucky, 1962.

Frankenberg, Ruth. *White Women, Race Matters: The Social Construction of Whiteness.* Minneapolis: University of Minnesota Press, 1993.

Frierson, Michael. "The Image of the Hillbilly in Warner Bros. Cartoons of the Thirties." In *Reading the Rabbit: Exploration in Warner Bros. Animation,* ed. Kevin S. Sandler, 86–100. New Brunswick: Rutgers University Press, 1998.

Genovese, Eugene D. "'Rather Be a Nigger Than a Poor White Man': Slave Perceptions of Southern Yeomen and Poor Whites." In *Toward a New View of Amer-*

ica — *Essays in Honor of Arthur C. Cole*, ed. Hans L. Trefousse, 79–95. New York: Burt Franklin, 1977.

Gitlin, Todd. "The Turn toward 'Relevance.'" In *Inside Prime Time*, 203–20. New York: Pantheon Books, 1983.

Glen, John M. "The War on Poverty in Appalachia — A Preliminary Report." *Register of the Kentucky Historical Society* 87 (Winter 1989): 40–57.

Glenn, Max E., ed. *Appalachia in Transition*. St. Louis: Bethany Press, 1970.

Goad, Jim. *The Redneck Manifesto*. New York: Simon and Schuster, 1997.

Goldstein, Kalman. "Al Capp and Walt Kelly: Pioneers of Political and Social Satire in the Comics." *Journal of Popular Culture* 25, no. 4 (1992): 81–95.

Gorn, Elliot J. "'Gouge and Bite, Pull Hair and Scratch': The Social Significance of Fighting in the Southern Backcountry." *Journal of American History* 90, no. 1 (1985): 18–43.

Goulart, Ron. *The Adventurous Decade*. New York: Arlington House, 1975.

Graham, Allison. *Framing the South: Hollywood, Television, and Race during the Civil Rights Struggle*. Baltimore: Johns Hopkins University Press, 2001.

Graham, Hugh D., and Ted R. Gurr, eds. *Violence in America: Historical and Comparative Perspectives*. New York: Bantam Books, 1969.

Graham, S. Keith. "Tale a Mixed Blessing for Rabun County." *Atlanta Journal and Constitution*, March 18, 1990, M1+.

Green, Archie. "Hillbilly Music: Source and Symbol." *Journal of American Folklore* 78, no. 309 (1965): 204–28.

——. "Commercial Music Graphics: Sixteen." *JEMF Quarterly* 7, no. 21 (1971): 23–26.

——. "Portraits of Appalachian Musicians." *JEMF Quarterly* 15, no. 54 (1979): 99–106.

——. "Farewell Tony." *JEMF Quarterly* 19, no. 72 (1983): 231–40.

——. "Graphics #67: The Visual Arkansas Traveler." *JEMF Quarterly* 21, no. 75/76 (1985): 31–46.

Green, Douglas B. *Country Roots — The Origins of Country Music*. New York: Hawthorn Books, 1976.

——. "The Singing Cowboy: An American Dream." *Journal of Country Music* 7, no. 2 (1978): 4–61.

Gregory, James N. *American Exodus — The Dust Bowl Migration and Okie Culture in California*. New York: Oxford University Press, 1989.

——. "The Southern Diaspora and the Urban Dispossessed: Demonstrating the Census Public Use Microdata Samples." *Journal of American History* 82 (June 1995): 111–34.

Grieveson, Lee. "Why the Audience Mattered in Chicago in 1907." In *American Movie Audiences: From the Turn of the Century to the Early Sound Era*, ed. Melvyn Stokes and Richard Maltby, 79–91. London: British Film Institute, 1999.

Griffis, Ken. "The Charlie Quirk Story and the Beginning of the Beverly Hill Billies." *JEMF Quarterly* 8, no. 28 (1972): 173–78.

——. "The Beverly Hill Billies." *JEMF Quarterly* 16, no. 57 (1980): 3–17.

Grundy, Pamela. "'We Always Tried to Be Good People': Respectability, Crazy Water Crystals, and Hillbilly Music on the Air 1933–1935." *Journal of American History* 81 (March 1995): 1591–1620.

Guy, Roger. "The Media, the Police, and Southern White Migrant Identity in Chicago, 1955–1970." *Journal of Urban History* 26, no. 3 (2000): 329–49.

Hackney, Sheldon. "The South as a Counterculture." *American Scholar* 42, no. 2 (1973): 283–93.

Hahn, Steven. *The Roots of Southern Populism—Yeoman Farmers and the Transformation of the Georgia Upcountry, 1850–1890*. New York: Oxford University Press, 1983.

Hahn, Steven, and Jonathan Prude, eds. *The Countryside in the Age of Capitalist Transformation: Essays in the Social History of Rural America*. Chapel Hill: University of North Carolina Press, 1985.

Hale, Grace Elizabeth. *Making Whiteness: The Culture of Segregation in the South, 1890–1940*. New York: Vintage, 1998.

Hall, Jacquelyn Dowd, et al. *Like a Family: The Making of a Southern Cotton Mill World*. New York: W. W. Norton, 1987.

Hammack, David C., and Stanton Wheeler. *Social Science in the Making—Essays on the Russell Sage Foundation, 1907–1972*. New York: Russell Sage Foundation, 1994.

Hansen, Miriam. *Babel and Babylon—Spectatorship in American Silent Film*. Cambridge: Harvard University Press, 1991.

Hardy, Charles. "A Brief History of Ethnicity in the Comics." In *Ethnic Images in the Comics*, ed. Charles Hardy and Gail F. Stern, 7–10. Philadelphia: The Balch Institute for Ethnic Studies, 1986.

Harrison, Dan, and Bill Habeeb. *Inside Mayberry*. New York: HarperCollins, 1994.

Hart, Henry. *James Dickey: The World as a Lie*. New York: Picador USA, 2000.

Hartigan, John, Jr. "Name Calling: Objectifying 'Poor Whites' and 'White Trash' in Detroit." In *White Trash—Race and Class in America*, ed. Matt Wray and Annalee Newitz, 41–56. New York: Routledge, 1997.

———. *Racial Situations: Class Predicaments of Whiteness in Detroit*. Princeton: Princeton University Press, 1999.

Harvey, Robert. *The Art of the Funnies: An Aesthetic History*. Jackson: University of Mississippi Press, 1994.

Harvey, R. C., Milton Caniff, and Al Capp. "Nightowls in the Bullpen." In *Li'l Abner Dailies: Vol. 2 (1936)*, 7–11. Princeton, WI: Kitchen Sink Press, 1988.

Hatfield, Sharon. "Mountain Justice: The Making of a Feminist Icon and a Cultural Scapegoat." *Appalachian Journal* 23, no. 1 (1995): 26–47.

Hauck, Richard Boyd. "A Davy Crockett Filmography." In *Davy Crockett: The Man, the Legend, the Legacy*, ed. Michael A. Lofaro, 122–23. Knoxville: University of Tennessee Press, 1985.

Herrin, Dean. "Poor, Proud, and Primitive—Images of Appalachian Domestic Interiors." In *Perspectives on American Furniture*, ed. Gerald W. R. Ward, 93–111. New York: W. W. Norton. Published for the Henry Francis DuPont Winterthur Museum, Winterthur, DE, 1988.

Hewitt, Barnard. *Theatre USA—1668 to 1957*. New York: McGraw-Hill, 1959.

Higgs, Robert J., and Ambrose N. Manning, eds. *Voices from the Hills—Selected Readings of Southern Appalachia*. New York: Frederick Ungar, 1975.

Higham, John. *Strangers in the Land—Patterns of American Nativism, 1860–1925*. New Brunswick: Rutgers University Press, 1955.

Himmelstein, Hal. *Television Myth and the American Mind*. Westport, CT: Praeger, 1994.

Hobson, Fred C., Jr. *Serpent in Eden: H. L. Mencken and the South*. Chapel Hill: University of North Carolina Press, 1974.

Holmes, William F. "Moonshining and Collective Violence: Georgia, 1889–1895." *Journal of American History* 67 (December 1990): 589–611.

Holt, Elvin. "*A Coon Alphabet* and the Comic Mask of Racial Prejudice." *Studies in American Humor*, n.s., 5 (1986–1987): 307–18.

Horn, Maurice. "*Li'l Abner* in Wartime: The Mystery of the Dog That Didn't Bark in the Night." In *Li'l Abner Dailies: Vol. 8 (1942)*, 5–9. Princeton, WI: Kitchen Sink Press, 1990.

Horn, Maurice, ed. *The World Encyclopedia of Cartoons*. Vol. 1–2. New York: Gale Research Company, 1980.

Horstman, Dorothy. *Sing Your Heart Out, Country Boy*. New York: Pocket Books, 1976.

Howd, Dean. "Esquire." In *American Mass-Market Magazines*, ed. Alan Nourie and Barbara Nourie, 108–15. New York: Greenwood Press, 1990.

Hsiung, David C. *Two Worlds in the Tennessee Mountains: Exploring the Origins of Appalachian Stereotypes*. Lexington: University Press of Kentucky, 1997.

Huber, Patrick. "A Short History of Redneck: The Fashioning of a Southern White Masculine Identity." *Southern Cultures* 1, no. 2 (1995): 144–66.

Hunt, Lynn, ed. *The New Cultural History*. Berkeley: University of California Press, 1989.

Hurst, Jack. *Nashville's Grand Ole Opry*. New York: Harry N. Abrams, 1975.

———. "'Barn Dance' Days—Remembering the Stars of a Pioneering Chicago Radio Show." *Chicago Tribune Sunday Magazine*, August 15, 1984, 11.

Hutson, Cecil Kirk. "Cotton Pickin', Hillbillies and Rednecks: An Analysis of Black Oak Arkansas and the Perpetual Stereotyping of the Rural South." *Popular Music and Society* 17, no. 4 (1993): 47–62.

Ignatiev, Noel. *How the Irish Became White*. New York: Routledge, 1995.

Inge, M. Thomas. "Sut and His Illustrators." In *The Lovingood Papers: 1965*, ed. Ben Harris McClary, 26–35. Knoxville: University of Tennessee Press (for the Sut Society), 1965.

———. "Comic Strips." In *Encyclopedia of Southern Culture*, ed. Charles Reagan Wilson and William Ferris, 914–15. Chapel Hill: University of North Carolina Press, 1989.

———. "Sut Lovingood and Snuffy Smith." In Inge, *Comics as Culture*, 69–77. Jackson: University of Mississippi Press, 1990.

———. "Sut, Scarlet, and Their Comic Cousins: The South in the Comics Strip." *Studies in Popular Culture* 19, no. 2 (1996): 153–66.

———. "Al Capp's South: Appalachian Culture in *Li'l Abner*." In *Li'l Abner Dailies: Volume 26 (1960)*, 5–26. Northhampton, MA: Kitchen Sink Press, 1997.

Inscoe, John. "Race and Racism in Nineteenth-Century Southern Appalachia—Myths, Realities, and Ambiguities." In *Appalachia in the Making—The Mountain South in the Nineteenth Century*, ed. Dwight B. Billings, Mary Beth Pudup, and Altina L. Waller, 103–31. Chapel Hill: University of North Carolina Press, 1995.

———. "Olmsted in Appalachia: A Connecticut Yankee Encounters Slavery and Racism in the Southern Highlands, 1854." In *Appalachians and Race: The Mountain South from Slavery to Segregation*, ed. John Inscoe, 154–64. Lexington: University Press of Kentucky, 2001.

———. ed. *Appalachians and Race: The Mountain South from Slavery to Segregation*. Lexington: University Press of Kentucky, 2001.

Isserman, Andrew M. "Appalachia Then and Now: Update of 'The Realities of Deprivation' Reported to the President in 1964." *Journal of Appalachian Studies* 3 (1997): 43–61.

Jacobson, Matthew Frye. *Whiteness of a Different Color: European Immigrants and the Alchemy of Race*. Cambridge: Harvard University Press, 1998.

Jenkins, Henry. *Textual Poachers—Television Fans and Participatory Culture*. New York: Routledge, 1992.

Jenkins, Henry, and Kristine Brunovska Karnick. "Introduction: Golden Eras and Blind Spots—Genre, History and Comedy." In *Classical Hollywood Comedy*, ed. Henry Jenkins and Kristine Brunovska Karnick, 1–13. New York: Routledge, 1995.

Johns, Elizabeth. *American Genre Painting: The Politics of Everyday Life*. New Haven: Yale University Press, 1991.

Johnson, Don. "Balancing Negative Stereotypes in *Deliverance*." *James Dickey Newsletter* 2, no. 2 (Spring 1986): 17–22.

Johnson, Victoria E. "Citizen Welk: Bubbles, Blue Hair, and Middle America." In *The Revolution Wasn't Televised—Sixties Television and Social Conflict*, ed. Lynn Spigel and Michael Curtin, 265–85. New York: Routledge, 1997.

Jones, Jacqueline. *The Dispossessed—America's Underclasses from the Civil War to the Present*. New York: Basic Books, 1992.

Jones, Jesse Aquillah. "Say It Ain't True, Davy! The Real David Crockett vs. the Backwoodsman in Us All." *Appalachian Journal* 15, no. 1 (1987): 45–51.

Jones, Loyal. "A Complete Mountaineer." *Appalachian Journal* 13, no. 3 (1986): 288–96.

Jones, Steven Loring. "From 'Under Cork' to Overcoming: Black Images in the Comics." In *Ethnic Images in the Comics*, ed. Charles Hardy and Gail F. Stern, 21–30. Philadelphia: The Balch Institute for Ethnic Studies, 1986.

Kahn, Ed. "Hillbilly Music: Source and Resources." *Journal of American Folklore* 78, no. 309 (1965): 257–66.

Kammen, Michael. *Mystic Chords of Memory*. New York: Vintage, 1991.

Kantrowitz, Stephen. *Ben Tillman and the Reconstruction of White Supremacy*. Chapel Hill: University of North Carolina Press, 2000.

S.v. "Kemble, Edward Wilson." In *The World Encyclopedia of Cartoons*, ed. Maurice Horn, 332–33. New York: Gale Research Company, 1980.

Kesterson, David B. "A Visit with Radio Humorist Chester Lauck (Lum Edwards)." *Studies in American Humor* 3, no. 3 (1997): 142–48.

Killian, Lewis. *White Southerners*. Amherst: University of Massachusetts Press, 1985.

Kingsbury, Paul. *The Grand Ole Opry History of Country Music*. New York: Villard Books, 1995.

Kingsbury, Paul, and Alan Axelrod, eds. *Country—The Music and the Musicians*. New York: Abbeville Press, 1988.

Klotter, James C. "Feuds in Appalachia: An Overview." *Filson Club History Quarterly* 56, no. 3 (1982): 290–317.

———. "The Black South and White Appalachia." In *Blacks in Appalachia*, ed. William H. Turner and Edward J. Cabbell, 51–67. Lexington: University Press of Kentucky, 1985.

Koszarski, Richard. *An Evening's Entertainment: The Age of the Silent Feature Picture, 1915–1928*. Vol. 3, *History of the American Cinema*. New York: Charles Scribner's Sons, 1990.

Lancaster, Bob. "Bare Feet and Slow Trains." *Arkansas Times*, June 1987, 34–41, 88–101.

———. *The Jungles of Arkansas: A Personal History of the Wonder State*. Fayetteville: University of Arkansas Press, 1989.

Langrall, Peggy. "The Evolution of Country Music." *Charlotte (NC) Observer*, October 16, 1985, E-1, E-6.

Levine, Lawrence. "The Folklore of Industrial Society: Popular Culture and Its Audiences." *American Historical Review* 97 (1992): 1369–1429.

———. "American Culture and the Great Depression." In Levine, *The Unpredictable Past—Explorations in American Cultural History*, 206–30. New York: Oxford University Press, 1993.

Lewis, George H., ed. *All That Glitters: Country Music in America*. Bowling Green: Bowling Green State University Popular Press, 1993.

———. "The Maine That Never Was: The Construction of Popular Myth in Regional Culture." *Journal of American Culture* 16, no. 2 (1993): 91–99.

Lightfoot, William E. "Belle of the Barn Dance: Reminiscing with Lulu Belle Wiseman Stamey." *Journal of Country Music* 11, no. 1 (1987): 2–15.

Linneman, William R. "Will Rogers and the Great Depression." *Studies in American Humor* 3, no. 2–3 (1984): 173–86.

Lipsitz, George. " 'This Ain't No Sideshow': Historians and Media Studies." *Critical Studies in Mass Communication* 5, no. 2 (1988): 147–61.

———. "Listening to Learn and Learning to Listen: Popular Culture, Cultural Theory, and American Studies." *American Quarterly* 42, no. 4 (1990): 615–36.

Lisenby, Foy. "A Survey of Arkansas's Image Problem." *Arkansas Historical Quarterly* 30, no. 1 (1971): 60–71.

Lofaro, Michael, ed. *Davy Crockett—The Man, the Legend, the Legacy*. Knoxville: University of Tennessee Press, 1985.

Lofaro, Michael A., and Joe Cummings, eds. *Crockett at Two Hundred: New Perspectives on the Man and the Myth*. Knoxville: University of Tennessee Press, 1989.

Lornell, Kip. "Early Country Music and the Mass Media in Roanoke, Virginia." *American Music* 5, no. 4 (1987): 403–16.

Lott, Eric. *Love and Theft—Blackface Minstrelsy and the American Working Class*. New York: Oxford University Press, 1993.

Lynn, Kenneth S. *Mark Twain and Southwestern Humor*. Boston: Little, Brown and Company, 1959.

MacCann, Richard Dyer. *The People's Films—A Political History of U.S. Government Motion Pictures*. New York: Hastings House, 1973.

MacDonald, Dwight. "Masscult and Midcult." In *Against the Grain*, 3–75. New York: Random House, 1962.

MacDonald, J. Fred. *One Nation under Television—The Rise and Decline of Network TV*. New York: Pantheon Books, 1990.

Magoc, Chris J. "The Machine in the Wasteland." *Journal of Popular Film and Television* 19, no. 1 (1991): 25–34.

Malone, Bill C. *Country Music USA: A Fifty-Year History*. Austin: University of Texas Press for American Folklore Society, 1968.

———. *Southern Music American Music*. Lexington: University Press of Kentucky, 1979.

———. *Singing Cowboys and Musical Mountaineers—Southern Culture and the Roots of Country Music*. Athens: University of Georgia Press, 1993.

———. *Don't Get above Your Raisin': Country Music and the Southern Working Class*. Urbana: University of Illinois Press, 2002.

Malone, Bill C., and Judith McCulloh. *Stars of Country Music: Uncle Dave Macon to Johnny Rodriguez*. Urbana: University of Illinois Press, 1975.

Marc, David. *Demographic Vistas—Television in American Culture*. Rev. ed. Philadelphia: University of Pennsylvania Press, 1996.

Marcus, Greil. "Review of *Elvis* by Albert Goodman." In *The Country Reader: Twenty-five Years of the Journal of Country Music*, ed. Paul Kingsbury, 298–305. Nashville: Country Music Foundation Press, 1997.

Marschall, Richard. "Al Capp (1909–1980)." In Marschall, *America's Great Comic-Strip Artists*, 237–253. New York: Abbeville Press, 1989.

Martin, Douglas. "Zeke Manners: 'Hillbilly' Who Ruled Radio, Dies at 89." *New York Times*, October 22, 2000, 46.

Mason, Bobbie Ann. "Recycling Kentucky." *New Yorker*, November 1, 1993, 50–56+.

Mason, Michael, ed. *The Country Music Book*. New York: Charles Scribner's Sons, 1985.

Mast, Gerald. *The Comic Mind—Comedy and the Movies*. Chicago: University of Chicago Press, 1973.

Masterson, James R. *Arkansas Folklore—The Arkansas Traveller, Davey Crockett, and Other Legends*. 1942. Reprint, Little Rock: Rose Publishing Company, 1974. Originally published as *Tall Tales of Arkansaw*.

May, Lary. *Screening Out the Past—The Birth of Mass Culture and the Motion Picture Industry*. Chicago: University of Chicago Press, 1983.

McCraw, Thomas K. *Morgan vs. Lilienthal: The Feud within the TVA*. Chicago: Loyola University Press, 1970.

McGee, Marsha G. "Prime Time Dixie: Television's View of a 'Simple' South." *Journal of American Culture* 6, no. 3 (1983): 100–109.

McIlwaine, Shields. *The Southern Poor-White: From Lubberland to Tobacco Road*. Norman: University of Oklahoma Press, 1939.

McKinney, Gordon B. "Industrialization and Violence in Appalachia in the 1890s." In *An Appalachian Symposium: Essays in Honor of Cratis D. Williams*, ed. J. W. Williamson, 131–44. Boone, NC: Appalachian State University Press, 1977.

McNeil, W. K. "Appalachian Folklore Scholarship." *Appalachian Journal* 5, no. 1 (1977): 55–64.

———. "'By the Ozark Trail': The Image of the Ozarks in Popular and Folk Songs." *JEMF Quarterly* (Spring/Summer 1985): 20–30.

———, ed. *Appalachian Images in Folk and Popular Culture*. Ann Arbor: UMI Research Press, 1989.

———. "Special Issue on the Weaver Brothers and Elviry." *Old Time Country*, Winter 1998.

McWhiney, Grady. *Cracker Culture — Celtic Ways in the Old South*. Tuscaloosa: University of Alabama Press, 1988.

Merrill, Hugh. *Esky: The Early Years at Esquire*. New Brunswick: Rutgers University Press, 1995.

Mertz, Paul E. *New Deal Policy and Southern Rural Poverty*. Baton Rouge: Louisiana State University Press, 1978.

Miller, Don. *B Movies*. New York: Ballantine Books, 1987.

Miller, Danny. "The Mountain Woman — In Fact and Fiction of the Early Twentieth Century." *Appalachian Heritage* 6 (Summer 1978): 48–73; (Fall 1978): 66–72; 7 (Winter 1979): 16–21.

Miller, Wilbur R. *Revenuers and Moonshiners — Enforcing Federal Liquor Laws in the Mountain South, 1865–1900*. Chapel Hill: University of North Carolina Press, 1991.

Mintz, Lawrence E. "Situation Comedy." In *TV Genres — A Handbook and Reference Guide*, ed. Brian G. Rose, 107–29. Westport, CT: Greenwood Press, 1985.

———. "Humor and Ethnic Stereotypes in Vaudeville and Burlesque." *MELUS* 21 (1996): 19–28.

Mitchell, Catherine C., and C. Joan Schnyder. "Public Relations for Appalachia: Berea's *Mountain Life and Work*." *Journalism Quarterly* 66, no. 4 (1989): 974–978, 1049.

Mordden, Ethan. *The American Theatre*. New York: Oxford University Press, 1981.

Morgan, Winifred. *An American Icon — Brother Jonathan and American Identity*. Newark: University of Delaware Press, 1988.

Morton, David C., and Charles K. Wolfe. "DeFord Bailey: They Turned Me Loose to Root Hog or Die." *Journal of Country Music* 14, no. 2 (1992): 13–17.

Munzer, Martha E. *Valley of Vision — The TVA Years*. New York: Alfred A. Knopf, 1969.

Nesbitt, Eddie. "A History of the Mountain Broadcast and Prairie Recorder." *JEMF Quarterly* 18, no. 65/66 (1982): 23–30.

Newby, I. A. *Plain Folk in the New South — Social Change and Cultural Persistence, 1880–1915.* Baton Rouge: Louisiana State University Press, 1989.

Newcomb, Horace. *TV: The Most Popular Art.* New York: Anchor Books, 1974.

———. "Appalachia on Television: Region as Symbol in American Popular Culture." *Appalachian Journal* 7, nos. 1–2 (1979–1980): 155–64.

Nye, Russell. *The Unembarrassed Muse — The Popular Arts in America.* New York: Dial Press, 1970.

Obermiller, Philip J. "Paving the Way — Urban Organizations and the Image of Appalachians." In *Confronting Appalachian Stereotypes — Back Talk from an American Region,* ed. Dwight B. Billings, Gurney Norman, and Katherine Ledford, 251–66. Lexington: University Press of Kentucky, 1999.

O'Connor, John E., ed. *American History American Television — Interpreting the Video Past.* New York: Frederick Ungar, 1983.

Oermann, Robert K., and Mary A. Bufwack. "Patsy Montana and the Development of the Cowgirl Image." *Journal of Country Music* 8, no. 3 (1981): 18–32.

Otto, John S. "'Hillbilly Culture': The Appalachian Mountain Folk in History and Popular Culture." *Southern Quarterly* 24, no. 3 (1986): 25–34.

———. "Plain Folk, Lost Frontiersmen, and Hillbillies: The Southern Mountain Folk in History and Popular Culture." *Southern Studies* 26, no. 1 (1987): 5–17.

Otto, John S., and Augustus M. Burns. "Black and White Cultural Interaction in the Early Twentieth-Century South: Race and Hillbilly Music." *Phylon — The Atlanta University Review of Race and Culture* 35, no. 4 (1974): 407–17.

Owsley, Frank Lawrence. *Plain Folk of the Old South.* Baton Rouge: Louisiana State University Press, 1949.

Paredes, Americo, and Morton Leeds. "The Process of Cultural Stripping and Reintegration — The Rural Migrant in the City." In *The Urban Experience and Folk Tradition,* ed. Ellen J. Stebert, 165–76. Austin: University of Texas Press for American Folklore Society, 1971.

Parish, James Robert, and William T. Leonard, eds. *The Funsters.* New Rochelle: Arlington House Publishers, 1979.

Patterson, Timothy A. "Hillbilly Music among the Flatlanders: Early Midwestern Radio Barn Dances." *Journal of Country Music* 6, no. 1 (1975): 12–18.

Pearce, John Ed. *Days of Darkness: The Feuds of Eastern Kentucky.* Lexington: University of Kentucky Press, 1994.

Peck, Elisabeth S. *Berea's First 125 Years, 1855–1980.* Lexington: University Press of Kentucky, 1982.

Pells, Richard. *Radical Visions and American Dreams — Culture and Social Thought in the Depression.* New York: Harper & Row, 1973.

Perdue Jr., Charles L., and Nancy J. Martin-Perdue. "Appalachian Fables and Facts: A Case Study of the Shenandoah National Park Removals." *Appalachian Journal* 7, nos. 1–2 (1979–1980): 84–104.

Peterson, Richard. *Creating Country Music.* Chicago: University of Chicago Press, 1997.

Peterson, Richard A., and Paul DiMaggio. "The Early Opry: Its Hillbilly Image in Fact and Fancy." *Journal of Country Music* 4 (Summer 1973): 39–51.

———. "From Region to Class, the Changing Locus of Country Music: A Test of the Massification Hypothesis." *Social Forces* 53, no. 3 (1975): 497–506.

Peterson, Richard A., and Marcus V. Gowan. "What's in a Country Music Band Name." *Journal of Country Music* 2, no. 4 (1971): 1–9.

Philliber, William W., Clyde B. McCoy, and Harry C. Dillingham, eds. *The Invisible Minority—Urban Appalachians.* Lexington: University Press of Kentucky, 1981.

Pieterse, Jan Nederveen. *White on Black—Images of Africa and Blacks in Western Popular Culture.* New Haven: Yale University Press, 1992.

Plater, Ormonde. "The Lovingood Patriarchy." *Appalachian Journal* 2 (Spring 1973): 82–93.

Porterfield, Nolan. "Mr. Victor and Mr. Peer." *Journal of Country Music* 7, no. 3 (1978): 3–21.

Precourt, Walter. "The Image of Appalachian Poverty." In *Appalachia and America—Autonomy and Regional Dependence*, ed. Allen Batteau, 86–110. Lexington: University Press of Kentucky, 1983.

Price, Michael H., and George E. Turner. "Abner Goes Hollywood; Gets Lost in Shuffle." In *Li'l Abner Dailies: Vol. 6 (1940)*, 5–13. Princeton, WI: Kitchen Sink Press, 1989.

Pugh, Ronnie. "Country Music Is Here to Stay?" *Journal of Country Music* 19, no. 1 (1997): 32–38.

Quinn, Arthur Hobson. *A History of America Drama.* New York: Harper & Row, 1923.

Radway, Janice. *Reading the Romance—Women, Patriarchy and Popular Literature.* Chapel Hill: University of North Carolina Press, 1984.

Randolph, Vance, and George Wilson. *Down in the Holler: A Gallery of Ozark Folk Speech.* Norman: University of Oklahoma Press, 1953.

Reed, John Shelton. *Southern Folk, Plain & Fancy—Native White Social Types.* Athens: University of Georgia Press, 1986.

Reed, John Shelton, and Daniel Joseph Singal, eds. *Regionalism and the South—Selected Papers of Rupert Vance.* Chapel Hill: University of North Carolina Press, 1982.

Reitberger, Rheinhold, and Wolfgang Fuchs. *Comics—Anatomy of a Mass Medium.* London: Studio Vista, 1972.

Rickels, Milton. *George Washington Harris.* New York: Twayne, 1965.

Riddell, Frank S. *Appalachia: Its People, Heritage, and Problems.* Dubuque: Kendall Hunt, 1974.

Rodgers, Daniel. "In Search of Progressivism." *Reviews in American History* 10, no. 4 (1982): 113–32.

Roediger, David R. *The Wages of Whiteness: Race and the Making of the American Working Class.* New York: Verso, 1991.

———. *Towards the Abolition of Whiteness.* New York: Verso, 1994.

Rogers, Jimmie. *The Country Music Message: Revisited.* Fayetteville: University of Arkansas Press, 1989.

Rosaldo, Renato. *Culture and Truth: The Remaking of Social Analysis*. Boston: Beacon Press, 1989.

Rosenberg, Bernard, and David Manning White, eds. *Mass Culture: The Popular Arts in America*. New York: Free Press, 1957.

Ross, Stephen J. *Working-Class Hollywood: Silent Film and the Shaping of Class in America*. Princeton: Princeton University Press, 1998.

——. "The Revolt of the Audience: Reconsidering Audiences and Reception during the Silent Era." In *American Movie Audiences: From the Turn of the Century to the Early Sound Era*, ed. Melvyn Stokes and Richard Maltby, 92–111. London: British Film Institute, 1999.

Rourke, Constance. *American Humor: A Study of the National Character*. New York: Harcourt, Brace, and Company, 1931.

Rouse, Sarah, and Katharine Loughney, eds. *Three Decades of Television—A Catalog of Television Programs Acquired by the Library of Congress, 1949–1979*. Washington, DC: Library of Congress, 1989.

Russ, John. "Dogpatch, U.S.A." (http://www.aristotle.net/~russjohn/attractions/dogpatch.html)

Sackett, Susan. *Prime Time Hits—Television's Most Popular Network Programs*. New York: Billboard Books, 1993.

Sagarin, Edward. "The Deviant in the Comic Strip: The Case History of Barney Google." *Journal of Popular Culture* 5, no. 1 (1971): 178–93.

Salstrom, Paul. *Appalachia's Path to Dependency: Rethinking a Region's Economic History, 1730–1940*. Lexington: University Press of Kentucky, 1994.

Saxton, Alexander. *The Rise and Fall of the White Republic: Class Politics and Mass Culture in Nineteenth-Century America*. New York: Verso, 1991.

Schneirov, Matthew. *The Dream of a New Social Order—Popular Magazines in America, 1893–1914*. New York: Columbia University Press, 1994.

Schreiner, Dave. "The Storyteller." In *Li'l Abner Dailies: Vol. 1 (1934–1935)*, 7–12. Princeton, WI: Kitchen Sink Press, 1988.

——. "1937: Sadie's First Run." In *Li'l Abner Dailies: Vol. 3 (1937)*, 8–9. Princeton, WI: Kitchen Sink Press, 1988.

——. "1938: Soap and Slapstick." In *Li'l Abner Dailies: Vol. 4 (1938)*, 6. Princeton WI: Kitchen Sink Press, 1988.

——. "1940: On The Road." In *Li'l Abner Dailies: Vol. 6 (1940)*, 14–15. Princeton, WI: Kitchen Sink Press, 1989.

Schudson, Michael. "The New Validation of Popular Culture: Sense and Sentimentality in Academia." *Critical Studies in Mass Communication* 4, no. 1 (1987): 51–68.

Schuster, Laura, and Sharyn McCrumb. "Appalachian Film List." *Appalachian Journal* 11, no. 4 (1984): 329–83.

Seeger, Charles. "The Folkness of the Non-Folk vs. the Non-Folkness of the Folk." In *Folklore and Society—Essays in Honor of Benjamin A. Botkin*, 1–9. Hatboro, PA: Folklore Associates, 1966.

Seiter, Ellen. "Stereotypes and the Media: A Re-evaluation." *Journal of Communication* 36 (Spring 1986): 14–26.

Selznick, Philip. *TVA and the Grass Roots*. New York: Harper & Row, 1966.

Shackelford, Laurel, and Bill Weinberg, eds. *Our Appalachia*. New York: Hill and Wang, 1977.

Shackford, James Atkins. *Davy Crockett—The Man and the Legend*. Chapel Hill: University of North Carolina Press, 1986.

Shapiro, Henry D. *Appalachia on Our Mind—The Southern Mountains and Mountaineers in the American Consciousness, 1870–1920*. Chapel Hill: University of North Carolina Press, 1978.

———. "John F. Day and the Disappearance of Appalachia from the American Consciousness." *Appalachian Journal* 10, no. 2 (1983): 157–64.

Silber, Nina. "'What Does America Need So Much as Americans?': Race and Northern Reconciliation with Southern Appalachia, 1870–1900." In *Appalachians and Race: The Mountain South from Slavery to Segregation*, ed. John Inscoe, 245–58. Lexington: University Press of Kentucky, 2001.

Simmon, Scott. *The Films of D. W. Griffith*. Cambridge: Cambridge University Press, 1993.

Slotkin, Richard. *Regeneration through Violence—The Mythology of the American Frontier, 1600–1860*. Middletown, CT: Wesleyan University Press, 1973.

Smyth, Willie. "A Preliminary Index of Country Music Artists and Songs in Commercial Motion Pictures (1928–1953)." *JEMF Quarterly* 19–20, nos. 70–73 (1983–1984): 88–18, 103–11, 188–96, 241–47.

Solomon, Eric. "Eustace Tilley Sees the Thirties through a Glass Monocle, Lightly: *New Yorker* Cartoonists and the Depression Years." *Studies in American Humor* 3, no. 2–3 (1984): 201–19.

"Special Hillbilly Issue." *Journal of American Folklore* 78, no. 309 (1965).

Speer, Jean Haskell. "'Hillbilly Sold Here': Appalachian Folk Culture and Parkway in Tourism." In *Parkways: Past, Present, and Future—Proceeding of the Second Biennial Linear Parks Conference*, 212–20. Boone, NC: Appalachian Consortium Press, 1987.

———. *The Appalachian Photographs of Earl Palmer*. Lexington: University Press of Kentucky, 1990.

———. "From Stereotype to Regional Hype: Strategies for Changing Media Portrayals of Appalachia." *Journal of Appalachian Studies Association* 5 (1993): 12–19.

Spigel, Lynn. *Make Room for TV—Television and the Family Ideal in Postwar America*. Chicago: University of Chicago Press, 1992.

Spigel, Lynn, and Michael Curtin. "Introduction." In *The Revolution Wasn't Televised—Sixties Television and Social Conflict*, ed. Lynn Spigel and Michael Curtin, 1–18. New York: Routledge, 1997.

Spigel, Lynn, and Michael Curtin, eds. *The Revolution Wasn't Televised—Sixties Television and Social Conflict*. New York: Routledge, 1997.

Staiger, Janet. *Interpreting Films—Studies in the Historical Reception of the American Cinema*. Princeton: Princeton University Press, 1992.

Stearns, Peter N., and Mark Knapp. "Men and Romantic Love: Pinpointing a 20th Century Change." *Journal of Social History* 26 (Summer 1993): 769–95.

Stott, William. *Documentary Expression and Thirties America*. New York: Oxford University Press, 1973.

Summers, Harrison B., ed. *A Thirty-Year History of Programs Carried on National Radio Networks in the United States, 1926–1956*. New York: Arno Press and the New York Times, 1971.

Susman, Warren. "The Culture of the Thirties." In Susman, *Culture as History*, 150–83. New York: Pantheon Books, 1984.

Terrill, Tom E., and Jerrold Hirsch, eds. *Such as Us—Southern Voices of the Thirties*. Chapel Hill: University of North Carolina Press, 1978.

Tindall, George B. "The Benighted South: Origins of a Modern Image." *Virginia Quarterly Review* 40 (Spring 1964): 281–94.

Titus, Warren. *John Fox, Jr.* New York: Twayne, 1971.

Toll, Robert. *Blacking Up—The Minstrel Show in Nineteenth-Century America*. New York: Oxford University Press, 1974.

———. *The Entertainment Machine—American Show Business in the Twentieth Century*. Oxford: Oxford University Press, 1982.

Toplin, Robert Brent, ed. *Hollywood as Mirror—Changing Views of "Outsiders" and "Enemies" in American Movies*. Westport, CT: Greenwood Press, 1993.

Tosches, Nick. *Country—The Biggest Music in America*. New York: Stein and Day, 1977.

Trachtenberg, Alan. *Reading American Photographs: Images as History—Mathew Brady to Walker Evans*. New York: Hill and Wang, 1989.

Tribe, Ivan M. "The Hillbilly versus the City: Urban Images in Country Music." *JEMF Quarterly* 10, no. 34 (1974): 41–54.

Usai, Paolo Cherchi, ed. *The Griffith Project*. Vol. 5 (Films produced in 1911). New York: BFI Publishing, 2001.

Verschuure, Eric Peter. "Stumble, Bumble, Mumble: TV's Image of the South." *Journal of Popular Culture* 16, no. 3 (1982): 92–96.

Walker, Brian. *Barney Google and Snuffy Smith—75 Years of an American Legend*. Wilton, CT: Comicana Books and Ohio State University Libraries, 1994.

Walle, Alf H. "Devolution and Evolution: Hillbillies and Cowboys as American Savages." *Kentucky Folklore Record* 32, no. 1 (1986): 58–68.

Waller, Altina L. *Feud—Hatfields, McCoys, and Social Change in Appalachia, 1860–1900*. Chapel Hill: University of North Carolina Press, 1988.

———. "The Hatfield-McCoy Feud." In *True Stories from the American Past*, ed. William Graebner, 35–54. New York: McGraw-Hill, 1993.

———. "Feuding in Appalachia—Evolution of a Cultural Stereotype." In *Appalachia in the Making—The Mountain South in the Nineteenth Century*, ed. Dwight B. Billings, Mary Beth Pudup, and Altina L. Waller, 347–76. Chapel Hill: University of North Carolina Press, 1995.

Waller, Gregory. "Hillbilly Music and Will Rogers: Small-town Picture Shows in the 1930s." In *American Movie Audiences*, ed. Malvyn Stokes and Richard Maltby, 164–79. London: British Film Institute, 1999.

Walls, David S., and John B. Stephenson, eds. *Appalachia in the Sixties—Decade of Reawakening*. Lexington: University Press of Kentucky, 1972.

Ward, William S. *A Literary History of Kentucky*. Knoxville: University of Tennessee Press, 1988.

Warfel, Harry R., and G. Harrison Orians, eds. *American Local-Color Stories*. New York: American Book Company, 1941.

Warren-Findley, Janelle. "Musicians and Mountaineers: The Resettlement Administration's Music Program in Appalachia, 1935–37." *Appalachian Journal* 7, nos. 1–2 (1979–1980): 105–23.

Watkins, Charles Alan. "Merchandising the Mountaineer—Photography, the Great Depression, and Cabins in the Laurel." *Appalachian Journal* 12, no. 3 (1985): 215–38.

Watson, Mary Ann. *The Expanding Vista—American Television in the Kennedy Years*. New York: Oxford University Press, 1990.

Wead, George, and George Lewis. *The Film Career of Buster Keaton*. Boston: G. K. Hall, 1977.

Weibe, Robert H. *The Search for Order, 1877–1920*. New York: Hill and Wang, 1967.

Whisnant, David E. "Finding the Way between the Old and the New: The Mountain Dance and Folk Festival and Bascom Lamar Lunsford's Work as a Citizen." *Appalachian Journal* 7, nos. 1–2 (1979–1980): 135–54.

———. *Modernizing the Mountaineer: People, Power, and Planning in Appalachia*. Boone, NC: Appalachian Consortium Press, 1980.

———. *All That Is Native and Fine—The Politics of Culture in an American Region*. Chapel Hill: University of North Carolina Press, 1983.

White, David Manning, and Robert H. Abel. *The Funnies—An American Idiom*. New York: Free Press, 1963.

Wiggins, Gene. *Fiddlin' Georgia Crazy—Fiddlin' John Carson, His Real World, and the World of His Songs*. Urbana: University of Illinois Press, 1987.

Wilgus, D. K. "An Introduction to the Study of Hillbilly Music." *Journal of American Folklore* 78, no. 309 (1965): 195–203.

———. "The Hillbilly Movement." In *Our Living Tradition: An Introduction to American Folklore*, ed. Tristram Potter Coffin, 263–71. New York: Basic Books, 1968.

———. "Country-Western Music and the Urban Hillbilly." In *The Urban Experience and Folk Tradition*, ed. Ellen J. Stebert, 137–59. Austin: University of Texas Press for American Folklore Society, 1970.

Williams, C. Fred. "The Bear State Image: Arkansas in the Nineteenth Century." *Arkansas Historical Quarterly* 35, no. 2 (1980): 99–111.

Williams, Cratis. "The Southern Mountaineer in Fact and Fiction." Edited by Martha H. Pipes. *Appalachian Journal* 3, nos. 1–4 (Fall 1975–Summer 1976): 8–61; 100–162; 186–261; 334–92.

Williams, John Alexander. *Appalachia: A History*. Chapel Hill: University of North Carolina Press, 2002.

Williams, Martin. "The Hidden World of 'Li'l Abner.'" *Comics Journal* 147 (1991): 74–76.

Williamson, J. W., ed. *An Appalachian Symposium: Essays in Honor of Cratis D. Williams*. Boone, NC: Appalachian State University Press, 1977.

Williamson, J. W. *Southern Mountaineers in Silent Films: Plot Synopses of Movies about Moonshining, Feuding, and Other Mountain Topics, 1904–1929.* Jefferson, NC: McFarland & Company, 1994.

———. *Hillbillyland—What the Movies Did to the Mountains and What the Mountains Did to the Movies.* Chapel Hill: University of North Carolina Press, 1995.

———. "Southern Mountaineers Filmography (1904–1995)." W. L. Eury Appalachian Collection, Belk Library, Appalachian State University (http://www.library.appstate.edu/appcoll/filmography.html)

Wilson, Charles Reagan, and William Ferris, eds. *Encyclopedia of Southern Culture.* Chapel Hill: University of North Carolina Press, 1989.

Wilson, Christopher. "The Rhetoric of Consumption: Mass-Market Magazines and the Demise of the Gentle Reader." In *The Culture of Consumption: Critical Essays in American History, 1880–1980,* ed. Richard Wightman Fox and T. J. Jackson Lears, 41–64. New York: Pantheon Books, 1983.

Wilson, Darlene. "The Felicitous Convergence of Mythmaking and Capital Accumulation: John Fox, Jr. and the Formation of an (Other) Almost-White American Underclass." *Journal of Appalachian Studies* 1 (1995): 5–44.

Wolfe, Charles K. "Nashville and Country Music, 1926–1930: Notes on Early Nashville Media and Its Response to Old-Time Music." *Journal of Country Music* 4, no. 1 (1973): 2–16.

———. "Clayton McMichen: Reluctant Hillbilly." *Bluegrass Unlimited* (May 1979): 56–61.

———. "Take Me Back to Renfro Valley." *Journal of Country Music* 9, no. 3 (1983): 9–27.

———. "The White Man's Blues, 1922–1940." *Journal of Country Music* 15, no. 3 (1993): 38–44.

———. "The Legend That Peer Built: Reappraising the Bristol Sessions." In *The Country Reader: Twenty-five Years of the Journal of Country Music,* ed. Paul Kingsbury, 3–18. Nashville: Country Music Foundation Press, 1997.

———. *A Good-Natured Riot: The Birth of the Grand Ole Opry.* Nashville: Country Music Foundation and Vanderbilt University Press, 1999.

Woll, Allen L., and Randall M. Miller. *Ethnic and Racial Images in American Film and Television—Historical Essays and Bibliography.* New York: Garland, 1987.

Wood, Gerald C. "The Pastoral Tradition in American Film before World War II." *Markham Review* 12 (Spring 1983): 52–60.

Woodward, C. Vann. *The Origins of the New South, 1877–1913.* Baton Rouge: Louisiana State University Press, 1951.

———. *The Burden of Southern History.* Baton Rouge: Louisiana State University Press, 1993.

Wray, Matt, and Annalee Newitz, eds. *White Trash—Race and Class in America.* New York: Routledge, 1997.

Unpublished Material

Campbell, Gavin J. "Fiddlers and Divas: Music and Culture in New South Atlanta, 1910–1925." Paper presented at the Graduate Student Conference on Cultural History and the South, Charlottesville, VA, April 1995.

Hsiung, David C. "Isolation and Integration in Upper East Tennessee, 1780–1860: The Historical Origins of Appalachian Characterizations." Ph.D. diss., University of Michigan, 1991.

Huber, Patrick J. "Rednecks and Woolhats, Hoosiers and Hillbillies: Working-Class Southern Whites, Language, and the Definition of Identity." Master's thesis, University of Missouri at Columbia, 1992.

Maxwell, Angela. "The South Beheld: The Influence of James Agee on James Dickey." Master's thesis, University of Texas at Austin, 2002.

McCoy, John. "The Art and Politics of Al Capp." Boston University, 1998.

McKinney, Edgar D. "Images, Realities, and Cultural Transformation in the Missouri Ozarks, 1920–1960." Ph.D. diss., University of Missouri at Columbia, 1990.

Perkins, Melody Joy. "Hillbilly Music and Its Components: A Survey of the University of Colorado Hillbilly Music Collection." Ph.D. diss., University of Colorado, 1991.

Pugh, Ronnie. "Personal Research for 'Country Music Is Here to Stay?'" Copy in author's possession.

Smith, Kermit Stephen. "What It Was Was Real Mountain Music: The Authentic Treatment of Music in the *Andy Griffith Show*." Appalachian State University, 1993.

Stoneback, Harry Robert. "The Hillfolk Tradition and Images of the Hillfolk in American Fiction since 1926." Ph.D. diss., Vanderbilt University, 1970.

Williams, Cratis D. "The Southern Mountaineer in Fact and Fiction." Ph.D. diss., New York University, 1961.

Motion Pictures

Ballad of a Mountain Man—The Story of Bascom Lamar Lunsford: Public Broadcasting System (The American Experience), 1990.

Stranger with a Camera: Appalshop, Inc., 2000.

Strangers and Kin: Appalshop, Inc., 1983.

index

Non-Print Cultural Productions

Page numbers in bold refer to figures.

Non-Print Cultural Productions Index

General Index

Abbott, Bud, 166
ABC-TV (American Broadcasting
    Corporation), 181, 189
Achenbach, Joel, 214
Acuff, Roy, 75, 101
Adkins, Hasil, 217
African-Americans, 13, 156
    influence on country music, 71, 72
    use of "hillbilly" by, 48, 237n. 3
    views of southern poor whites, 13, 16, 17, 25
Agee, James, 164–65
Alabama, 47, 49, 50, 55
Alamo, 22
Alderman, Tony, 77, 78, 79, 80, 81
Allen, James Lane, 30, 31
Allen Brothers, The, 75, 242n. 10
American Folk Song Festival, 91, 249n. 26
American Gothic (painting), 192
Andy Griffith Show, The, 10, 174, 181–84,
    183, 184, 186, 187, 197, 199, 202
    hill folk characters, 181–82, 184
    "mountaineer" episodes tied to War on
        Poverty, 184
    positive view of small town, all-white
        South, 197
    ratings, 181
    town characters, 182
    See also Bass, Ernest T.; Darling,
        Briscoe; Darlings, The; Taylor, Sheriff
        Andy
Animated cartoons. *See* Cartoons, animated
Appalachia, 8, 9, 10, 13, 22, 41, 42, 54, 120,
    199, 201, 202, 203, 214, 224
    defined as a distinct locale, 33, 35, 47
    defined as a troubled region, 96, 160,
        174, 184–85, 186
    events, 35, 160, 184–85
    envisioned as survival from a romanti-
        cized past, 82, 91

geographic definition, 229n. 2
literature and non-print media set in, 19,
    60, 112, 125, 137, 151, 160, 186
media construction of regional image,
    30, 236n. 46
Appalachia, Virginia, 224
Appalachian Regional Commission, 185
Appalachian State Teacher's College, 137
Appalachian Studies, launching of, 213
Appal-PAC, 213
Arbitron ratings, 198
Arbuckle, Fatty, 62
Area Development Administration, 185
Arkansas, 9, 13, 21, 22, 28, 47, 203, 214
    and Bill Clinton, 214
    comedians, 160–61
    literary portrayals, 25–27, 29, 50–52,
        54–55
    media productions connected to, 123,
        174, 223
Arkansas Traveller, The, 26–28, 27, 28,
    182
    changing versions, 27–28, 234n. 28
    nickname of Bob Burns, 160
    possible origins, 233n. 24
Arnow, Harriete, 138
Arnow, Pat, 206
Asheville, North Carolina, 64, 67, 69, 91,
    137, 150
Ashland, Kentucky, 91, 218
Atlanta, 73, 76, 78, 209
Audience
    declining interest in mountaineer films,
        63, 142, 143, 151–52, 167
    growing unacceptability of filmed hill-
        billy image, 165
    mass media, nature of, 221
    for mountaineer films, 163, 168
    reader reactions to hillbilly image, 177

311

Country Music (*continued*)
  comedic tradition, 76
  connected to pioneer heritage, 82
  costuming and appearance of musicians,
    77, 79, 80, **81**, 84, 87–88, 90, 92, 95,
    97
  and critics' derision, 84, 89, 90, 91, 99
  and economic, cultural and technologi-
    cal influences, 72–73, 89
  expansion, 84, 99
  and folk musicians' scorn for, 91
  and Great Depression, 89
  and "hillbilly." See "Hillbilly"
  instrumentation, 79, 82, 99
  musical origins, 72
  press coverage, 75, 76, 78, 84, 86, 87–88,
    89
  shift from hillbilly to cowboy image, 88,
    89, 95–96, 97
  themes in songs, 89
  and "whiteness," 74, 76, 82
Country musicians
  and Great Depression, 92
  and rustification, 78, 79, 80–84
  See also Country music
Coward, Herbert "Cowboy," 208, **209**
Cox, Ronny, 208
"Cracker," 17, 43, 211
Craddock, Charles Egbert. *See* Murfree,
    Mary Noailles
Crawford, T. C., 36
Crazy Blue Ridge Hillbillies, 92
Crazy Water Crystals, 91
Crenna, Richard, 178
Crichton, Kyle, 75
Crist, Judith, 201
Crockett, David (Davy), 21–22, **23**, 232n. 16,
    115, 116
Crosby, Bing, 188
Cross, Hugh, 83
Crowther, Bosley, 161
Cultural "brow-levels," breaking down of
    190, 201
Cultural conflicts of 1920s, 73, 109
Culture, boundaries between folk, mass,
    popular, 221
Cumberland Gap, Kentucky, 21
Cumberland Ridge Runners, 82, 182
Cumberland Vendetta, A [Fox, Jr.], 39
Cummings, Bob, 174, 175
Currier and Ives, 26

Daisy Mae Scragg, 125, **131**, 132, 133, **135**,
    188
Daley, "Blind Billy," 91
Damrosch, Dr. Walter, 243n. 26

Daniell, George, 92
Darling, Briscoe, 182
Darlings, The, 182–83, 184
Daughters of the American Republic, 155
Davenport, Homer, 49, **50**
Davis, Elmer, 158
Davis, Jefferson, 197
Davis, Jimmie, 76
Davis, Karl, 81, 82, **83**
Davis, Mrs. S. M., 43, 236n. 53
Davis, Rebecca Harding, 30, 31
*Davy Crockett; Or Be Sure You're Right,
    Then Go Ahead* [Mayo], 22
Dayton, Ohio, 213
Dayton, Tennessee, 110
DeBeck, Billy, 9, 103, 104, **114–17**, 115,
    116, 118, **119**, 121–24, 135, 148, 152, 154,
    251n. 49
  audience reception of comics, 124
  biographical background, 113–14, 248n.
    15, 248n. 22
  comments on work, 248n. 19
  influence, 136, 139, 154
  origins of hillbilly characters, 114
  and parodying of hillbilly stereotype,
    122–23
  portrait of mountain communities,
    122–23, 124
  portrayal of African-Americans, 118–19
  use of dialect, 114, 121–122, 124
Decca Records, 74, 86, 95, 97, **98**, 99
Dees, Ashley "Jad," 88
Deliverance (book) [Dickey], 205, 206–7
  ambiguity, 206
  contrast to film, 207, 208–9
  sales, 209
  use of author's experiences, 207
Deliverance (film), 3, 10, 184, 205, 206,
    207–10, **215**, 237n. 8
  albino banjo player scene, 206, 208,
    262n. 9
  audience reaction, 209: in Georgia, 209
  box office returns, 209
  contrasts to book, 207, 208–9
  and "Deliverance syndrome," 210,
    262n. 14
  influence on other films, 210–11
  relation to Southern mountain people,
    208
  sodomy scene, 206, 208–9
  "squeal like a pig," 208, 210
Democracy on the March [Lilienthal], 159
Depression, Great, 4
  celebration of common folk, 160, 163
  and hillbilly image, 9, 10, 72, 103–4, 112,
    206

Gooch, Abijah, 133
Good, Millie and Dolly. *See* "Girls of the
  Golden West, The"
Goodrich, Frances Louise, 249n. 26
Google, Barney, 113, 114, 116, 117, 119, 122,
  124, 251n. 49
Gorcey, Leo, 166
Graham County, North Carolina, 150
Granny (Daisy Moses), 187, 188, 192, 194,
  197, 198, 200, 202
Grant, Allan, 192
Grapes of Wrath, The [Steinbeck], 130–31,
  163. *See also* Joads, The
Green, Abel, 90
Green, Archie, 48, 75
Green, Douglass, 96
Greenbaum, Everett, 181
Greenbrier County, West Virginia, 237n. 4
Griffith, Andy, 181, 183
  comedy routine "What it was was
    Football," 181
  comparison to Li'l Abner, 181
Griffith, D.W. (David Wark), 58, 59, 61–62,
  114
Gross, Clifford, 96–97
Gully Jumpers, The, 80

Hammid, Alexander, 159
Hamner, Jr., Earl, 205
Handy, W. C., 76
Hano, Arnold, 196
Harben, William Nathan, 48
Harlan County, Kentucky, 120
Harmon, Roy Lee, 139
Harney, William Wallace, 30
Harrington, Michael, 185
Harris, George Washington, 19, 31, 107, 114,
  167
Harris, Jim, 218
Hatburn, Luke, 144
Hatburns, The, 3, 184, 251n. 47
Hatfield, Johnse, 182
Hatfield, William Anderson "Devil Anse,"
  36, 37–38, 155
  media construction of, 37–38
Hatfield-McCoy Feud, 36–38, 152, 235n.
  40.
  See also Hatfield, William Anderson
    "Devil Anse"; McCoy, Randolph "Old
    Ranel"
Hathaway, Jane, 195, 196
Hatton Gap, Arkansas, 52
Hawthorne, Julian, 49
Hay, George Dewey, 80, 81, 86, 99
  comments on "hillbilly," 84–85
  naming of *Grand Ole Opry*, 243n. 26

and rustification of country performers,
  80
Haynes, Henry. *See* Homer and Jethro
Hazard, Kentucky, 213, 225
Hemphill, Paul, 212
Henning, Paul, 175, 181, 187–89, 191, 192,
  194, 198, 201, 203
  biographical background, 187–88
  commentary on *The Beverly Hillbillies*, 193
  efforts to present characters as real
    mountaineers, 189
  fascination with hillbilly characters, 188
  origins of idea for *The Beverly Hillbillies*,
    188–89
Henry, Thomas, 110
Hepburn, Katherine, 156
Hergesheimer, Joseph, 143
Hibler, Charles S., 50–51
Hicks, Granville, 163
Highland County, Virginia, 143
"Highlanders," 44–45
Highlands, North Carolina, 263n. 26
Hildreth, Richard, 18
Hill, Billy, 91
Hill, George, 146
Hill Billies, The, 74, 77, 78, 80, 81, 93, 101,
  182
  naming, 78–79
Hillbillies from Mars, 219
"Hillbillies Invade Chicago, The" [Votaw],
  176–77
"Hillbilly"
  absence from early twentieth-century
    media, 57, 64, 69, 238n. 15, 240n. 28
  in country music: audiences' use of, 79,
    98; band names using, 74, 76, 86,
    87–89, 243n. 27; performers' reaction
    to term, 79, 91–92, 99, 101; performers'
    use of, 78–79, 90, 92, 93, 94–95, 98;
    press stories on country music employ-
    ing term, 76, 78, 84, 86, 90, 99; pro-
    ducers' use of, 79, 82, 84, 87–88, 91,
    101, 242n. 16; song titles with word, 76,
    86, 87, 244n. 29 (*see also* "Hillbilly
    music")
  defined as a slur, 48, 79, 138, 175, 176
  definitions, 49, 51, 55, 191–92
  difference from "redneck," 6
  first appearance in print, 49
  early uses in film, 145, 146–47, 153–54,
    156, 253n. 6
  early uses in print media, 48, 50–51, 55,
    57, 64, 176
  localized use of term, 93, 212
  opposition to use of term, 69, 91–92, 138,
    205, 212–13, 218–19

Norfolk, Virginia, 15
North Carolina, 15, 64, 67, 78, 90, 121, 223
  literary references to, 23, 25, 40, 44, 147
  media settings in, 114, 123
Norwood, Ohio, 219

O'Daniel, Wilbur Lee "Pappy," and Hillbilly Boys, 97, 245n. 46
Odum, Howard, 138
Office of Economic Opportunity, 185
Office of War Information, 158
Ohio, 44, 175, 176
O'Keefe, Walter, 89
Okeh Records, 73, 74, 78, 86, 95, 101
Oklahoma, 131
Olmsted, Frederick Law, 24–25
On a Slow Train through Arkansaw [Jackson], 51, **52**
O'Neill, Rose, 238n. 15
Other America, The [Harrington], 185
Ott's Woodchoppers, 92, 94, 95
Oudeans Hill Billy Boys, The, 86
"Our contemporary ancestors" [Frost], 43
Our Southern Highlanders [Kephart], 147, 150, 240n. 28
Oxford, Vern, 211
Ozark Hillbillies, The, 243n. 27
Ozarks, 5, 22, 55, 60, 62, 65, 88, 120, 121, 127, 139, 156, 174, 176, 187, 191
  comic associations, 240n. 29
  geographical definition, 229n. 2
  humorists, 160

Paley, William, 203, 205
Paramount Studios, 148, 151, 156, 161
Parker, Linda. See Meunich, Jean
Parton, Dolly, 215
Paulding, James Kirke, 22
Paulette, Cyprian, 87, **88**
PCA (Production Code Administration), 155
Peer, Ralph Sylvester, 73, 74, 75, 241n. 4
  attitudes toward country musicians, 74
  and Fiddlin' John Carson, 73–74, 241n. 5
  and The Hill Billies, 74, 78–79, 81
  rustification of performers, 78, 79, 242n. 16
Pennsylvania, 34
Pepsi Corporation, 199
Perkins, Carl, 101
Pickford, Jack, 145, **146**

Pickford, Mary, 58, 145
Pigeon Forge, Tennessee, 215
Pikeville, Kentucky, 11, 225
Pincus, Irving and Norman, 180
Pinex cough syrup, 84, **85**
Plays, hillbilly, 166, 256n. 37
Polhemus, Minister J. H., 41
"(Poor) white trash," 90, 110, 147, 224
Pop Art, 201
Popular Front, 163
Populist Party, 56
"Porte Crayon." See Strother, David Hunter
Porter, William T., 19
Pound, Virginia, 156
Poverty, portrayed as simply part of "mountain culture," 179. See also Hillbilly image
Prairie Ramblers, 96
Presley, Elvis, 101
Pride, Charley, 241n. 8
Progressive Era, ideological atmosphere, 56, 60
Prophet of the Great Smoky Mountains, The [Murfree], 30
Pyle, Denver, 182, 214

Quare Women, The [Furman], 147
Queen, Adeline, **148**

Rabun County, Georgia, 207, 210
Race and southern mountaineers
  comparisons to Africans Americans, 43, 49, 51, 53, 60, 118, **119**, 165, 176, 177, 197, 198, 224
  comparisons to American Indians, 15, 16, 17, 25, 35–36, 60, 119, 233n. 24, 256n. 38
  comparisons to Mexicans and Latinos, 17, 60, 176
  comparisons to other non-whites, 60, 155
  connections to racial and ethnic stereotyping, 63, 130, 220
  See also African-Americans; Whiteness; "White other"
"Race" records, 73, 241n. 4
Radio, growth in stations and sales, 73
Railroads
  influence on country music songs, 73, 243n. 26
Raleigh, North Carolina, 224
Ranch Boys, The, 86
Randolph, Vance, 57, 138, 139, 249n. 26
Rasahoff, Martin, 189

General Index

have played a critical role in the construction of whiteness and modernity in twentieth-century America. Though the hillbilly has eighteenth-century literary antecedents, the stereotype became popularized in the twentieth century as a foil to increasingly urbanizing and industrializing America. Middle-class Americans viewed hillbillies, with their supposedly pure Anglo-Saxon or Scottish origins, as an exotic race, akin to blacks and Indians, but still native and white, as opposed to the growing influx of immigrants in the first half of the twentieth century. At the same time, the image's whiteness allowed crude caricatures to persist long after similar ethnic and racial stereotypes had become socially unacceptable.

Richly illustrated with dozens of photographs, drawings, and film and television stills, this unique book stands as a testament to the enduring place of the hillbilly in the American imagination.

Anthony Harkins is an Assistant Professor of History at Western Kentucky University.

Jacket design: Tracy Baldwin

Jacket art: *The Mountain Boys*. By Paul Webb, *Esquire*, November 1934.

OXFORD
UNIVERSITY PRESS
www.oup.com